Thinking ahead

Thinking ahead

Unesco and the challenges of
today and tomorrow

unesco

1830

Published in 1977 by the United Nations
Educational, Scientific and Cultural Organization
7 Place de Fontenoy, 75700 Paris
Printed by Imprimeries Populaires
ISBN 92-3-101525-7
French edition: 92-3-201525-0
Spanish edition: 92-3-301525-4

Preface

The purpose of this work is to present to the public Unesco's Medium-Term Plan for 1977-1982. It contains a set of texts—slightly re-edited for easier reading—which were prepared at the beginning of 1976 to enable the governing bodies of Unesco to take decisions concerning the Organization's action during the six-year period 1977-82, covered by the Plan. These texts give a comprehensive account not only of the main guidelines for the Organizations's activities in the next six years, but also of the reasons which dictated their choice. In fact the reader is presented at the same time with a certain view of the world of today.

The Medium-Term Plan is based on an analysis of the major world problems which come within the Organization's field of competence, the purpose being to define Unesco's possibilities and intentions regarding its contribution in the next few years towards their solution—in other words, to define the aims which the Organization has set itself.

The authors of the Plan were therefore led to prepare a series of studies to identify and situate the various problems, to evaluate the work already accomplished and to establish principles for future action. Each of these studies has been carried out at two levels—one, very general, which relates to the *problem* and the other, more specific and concrete, to the *objective*, leading to the outline of a programme of action and proposals for the allocation of resources.

The Medium-Term Plan has been adapted for publication by the Secretariat of Unesco. The analyses of matters of substance have been reproduced mostly in their original form. These analyses, in which care was taken to reflect the many and varied aspects of the work of an Organization almost universal in character, since it now totals 142 Member States, enabled the representatives of those States at the nineteenth session of the General Conference of Unesco in October-November 1976, to approve unanimously the objectives and main guidelines of the Medium-Term Plan. The detailed descriptions of proposed activities, on the other hand, have been summarized briefly and information of a purely methodological or budgetary nature, which concerns mainly the internal functioning of the Organization, has been omitted. Chapter and section headings have also been simplified: briefer formulae have been found to replace the long, somewhat complicated titles of the Medium-Term Plan, which correspond to the description of the Plan's objectives. Sub-headings have been added to link up the different parts of the text more flexibly.

The work follows the general structure of the Medium-Term Plan. It begins with an introduction by Mr Amadou-Mahtar M'Bow, Director-General of Unesco, written in March 1976, which gives an overall view of the world problems upon which the Plan is based. The ten chapters which follow correspond to the ten major problem areas with which the Plan is concerned and each chapter is divided into sections corresponding to the different objectives.

These clarifications on the origins of the work were in a way necessary in order to explain certain of its characteristic features. And yet its significance emerges from the text itself, as it stands: the reader will find here a wide-ranging reflection on contemporary problems and the challenges of the future, placed within the practical context of international co-operation, with the main emphasis on action.

Contents

Introduction

The situation at the present time, as we stand on the threshold of the last quarter of the twentieth century, can probably best be summed up by saying that never has the world been such an integrated whole, never has its diversity been so evident.

The interdependence of societies is coupled with an interdependence of the problems which man is now facing. At a time when the world is constantly growing smaller as regards both information and action a global viewpoint becomes mandatory. World problems cannot be considered in isolation; they are closely bound up with each other. For contemporary thought the world forms a whole, a unity of interrelated parts; a global approach to world problems is manifestly the only approach which comes to terms with their real nature.

At the same time, modern societies display the greatest diversity—whether as a result of events outside their control, as with the growing differences in levels of development and living standards, or whether such diversity is actively sought, like that stemming from the desire of individuals and groups to assert their identity and originality.

The crux of the problems facing the modern world lies perhaps in this constant tension between a unity which, rising above disparities, seeks realization in a respect for differences, and a diversity which, transcending inequalities and conflicts, draws inspiration from man's common vision of the future. What is at stake is an authentic human fellowship embracing all societies.

The very fact that the international community has clearly expressed a desire to link the programme of an organization such as Unesco to consideration of major world problems is proof of the unity of those problems. The body of the text which follows contains numerous analyses which, in connection with a particular problem or medium-term objective, draw attention to the need for an overall view and to the interdependence of problems.

This is the case as soon as one broaches the—from every point of view, primordial—issue of human rights which are now acknowledged to be indivisible and universal in their application. Even partial and localized violations of those rights undermine and negate their very principle. Peace also displays the same characteristics of indivisibility. Every individual conflict seriously threatens world peace in so far as it is a manifestation of tensions and friction on a world-wide scale. Peace itself can only be conceived on a basis of justice, that is to say on the basis of respect for human rights and the right of self-determination of peoples. Peace is more than simply a matter of refraining from war; there can be no lasting peace if individuals are deprived of their rights and liberties, if peoples are oppressed by other peoples, if populations are beset by poverty or suffering from malnutrition and sickness. There can be no peace if there is no determination to build a just world. The arms race, which is the most obvious symptom of the present tensions throughout the world, devours vast resources which, if they were used for other purposes, would be capable of substantially improving the lot of the most seriously disadvantaged peoples and giving a possibly decisive impetus to the development of the societies to which they belong. The unity of the world is also evidenced by the world-wide crises which jeopardize the future of mankind: problems arising from population growth, the risks of exhausting natural resources by despoiling the heritage of mankind and by continual damage to an environment which is the collective and irreplaceable setting for all human life. The dangers threatening the world in which we live are of concern to each and every one of us. Lastly, development, as the international community must now conceive it, is a global, multi-dimensional process taking into account simultaneously economic, political, social and cultural factors with reference to a society which is considered not in isolation but as one part of a complex network of relations and forces which characterize the world situation. Development is an all-embracing concept, applying to all societies, those which from the economic point of view are most advanced as well as those which, in this respect, are the most deprived. Development is therefore justifiably one of the major themes in terms of which several of the objectives occupying a central place in the Organization's Medium-Term Plan are defined.

Over and against these ties which necessitate a unified and global view of world problems, there are the contradictions, the confrontations, the tensions and the profound and numerous disparities which typify the present situation and one or other aspect of which is highlighted by each of the analyses which follow. Threats of confrontation subsist and sometimes lead to open conflicts which, even when they occur in the most seriously disadvantaged regions, are evidence of the profound divergencies which still divide the world. Violations of human rights in association with certain conceptions of power and various forms of racialism or intolerance emphasize the aberrant nature of inhuman practices and the difficulties which beset the advance of the idea of human unity and solidarity.

The inequalities in the modern world have reached unprecedented dimensions because of the very fact that economic growth, in favouring particular societies, has often taken place to the detriment of other specially numerous and deprived groups.

Such inequalities take various forms. They may consist in overall disparities in income between countries—as in the case of developed and developing countries—which are due not only to historical factors but also to differing conditions for the production of material goods and to the frequently inequitable terms of international trade. It has been noted that, in the past, the inequalities existing between societies were relatively minor, since all these societies were at the pre-industrial stage; and the ratio between the average income of the richest and the poorest was approximately 3 to 1. At the present day, however, the ratio between average per capita income, as between the most and least developed countries, is often in the region of 30 to 1, rising in extreme cases, to as much as 80 or 90 to 1. There are also, within each nation, inequalities as between the different social categories. It is, in particular, in the rural areas or in certain large towns in the developing countries that the most distressing poverty is to be found, with some people living in utter deprivation, a prey to hunger and chronic disease, permanently in conditions below the minimum level which man could at most bring himself to regard as tolerable on a purely temporary basis.

In addition to these material inequalities in regard to the possession of and access to consumer goods and standards of living, there are also other equally serious inequalities as to the possession of and access to cultural goods and amenities. The very fact that there are still some 800 million illiterates and that this number, far from decreasing, has, because of the population growth, slightly increased over the past few years constitutes the most glaring inequality in the matter of education. The right to education, even elementary education, has not yet been universally established as a practical reality; it is estimated that in 1975 over 130 million children of between 6 and 11 years of age were receiving no schooling. Inequality between the sexes in regard to education also continues to be widespread. Analysis of scientific development shows that research potential, measured either by the number of research workers or by the level of research expenditure, is concentrated in the industrialized countries: the developing countries, though inhabited by a large majority of the world's population, possess only a very small fraction of this potential, between 5 and 10 per cent, depending on the criterion used. The inequalities in regard to the production and use of information media are no less glaring, these media also being concentrated in the hands of the developed countries.

To eliminate inequalities, and reverse the present alarming trend towards a widening of the gulf between developed and developing countries, due largely to the world economic crisis and the acute worsening of the terms of trade, is a prime necessity.

This is not to advocate integration in a system in which all distinctions would be obliterated; for, alongside the disparities which must be eliminated, there also exist certain deliberate, positively sought differences. Individuals and groups, in a great variety of circumstances, affirm their desire to remain themselves, to avoid standardization leading to loss of their cultural characteristics, their way of life and their own particular conception of the well-being of the individual and his relations with his fellow men. This fundamental diversity, which is in no way incompatible with the aspiration to universal human solidarity, has come to be focused round the idea of cultural identity, a notion which, as will be seen, looms large in the Medium-Term Plan, forming one of the key ideas on which a considerable part of the programme is based.

Thus an essential problem appears to be how to remove disparities whilst maintaining differences, how to pass from a contingent interdependence, which favours certain elements to the detriment of others, to an actively sought solidarity. The problem is to replace a system submitted to as the inevitable outcome of uncontrollable forces by an axiologically guided system reflecting the broadest possible measure of agreement on the aims the human community should pursue.

Whatever field one is considering, the problems are set in a context of change. Our age is perhaps more than any other a period of profound and rapid mutations. The transformations are extremely varied, but what they appear to have in common in most cases is a growth dimension. It thus seems essential to meditate on the phenomena of growth, in the broadest sense, as a prelude to analysis.

In the past there were periods of relative stability or slow transformation, sometimes with regressions, but the modern age has been marked and, despite certain doubts which are beginning to surface, continues to be marked by virtually constant growth: economic growth, mainly exemplified by more material goods and higher GNPs, but also in many cases by inflation and an increase in the amount of money in circulation; population growth; technological growth permitting, for instance, higher speeds or increased capacities; growth of knowledge with an unprecedented accumulation of skills conjoined with also unprecedented accumulation of the mass of information actually or potentially available. We also have the growth of educational systems which take in more pupils or students than ever, under the dual effect of population growth and the demand for education, which itself goes hand in hand with the growing democratization of society. But the process, directed as it is towards quantitative increase, also results in other, less desirable, disquieting forms of accumulation. There again there are deliberate types of accumulation like the constantly increasing production and stockpiling of nuclear weapons and missiles capable of carrying warheads of ever greater destructive power. Then there are the consequences of growth itself, namely the waste products, the pollution and, generally speaking, those effects of human activity which strike at the overall balance of the planet.

The various phenomena just mentioned may all stem from growth, but the connections between them are far from simple. Besides, all growth problems raise a number of fundamental questions. First, there is the question of inequality. Far from diminishing it, growth really seems to make for greater inequality.

Economic growth has undoubtedly conferred major benefits, particularly in the now industrialized countries, where people can on the whole satisfy their basic needs in terms of food, housing, clothing and education; but this is not so in the developing countries, one possible definition of which is in fact that they cannot provide their inhabitants with these fundamental requirements of life. But in these countries there are often very great disparities as well between those at the helm in economic, administrative or political affairs and the broad strata of the population. In this connection, it is a fact that even when rapid economic growth is patterned on that of certain industrialized countries, it has very little effect in the developing countries on the people at large.

But within many developed countries themselves, there is malaise and deep-seated dissatisfaction due to uneven distribution of the benefits of growth. There are still inequalities based on sex since, despite progress made and the fact that all the stigmas which attached to them have to a greater or lesser extent disappeared, women often continue to be at a disadvantage, particularly in matters of income; there is also a great deal of inequality between social categories. Poverty areas still exist in the most developed regions, whether in the centre of the towns or in distant, neglected and marginal provinces. The poverty of the most disadvantaged sections of the population is of course much worse in the developing countries, whether it is a question of the rural masses or the often unemployed inhabitants of the over-populated outskirts of the large towns. The phenomena of unemployment, which are particularly serious in developing countries where growth, often limited to the modern sector, has not succeeded in ensuring full employment of human resources, have also taken on such dimensions in the last few years in certain developed countries that they constitute a major source of concern.

Equally serious are the questions which arise concerning the relationship between economic growth and the well-being of the individual. It is not a question only of the various deleterious effects of economic growth and industrialization, such as pollution of air and water, a use of space and of land which destroys the environment, rapid urban development and its many consequences. There is also the equally fundamental question of the way of life brought about by economic growth, which is giving rise to increasing concern in regard to the final aims of development. Often consumption, which is an essential element in sustaining economic growth, finds itself diverted to the satisfaction of needs which are not essential; more precisely, it is products and material objects which ultimately arouse needs whereas, logically, it should be needs which determine economic choices. This is doubtless the source of the alienation which many people feel when faced with the mechanisms of the consumer society. This feeling is all the more significant in that it finds complementary motivations in the way in which men experience their working time and their leisure time—they may feel dissatisfaction because their work is uninteresting, repetitive and offers no possibility for initiative or true self-fulfilment, or because their leisure time, always supposing that it is not just what is left over from the time absorbed by the various obligations of everyday life (transport for example) on top of working hours, may also be given over to satisfying artificial needs. To these various dissatisfactions may be added in many cases the feeling of not being in a position to play any part in defining and directing the process of growth. All in all, what is at stake is people's ability to influence their own destiny, to build a significant life and future and to establish creative relationships with others.

Moreover, growth brings about deep transformations in the social structures and the relationships between the different strands which make up the fabric of society. Thus it can upset the balance between groups or generations and create situations of maladjustment, tension or discord. The often difficult situation of old people in industrial societies bears witness to such discord. At another level, manifestations of maladjustment of all kinds may be noted, whether they are expressed through various types of violence, through asocial behaviour or through recourse to drugs.

These various problems internal to growth are undoubtedly as important as the external problems of its global limits, which aroused considerable attention some years ago. While there are certainly ultimate limits to growth, external limits determined by the finite nature of all human endeavour and by the equally finite dimensions of our planet (what is surprising is that men have acted without regard to so evident a fact), it is none the less undeniable that the question cannot be isolated from the whole nexus of problems raised by growth. Care not to go beyond the external limits—that is, not to produce serious or fatal deteriorations in the biosphere, and not to exhaust the natural non-renewable resources at the disposal of mankind—must go hand in hand with care to respect what may be termed the 'internal limits', that is the levels below which (it must be stressed once again) too numerous human groups are still living.

In any case, it is insufficient, as has already been seen, to consider the problem in quantitative terms. Growth refers back to something other than itself, for its significance cannot be found merely in its own logic, a logic which would be totally self-contained and would be no more than its own self-justification. The real problem is to know in what direction growth points, what are its final aims, how is man to find self-fulfilment through this process. This is the question that confronts all societies, whether developed or developing, when they seek to discover new types of growth or when they contrast imported models with the demands of their own structures and socio-cultural values, the factors that alone make true endogenous development possible. When and only when growth is directed towards the ends which individuals and groups fix for themselves, can it become development in the full sense of the term, that is, the full flowering of everything which exists in man in a latent state, the realization of his creativity in all its many forms and aspects.

The means and ends of development are thus the questions which are involved in the analysis of growth problems as they interact with each other. The analysis of such problems cannot be other than an abstract exercise if the phenomena are considered out of their specific context. It is within a given society, within a culture in the broadest sense, that questions of growth arise and have to be integrated into the overall project represented by development. The significance of these phenomena can be fully understood only in terms of an overall view of the knowledge, skills, attitudes and values which are characteristic of the various societies and of the period of history through which we are living.

It is thanks to the powers given to mankind by science and technology that societies have changed decisively over the last few centuries and are continuing to make progress in the contemporary world. Science and technology have brought great benefits to the human race and have contributed to freeing men—or at least many of them—from the constraints imposed by nature. They have given them considerable means of controlling natural phenomena and exploiting the earth's resources. However, this power itself is fraught with dangers, either because of the damage inflicted by man on the natural world, of which he forms part as a living creature and whose very survival is threatened by the harm he does, or because of the more effective means he has acquired for dominating his fellow-men, the extreme instances being the destructiveness of modern weapons or the possibilities for carrying out disturbing experiments which affect the biological or social existence of individuals. Science and technology are therefore at the heart of the problems stemming from the aspiration for a better future and the concern to avert the dangers hanging over the destiny of mankind.

It may be thought that science, in following its special process of development and as an intellectual structure, obeys nothing but its own internal logic, its autonomous dynamics. The nature of scientific research work is such that scientists are obliged to accept a code of ethics which sets the quest for knowledge for its own sake above all other considerations in the scale of values.

Because of its effects, science is not neutral, however. The activity of the scientist is a social fact, in the same way as the search, transmission and storage of knowledge, which are the responsibilities of institutions integrated within society. Seen from this angle, science cannot be regarded as developing independently from the other elements in the social process, by which it is greatly influenced. In this respect, it has political implications.

Here we have two points of view which are actually complementary, though entirely different. It cannot be said that one is right and the other wrong. The conflict between an approach which lays the emphasis on scientific objectives and an approach which lays the emphasis on economic and social objectives cannot be settled, nor can the discussion which regards the freedom and the planning of research as alternatives for the problem is not stated in the same terms in both cases. Moreover, the two points of view overlap. To the scientist, the planning of science is an activity having its theoretical bases in sociology, economics and other disciplines which themselves belong to science. To the politician, on the other hand, science is one of the sectors concerning which forecasts, choices and decisions are made, just like any other sector of the social system, of which it is an essential part. The universality of science, both as knowledge and as a common factor in the evolution of all societies, makes it imperative to reconcile these two points of view, which are not mutually exclusive. Two fundamental aspects of this universality illustrate the complementary nature of the two points of view.

The universality of scientific knowledge, which goes hand in hand with its objectivity and disinterested character, should lead us to consider the whole stock of such knowledge as the common heritage of mankind and to challenge any move which is seen to aim at the exclusive appropriation of scientific knowledge. If we adopt this attitude, it is right that such knowledge should be made available to all without reservations of any kind. This demand stems from the very code of ethics of the world of learning: the findings of research work should be accessible to the whole of mankind. This demand has implications, however, for the institutions and services which have to process scientific information and to organize its transfer and exchange at both the national and the international levels by means of effective tools and methodologies.

Here, without the slightest doubt, is a field of activity whose importance cannot be exaggerated. It affects relations between developed countries just as much as relations between developing and developed countries and is a major concern both in national policies and in international co-operation.

Conversely, a science policy directed towards goals bound up with economic and social development must respect the freedom and ultimate purposes of fundamental research, which is the hub of creative work irrigating the whole system of science and technology. All sectors of activity might be seriously disturbed if the stream of new knowledge ceased to flow from its source in fundamental research. Despite the universality of science, it must be admitted that the scientific and technological potential is unequally distributed throughout the world and that this is one of the most serious disparities of our time. To possess a high potential gives a society a dominant position in international relations; to be disadvantaged in this respect is one of the worst handicaps.

The effort to establish a more fair and equitable world order therefore highlights the problems of science and technology. While it is necessary for all countries to develop their scientific and technological potential, this is a task of particularly vital and urgent importance for the developing countries. The very possibility of ensuring that knowledge and techniques available elsewhere in the world and acquired by transfer are used in a way which meets the receiving society's real needs depends on research efforts made by that society itself. It means keeping abreast of the status and trends of scientific and technological development all over the world and, at the same time, adopting criteria for the selection of the technologies best suited to the country's needs. Accordingly, the existence of indigenous structures is a prerequisite for creating the receptivity which is essential if transfers are to be correctly assimilated by countries seeking to use technologies developed abroad.

Furthermore, it is not simply a matter of choosing technologies which offer an effective solution to urgent material problems such as those of industrialization and agricultural production. It is also a matter of facilitating their establishment by devising methods of transfer and adaptation which take account of the economic and socio-cultural characteristics of the importing country.

So, instead of importing technologies designed for another environment, it is better to try, whenever possible, to work out appropriate technologies in the developing countries themselves, taking into account a set of specific factors, including available resources, forms of energy to be used, the country's human potential. The establishment of a scientific and technological basis in every country must be regarded as a high priority task. The endogenous development of the appropriate techniques must be the culmination of an educational and cultural effort combining scientific lines of approach with the heritage of the past. In this connection, it is advisable to consider assigning a significant role to endeavours to reinstate technical traditions based on age-old skills which have long been neglected in the name of modernity. Because they tend to be regarded as a way of reasserting the cultural characteristics of a society, they can be an excellent means of winning the confidence of the whole population, and not just of an élite, so as to start a general movement towards a form of development benefiting widely from the participation and initiative of every individual. This approach is likely to prove successful in stimulating endogenous creativity. It is perhaps because it is rooted in a specific culture that this endogenous creativity can make a contribution which may prove to be of universal value.

But we must go further. Through their own scientific and technological potential, the developing societies should be able to make a substantial and original contribution to the joint creative effort whereby the whole complex structure of science and technology is built up. This concern for universality links up with the question of the action demanded in order to meet the specific needs of the developing countries themselves. From whatever angle this problem is approached, research options and priorities must not be limited to reflecting the trends that can be observed in the most advanced countries. On the contrary, it is to the extent that options and priorities take fully into account the specific objectives and requirements of the societies concerned, that research and development work will be able to operate on original lines and thus make a constructive contribution both to the development of these societies and to overall scientific and technological development. This is where the dimension of universality and cultural specificities come together; in striving, through their scientific and technical progress, to make the best possible use of their natural resources and human potential, the developing countries have several closely related objectives in view: to be independent of foreign technologies, to achieve the harmonious integration of cultural traditions with modern ideas and attitudes, to participate fully in the ongoing creative work of the whole international scientific and technological community.

It should be possible for the efforts of the developing countries to benefit from complementary activities initiated by the developed countries, which should themselves direct part of their scientific and technological research towards the solution of problems concerning the developing countries. This convergence of efforts is one of the elements that can give a real meaning to the sense of a world community.

It has to be admitted that it is rather the conflictual aspect of the contemporary world that has been the determining factor in the recent science policies of a large number of industrialized countries where the allocation of the largest proportion of resources has been governed by the imperative requirements of political rivalries or the pursuit of military aims. Vast sums have been devoted to research and experimental development for exclusively military purposes, amounting in some cases to from 30 to 50 per cent of national research expenditure. Further substantial resources have been allocated to major scientific and technological projects such as space programmes, as part of policies not unalloyed by prestige-seeking considerations. Lastly, it may be asked whether it was worth while to invest so heavily in the development of products designed to meet a consumer demand which is often artificial and a travesty of the real aspirations of man. Science has been associated too often with a certain model of society offering especially favourable conditions for the pursuit of political and military power, and for the consumption and wastage of natural resources.

In this way people have come to mistrust and even fear science—and their feeling is strengthened, furthermore, by the growing awareness of certain important consequences of scientific development such as, for example, the possibilities for interfering with the genetic code, deliberately changing atmospheric conditions, using omnipresent information systems on a large scale, and so on.

As a result, there is a more acute need to integrate the development of science more effectively with the whole range of society's ultimate aims. It is absolutely essential to reconcile the claims of the world of learning and those of policy-makers. Science and technology cannot be regarded as factors whose development can be left to chance or to forces which would use them for their own ends. Science and technology must serve the development of man and society as a whole and not merely certain restricted sectors, particular interests or specific aspects of the life of societies. In promoting development, it is necessary to take greater account of the whole complex of social needs, and to adopt courses of action consonant with the fundamental values of human life and the aspirations of the majority of human beings.

The fundamental problem now consists in taking action directed concurrently towards ensuring the development of science and technology, particularly through increasing the number and diversity of centres calculated to contribute to the advance of knowledge and its applications, and towards gaining real control of their evolution. Both these objectives, which imply a clearer and more penetrating vision of the rôle of science in society, make it imperative to develop the social sciences in such a way as to keep pace with the development of the exact and natural sciences and the various technologies. Greater importance should accordingly be given to the social sciences, for they can play a crucial rôle in the present situation. They are in a fair way to becoming the key factor in an approach that is common to the two vantage points—one founded on the claims of the world of learning and the other on those of policy-makers—from which science can be considered.

In the course of the foregoing analyses the importance of cultural factors has been repeatedly emphasized. Neither economic growth nor the development of science and technology should be achieved at the cost of sacrificing a people's cultural identity. A future world civilization would be devoid of meaning if it were to be based on standardization and banality and not on a wealth of original cultural features.

Inasmuch as it is rooted in tradition, culture has sometimes been regarded as an obstacle to modernization. But far from being a drawback, the fact that countries refuse to lose their identity by accepting alien models should be welcomed both from the national and from the global point of view. For what is rejected never amounts to more than an imitation lacking the authenticity that gives human enterprises their vigour and value. On the other hand—and there are examples to prove it—the conquest of modernity in the Third World countries can be achieved by other means than the passive adoption of a process copied from foreign models. A people's awareness of its cultural identity can be a force that supports economic development and modernization and gives them a special dynamic quality. Modernity is then regarded as the stage of reactualization of the forms, relationships and symbols constituting the specific style and meaning of a culture, which is reached after a stage of interrogation when obsolete elements are discarded as no longer relevant to contemporary conditions.

The demand for recognition of cultural identity, which is one of the most characteristic features of our time, is not a futile, nostalgic attachment to the vanished past. It is, of course, linked with tradition, that record of experience accumulated throughout the course of history by a community. But its real significance lies in the use of the past as leaven for the future. The notion of cultural identity, which crystallized the aspirations of the peoples of the Third World once they had been liberated from colonial domination, is still a decisive factor in their determination to tackle the future in their own way, one that is free from the various—and sometimes insidious—forms of alienation that may be imposed upon them by societies whose structures and ways of life and development set themselves up as models at a given point in history.

To assert one's cultural identity is to resolve to be one's self, but this does not imply withdrawal and isolation. On the contrary, it is by remaining true to themselves that cultures can evolve harmoniously, grow stronger and maintain a fruitful give-and-take relationship with other cultures. Thus, the preservation of the cultural heritage, in its most diverse aspects—whether it be a matter of safeguarding monuments and towns from the ravages of time, pollution or the effects of human action, or of ensuring the vitality of languages, oral traditions and performing arts and music—is at one and the same time, and inseparably, an endeavour to strengthen cultural identity, the prerequisite for making a culture available and receptive to all the others, and an enrichment for mankind as a whole. It is accordingly by mutual knowledge of, and respect for, different cultures that a genuine cultural symbiosis can be built up on a world scale, which will involve neither the domination of a particular form of culture covering a range of limited values, nor a kind of cultural cosmopolitanism resulting from a pooling of that which, in each culture, is non-essential and verges on the commonplace. When it comes to the world scale, only that which is of value in each culture can be included in the notion of cultural identity.

Nothing is more difficult to define, however, than the reality of a culture and of culture in general. Narrow, élitist definitions of culture, viewed as the system of fine arts and literature, a luxury reserved for the privileged few, must be superseded. Culture, in the full sense of the term, is a fundamental component of the vitality of any society; it is the sum total of a people's creative activities, its methods of production and of appropriation of material assets, its form of organization, its beliefs and sufferings, its work and its leisure, its dreams and its successes. This being so, in addition to the policies governing culture itself, policies in other spheres of human activity, and particularly in education and communication, must be worked out.

For concomitant with the search for cultural identity is the henceforth clearly affirmed determination of each society to plan and carry out educational action geared to its own particular objectives, rejecting anything that may imply imposing knowledge, attitudes and behaviour patterns inconsistent with its real aspirations and needs. Very often, the educational systems of the developing countries are mere copies of the systems devised in the industrialized countries for the benefit of other societies, employing other means and serving other values. It is an essential task of educational policy-makers to redefine and remodel their educational systems in the light of their countries' own aims and their actual socio-economic and cultural conditions.

As for communication, a parallel requirement is to steer clear of the risks of cultural extroversion which may arise from the fact that all countries are not equally well equipped with communication media. At the present time, the dissemination of information is largely a one-way process, issuing from a few centres mainly located in the industrialized countries. Such information perforce reflects the concerns, aspirations and even the point of view of the societies from which it stems and on whose media it depends, and their mass communication organizations have a tendency, whether they will or no, to exercise *de facto* domination which may impose cultural models. It is vitally important to establish the necessary conditions for a truly balanced exchange of information, which is the only base for any attempt to create genuine international solidarity.

Education and communication should play a decisive part in preserving or giving fresh significance to men's relationships with their environment and with the communities to which they belong. All too often, education appears to do just the opposite, thus leading to alienation. This is sometimes the case, in the developed and developing countries alike, when education seems to be cut off from the important things of life and consequently tends to create passivity and indifference. Ways of remedying such situations depend, of course, on having policies adapted to the cultural conditions and objectives of each society. However, among the efforts to make education more meaningful and to integrate it more closely with the real life of society, attention should be drawn to measures designed to associate productive work with education. Such programmes may make an important contribution to the renewal of educational curricula and methods, forge closer links between intellectual and manual occupations and enable young people, through productive work, to contribute to the development of their society and even to create resources which help to cover the cost of their education. This is but one example of the sort of education which would foster creative capacities.

Education which stimulates social awareness and public participation to tackling communal problems helps to increase the ability of each people to produce new ideas and create new resources and techniques; it also facilitates the latter's utilization in the interests of society as a whole.

Communication policies should likewise be aimed at fostering creativity, in order to react against the tendency to receive messages passively. The mass media today are a powerful means of expression and it is important to make it possible, on as wide a scale as possible, to master their techniques and use the means of intellectual and artistic expression which they offer.

Each of the foregoing analyses, bearing on some particular aspect of the problems arising in the modern world, leads up to a more general, overall subject, that of *the development of people and societies*. For that is the widest concept of all, taking in the different aspects of world problems—whether quantitative or qualitative, whether they concern the industrialized or the developing countries; it is a global notion, considered in a multidimensional context, economic as well as social, scientific, technological and cultural. In a word, it is a process which necessarily involves a diversity of paths and goals, adjusted to the different sets of values peculiar to each society. Development viewed in this light incorporates the characteristics of unity in diversity which are peculiar to the current world situation.

Although the problems of development are foremost among the concerns of the less advanced countries, they also concern the so-called developed countries. It has rightly been said that the world contains only developing countries. Many industrialized countries are going through economic and monetary crises, experiencing serious shortages in a given sector of production, and are facing environmental problems or difficulties affecting this or that part of the national community. They are obliged to think about the ways, means and goals of integrated, harmonious development. Faced with the standardizing process of the industrial model, worsened by the insufficiently controlled pre-eminence of the mass communication media, with the changes in economic or social structures which cut the individual off from his roots, with the critical situation in regard to young people, towns or popular culture, many of the developed countries are having to seek for a new type of development. The ultimate aim of such development must be to restore man to himself, that is to say, to give him space which broadens his existence instead of restricting it, time which allows for his needs and wishes, a town into which he can fit instead of being rejected, a community henceforth at one, and work which accords him dignity and freedom. Growth has no meaning unless it contributes to the fulfilment of individuals and of the community, unless it offers greater chances to be human and to create.

Such a view of development is obviously far removed from one that takes into account only its economic dimension, i.e. growth measured in quantitative terms, by the level of the Gross National Product, for example. Development of this kind, based solely on market forces, can only lead to greater disparities and more dissatisfaction of all sorts. The process of development, as we have seen, is necessarily multidimensional. It involves not only a community's economic potential and activity, but also its social cohesion and cultural values. Taken in the broadest sense of the term, the process of development should be the concrete expression in social practice, through words and actions, of a particular interpretation of the universe and man's situation in it.

In other words, this multidimensional, global process, considered from the point of view of the factors of which it is made up, cannot be identical in differing societies. Development can only be endogenous, precisely because it must take account of all the components that go to make up the particular pattern of this or that society and give it a character or style which is unlike any other. Hence it is a mistake to think that the developing countries should necessarily copy in every respect the development models worked out at other times and in other places by the countries that are now industrialized. The centres of economic power today are not in a position to provide us with methods that can be generalized. It is for each society to search for and work out the style of development that best suits its social structures and their underlying attitudes and forms, as well as the values which they determine.

Development in its universality and diversity is a process which is found everywhere, but its centre is nowhere. The conviction that this is so—a conviction based on an attentive analysis of the problems of the world situation—naturally leads us to doubt the validity of an international system which, explicitly or implicitly, assumes that certain centres of economic power are pre-eminent and that international relations have a rationale of their own. Recent crises, such as the monetary crisis and the energy crisis, have indeed shown the limitations of this system.

Most countries, whether developed or developing, have been affected to some degree by the manifestations of a crisis affecting international relations. Unemployment, recession, inflation, the deterioration of the situation of the least advanced countries— these are symptoms of the various forms of imbalance in the international economic system. In point of fact, there is a deep-seated contradiction between the logic underlying the present international system, centred as it is round the industrialized countries, and the demand for an overall solution of the problems, based on solidarity and justice. The clearest proof of this contradiction lies in the demand of the developing countries for a new kind of economic relations with the industrialized countries, which would ensure that each country controlled its own natural resources and could use them for the benefit of its people, participating on an equal footing in the decisions which affect the operation of the international economic system—a demand, in short, for the adoption of new and more equitable rules in national economic relations. These aspirations have centred around the idea of a new international economic order, the formulation of which by the international community has led to the adoption by the United Nations General Assembly of the Declaration and Programme of Action on the Establishment of a New International Economic Order (1 May 1974) and the Charter of Economic Rights and Duties of States (12 December 1974).

In reality, if we take an overall view of these problems, one which is consistent with Unesco's specific mission—that of reflection upon the various problems of our day in so far as they are concerned with science, culture, education or information—we shall conceive of the movement towards a new international economic order in its broadest sense, i.e. as a movement towards a world order embracing its economic, social and cultural dimensions and satisfying the basic human aspirations towards progress, peace and justice.

It should be emphasized that to accept this principle is in no way to underestimate the importance of urgent economic problems the solution of which is a necessary condition of any other form of progress. In stressing the social and cultural aspects, there is no intention whatsoever of committing Unesco to some sort of superficial idealism which would lead only to ineffectiveness or to what might be called 'other worldliness' that leaves the various facts of economic life out of account. Nothing would be more dangerous than to allow emphasis on questions of a socio-cultural nature—for example, the fact that the idea of economic rationality is foreign to certain developing societies—to be used as an argument in favour of the forces which tend to maintain what may be called economic hegemony in the world.

To see the problems of international economic relations in a broader framework is, in reality, both to demonstrate the importance of social and cultural factors in the attainment of purely economic objectives and to emphasize the fact that economic concerns are part of a multidimensional whole made up of human requirements and values.

In the last analysis, the concept of a new international order is something more than a certain way of organizing the relations between States, something more than a set of legal rules based on the recognition of rights and duties; it is the acceptance of a certain system of values, the values of justice, equality, liberty and solidarity, and the will to give them real effect. These values will be based on a new awareness in two respects, viz: recognition of the unity of mankind, with all its diverse peoples, races and cultures; and the assertion of a desire to live together, actually experienced not simply as a necessity for survival or coexistence but as the deliberate choice of fashioning a common destiny together, with joint responsibility for the future of the human race.[1]

AMADOU-MAHTAR M'BOW
Director-General of Unesco

1. *Moving towards Change: Some Thoughts on the New International Economic Order*, p. 25, 26, Paris, Unesco, 1976.

1 Universal affirmation of human rights

The universal assurance of human rights is not only a major necessity of our time, but its very hallmark, distinguishing it from earlier ages. People today, in their attitudes towards the recognition and application of human rights, are no longer prepared to accept without question a universality which represents no more than an ideal, abstract principle to be put into effect in the unforeseeable future and the mere affirmation of which would be sufficient to sanction the existence of privileged enclaves of achievement and vast areas of darkness, stagnation and despair. Effective universality is now the yardstick for measuring the conditions of human existence, and by that standard the public conscience cannot fail to be shocked by the fate of part of mankind. This awakening consciousness and this demand of our times are reflected in the fact that the international community has proclaimed the principle that all are entitled to the same rights, and has pledged itself collectively to work together to achieve those rights for all, 'without distinction of any kind, such as . . . colour, sex, language, religion, political . . . opinion, . . . birth or other status', and without acceptance of any special circumstances, historical, social, or other, as warranting or excusing any violation of those rights, disregard of them, or failure to make resolute efforts to secure their gradual achievement.

Effective universality of human rights—a fundamental necessity

Immediately after the end of a world war which, with all its train of suffering, had sprung from denial of human rights and had itself carried that denial to the extreme, the pressing need to reaffirm those rights in all their aspects was seen to be essential as the only possible foundation for the building of a just and lasting peace. From then on, an all-embracing conception of human rights began to emerge: civil and political rights, economic, social and cultural rights gained recognition and demanded action to sustain them as interrelated components of a single whole, transcending the level at which their requirements might appear to compete with one another.

The struggles of various peoples for their liberation, the emergence of new independent nations, the establishment, gradually covering the whole of the planet, of an international community pledged to the pursuit of common ideals, the revolt, or the clamant sufferings, of oppressed or exploited minorities, all combined to complete this process of developing awareness and to give this demand its full impact, from the three standpoints of effective universality in the application of human rights; indissolubility of civil and political rights and economic, social and cultural rights; and the necessary rôle of men and women themselves—individually and in groups—in the struggle for human dignity, and in the development and building up of a world order and a social order in which their rights and those of others would be guaranteed. For it is a mockery to grant explicit freedoms to those who are prevented, by destitution, from exercising them; but, on the other hand, to improve the material well-being of the prople at large while they are kept in bondage and in ignorance, excluded from the community of human relations and the mainstream of history, would also be a denial of the dignity of man.

Recent decades, then, have seen a decisive advance in the full affirmation, for the whole of humanity, of that respect for man without which there can be no public morality; and in the recognition of the fact that human rights are necessarily indivisible: their violation in the case of a single human being implies the flouting and denial of the very principle from which they spring; if only certain rights are recognized and guaranteed, the denial or disregard of others is a sufficient denunciation of the illusory character of such partial observance.

Realities that fall far short of aspirations

And yet, in comparison with this clear need, what blemishes mar the picture that the actual situation presents! Not only are human rights still not effectively assured in practice in most of the world's countries, but there is nothing to suggest that any steady, undeviating progress is being made towards improvement: clashes of interest, overriding reasons of State, sudden, sharp changes in the economy and in social relationships, the vicissitudes of national and international policy, inter-group antagonisms, fluctuations in power relationships, the pressures of egoism, intolerance or obscurantism, the pretexts afforded by circumstances—all these are continually responsible for shameful retreats which may well produce indignation and alarm. It would indeed be disastrous if, in the end, these retreats were to be met by the false wisdom or illusory realism of resigned acceptance.

Specific violations of human rights take many different forms in our present-day world: deliberate violations that State authorities, claiming to be the sole judges of their legitimacy, justify on the grounds of particular circumstances of political or social crisis, the need for the maintenance of order or the safeguarding of national unity; flagrant violations (although there is often an attempt to conceal these beneath a travesty of the very principles that are being trampled underfoot) such as those revealed in exceptional, localized situations—apartheid, vestiges or upsurges of colonialist or neo-colonialist oppression, foreign occupation; less obvious violations, embodied in the structures or the functioning of unjust societies which, under the veneer of formal democracy, engage in forms of oppression and exploitation that bear particularly heavily on underprivileged groups or on certain categories of individuals, including the great mass of women; interference with freedom of thought, conscience or religion, or with the possibility of seeking, receiving or spreading information or ideas; violations of which the community has more recently become conscious, such as those involved in the unjustified appropriation of natural and cultural resources or the despoiling of the environment or, again, those that may, for individuals and nations, attend the consequences of scientific and technological progress; violations arising from contempt for or rejection of cultural identity, or from the tensions present in multi-ethnic societies; and so on. The problem of the protection and application of human rights is immense, since it covers every aspect of the life of individuals and groups.

The full achievement of human rights and its implications

The determination to promote human rights is at the basis of all the great purposes by which mankind is motivated at this point in its history; it gives them their significance, sets their trends and likewise imposes certain criteria for the action to which they give rise. The assurance of human rights and the *construction of peace* are tasks that go hand-in-hand, no doubt because any war irremediably compromises the exercise of rights of all kinds, while denial of rights, in itself, inevitably ends by engendering violence; and because a peace based on inequality, domination and exploitation, even if it could be maintained by compulsion, would be peace in name only. But an even deeper reason is that the universal application of human rights coincides with the building up, both materially and spiritually, of a genuine human community taking in all mankind. The achievement of human rights on the scale of mankind as a whole also implies that all should enjoy living conditions that will not expose them to hunger, destitution, apprehension for the future, the extremes of ignorance and social exclusion, or condemn them to distress and despair. It accordingly implies the *development of all nations*; it further implies their independence in co-operation, and mutual recognition of their dignity. At the same time, it is by his very efforts in the cause of development, in the achievement of independence and in the practice of discussion on equal terms, that man, with his inherent rights, gains stature, and fulfils his potential. Springing from the dialectic of development taken in its fullest sense, the desire for *balance* and *harmony between man and his environment* (both natural and socio-cultural), the striving after *communication* which will provide the foundation for a real life in common, the determination to establish a *new economic and social order* on a world scale that will be an order based on justice and co-operation for common purposes—all these reflect at different levels the demand for the full and universal implementation of human rights.

While, then, the fate of men and women is in their own hands, no international organization is better placed than Unesco to appreciate the vital and fundamental importance of the promotion of human rights, to bring it home to people, and to translate it into practical programme terms. Indeed Unesco, by appealing to men's minds and calling upon intellectual resources, seeks to help in giving all men the means for their own liberation, their accession to a better life, and the building up of a real community among them. The problem of the promotion of human rights is naturally in the forefront of those on which the Organization intends to focus its action, as a reference to the ultimate purpose of such action. But at the same time, the promotion of human rights takes a practical form *vis-à-vis* the specific problems with which mankind is confronted today. Ultimately it involves the whole range of Unesco's activities directed to achieving a host of particular objectives; conversely, concern to secure the observance and achievement of human rights is bound to qualify and determine, in various specific contexts, the way in which Unesco deals with the other problems claiming its attention. It is no accident that, in listing the aspects of our present human problems with which the question of the full exercise of human rights is linked, we should have come back to the main lines of the schedule of problems that Unesco has resolved to tackle. Alone among all the organizations belonging to the United Nations system, Unesco can lay claim to a dual mission: it has to work for the promotion of human rights in the particular fields of its competence, and it must have a place at the very centre from which particular rights emanate, clarifying them, ensuring their recognition, and promoting them, and the principles behind them, as a whole.

It is none the less true that, while the full achievement of human rights presupposes patient efforts in the furtherance of development, the dissemination of knowledge and the equalization of opportunities for acquiring it, the humanizing of the environment and the background to life, the enhancement of cultures and communication between them and the promotion of a genuine mutual communication system among people, this does not mean that active measures for the protection, achievement and extension of human rights can be put off until tomorrow except at the cost of an intolerable abdication. It is one thing to take into account, as we must, the fact that circumstances are difficult, the need for patient improvement of the conditions determining the life of every society and the extent and level of what it can achieve, the limited amount and precarious nature of the resources that can be mobilized for this purpose, and the need for a determined and prolonged effort to build a better and a juster world. It would be quite another to disregard the obligation, admitting of no compromise, to tackle without further ado all the clear denials of human rights which are already such a scandal. In the first case, what is involved is a question of degree—a more or less satisfactory position as regards the possible achievement of rights. In the second instance, a question of principle is at stake: the question of respect for man, which is indivisible. The difficulties of the times do not remove the scandal of inequality—rather the reverse; the requirements of public order and safety—not to mention the will to power—can neither justify nor excuse arbitrary arrest and the use of torture, any more than concern for growth—not to mention the lure of gain—can make the subjection and exploitation of human labour acceptable, or than the desire to build up an intellectual elite can warrant keeping the mass of the people in ignorance. Without prejudice to the persistent efforts needed to build a world more conducive to the full enjoyment of human rights, the protection, consolidation and extension of those same rights call urgently for resolute, specific, direct action.

The first aspect of the programme relates to research: research directed to increasing our knowledge about human rights, their content and interrelations, studying the necessary conditions for their achievement, and identifying and denouncing violations of those rights in the day-to-day functioning of societies; research of a more formal, legal nature, which relates to the methods of official recognition, institutional measures calculated to guarantee the protection of rights by the public authorities and to ensure that individuals whose inherent rights may be endangered have the possibility of remedy at law.

The second is concerned with respect for cultural identity as the basis of the free self-determination and self-fulfilment of individuals and groups. It draws on experience of two kinds: favourable, in the appreciation of the values inherent in each culture and the importance for individuals and groups of unfettered participation in the values of their own particular culture; and unfavourable, in the case of peoples or groups who have been under domination and deprived of that culture, and of individuals, excluded from society, with the impoverishment and far-reaching disturbances that result from such alienation, and the forms of protest and cultural metamorphosis that go with it. A definition must, however, be given of the purposes for which cultural identity is to be defended and promoted: not introspective withdrawal but increased participation in larger communities, mutual appreciation of the values of all peoples, fuller integration in development and, in the case of communities that are today rejected or in a marginal position, the right to existence and dialogue on a footing of equality.

A third aspect relates to a part of humanity that has for too long been subject to discrimination, or even exploitation: women. It combines the vital need to ensure that women can exercise human rights to the full, with the requirement that there should be a far-reaching improvement of their status. The programme is designed to bring to light, so that they can be eliminated, the factors which have led to the inferior status of women and still jeopardize the full exercise of their rights, and is also concerned with the positive definition and application of measures designed to bring about a change for the better in the status of women in various societies, which is linked up with the need to promote active participation by women in the work of development.

Special attention is to be given to the defence of the rights of a category of human beings who are particularly wronged or threatened—refugees and members of national liberation movements. The right to education, in particular, as an instrument of emancipation, is especially important in this context, as well as the right to cultural identity. This is a particular, and specially acute, instance of the denial of human rights.

The last aspect deals with the mobilization of the means afforded by education and information for spreading awareness of the vital need for universal observance of human rights, explaining the content and interrelations of those rights, and giving people the means and the desire to go more deeply into the conditions required to secure human rights and to work for their achievement.

Understanding and ensuring human rights

With perhaps greater vigour than ever, the international community is at present manifesting its resolve to promote the universal consummation of human rights, understood in the widest and fullest sense of the term. However, it finds itself today, in a manner of speaking, at a crossroads.

Work achieved since 1945

Normative work was undertaken on an international scale in 1945 following a war which was, first and foremost, a fight for man. This work, of which the linchpin is the 1948 Universal Declaration of Human Rights, is, to a certain extent, complete. It takes the form of an apparently all-embracing series of international standards defining human rights, set out either in declarations or in the fifty or so treaties and conventions on human rights, and backed by an impressive number of public bodies (intergovernmental bodies like the United Nations Commission on Human Rights and also independent bodies such as, in the case of Unesco, the Conciliation and Good Offices Commission set up in connection with the Convention against Discrimination in Education) as well as several private non-governmental organizations. These various bodies or organizations have been given the task, or have taken it upon themselves, not to penalize but simply to identify by a very varied range of methods (judicial, semi-judicial, consultative, administrative, political) the most serious violations of human rights in the world.

The feeling that a stage in the international protection and promotion of human rights is coming to an end, is further strengthened by the entry into force of the International Covenants on Economic, Social and Cultural Rights (3 January 1976) and on Civil and Political Rights (23 March 1976). These two instruments have for the international community the value of constitutional texts inasmuch as they provide, with the Universal Declaration, a universally valid set of criteria which must henceforth be used to guide all action or evaluate every situation.

Recurrent infringements of human rights

Nevertheless, the 'peoples of the United Nations' in whose name the San Francisco Charter was drawn up and adopted, all feel the need for new measures which would make it possible for human rights to become a reality generally observed. The truth is that deeds and practices still fall far short of ambitions and declared intentions. Violations of human rights remain a common event, whether they are open and deliberate or more covert. To begin with, particular situations still exist which provide an opportunity or pretext for a radical denial of human rights, as in southern Africa where racial discrimination is systematic. In other places, the exercise of civil and political rights is hamstrung by infringements of the freedoms normally accorded to individuals and groups. On other occasions still, there are forms of discrimination which affect people's place of residence or access to employment. Finally, there is evidence of the practice of torture, so much so that the General Assembly of the United Nations was led, at its 30th session, unanimously to adopt a resolution condemning torture in all its forms.

The recurrence of these situations has recently led the majority of worldwide or regional international organizations to take a variety of steps, such as the adoption by the United Nations General Assembly of resolution 3221 (XXIX) which urges the desirability of exploring alternative approaches and ways and means in the field of human rights.

Towards a focusing of activities

At the start of this new move in favour of human rights, one concern in everybody's mind is that these rights should not be devalued by a multiplicity of declarations conveying false hopes and ill able to mask the sad facts. What is rather needed is a *deepening of the knowledge of human rights and a consolidation of what has been achieved in the way of standards and institutions* during the period which has only just ended. The task first of all is to protect man as he is, man with a situation and a place in history, through the rights provided for by the declarations in force, and only then to consider new rights for man in the abstract.

The task is first of all to enlarge the legal, indeed too legal, notion of human rights through contributions from other disciplines, chief of which must be the social sciences, before proposing new legal standards for adoption by States. The main aim of work in the social sciences in this connexion is to throw light on the specific circumstances in which individuals and groups can effectively enjoy their rights. The social sciences essentially attempt to analyse social relationships and practices, including those that determine the way in which the machinery and institutions for guaranteeing the exercise of human rights actually function. The sociological examination of violations of human rights, and more generally, of situations in which these rights are denied, is thus of crucial importance. It is in the light of this work that the functioning of existing machinery and procedures for the international protection of human rights should be consolidated before recommending States to adopt new measures.

This period of study and consolidation provides Unesco with a real opportunity for illuminating and focusing more effectively the various international activities undertaken on behalf of human rights. The work which has just been completed is in fact somewhat fragmentary: the instruments adopted by various international and national organizations contain a number of contradictions and liaison is awkward between the different world-wide or regional bodies set up to secure the recognition of, or respect for, human rights; accordingly public opinion frequently has difficulty in grasping the necessarily global character of the efforts made to promote these rights by the United Nations agencies and by other organizations.

Unesco, by the very nature of its tasks, is ideally suited to assume responsibility, during this period of study and consolidation, for advancing the cause of human rights taken in their entirety, by encouraging and assisting the international community to use, in the service of this cause, whatever educational, research and information resources it can muster.

The institutional framework

Research into human rights and into the best ways of enforcing them is indissociable from the principle of an organized international community.

International organizations with responsibility for human rights have sometimes entrusted this work to a specialized body. In the case of the United Nations, it is the Commission on Human Rights—and more especially its Sub-Commission on Prevention of Discrimination and Protection of Minorities—and the Commission on the Status of Women. In the case of the League of Arab States, it is the permanent Arab States Commission on Human Rights; with the Organization of America States it is the Inter-American Commission on Human Rights and with the Council of Europe, its Committee of Experts on Human Rights. Other organizations, like the International Labour Organisation and Unesco, have relied more on the appropriate units in their secretariats. The United Nations has combined both methods.

The research conducted by these bodies or administrative departments was hitherto concerned with defining rather than enforcing the legal standards of human rights.

The studies and investigations directed towards the guaranteeing of human rights are entrusted preferably to specialized bodies set up on an *ad hoc* basis or according to the terms of particular provisions made in an international human rights convention. In the United Nations for instance there are the Special Committee on Apartheid, the Special Committee on Decolonization, the Committee on the Elimination of Racial Discrimination and the Committee on Human Rights. In ILO, there are the bodies provided for under its Constitution, and also its Governing Body's Committee on Freedom of Association. The Organization of African Unity has its Liberation Committee while the Council of Europe has the bodies set up under the European Convention on Human Rights, the Commission and the Court, as well as those associated with the European Social Charter. Lastly, there are the bilateral methods employed by the socialist States for the international promotion of human rights, particularly cultural rights.

Whether directed towards setting standards for the promotion of human rights or ensuring their enforcement, international studies and investigations have always been supported and sustained and sometimes even initiated by a host of national and international movements, organizations, groups and institutes, most frequently of a private nature. And it will be to their eternal honour to have originated the Universal Declaration of Human Rights.

Unesco's action and the contribution of the social sciences

This proliferation of instruments and institutions none the less gives to even the most optimistic an impression of confusion and weakness, and to others a feeling of failure. The excessive dispersion of effort will thus have to be overcome by means of an overall approach to all the aspects and implications of the problem of human rights in order that this feeling of failure shall not become the acknowledgement of a reality.

In so far as regards Unesco, which by its very purpose has always been dedicated to the cause of human rights and peace, its most recent activities extend in two directions. First it operates a major *programme of social studies* devoted to the elucidation of certain general factors conducive or inimical to the advance of human rights and to the analysis of certain specific social situations entailing serious violations of human rights, particularly in connexion with colonialism and racial oppression, and especially to unmasking and condemming the social institutions and practices which perpetuate these grave injustices. The first group of studies has borne mainly on ways of eliminating racism and racial discrimination and has led to meetings of experts and to studies and publications either of general significance or applying to particular situations, especially those found in southern Africa. Other questions studied have been inter-group relations in multi-ethnic societies, the role played by the various factors making for discrimination and inequality and ways and means of establishing more equitable social relationships which are more in conformity with human dignity and human rights.

The second direction in which Unesco's activities have been turned in recent years has been towards *defining in greater depth the rights existing within its fields of competence* and examining the optimum conditions for their enforcement. The Organization has attempted to improve the working of existing legal instruments, particularly the Convention against Discrimination in Education, and to prepare new instruments concerning education, access to culture and the protection of the cultural heritage. A start has also been made on examining problems not all of whose aspects are as yet fully explored, and particular mention may be made of a meeting of experts on 'Human Rights and Population' and a symposium on biology and ethics. Akin to this work to clarify and illustrate human rights and ways of implementing them, particularly at international level, is the encouragement given by Unesco to furthering the advanced study of these rights, either through surveys concerning the organization of university research and teaching on these subjects, or through the development and dissemination of methodological guides, handbooks, etc.

The two broad series of activities just described have been supplemented over the last two years by Unesco's *increased participation* in the work of all the United Nations bodies with responsibilities for human rights.

Overall approach and specific studies

Under its Constitution, Unesco has special responsibility for everything involving prevention of the various forms of discrimination and promotion of the rights to education, science, culture and information in the service of peace. With the passage of time, however, extra tasks have been entrusted to it, either by its own General Conference or by the United Nations' General Assembly or Economic and Social Council (ECOSOC), in regard to the race problem, apartheid, the preparation of textbooks on human rights for higher education, or surveys on particular issues.

In the coming years, Unesco's action should be guided by three principles.

First, in the light of Unesco's particular responsibilities, an *overall approach* to human rights will have to be encouraged in order to gather together the fragmentary components—as regards both international standards and their implementation—so that they can be better known and more effectively taught. Without abandoning the search for solutions to the eternal conflict between the individual and the State, it is also necessary to promote knowledge and recognition of human rights as an arena affording the possibility of co-operation between the individual and the State when faced with the abuse of private power (e.g. by multinational corporations) or within the framework of a new economic order. Finally, only this overall approach will enable human rights to be made personal by adapting their requirements to particular situations relating, for example, to multi-ethnic or multi-racial societies, socially excluded groups or groups which have been relegated to an inferior position.

Secondly it will be necessary to further the *specificity of cultural rights*, taken in the broad sense of the term, since these are rights for which Unesco bears particular responsibility. As cultural rights denote inherent qualities of man *vis-à-vis* organized society and at the same time reflect man's beliefs as to the nature of that society, they are both individual and collective in character, culture truly deserving its name only if it belongs to everyone and if it is expressed for the benefit of all: in short, only if it is shared. This will be the principle which must for example govern Unesco's contribution to the human rights activities of the United Nations, and primarily with regard to implementation of the world code of human rights formed by the two Covenants of 1966.

Thirdly, there must be a redoubling of vigilance and of the spirit of accuracy and objectivity in the *scientific* study of the complex problems raised by the effective implementation of human rights, which must include an analysis of the underlying reasons why they are so frequently flouted. Knowledge of the social structures which provide the backcloth for any ethical assertion and any formulation of human rights, as for any attempt to promote them, requires to be taken further and also extended to cover other societies and other aspects. Elucidation of the philosophical and cultural attitudes subtending acceptance or refusal or standard-setting activities is also of major importance. Unesco is here again fulfilling a task specific to it. In the final analysis, the effort called for will have to be directed, on the one hand, to adopting a rigorous scientific approach to all Unesco's human rights activities and, on the other, to infusing research in all Unesco's fields with the concern to illuminate and to serve human rights. Human rights are neither a new morality nor a lay religion and are much more than a language common to all mankind. They are requirements which the investigator must study and integrate into his knowledge using the rules and methods of his science, whether this is philosophy, the humanities or the natural sciences, sociology or law, history or geography. In a word, the task is gradually to build up or promote a genuine scientific formulation of human rights.

These three principles of action should guide Unesco in the two aspects of its practical activities on behalf of human rights which are defined in the above analysis: deepening the knowledge of human rights and consolidating what has been achieved.

Deepening . . .

Action in favour of *deepening the knowledge of human rights* should thus be centred on an analysis of the violations of these rights and the manifestations, causes and effects of these violations, with particular reference to racism, colonialism, neo-colonialism and apartheid. It should also form part of the Decade for Action to Combat Racism and Racial Discrimination and have recourse particularly to the social sciences in which important research work has been carried out. Sociological examination is also very much needed for the necessary study of the socio-economic phenomena which affect the exercise of human rights, particularly those of groups and especially socially excluded groups such as minorities and migrant workers.

Between now and 1982, appropriate programme action will be directed specifically towards:

Acquiring a better understanding of the main socio-economic processes at work in situations of racial discrimination, apartheid, colonialism and neo-colonialism.

Building up a body of knowledge which will throw light on the functioning of the principal types of multi-ethnic societies and the ideological and cultural aspects of ethnic awareness, thus encouraging the adoption of social policies better able to guarantee the exercise of human rights in the societies in question.

Shedding light on the relationships existing between certain socio-economic and cultural phenomena (especially those associated with rapid technological change and accelerated urban development) and the exercise of human rights in general and the rights of socially excluded groups in particular. This additional knowledge will have been put to use more especially in connection with the efforts to establish a new international economic order.

... consolidating

Action to *consolidate what has been achieved in the way of standards and institutions* should be aimed at developing a specialized study of human rights, along lines directed towards the guaranteeing of such rights in a manner which will have to be, if not integrated, at least co-ordinated among all international organizations. Unesco intends, within its fields of competence, to improve existing legal instruments, having regard to the appropriate articles of the Universal Declaration of Human Rights and the Covenants. At the same time, it will participate in systematic development of the various research activities relating to human rights at international level, both as regards improving the conceptual framework and in the matter of establishing a network of institutions.

Unesco will seek to initiate a wide-ranging debate at international level on the problems raised by the right to communication and ways of promoting it.

... through teaching

Between now and 1982 efforts will be made to encourage the development of courses and research programmes on human rights, the setting up or enlargement of specialist departments in university and scientific establishments and the training of teachers and research workers in this field.

Unesco's action will also be aimed at developing methods for the advanced study of human rights and preparing the necessary teaching material and reference works.

... and co-operation

Steps will be taken to make the Organization's standard-setting activity more effective and to secure better co-ordination with similar activities carried out by the other agencies of the United Nations system, particularly by participation in the implementation of the International Covenant on Economic, Social and Cultural Rights, under the auspices of the Economic and Social Council, and by the study of reports and in information provided by governments on measures adopted, progress made and obstacles encountered in securing the rights which fall within Unesco's purview.

Cultural identity and cultural pluralism

The assertion of cultural identity is now widely recognized as a powerful factor in the life of the nations as well as in international relations. Firstly as a factor making for liberation, cultural identity provides a justification for independence movements and resistance to colonialism. For newly established States cultural identity remains a guarantee of their very existence as a nation. The right to one's own culture is invoked throughout the world, in the fight against racial, ethnic, linguistic or cultural discrimination, as a basic human right. Apart from the profound imprint it has already made in recent years, with the accession of newly independent States to political life, the assertion of cultural identity is still exerting a decisive influence on liberation movements, particularly in Africa.

A factor of liberation and development

Indeed the most recent trend is for cultural identity to take on a new and even wider significance: without losing its political, liberating function, it is now impinging on the economic and social fields, with the current search for a new international economic order. This search presupposes a new viewpoint, transcending considerations of economic growth alone. From this new point of view, cultural identity can be seen to form an essential component. Whereas earlier strategies for international aid were based mainly on the transfer of technology and foreign models, the new conceptions are characterized by a dual insistence on endogenous development and integrated development.

Endogenous development, summoning up from within the whole spectrum of resources, beginning with the untapped energies and capabilities of the peoples themselves, must take full account of their specific cultural values and aspirations. Development will thus be achieved at international level on the basis of mutual respect between nations and at national level on the basis of respect for social justice, instead of leading, as is too often the case in the countries concerned, to disequilibrium or even subjection to external interests.

In the same way, the quantitative definition of growth is gradually being replaced by the richer concept of integrated development, which gives the cultural dimension its full significance. For it alone makes it possible for the work of development to become a design for civilization based on truly human values, involving social progress, moral values and the broadest participation in an authentic cultural life.

This is why it is becoming increasingly obvious that the introduction of a new international economic order implies that each nation should have an ever clearer sense of its identity and vocation, as seen within the worldwide context. The identity of the nations, which is the basis for their sovereignty and a precondition for dialogue, draws its strength from the intensity and authenticity of their cultural life. Cultural identity is thus ensconced at the very heart of the new international economic order, and this imparts to it a new dynamism whose implications for the future are only now beginning to emerge.

The trend of international affairs over the last few years is consequently far from having led to the 'lowest common denominator' of cultural conformity and banality prophesied by some. Neither world economic expansion, which has removed all possibility of autarky, nor the power of technology nor the ubiquity of the media have seriously affected the cultural specificity and creativity of the different peoples. In fact in the developing countries there has been a new awareness of identity, coupled with a new respect for their own cultures and a desire to join in the dialogue between the different cultures as full partners.

Avoiding stereotyped culture: an open, operational concept . . .

The assertion of cultural identity cannot, therefore, be regarded as a form of intro-spection or even chauvinism. On the contrary, it betokens a desire to join in and to share, giving substance and, at last, a truly universal dimension to international cultural co-operation. Far from being merely a pious hope or, worse still, based in fact on the hegemony of a single form of culture, which arrogates to itself the quality of universality, international understanding is shaped and its practical reality strengthened by the individual contributions of the different peoples with their cultural traditions, their historic heritage, their human values and their specific forms of artistic expression. For each nation, whether or not it is its own master politically, whether or not it is a great power, whether it has a full range of resources and skills at its disposal or is still in the stage of development, the assertion of cultural identity is the basis for cultural pluralism. Acceptance and respect for such pluralism, with equal rights and on an equal footing, is today manifestly a factor contributing towards peace and under-standing between nations.

It should be stressed that problems of cultural identity affect countries with strongly expanding economies and a dynamic technological potential as well as those which are only starting along the path to development. They are sometimes of a different nature, but they are no less serious and far-reaching.

In a number of highly industrialized countries many people, and particularly young people, are seeking for a new quality of life, based on values other than those of production and consumption. They are beginning to criticize all the modern forms of individual or social alienation and the triviality of everyday life. There is an increasing conviction that economic growth has no meaning unless it contributes towards the fulfilment of the individual and of the community and generates a surplus of humanity and creativity.

Another major problem of technologically developed societies is that of the cultural levelling down which is all too often promoted by the mass media. Stereotyped ideas, the predominance of commercial or advertising interests, programmes intended for entertainment but in fact creating an even greater cultural vacuum, these are all too often factors which discourage creativity and initiative.

... which establishes the right to culture and the respect for pluralism

International action has been too limited to the technical aspect of these problems, to the means whereby communication takes place. Despite the tremendous difficulties involved, much more attention should be paid to the substance, the cultural content of these means of mass communication which are now the main and sometimes the only access to culture available to the majority.

On the other hand a trend has recently emerged and is becoming quite marked in a number of countries which have reached a high level of development: the tendency, in the face of all-enveloping industrialization or urban centralization, for smaller but warmer communities to form, making possible more direct communication and a culture which is more specific and concrete and lived more in the here and now. Hence the increasing importance attributed by the public authorities to the cultural life of regions, provinces and local communities. Hence also the new importance attributed to the cultural identity of ethnic, linguistic or other minorities. On the one hand we are witnessing a deeper awareness of their specificity on the part of the minorities themselves and on the other the principle of cultural pluralism is beginning to be accepted as an enrichment of the national heritage in the same way as it is conceived as a principle of international relations. The right to culture as a basic human right implies the right of each community to its own culture no less than the accessibility of all cultures.

A new awareness linked to contemporary history

The situation analysed above is primarily the result of the very marked and definite change which took place in international relationships during the period of decolonization, when political independence was closely linked with the growing awareness of one's own culture. It is thus essentially born of the will of the Member States, while to trace its evolution would be to go over the history of international co-operation during the last few decades.

However, if it were necessary to pinpoint more precisely the *terminus a quo* and *terminus ad quem* of the process, these could be identified respectively in the Bandung Conference of 1955 and the action initiated by the United Nations in 1974-75 towards the establishment of a new international economic order. The periods of most intense activity were those marked by the struggles against colonialism in Africa and South-East Asia, while on the international plane the sixties saw many African countries become members of the United Nations and their rapid progress as independent States.

All these events find their direct inspiration in a growing awareness and assertion of a specific cultural identity. Already in the spirit of the Bandung Conference the countries of Asia were claiming their say as both the centres of a specific culture and active partners in international co-operation, the two concepts being closely linked. This stance was to be reflected in Unesco's programmes by the Major Project on Mutual Appreciation of Eastern and Western Cultural Values, adopted by the ninth session of the General Conference held in New Delhi in 1956 and prepared by the first session of the Asian National Commissions held in Tokyo. It is interesting to note that the movement to transform Unesco's programmes, under the influence of the principle of cultural identity, came from within the countries concerned, and was expressed in discussions held and decisions taken in Asia.

Just as the promotion of the cultural dialogue between East and West on an equal footing was a feature of Unesco's programmes from the mid-fifties, the second assertion of the principle of cultural identity came strong and clear from Africa in the sixties. One of the most significant aspects of the General Conference of 1960, which saw the accession to membership of many newly independent African States, was undoubtedly the stress laid on cultural identity. Some had thought that Africa would have no hesitation in assigning the highest priority to technical aid in favour of development. But although this aspect was important it immediately became clear that for the new delegations from Africa all development had first and foremost to be rooted in the cultural and social realities of their nations' life.

In the same way it was plain that the African Member States desired not only to receive aid of a purely technical nature, but also, and above all, to share their views of man and society and to gain recognition of the spiritual and ethical content of their traditions.

This led to the establishment, in rapid succession, of programmes such as the overall plan for cultural co-operation with Africa, the General History of Africa and the ten-year plan for the promotion of African languages as vehicles of education and culture, along with activities concerned with the collection, conservation and presentation of the oral tradition.

Mutual recognition and appreciation of cultures

During this period, the emergence of many former colonies as independent entities able to play an active part in co-operation between sovereign States enabled the international organizations to attain universality. The scope of this transformation has often been commented upon. But it is perhaps in the field of the different cultures, their mutual recognition and appreciation, that this widening of horizons was destined, by virtue of its nature, to exercise the greatest influence. For it was not only a question of geographical extension, but a genuine and far-reaching transformation of the meanings and importance represented by the various peoples and cultures for each other. The original Unesco reflected, preponderantly, one form of civilization, rich in humanist values though it was, and largely universal in its scope. But, in the nature of things, the standards, criteria and methods which it used inevitably coloured the design for international co-operation in terms of its own experience and its own ideals. It was when very different and autonomous poles of influence emerged in international relations as sources of ideas and values and initiators of action and decisions that the principles of cultural identity and pluralism came into their own. The universality of each culture could now be constantly enriched by contact with others.

Thus it is that Unesco's programme is now based to a large extent, and in the most diverse cultural spheres, on the recognition of cultural pluralism, standing foursquare in consequence on the practical realities of cultural identity—specific in its nature yet universal in its human values—as experienced by the different peoples, groups and nations.

Return to sources

The presentation of cultures in their authentic form must essentially come from within; cultural values must be interpreted and brought up to date by the people who are actually living them. The adoption of this conceptual standpoint will have repercussions on the actual procedures adopted. On the one hand it will be necessary to increase the number of research institutions or cultural centres, encourage first-hand studies, often on the basis of unpublished sources and data, and give wide publicity to their findings, not only among scientific circles but also among the general public—within the region in question in order to increase cultural awareness, and outside the region with a view to truer appreciation of the culture concerned. On the other hand, this mobilization of each region's internal intellectual and scientific resources must go hand in hand, as regards programme organization, with greater decentralization of activities and even of structures so as to make possible a closer insight into the characteristic features of cultural identity in each country and each community. This is a natural corollary of the initial concept: specific projects in keeping with the realities of the local situation cannot be initiated by an organization which is excessively centralized.

Dialogue

Intra-cultural authenticity must necessarily be supplemented by inter-cultural dialogue. For unless one is to run the risk of encouraging national compartmentalization and sectarianism in one or other form, it is important to ensure that each culture is open to the influence of all the others within a broad international framework, by promoting and increasing the number of approaches which enable comparisons to be made between sub-regions, paying special attention to the study of areas where different civilizations adjoin, such as the Caribbean and South-East Asia. Specificity on the one hand and inter-cultural relations on the other are thus seen as two complementary terms, giving poise and balance to this group of activities taken as a whole.

Unesco will therefore take steps to promote the study of cultural identity as a factor of independence and community of interests, but also as a factor of mutual appreciation among individuals, groups, nations and regions, with particular reference to those affected by the social exclusion phenomenon within developed or developing societies. Lastly, Unesco will seek to promote the concept of cultural identity as part of an overall strategy for balanced, integrated development.

Action for women and by women

According to the most recent estimates [1] 49.9 per cent of the world's population are women; 70 per cent of them live in developing countries and more than 60 per cent in rural areas.

Although their situation varies considerably according to the various natural and cultural regions of the world, and also within each region, women often continue to be at a disadvantage with regard to the enjoyment of their rights. The principle of non-discrimination is whole-heartedly acknowledged and does not appear to be called in question; most States have incorporated it in their laws or their constitution. Nevertheless, certain legal provisions unfavourable to women still remain in force, and, in any case, there is a wide gap between *de jure* and *de facto* equality.

The main causes of inequality of women

Despite all the progress and efforts made, the three main causes of women's inferior position in the world, viz. weight of family responsibilities, particularly those connected with domestic activities, inequality in education and discrimination in employment, have by no means disappeared.

In a number of countries, the burden of repeated childbearing and children too numerous to bring up weighs extremely heavily on the health and capacities of women, who are worn out before their time by the disparity between resources and responsibilities, especially since fertility rates are highest in the poorest classes.

In the field of education, there is glaring inequality between men and women. In 1970, of the 783 million illiterates throughout the world, 468 million were women and, as a rule, women benefit less than men from adult education. In many countries, obstacles to equality of access to education take the form of traditions and preconceived ideas, stereotyped distinctions and excessive differentiation between the roles of men and women as they are usually portrayed by the media and by school textbooks. Besides the fact that fewer girls than boys attend school, a higher percentage of girls

1. Demographic forecasts made by the United Nations on the basis of 1973.

drop out, and drop out earlier, so that the difference becomes more marked as they grow older. The school wastage rates for girls may vary, according to the country concerned, between 5 and 70 per cent; drop-outs are more frequent in rural areas than in an urban environment. Women who wish to continue their studies encounter socio-cultural and economic conditions which are often unfavourable to education for women: indifference, tradition, customs, early marriage, domestic drudgery, work in the fields, underestimation of the needs for education for women and priority given to boys' education, often recognized by parents as a more profitable investment, etc. Inequality also resides in the type of education received. Girls who enter secondary and higher education do not take the same courses of study as boys, and do not have the same employment opportunities.

The working population of the world numbers 1,637 million, 562 million of whom, i.e. approximately one-third, are women. Women make up 34 per cent of the working population in developed areas and 26 per cent in developing areas; moreover, the general trend is for the proportion to increase. The percentage of women employed varies a great deal from country to country, since it ranges from nearly 50 per cent, in some industrialized areas, to less than 5 per cent. But all these figures only partially reflect the facts, since women go on record as working only if they are in full- or part-time employment. Housework does not therefore qualify a woman as a 'working' individual. Similarly, the countless women who do regular or occasional unpaid work in the farming, handicraft or commercial business of the head of the family are not included in the working population. Although only scanty data are available on this score, the economic and social importance of these two forms of work is undeniable.

In the developing countries, the proportion of women working in agriculture has always been considerable. For example, they take an active part in agricultural work in Africa, where they do much of the labouring in the fields and sell the produce at the market. In Asia, they are proportionally fewer, and their participation has also diminished with the modernization of machinery and methods. In Latin America, on the other hand, there is much female labour in the tertiary sector.

But in most cases, and in nearly all regions of the world, in the various fields of agriculture, industry or services, women are usually at the bottom of the qualifications ladder and are paid less than men for work of equal value; they climb the rungs of promotion more slowly than men, they are more readily fired in a crisis or a slump, and, with the exception of a few countries, they very seldom occupy posts of responsibility.

'Machismo' and the weight of tradition

One of the major difficulties in the battle to combat discrimination against women, as it should be waged today, arises from the insidious, not to say intangible, nature of many of the obstacles to be overcome. Attitudes and behaviour, such as 'machismo', to mention only one example, which help to perpetuate the domination of one sex over the other, assume the most varied and subtle forms; they affect all aspects of women's daily life.

The injustices and inequalities endured by the female population constitute a formidable obstacle to development. Some economists take the view that, if the labour reserve represented by women were to be tapped, the national income would show a marked increase. Moreover, a better integration of women in economic and social development might result in a more equitable distribution of income. Their active participation, on a completely equal footing with men, is therefore becoming an increasingly vital necessity if solutions are to be found to national and world problems.

At present, the main obstacles to women's economic participation are seldom of a legal nature. Rather, they are traditional views as to the role of women in society on the one hand, and, on the other, situations of unemployment and underemployment, combined with the idea that women are of marginal importance in occupational activities and that, in such situations, it is therefore preferable to employ men.

It is chiefly as a result of conceptions and attitudes of this kind that most development plans have, hitherto, paid little attention to ways of making the best and most advantageous use of the human potential contained in the female population, with a view to speeding up economic and social development.

The practical difficulties in the way of women's full integration in economic life are many: lack of information; non-existence or inadequacy of social services, communal facilities and nursery schools; distances to travel to work; lack of qualifications; in some cases, reluctance on the part of employers to hire women owing to the social security protection due to them, etc.

Obviously, the problems vary greatly in kind and scope according to political and social policy trends, cultural factors, the level of development and whether the environement is rural or urban. In a rural environement, women's participation in the economy sometimes runs up against the idea that an agriculture which employs them is a primitive agriculture and that they must be progressively replaced by male manpower as modernization advances. In urban environments, the traditional division of labour, which could be justified for economic reasons in small, self-sufficient units, has tended to survive despite the disappearance of the rational grounds for its existence.

How women could contribute to development

Women's full contribution to the progress of society also presupposes their ability to gain a hearing in the groups and assemblies which make the decisions, from the village council or co-operative association to the highest administrative bodies of the country. The gap between official recognition of women's fundamental political rights and their effective participation in political structures is considerable: when women are represented, their representation is scarcely ever proportional to their numbers or their abilities.

Furthermore, greater participation by women in decisions concerning development would undoubtedly give development a new dimension, with more attention, as part of an integrated approach, to such matters as health, education and culture. These, indeed, are fields in which women certainly have special experience and to which they pay particular attention, precisely because of their present role and place in society. They can also impart a distinctive stamp to the character of development, helping to ensure that it is endogenous and rooted in socio-cultural values. Lastly, their participation in all cultural aspects of development is as important as their integration in and contribution to economic progress; this is a field in which women's talents and creative abilities both can and should find an outlet for the benefit of society as a whole.

Awareness of discrimination against women has dawned slowly, for many reasons. One of the most important is probably the fact that resistance to equal rights for women and opposition to their self-fulfilment, both individually and as a group, arise not only from economic causes, but also from irrational motives, superstitious fears and prejudices which are as difficult to uproot as racial prejudice. Secondly, the battle for women's rights has long been confused with the revolutionary struggle in general, and although it is true that it has reaped the benefits of that struggle, it can also choose other paths.

The evolution of ideas—militant attitudes and new awareness

It is beyond question, however, that the evolution of ideas has now taken a favourable turn. Comparison with the situation ten or fifteen years ago shows that International Women's Year, 1975, has highlighted two phenomena: firstly, women are militating resolutely and in growing numbers against their exclusion from the political, economic, social and cultural life of their time; secondly, governments and national leaders are becoming increasingly aware of the fact that it is indispensable to improve the status of women, not only for the sake of justice and equity, but also in order to avoid wastage of human resources.

In the industrial countries, where most working women are wage-earners, equality of civil and political rights, the improvement of working conditions and the provision of social and educational services for young children are the subjects which have led to reforms and which continue to form the mainstream of reform-directed activity.

In the countries which are most advanced in this respect, the progress achieved may be measured by various indicators, such as: access to the same jobs, identical education for girls and boys, numbers of nursery schools and childcare centres, development of communal facilities (family restaurants, launderettes, etc.). In certain industrial countries, legislation has been revised or extended, chiefly with a view to eliminating discrimination in the field of legal and commercial rights and in matters of employment, and to achieving a better balance of rights and responsibilities within the family.

In developing countries, the reforms already carried out have taken place against an altogether different background, owing to the struggle for independence and physical survival. The emergence of newly independent States has certainly served the cause of women, who have often gained the right to vote and access to certain political responsibilities more rapidly than in other countries.

However, the harsh everyday realities of underdevelopment continue to weigh heavily on both men and women. Women therefore direct their demands first of all to the improvement of overall conditions and the elimination of undernourishment, illness, poverty, illiteracy, etc., without however losing sight of their own specific problems, which must be treated as such, and whose solution must not be postponed until such time as these broader objectives have been attained.

The efforts expended in developed regions have aimed first and foremost at the improvement of health and education (wider access to all levels of education, vocational training courses, educational and vocational guidance services, etc.) and the expansion of employment opportunities. Progress has also been made in integrating women into local and national political life.

For world-wide action

Throughout the existence of the United Nations system, the United Nations and its various branches, including the Specialized Agencies in their respective fields of competence, have made incalculable efforts on behalf of women's rights and the improvement of their status.

Immediately after the founding of the United Nations, a Commission was given special responsibility for the status of women. This Commission has achieved a great deal; among other things, it has compiled various legal instruments relating to most aspects of women's status. Indeed, it rapidly came to light that women suffered even more than men from lack of respect for the freedoms and rights set out in the Universal Declaration of Human Rights. This discovery, especially, led the United Nations General Assembly to adopt, on 7 November 1967 (resolution 2263 (XXII)), a Declaration on the Elimination of Discrimination against Women.

The idea that the full development of a country and the well-being of the world call for women's active participation, an idea already contained in the Preamble to that Declaration, was to be made fully explicit in the context of the International Strategy for the Second United Nations Development Decade, one of the aims and objectives of the Decade being to encourage the full integration of women in the world-wide development effort.

In December 1972, the General Assembly, by resolution 3010 (XXVII), decided to proclaim 1975 International Women's Year, and invited all the Specialized Agencies to participate in its preparation and celebration. The International Year has had major repercussions throughout the world and has inspired the launching or strengthening of all sorts of activities; its culmination was a World Conference (Mexico City, 19 June-2 July 1975) which, among other things, drew up a World Plan of Action with a view to the full integration of women in an international community based on equality and justice and reflecting the many-sided contribution women can make. The implementation of the principles and guidelines contained in this Plan, together with the results obtained and the progress achieved, are to be assessed at a second world conference on women, which will be held in 1980, i.e. half-way through the United Nations Decade for Women: Equality, Development and Peace (1976-1985) which the General Assembly prcolaimed in December 1975.

From its earliest days, Unesco has worked in its fields of competence for the advancement of women. In 1967-1968, a long-term programme was launched to facilitate women's access to education and to scientific and technical careers, and to study the socio-economic obstacles to such access. The Organization's activities have taken various forms: collaboration with women's non-governmental organizations, educational projects, seminars, and studies on the access of girls and women to all levels and types of education and to literacy training.

Social science studies have also been undertaken or encouraged, particularly on the status of women in various Asian countries, women's participation in political life, and television and the social education of women.

Three major experimental projects were launched in three countries towards the end of the 1960s, aiming to improve conditions of access to education for girls and women: the first project concerned technical education, literacy training and the education of women in rural areas; the second dealt with primary education for girls and the training of primary school teachers; the third aimed to improve the technical education provided for girls, so as to enable them to take up skilled employment in industry. A critical assessment of these three projects was published in 1975 under the title *Women, Education, Equality*.

Regarding the education of girls and women in a rural environment, Unesco's work has been increasingly closely co-ordinated with that of the Food and Agriculture Organization of the United Nations (FAO) and the International Labour Organisation (ILO). In 1973, it submitted to the Commission on the Status of Women a study on the equality of access of girls and women to education in the context of rural development

As it has gained greater experience in regard to the advancement of women through education, Unesco has become aware of the numerous ramifications of this type of activity. Hence, the programme has tended more and more to encourage equality of educational opportunity for girls and women, a trend which was officially approved by the General Conference in 1972. It was in this spirit that in 1973-1974, the Organization made arrangements with ILO for a joint study to be conducted in five countries concerning education, training and employment opportunities for women.

On 18 November 1974, following the proclamation by the United Nations General Assembly of the International Women's Year, the General Conference of Unesco unanimously adopted resolution 16.1 on Unesco's efforts concerning the improvement of the status of women, thereby mapping out for the Organization a detailed frame of reference for its future activities. A large-scale movement was under way; Unesco has taken an active part in the International Year and is preparing a programme to meet the requirements of both this General Conference resolution and the World Plan of Action, adopted in July 1975 in Mexico City and approved by the United Nations General Assembly. Indeed, the situation is now dominated by the necessity of implementing the World Plan of Action, in the light of the guidelines laid down by the United Nations General Assembly at its thirtieth session for the United Nations Decade for Women: Equality, Development and Peace, and by the serious concern to which the plight of a great many women throughout the world gives rise.

Two complementary lines of approach: denunciation of discriminatory practices; legal action and information services

Unesco's contribution to the task of improving the status of women—placed within the context of extensive inter-Agency co-operation—must follow two different, but complementary lines of approach.

The first, which is the more general of the two, concerns the values and myths, economic data and cultural attitudes, structures and social practices which, in their origins, their present form and their tendencies underlie the present status of women in society and form the substrate on which remedial action must be based. In this connection, efforts will be made through statistical studies and publications, to bring to light all the discriminatory practices to which women are subjected in the fields of education, science, culture and communication. In particular, the image conveyed in school textbooks of the respective roles of men and women will be analysed, for example through regional conferences, with a view to proposing more realistic descriptions and illustrations.

This action will be accompanied by a programme aimed at promoting the preparation and implementation, on the one hand, of legal and administrative measures which are more conducive to women's enjoyment of their fundamental rights, and, on the other, of policies for the advancement of women designed to create *de facto* conditions of genuine equality in the Organization's fields of competence. Thus Unesco will contribute to the drawing up, under United Nations auspices, of the draft convention on the elimination of discrimination against women and to the dissemination of that convention; it will also organize conferences and exchanges of information and, at Member States' request, will provide advisory services for the preparation and implementation of policies for the advancement of women in the fields of education, science, culture and communication.

The Organization's activities in this field will be based on the principle that women themselves must work to improve their situation. Indeed, it is essential to respect the distinctiveness of the female viewpoint and to avoid the application to women's problems of abstract solutions, imposed from outside, which are very ill-suited to contemporary developments and which would constitute a new form of domination. The principle of action implies not only that women should participate in working out reforms designed to grant them a fair deal, but also that they should be the principal agents of their implementation.

Ensuring, through education, women's full participation in development

The second approach is more specific, involving various ways and means of ensuring the full participation by women in economic, social and cultural development. These measures are mainly educational, on account of the fact that in the integration of women in development, which is part and parcel of the improvement in the status of women, very special importance is attached to education.

Unesco will continue its efforts to increase the participation of girls and women in both formal and non-formal education, especially in rural areas. Emphasis will also be placed on their admission to those types and branches of education in which inequality is particularly great, with all that such inequality implies in the field of employment. Research, followed by experimental application, will be carried out on educational and vocational guidance for girls and women. The Organization will make parallel efforts to prepare and disseminate standardized curricula suitable for application in co-educational schools, within the wider context of a revision of curricula and educational standards in order to preclude any distinction based on discrimination between the sexes.

The cause of refugees and national liberation movements

The international community assumes responsibilities for about five million refugees throughout the world. Because of sudden changes resulting from the political and economic situation, or occurring as a consequence of natural disasters, conflicts or war, it is difficult to establish statistics concerning the exact number of refugees and their location. In 1975, the number of refugees was estimated to be 1,062,000 in Africa, 997,000 in Asia, 310,150 in Europe, 110,000 in Latin America, 2,000,000 in the Near East and 146,000 in the United States of America.

The uprooted millions

Refugees may wish to settle in the country of asylum or to return to their country of origin; in either case, they are faced with particular situations which have political, human, cultural and educational implications. The tragedy of exile touches them all, whether they have been deprived of their homeland or have left their country or been deported for religious, ideological, political or racial reasons, or as a result of natural catastrophes.

The right of asylum does not always ensure that they find themselves in an acceptable situation. In addition to the problems of settling in the host country and securing acceptance by the community of that country, they encounter difficulties in finding employment and housing, have to adapt themselves to a new environment, and suffer emotional isolation. The way of life, ideas about values and customs, and often the use of a new language create a feeling of non-participation and not belonging which often leads eventually to real cultural rootlessness.

The rootlessness consequent upon the transfer of refugees to cultural environments which are sometimes very different from their own should call forth concerted action on the part of international bodies—and lead to its being more energetically prosecuted—with a view to the preservation of the original cultures, especially when those cultures are oral and hence threatened with disappearance. This should be done by developing, among the refugees, the study of their languages, cultural traditions, ethnic characteristics and national history.

With regard to education, refugees have to overcome difficulties such as the problem of admission to schooling, owing to the fact that there are not enough places in a nation's schools; the problem of equivalence of diplomas and degrees, and differences in scholastic and linguistic standards; vocational and technical training for adults and, in some cases, the need for literacy instruction. 'Temporary' refugees waiting to go back to their country of origin find that the curricula in the country of asylum are ill-adapted to their needs and this, in many cases, is a major source of anxiety for them when they wonder how they will fit back into their original environment.

In addition to these general problems which concern all refugees, whatever the reason for their situation, there are specific problems which concern those among them who have chosen exile rather than accept foreign domination. Certain groups of refugees, for instance, have organized themselves into liberation movements with programmes of action, recognized at regional level by intergovernmental organizations. Most of these movements have been recognized by the United Nations and its Specialized Agencies and are thus empowered to take part in the discussions of those organizations to which they look for aid.

Organizing aid and protection: the United Nations in the forefront

Refugees and recognized liberation movements receive assistance from the United Nations and, within their special fields of competence, from bodies such as the Office of the United Nations High Commissioner for Refugees (UNHCR), the United Nations Relief and Works Agency for Palestine Refugees (UNRWA), the United Nations Educational and Training Programme for Southern Africa (UNETPSA), the United Nations Council for Namibia, the United Nations Disaster Relief Office, the United Nations Children's Fund (UNICEF), and the United Nations Development Programme (UNDP). In addition, almost all the Specialized Agencies of the United Nations provide assistance to refugees and liberation movements in their respective areas of competence. It is obvious that account is taken, in the work of the international community, of the facilities made available by the countries of asylum and of the bilateral assistance provided by certain donors (non-governmental organizations and private foundations) which, in some cases, may be quite substantial.

It is scarcely possible to evaluate the full extent of the substantial efforts made, directly or indirectly, by Member States on behalf of refugees and liberation movements. But it may be recorded that the influence this assistance has had on the refugees' situation is noteworthy. States have often granted the right of asylum or citizenship to refugees or groups of refugees seeking to resettle. They have generally made education available to them on the same footing as to their own nationals or have made them substantial cash grants.

Ever since it was set up, the United Nations has striven for the recognition and observance of the fundamental rights of refugees throughout the world. In the years following the end of the Second World War, for instance, the United Nations Relief and Rehabilitation Administration (UNRRA), addressed its efforts to assisting displaced persons and the war-devasted areas of Europe.

In 1949, the General Assembly established the United Nations Relief and Works Agency for Palestine Refugees in the Near East (UNRWA), to be responsible for the Palestinian refugees in the Near East whose presence was a result of the 1948 war.

In 1951, the Conference of Plenipotentiaries organized by the United Nations, adopted a Convention relating to the Status of Refugees, to which nearly half the Member States of the United Nations have so far acceded. A Protocol, the object of which was to provide protection for people who had become refugees after 1 January 1951, was adopted in 1967.

The Office of the United Nations High Commissioner for Refugees, replacing the International Refugee Organization (IRO), is responsible for the application of the Convention and Protocol; this is the body generally responsible for material aid to refugees and their protection at the international level. (This responsibility does not, however, extend to Palestinian refugees, who come under UNRW.) The Office of the High Commissioner co-operates with other United Nations agencies in their particular fields of competence.

The United Nations has constantly encouraged and helped the peoples of trust and non-self-governing territories to secure their independence. During the last ten years, high priority has been accorded to measures to mobilize international public opinion and assistance on behalf of peoples still subject to colonial domination and on behalf of their national liberation movements. In October 1970, the United Nations General Assembly recommended that positive steps be taken by the Specialized Agencies to assist in the provision of practical assistance to the colonized peoples of southern Africa and their liberation movements.

The Organization of African Unity (OAU) and the League of Arab States support the national liberation movements and organizations in their struggle for international recognition of the right of their peoples to self-determination.

Unesco at work: priority to educational action

Unesco has been working to assist refugees ever since its foundation: during the years following the end of the Second World War, for instance, it supported UNRRA, while in 1950, following the appeal launched by the United Nations General Assembly, it undertook activities on behalf of the Palestine refugees in the Near East. At its sixth session, the General Conference adopted resolution 7.1.5 authorizing the Director-General 'to continue and intensify, in collaboration with the United Nations Relief and Works Agency, the activities already undertaken on behalf of Palestine refugees'. An agreement was then signed with the Commissioner-General of UNRWA.

Under the terms of this agreement, which is renewable every two years, Unesco assumes technical responsibility for the educational services provided by UNRWA for the children of the million-and-a-half registered Palestine refugees. This assistance takes the form of seconding to UNRWA twenty Unesco specialists, among whom are the Director and administrative staff of the UNRWA/Unesco Department of Education, and providing the assistance of twelve associate experts recruited by Unesco, whose services are, however, made available by the donor countries (associate expert system). Unesco is technically responsible for the running of 580 UNRWA/Unesco schools, four teacher-training colleges, and seven vocational and technical training centres, attended in 1975 by a total of just over 285,000 students in Lebanon, Jordan, Syria, the occupied territories on the West Bank of the Jordan and in the Gaza Strip. The UNRWA/Unesco Institute of Education, which receives financial assistance from UNDP, provides in-service training for more than 1,000 student teachers annually. Following the difficulties which arose in the Gaza Strip after the Israeli occupation in 1967, Unesco secured the agreement of the authorities concerned for the organization and supervision, in this region, of the Egyptian secondary school-leaving examinations. The first of these examinations took place during the summer of 1969. Since then, 7,000 to 8,000 students have sat this examination each year. A certain number of those who pass receive scholarships from the Egyptian Government.

In 1967, following consultations between the Office of the United Nations High Commissioner for Refugees and Unesco, the two organizations signed a Memorandum of Understanding which specifies the arrangements for co-operation between them in the sphere of education. The Memorandum was originally drawn up to cover groups of African refugees only but since 1973 it has been applied to refugees from other regions of the world as well. This co-operation involves the secondment of Unesco staff members to the Office of the High Commissioner for Refugees, whenever necessary, to provide advice on any educational work undertaken, and the recruitment of associate experts for the High Commissioner.

In 1971, in pursuance of resolution 8 adopted by the General Conference of Unesco at its sixteenth session, a special programme of aid to African liberation movements recognized by the Organization of African Unity was begun. This programme of activities was subsequently expanded following the approval by UNDP, first of a regional aid programme for African refugees and then, in 1975, of ten separate projects (totalling $2 million) for movements which had requested assistance from Unesco.

Unesco's activities consisted first in providing assistance to PAIGC (representing Guinea-Bissau and the Cape Verde Islands), FRELIMO (Mozambique),

MPLA (Angola) and certain liberation movements in Zambia. More recently, assistance has been provided for the following movements: ANC and PAC (South Africa), ANC/Zimbabwe (resulting from the merging in 1975, of ZANU and ZAPU), FNLA (Angola), MOLINACO (the Comoros) and SWAPO (Namibia). As the territories formerly under Portuguese domination have now become independent, Unesco's activities in the coming years will be centred mainly on assistance to the liberation movements of Namibia (SWAPO), Zimbabwe (ANC/Zimbabwe) and South Africa (ANC and PAC).

Negotiations have been started with the United Nations Council for Namibia with the object of arranging for co-operation which should lead to an expansion of educational activities for Namibian refugees who have found asylum in certain African countries; these activities will be additional to those already undertaken on behalf of SWAPO. The United Nations Educational and Training Programme for Southern Africa (UNETPSA) and Unesco are, furthermore, already co-operating over the award of study grants.

Lastly, the General Conference of Unesco, at its eighteenth session (1974), expressed a desire that the resources made available to assist the Palestine Liberation Movement, the liberation movements recognized by the Organization of African Unity and the peoples of liberated areas should be increased.

Ensuring equality of opportunity and preserving cultural identity

Unesco's action is based on two major principles, namely fuller observance of human rights and promotion of equality of opportunity in education. One of the aims of action in this respect is to ensure that the character of the education provided is consonant with the national, religious and linguistic traditions of the refugees and liberation movements and organizations, whose cultural identity must be preserved. In addition, Unesco must see that arrangements are made to ensure the unity necessary in any education system if pupils are to be able, in case of need, to continue their studies in educational establishments of a higher level forming part of the same system as the schools they attend, or of a system with the same social, cultural and, more particularly, linguistic characteristics.

The assistance afforded by Unesco covers the following categories of persons: (a) child and adult refugees who come under the Office of the United Nations High Commissioner for Refugees and UNRWA; (b) children and adults from colonial countries who are unable to avail themselves of the provisions of the United Nations Convention and Protocol, but who are considered by OAU to be refugees; (c) children and adults who are either in camps in frontier zones or in the interior, in the liberated areas of colonial territories; (d) young people and adults belonging to liberation movements and organizations recognized by regional intergovernmental bodies.

This aid takes different forms according to the groups to which it is given. Educational and cultural assistance to national liberation movements and organizations consists, in particular, in the provision of teaching materials, study grants and advisory services, the organization of literacy programmes, the conclusion of contracts with liberation movements for research into the oral traditions and cultures of the regions represented by these movements, etc. Under the educational programmes for Palestine refugees carried out in co-operation with UNWRA, Unesco arranges for education specialists to take charge of activities, provides teaching materials and fellowships, and organizes State examinations. Unesco also carries out, in co-operation with SWAPO and the United Nations Council for Namibia, a programme of aid for Namibia for the training of specialized staff. The Organization continues to provide the services of specialists to advise the Office of the United Nations High Commissioner for Refugees on the education programmes it is carrying out. Lastly, with a view to achieving equality of treatment of refugees within its fields of competence, Unesco intends to insert in its normative instruments, when they are revised, specific clauses relating to refugees.

Education on human rights

The promotion of human rights and the elimination of colonialism and racialism are essential to the establishment of a new international economic, social and cultural order. This proposition is equally true if put conversely: the establishment of such a new order is essential to the promotion of human rights and the elimination of colonialism and racialism.

The importance of the part to be played by education and information is clear. Among the obstacles to both the realization of human rights and the establishment of a new international economic and social order are widespread ways of thinking which must be changed if these objectives are to be achieved. Many people are not yet ready to accept the practical consequences involved. Transforming such attitudes and strengthening understanding of the related problems in a global perspective will require an intensive effort in education and information. Human rights and their implications must be shown in a new light. At the same time, education and information have a crucial role of training to play as societies advance towards the goals set, for the assurance of human rights will depend to a considerable extent on educating and informing people so that they are aware of their rights and know how to exercise them in an effective and responsible way. They will thus be prepared to participate in the management of their society and in the establishment of a new order in which there is 'unconditional recognition of and respect for the dignity of the individual and equality among men' (18 C/Resolution 11.1).

Problems and difficulties

Many problems are involved in promoting education and wider information concerning human rights. In developing school education about human rights the difficulties commonly attendant upon any kind of educational change and advance, further complicated by some special technical problems, are encountered. Curricula and syllabuses must be opened up to accommodate new subject-matter. Suitable teaching materials must be produced. Teachers must be prepared for new tasks, and in this field in particular such preparation may necessitate not only mastering new bodies of information but also adapting teaching methods and approaches to new purposes. Education aimed at developing an attachment to the principles of human rights and the relevant attitudes and behavioural traits cannot be a purely cognitive process. It must also have affective impact and moral effect—results which cannot be achieved simply by transmitting information. The traditional range of teaching methods may consequently need to be broadened to include new ways of working and even new teacher/pupil relationships. In this matter, methods and approaches, the general atmosphere of the school, the personality of the teachers, the respective roles played by teachers and pupils and similar factors are of paramount importance. The school, in other words, should be a place where the rights of all are seen to be respected and where each has the opportunity for direct experience in exercising rights and carrying out responsibilities.

At the university level, a central problem is to develop and generalize coherent programmes of teaching about rights.[1] At present specialized courses on the subject, although increasingly offered, are relatively rare. It is more common for aspects of human rights to be dealt with in courses of international law, international relations and political science. The part played by universities in producing community leaders and shaping the intellectual character of society makes it particularly important that they present programmes broad enough to reach all students regardless of their specialization.

In most countries, out-of-school education, though progressing, is still without adequate institutions, personnel, installations and equipment. These factors limit possibilities for education concerning human rights as well as education on other matters. It is evident, moreover, that education about human rights has not always been placed among the highest priorities. In this situation organizations for young people and adults, which in many instances conduct their own education and information programmes, assume a special importance. Thus, in efforts to reinforce the contribution of out-of-school education attention must be given not only to strengthening institutional resources (not overlooking the possibilities for extending the extramural range of school and university programmes) but also to encouraging the work of organizations active in this field.

1. See the publication *Human Rights Studies in Universities*, which contains a world survey of teaching and research on human rights conducted by the International Institute of Human Rights and International Law Association in 1970 under contract with Unesco and published in 1973.

It is difficult to generalize about the role of public information in promoting human rights, as it varies widely from one country to another in function, resources and objectives. The main problem in assisting Member States in their efforts to promote human rights through public information is one common to all Unesco's information activities: it is difficult for a centralized service of material to meet the varying needs of Member States. Further problems are of a mechanical and technical nature. Campaigns of information imply that action should be programmed, but this is hindered by delays in communication and by lack of feedback. Experience has shown that while the media in developing regions are more receptive to Unesco information than those in industrialized areas, it is precisely from the Third World that indications of utilization of Unesco information are most lacking.

Since all Unesco undertakings are essentially human-rights oriented, the range of information possible is extremely wide. The fundamental challenge is to make the human rights element of particular programmes emerge in a manner which the general public will appreciate.

Progress in school, university and extra-curricular education

Surveys of teaching about human rights conducted in 1951 and 1967 by international non-governmental organizations of teachers in co-operation with Unesco show a steady if unspectacular progress over the years in the development of educational methods and programmes in this field. This progress is confirmed by more recent joint Unesco/United Nations surveys in 1969 and 1974 of teaching about the United Nations and its Specialized Agencies, which covered this subject as well as others.

As regards school education, explicit official instructions have been issued by central educational authorities concerning teaching about human rights in many countries where such directives are a feature of the educational system. Moreover, in numerous instances provisions emphasize the need for schools at all levels to give attention to the subject. In a number of other countries where the issuing of such official instructions is not the practice, educational authorities nevertheless encourage teaching about human rights through curricular or extracurricular activities. Annual observance of Human Rights Day, for example, is characteristic of school programmes in the great majority of Member States. The extent of interest and action can be judged by the fact that approximately four-fifths of the Member States which provided data for the 1974 study [1] reported on programmes of teaching about human rights. The information available indicates that programmes are strongest at the secondary and higher levels of education.

As regards out-of-school education for young people and adults, the aforementioned studies show that inclusion of education about human rights in programmes is still comparatively rare. This is an area where possibilities could be more fully utilized. One of the most encouraging facts to emerge from the studies, however, is that inter-

---

1. United Nations Economic and Social Council, fifty-eighth session (Doc. E/5610 of 27 January 1975).

national and national non-governmental organizations have reached literally millions of young people and adults with information about the United Nations and its related agencies, which in general includes material on their work to promote human rights. Non-governmental organizations have in fact often played a leading role in the defence and promotion of human rights and their action frequently includes educational campaigns on human rights in general or on particular issues. A number of organizations having consultative relations with Unesco have undertaken, sometimes with Unesco's collaboration, projects of this kind.

The overall impression conveyed by the data available is that, while much effective work has been done, the promotion of education and information about human rights remains a peripheral concern in a large majority of Member States, with even its marginal position sometimes threatened by competition with other claims on education and information, by weakness of administrative and professional stimulus and by inadequacy of technical and material resources. It would appear that the most sustained efforts have been made in the field of school education, but even here the work done has often been unsystematic and improvisatory. What is clear, in sum, is that in most countries a stronger stimulus and a general development of programmes, methods, approaches and materials will be needed if the demands implicit in this objective are to be met.

The organizations of the United Nations system have been active from the outset in promoting education and information on human rights. While some are by their very nature concerned only with the realization of certain of the rights proclaimed in the Universal Declaration, and with education and information bearing upon them, the United Nations itself and Unesco have taken the lead in promoting education and information about the full range of human rights. The work of the United Nations has been done mainly in the area of public information by, for example, disseminating in large quantities and many languages such instruments as the Universal Declaration and the Covenants on Human Rights, issuing reports on progress towards the achievement of human rights, publicizing activities of the United Nations family of organizations in the field of human rights, and promoting observance of Human Rights Day and special events such as International Human Rights Year.

Unesco's dual responsibility: education . . .

As regards Unesco, numerous General Conference resolutions adopted over the years, have aimed at promoting widespread knowledge and understanding of the principles of human rights. Pursuant to these resolutions, a continuous effort has been made to encourage teaching about human rights and related issues in schools, in programmes of youth and adult education and through public information.

Measures to stimulate teaching about human rights in schools have formed an integral part of Unesco's programme of education for international understanding (see Chapter 2, pages 79-82). Within this framework, various kinds of action have been concerned specifically with human rights education in school. Activities have included surveys of methods and programmes, seminars, and the production of teaching aids. At the beginning of the Associated Schools Project (see Chapter 2) human rights was chosen as one of the main themes for special programmes, and many of the participating educational institutions, from that time to the present, have concentrated their work on human rights.

At the level of higher education, at Unesco's request pursuant to resolution 11 (XXVII) of the United Nations Human Rights Commission, the International Institute of Human Rights (Strasbourg), in collaboration with the International Law Association, conducted a two-year survey on the university teaching of human rights, covering every faculty of law in the world. After considering the report prepared on the basis of the survey, the Commission requested Unesco 'to encourage teaching and research in human rights in universities and to this end to accelerate the preparation of appropriate material for the teaching of human rights . . .'. (resolution 17 (XXIX). Accordingly, fellowships were provided to the International Institute of Human Rights to allow teachers to participate in a special training programme for university human rights teaching created in 1973 and a university textbook, *International Dimensions of Human Rights*, was prepared by an international team of experts. In addition, a programme designed to intensify teaching and research in international humanitarian law was prepared.

In the field of youth and adult education a series of projects has aimed at the promotion of civic and social education as an integral part of out-of-school education programmes. These have been conducted generally in co-operation with international non-governmental organizations. Questions of human rights have often been discussed at seminars on youth and adult education and have formed a theme for such activities as the Associated Youth Enterprises. Current action in the area of adult education includes the provision of aid to Member States for projects on innovative educational activities concerned with human rights and their exercise and educational activities to encourage the participation of citizens in the administration of society's affairs.

An important contribution to the establishment of international standards in this field was made with the adoption by the General Conference at its eighteenth session of the Recommendation concerning Education for International Understanding, Co-operation and Peace and Education relating to Human Rights and Fundamental Freedoms. This recommendation is intended to apply to all stages and forms of education. A further step was taken when the General Conference adopted at its nineteenth session the Recommendation concerning the development of adult education, aimed in particular at promoting the exercise of human rights through educational action.

. . . and information

Public information about human rights formed part of Unesco's earliest programmes (the first of the Unesco Clubs were founded precisely to spread knowledge of the Universal Declaration). The Organization's exposure of the mythology of racial supremacy in the 1950s received wide media coverage and helped to arouse public opinion against the racial policies of South Africa. The struggle against discrimination has been a constant theme of information supplied to Unesco Clubs, while *Unesco Features* began special issues on human rights in 1951. Most consistent coverage has been given to the right to education. Of recent years, Unesco publications and radio and visual productions have been geared to the needs and opportunities of international years promoting specific rights. Thus, apart from other numbers concentrating on these issues, the Unesco *Courier* brought out a special number on the occasion of the International Year of the Struggle against Racism (1971). During International Women's Year (1975), the *Courier* devoted two special issues to the theme and *Unesco Features* one. The *Unesco Chronicle* published special articles; press kits of background documentation were issued, and a meeting of representatives of the media was organized to follow the United Nations Conference in Mexico City. In addition, a colour film was produced, a symposium on women film-makers was organized and a series of supporting actions was carried out.

During the next six years Unesco will concentrate its effort, *in the education programme*, on the implementation at different levels and in different fields of education, of the Recommendation concerning Education for International Understanding, Co-operation and Peace and Education relating to Human Rights and Fundamental Freedoms. Assistance will be given to Member States for dissemination of the Recommendation and activities to implement it. National studies will be made and regional meetings held on the implementation of the Recommendation.

Experimental projects will be carried out on education for peace and respect for human rights; regional meetings will be held and a source book published on the role of social studies in this type of education. Similarly, studies and pilot projects will be conducted on education concerning problems of development. Unesco will also continue to produce specialized educational materials, including a manual on international humanitarian law for use in higher education. These activities will be organized chiefly within the framework of the Associated Schools Project, which is to be extended to the university level. Special attention will also be given to the treatment of contemporary world problems in school programmes and teaching materials.

In the field of *information*, the dissemination of information concerning human rights and the furtherance of peace will be increased, by means of: Unesco publications and periodicals, such as the *Courier*; services to the mass media, including press releases and articles, particularly those published in *Unesco Features*; public liaison activities, such as Unesco Clubs and associations. A number of themes will be developed, including that of the essential conditions for the establishment of a new international order.

The close links which are formed, in the educational sphere, between action for the promotion of human rights and action for the reinforcement of peace, reflects the fundamental unity of these two problems. They are not, of course, to be confused. But in the final analysis, universal respect for and assurance of human rights are the very foundation of real peace, and the maintenance of a just, lasting and constructive peace at the level of groups, societies and the world is the necessary condition for the achievement of human rights. And indeed, peace is the subject of the following chapter.

2 The path towards peace

Unesco came into being as a direct result of the work which had been initiated in wartime by the Allied Ministers of Education, in a capital badly damaged by bombing. It was officially founded directly after the termination of this world conflict that its Constitution refers to as a 'great and terrible war', at a historical moment when the return of peace entailed a twofold task: in the immediate future, that of rebuilding what had been destroyed by war; in the longer term, that of building a world from which the spectre of war was banished. The paramount importance and the eminently positive nature of this long-term work of consolidating peace were to govern Unesco, according to the terms of its Constitution, in carrying out its mission, as a Specialized Agency of the United Nations, in its fields of competence and by the ways and means specifically assigned to it.

The Organization has remained true to this original conception at the same time as its range of action was progressively broadening to embrace the new and large-scale tasks generated by the requirements of development. The General Conference has been constantly concerned to refer to this original conception and to reactivate it as both a prime necessity and an ultimate objective: the series of general resolutions adopted by it at different sessions bears witness that, whatever the arrangements that may be made by governments, the true foundations of peace are rooted in the minds of men, that the maintenance and strengthening of peace rests upon mutual knowledge, understanding and respect and on the development of friendly relations between nations and that in the final analysis there can be no true and lasting peace not based on popular support. Without the guarantee of peace and the reduction of tensions, the solution to all the problems facing mankind would be seriously and without doubt irrevocably jeopardized. At the same time, no international settlement secured at the cost of the freedom and dignity of peoples and respect for individuals can claim to be a truly peaceful settlement, either in its spirit or in terms of its durability. In the resolutions which it has adopted respecting this problem, particularly those adopted at its most recent sessions, the General Conference has associated the struggle for peace with a condemnation of all forms of oppression, discrimination and exploitation of one nation by another, not only because they inevitably generate violence but also because they themselves constitute a form of violence and partake of the spirit of war. Finally, while it explicitly condemns in this context colonialism, neo-colonialism, imperialism, racism and apartheid, foreign occupation and all violations of the right of peoples to self-determination, the General Conference thereby also condemns all violations of human rights as a threat and contrary to its very spirit. The struggle for peace and action to promote human rights are recognized as being inseparable: their linking together in the same programme 'constitutes a coherent conceptual framework'.

The past three decades have seen a notable change in the way in which the problem of peace is conceived; in particular, the approach to the problem has been markedly consolidated and enriched as a result of the new developments that have occurred in the world situation as also thanks to the growing awareness that has been gained of the factors involved.

The changing world situation

The Second World War had dramatically laid bare the devastating nature of war, while recourse to the atomic bomb during the final stage of hostilities had given a glimpse of even more terrifying prospects of mass destruction. However, even the boldest forecasts of that time pale beside the reality of the arsenal of weapons that scientific and technological progress has since made available to, or placed within reach of, human societies, and which harbours the threat of total, irrevocable annihilation. There can be no overlooking the fact that when it is a matter of war or peace, what is at stake today is the survival of the human species, or at any rate the survival of man as the vehicle of civilization.[1]. Accordingly, it is essential, for the sake of mankind's very survival, that everything be done to obviate a new world-wide conflagration and to check all escalation of violence. Fear, however, which is a purely negative emotion, is not in itself sufficient to provide a guarantee against catastrophe. It is becoming increasingly widely accepted that the maintenance and consolidation of world peace call not only for constant and sincere recourse to ever more effective procedures for

---

1. Existing stocks of nuclear weapons are already sufficient to destroy the world's population several times over. The bomb which wiped out Hiroshima, causing the death of some 100,000 persons, appears a relatively modest weapon today, despite its power equal to 15,000 tons of TNT, in comparison with the hundredfold more powerful hydrogen bombs, several of which are manufactured daily. It is also a known fact that the technical and economic obstacles to the manufacture of nuclear weapons are disappearing progressively, with the result that by 1980, it is quite possible that 12,000 such weapons may have been produced by countries which at present possess none. Reference must also be made to the horrifying possibilities that are opening up in the field of bacteriological, climatological and even psychological warfare.

achieving conciliation among nations but also for the joint adoption and prosecution of a positive scheme designed to marshall energies and transcend oppositions.

The building up, in recent years, of a spirit of detente and peaceful co-operation in place of the climate of tension and overt or covert confrontation which had reigned for many years between the major powers—and which had won for itself the term of 'cold war'—holds out in this respect promises of great moment, particularly when this determination to seek peaceful solutions is considered in its repercussions not only on bilateral negotiations but also on the actual fabric of relations among all the world's nations. For the building of peace must henceforth be seen as an effort to establish a multidimensional whole within which each nation must be free to develop and express itself in conformity with its own aspirations while respecting the integrity of other nations and co-operating freely and fruitfully with them. Moreover, it is clear that, if the reform of political relations between States is to be fully effective, it must be paralleled by intensified exchange and co-operation at the economic, social and cultural levels: peace is one and indivisible. In this connection, the transactions and conclusions of the recent major regional conferences, especially the Conference on Security and Co-operation in Europe, merit particular attention.

Furthermore, as is noted in the Preamble to Unesco's Constitution, the Second World War provided a striking illustration of the denial of human rights and democratic values going hand in hand with the spirit of domination, violence and war, thereby laying bare the inadequacies of a theoretical pacifism which merely exorcised war without analysing its underlying causes and roots, condemned violence without distinguishing between aggression and popular resistance and invoked the reign of concord without proposing, much less initiating, effective remedial action for situations in which injustice and oppression prevailed. World developments were to underline this lesson, demonstrate its validity and broaden its reference.

The victory of the democracies and the reaffirmation of human rights were soon to be followed by a vast movement of popular liberation, destined to break the colonial yoke and, through the accession of many newly sovereign States, make international dialogue and co-operation truly universal. The international community, in the full dimensions of the term, was born, and with it a new hope. However, war had not thereby been banished, even if its main theatre had been shifted to the poor countries. As a result of the persistence of factors making for tension and turmoil in one area or another, it has continued to break out intermittently in the form of conflicts which, while localized as far as their theatre is concerned, are none the less part and parcel of the major confrontations of world politics. These conflicts, while demonstrating the capacity for heroism, sacrifice and resistance of the peoples directly concerned in their struggles to achieve independence, have been settled only at the cost of grievous sufferings.[1] Moreover, despite the determination to contain them, there has been a constant and serious risk of these conflicts spreading and becoming general.

---

1. It is a known fact, for example, that the total number of deaths—military and civilian—since the end of the Second World War in the Indo-Chinese peninsula alone can be estimated at 2,600,000.

The dangers of flagrant injustice

The flagrant and continuously aggravated inequality among nations, the persistence of international injustice in regard to the distribution and disposal of resources, the perpetuation of overt or covert relations of dominance, corrupting the nation's very life, have emerged increasingly clearly as factors giving rise to serious tensions and grave disorders, whose long-term effect is to jeopardize the achievement of a true and world-wide peace. However hampered it may be by the constant pressures of self-interest, however inadequate its results may still be, the joint quest for development constitutes a positive response to this situation, an essential contribution to the work of building peace. In this respect, the decision of the United Nations to work together to institute a new international economic order replacing relations of inequality and exploitation by a system of co-operation based upon community of interests and designed to achieve international equity and social progress for all peoples promises to be of decisive importance.

Given the destitution and stagnation to which a considerable section of mankind is doomed, and given the need to marshall all available resources in order to satisfy the vital needs of a world population that is rapidly expanding,[1] the frantic arms race, which in itself comprises a serious threat to world peace, increasingly stands condemned as a scandalous squandering of energies and resources which should be redeployed in order to improve the living conditions of the most disadvantaged nations, to open their paths into the future and thereby to secure the conditions for the establishment of a profound and lasting peace.[2]

It is in the light of these developments that it becomes possible to discern the principles which must today govern all coherent action to strengthen peace.

First and foremost, however complex may be the factors involved in the system of international relations, the desire for, and spirit of, peace require to be cultivated and consolidated as one of its prime components and essential foundations. To overcome aggressivity and mistrust, to promote and nurture feelings of fellowship and friendship among men, mutual respect for other peoples' personality and values and the desire for concord remain today, no less than thirty years ago, a fundamental task. And, provided the stage of self-interest and cynicism is transcended, the daily experience of international life continually brings confirmation and encouragement to the development of these constructive attitudes, which are henceforth called upon to be world wide in their concern.

---

1. According to ILO data, during the next ten years some 300 million people will be seeking employment. World agricultural production is likely to increase at a rate of 2.6 per cent annually, up to 1985, while the world population will rise at an annual rate of 2.7 per cent.
2. In 1974 over $210,000 million— that is, a sum equivalent to the total national income of countries populated by the major section of mankind or twenty times the total amount of aid given to the poor countries—were devoted to arms expenditure. And this at a time when 2,500 million men and women are in large measure leading a precarious existence, below the minimum acceptable subsistence level. The growth rate of the populations concerned is such that their number is likely to double by the end of the century.

Beyond the 'absence of war' . . .

However, this desire for peace is not in itself sufficient to secure the settlement of disputes and to obviate the threat of catastrophe linked to the process of escalation and continually increasing the stakes. It is essential to have smoothly running, universally available machinery and procedures for direct negotiation and conciliation, failing which any conflict of interests may become envenomed to the point of no return. It is equally essential that a permanent institutional framework for joint international consultation be provided, within which the entire community of nations can take a common stand in face of a crisis or an impending crisis, even at the local level, and together devise means of countering it.

However, it is not enough to counter the threats of irremediable catastrophe whenever and wherever they occur; this type of operation amounts to no more than papering over the cracks unless it stems from a positive framework the effect of which is to regulate the relations between States and make them subject to the rule of law. It would be equally pointless to foster feelings of fellowship which were then flouted and belied by the maintenance of an iniquitous state of affairs, or too sorely strained by the persistence or exacerbation of factors making for tension. As the General Conference strongly emphasized at its eighteenth session (resolution 11.1), 'peace cannot consist solely in the absence of armed conflict but implies principally a process of progress, justice and mutual respect among the peoples designed to secure the building of an international society in which everyone can find his true place and enjoy his share of the world's intellectual and material resources . . .'. There is no point and no meaning in preaching peace unless and until a programme of effective action is devised and implemented with a view to building a peaceful order. Such a peaceful order, which must perforce be world wide and necessarily affects relations between men in all their dimensions, must be both an order of security and an order of justice, and must open upon a future to the building of which each and every nation must be able to contribute according to its own genius and aspirations.

It is clear that the international organizations are called upon to play a paramount and increasingly constructive role in an area in which, to the superficial observer, the actions taken and arrangements made by governments would alone appear to be decisive. It is within these world-wide agencies, that is, the United Nations system, the product of the common will of States, that disputes can be settled from the broadest and most equitable standpoint, that a veritable code of conduct, at once legal and political in character, is being progressively defined and adopted, that peaceful co-operation between countries possessing different social structures can be developed, and that national policies can, without infringement of sovereignties, go on from the pursuit of steady-state equilibria to dynamic collaboration for the purpose of building a more harmonious world. It is within these organizations, too, that the major debates concerning the construction of peace receive the publicity capable of arousing and clarifying public opinion and enlisting active popular support for a common undertaking.

... the patient disarmament of minds

Of the different agencies of the United Nations system, Unesco has a mission to serve in the fundamental work of strengthening peace which is at once quite specific and extremely general in its bearing. Clearly, it is not competent to settle specifically political disputes between States, still less so to seek solutions to open conflicts, nor even to take action directly aimed at progressively establishing, at the institutional level, a rule of law to govern international political relations. Responsible, like the other Specialized Agencies, to the Economic and Social Council, Unesco exercises direct competence first and foremost in the social sphere in general and in particular in questions respecting intellectual life, its promotion and its various media: education, science, culture, communication. In this respect, the work which it carries out with a view to fostering the advancement of nations, the equalization of their opportunities and the intensification of co-operation between them can claim to be regarded as a positive contribution to the building of a world capable of establishing true peace.[1] As the General Conference has stressed on many occasions, it is its programme as a whole, and particularly its action to promote the development and generalization of international exchanges, which constitutes, implicitly yet pervasively, a contribution to the building of peace, and which is actuated and guided by this essential mission. Stress must, however, be placed on the extremely close and evident interrelationship existing between the reinforcement of peace and the defence of human rights: through the defence and promotion of human rights, the condemnation of violations thereof and analysis of the underlying structural causes of the realities of discrimination, oppression and exploitation, through the study and dissemination of means of redressing such situations and through the awakening of public opinion to these problems (see Chapter 1). Unesco is explicitly working to achieve the maintenance and reinforcement of peace, according to the terms of Article I of its Constitution, as well as highlighting the way in which peace conduces to the increasingly full observance of human rights.

Among these rights is the right to respect for the cultural values of the world's peoples (Chapter 1, page 37), which constitutes the basis for the development among them of relations of understanding, friendship and mutual enrichment, and for the assertion of that intellectual and moral fellowship of mankind which Unesco has from the outset continued to look upon as the bedrock of peace. Within the United Nations system, Unesco is assigned here a unique role which endows its work on behalf of peace with a considerable and indeed unequalled significance.

However, it is also Unesco's mission to work directly and explicitly for the strengthening of peace. In doing so, it is operating in an area which, while lying specifically within its competence, is nevertheless of extremely general import. As its founders stressed, Unesco is in fact concerned primarily with the minds of men, and 'it is in the minds of men that the defences of peace must be constructed'. It is for Unesco to under-

---

1. Its normative action and the assistance it gives individual States in concluding mutual arrangements can even be regarded as an effective, though strictly specialized, contribution to the United Nations political and legal work.

take, on behalf of the United Nations system as a whole, the work of educating young people and adults, which is in no way a form of indoctrination but an appeal to freedom, the exercise of judgement and generosity, for the purpose of causing the reign of fellow-ship to prevail and providing the public at large with an informed understanding of the conditions for achieving a just peace founded on mutual respect. Responsible as it is for promoting intellectual advancement and evolving a thorough-going form of constructive humanism corresponding to the needs of our age, it behoves the Organization to encourage thinking and discussion on the ideals of the different civilizations and on the significance of peace for the future of mankind and to address itself to public opinion as well as to the specialized circles with which it maintains relations. It is also its task, as the organization responsible for promoting the advancement of scientific knowledge and its contribution to human well-being and progress, to encourage research designed to elucidate the conditions and principles governing international action to build peace and, by seeing that such action matches up to the complexity of the factors involved, ensure its increasing efficacity.

It is to these modes of direct, problem-focused action by Unesco in the cause of peace that are related the three sections of the present chapter. These three sections approach the question of reinforcing peace from three standpoints which are mutually complementary: *peace research*, which makes possible an overall grasp of the decisive structures and processes governing negative peace (absence of direct violence) and positive peace (development of relations of co-operation founded on justice); *study of the international system*, which calls for new directions to be taken in the study of international law and of international organizations as subsystems of the international system; lastly, *education for peace*, which concerns both the development of international understanding by means of education and the most diversified forms of action to promote an awareness among all sectors of society such as to encourage the radical changes of attitude and practice which the institution of a peaceful world calls for.

... and alerting of public opinion

True peace, in the sense intended by Unesco—'just, lasting and constructive'–must be conceived of not merely as the absence of war but as an equitable and democratic system of international relations, and as entailing the establishment and maintenance of an order of friendly understanding and co-operation based upon a community of interests among peoples, rooted in respect for and the promotion of human rights and keyed to the achievement of progress and well-being for all.

The three groups of activities described in the present chapter are designed to contribute to the maintenance and reinforcement of this peace through a better understanding of the nature of the problems involved and of the means of solving them, as well as through the moulding of minds and the alerting of public opinion. They approach the question of peace in the most concrete terms, in the context of the life of communities, of their relations and exchanges. They cannot therefore be wholly divorced from the overall programme of action carried out by Unesco as an institution for international co-operation. The effectiveness of this effort will depend on its organic links with the rest of the programme, as also on the attention that will be paid to the work of the United Nations and the United Nations system as a whole and to the similarly directed efforts made and progress achieved by Member States, acting jointly or on their own. The ultimate justification for these objectives is that the work done will help to sustain, illuminate and facilitate this action through a contribution which only Unesco can make, and to develop among the public a sense of the responsibilities which are incumbent on each and every one. For, in the final analysis, the effective establishment of peace will depend on the enlightened resolve and concerted action of Member States— of their governments and their peoples.

Peace research

As we have just seen, the maintenance and reinforcement of peace are among the major goals of world politics in these last decades of the twentieth century. Mankind is now aware of the dangers which threaten it: it knows that the scientific and technological revolution, while opening new horizons for social progress, makes possible the mass destruction of the human species through the use of nuclear, biological and chemical weapons. The arms race represents a real and constant threat to its survival. It is already a contributory factor in the ecological damage being done to the planet and is compromising or limiting the chances of development. Public opinion is increasingly shocked by the absurdity and the danger of this appalling waste. The objective of maintaining and reinforcing peace is continually being proclaimed by governments themselves at many international meetings.[1]

The achievement of a real, lasting peace runs, however, into many powerful obstacles in the present state of international relations, the root cause of which must be seen in the persistence of inequalities between nations and within nations, leading to the perpetuation and even extension of conflicts and tensions between present-day societies.

In the course of history, wars, mass destruction and even genocide have wreaked havoc among mankind. Twice in less than fifty years, in the recent past, con-

---

1. The Conference on Security and Co-operation in Europe (Helsinki, July-August 1975) affords a recent and striking example. The General Conference, at its eighteenth session, considered that the European Conference was a factor in the continual strengthening of the security of all peoples and that Unesco should take into account the decisions and recommendations of this and similar conferences directly related to its fields of competence (18 C/Resolution 11.1). Various activities are envisaged under this and other objectives to implement the Final Act of the Helsinki Conference and other similar resolutions.

flicts originating in Europe have extended beyond that continent, bringing death to millions. In the last thirty years, there have been no recurrences of these conflagrations and machinery for concliation and concertation at international level has been set up to obviate any such recurrence. However, the relative calm in relations between the industrial nations—due, at least in part, to the balance of atomic terror—should not inspire any undue optimism for the future or any blind confidence in the automatic working of the mechanisms for maintaining world peace. Above all, it should not delude us as to what is happening here and now, as to the scope and significance of the conflicts which follow one upon the other: war continues to wreak havoc, the only difference being that the theatre of war has moved to the poor countries, where the effects of the major international antagonisms continue to be felt in one way or another. As for the disarmament negotiations, their results must not be underestimated, inasmuch as they limit the accumulation by the great powers of more and more sophisticated, lethal and costly means of destruction; but for the time being they are not enough to prevent a widespread arms race.

Tensions, imbalances and violence: a set of complex problems

Present-day thinking takes full account of the complexity of the interplay of factors of tension and factors of harmony in the world and takes pains to identify the prerequisites for the establishment of a genuine peace. That a genuine peace implies the establishment of an underlying harmony in the relations between nations, groups and individuals in general and that it can only come about when a just order has been universally established are principles which have been repeatedly proclaimed by the international community and which are illustrated in particular by the Declaration and Programme of Action on the Establishment of a New International Economic Order. Important as this new awareness is, it is not in itself sufficient for the building up of the corpus of practical knowledge on which the effort to establish peace needs to be based if it is to give peace firm roots in human relations.

Such knowledge has to be built up by means of a patient and systematic effort of scientific thinking applied to the world situation—an undertaking now known as 'peace research'. It is true in a sense that the sources of conflict in the modern world have become more obvious, or more a matter of public knowledge, than they used to be, since today they are expressed and transmitted by highly developed mass media and information networks. However, this really only applies to the proximate causes, which, as we have just seen, are generally only a reflection of the deeper and more complex phenomena constituting the very substance of relations between nations and between groups. In this world of ours, every part of which, because of the advances in the techniques of material civilization and the extension of communications, interacts with and is inseparable from every other part, the affinities and tensions existing within societies and the kaleidoscopic changes of international politics all form part of a single network of actions and reactions. This complex situation, which seems to defy analysis, is also marked by the profound inequality prevailing between nations and deeply affecting the fabric of the relations between them; its direct or indirect repercussions affect every aspect of international relations and what is more it makes it impossible to dissociate the question of ways and means of organizing a peaceful world order from that of the values which such an order should embody and promote.

These inequalities are in themselves sufficient to demonstrate the highly multi-dimensional character of the phenomena requiring rational, methodical investigation, taking due account of past experience; for the economic imbalances, so complex in themselves, are further complicated by all the other factors—social, political, scientific, cultural, etc.—involved in the present unequal distribution of potentialities and re-sources in the world which must be given priority when the problem of reducing ten-sions and building peace is being considered. There are, however, other aspects or other levels which can no longer be overlooked in the statement of this problem: there are the interests of States and the conflicts and convergences of those interests, the components of world strategies and their domino effects, the mindless machinery of escalation and overbidding, the factors involved in the arms race, the methods and procedures used in negotiation, mediation and concertation; there are also the domestic problems of societies—social inequalities, social demands and movements, states of tension between groups, etc., and their repercussions on international politics and vice versa; there is the underlying psychological basis of the tendencies towards violence and also of the tendencies towards the extension of the bonds of solidarity, which needs to be carefully studied, in close relation to the social conditions in which it arises; there are the ways and means—institutions and regulatory instruments in particular—whereby inter-national relations can gradually be brought under the rule of law; and so on and so forth.

The conditions for objective peace research

Research applied to peace problems must show itself capable of dealing effectively with these many different aspects with a view to gradually building up a comprehensive body of knowledge which would be regarded as valid by all nations and would be capable of guiding and staying them in their joint effort—transcending the differences in their political and social structures, their degree of development, their situation, their resources and their aspirations, their capacity to influence world politics, their traditions and their values, etc.—to build a just, lasting and constructive peace for groups, societies and the world.

This research must therefore be:

Pre-eminently interdisciplinary, practical (i.e. not confining itself to generalities, but showing itself capable of getting down to the analysis of particular situations) and systematic (i.e. taking as scientifically strict a view as possible of the infi-nitely complex interaction of all the relevant factors, however heterogeneous they may be).

Motivated by a concern for inspiring and providing a basis for action, taking as its points of reference the values of civilization and the imperatives of equity and mutual respect, but at the same time genuinely scientific io its approach and free from any biased preconceptions and from any particular allegiance or initial ideological slant.

Universal, i.e. tackling the problem at world level (without any arbitrary reduction to uniformity or unity) and incorporating the approaches of all peoples.

Co-operative, i.e. based on the contributions of all countries and encouraging the strengthening of the facilities for investigation and systemization of those nations which are still inadequately provided with research institutions.

Dedicated simultaneously (and indissociably) to: (a) analysing the effects and repercussions of war—and the constant threat of war as a result of the permanent character of the tensions and inequalities and of the arms race—on people's lives, on social progress and the future of civilizations; (b) laying bare the direct causes and indirect factors of conflicts in their multiplicity, diversity and interrelatedness; (c) identifying and co-ordinating the means capable of promoting and consolidating the rule of peace, including in particular means to pursue in-depth action directed towards the establishment of international equity and social justice and real respect for the legitimate aspirations of all peoples and groups; (d) drawing attention to positive achievements, examples of co-operation, etc., which already give concrete expression to the spirit of peace and which, if undisturbed peace were to be established, could be repeated as a matter of course; and also demonstrating the advantages of peace in general and the prospects it opens up for human progress.

Here more than anywhere else Unesco emerges as a focal point for the United Nations system in general and for all the professional and scientific bodies currently active in this field. It should organize, stimulate and implement integrated peace research on an international scale.

Growing interest in analyses, conflict studies and peace research

Since the dawn of human history, attempts have continually been made to explain and to avoid the antagonisms which divide families, clans and ethnic groups and which set the inhabitants of different regions against each other. The phenomena of domination and exploitation have been analysed as well as the reasons for wars and aggressions. Since the end of the Second World War, a new impetus has been given to this work, and the scientific study of the nature and effects of war (conflict studies) and that of the conditions for peace (peace research) have found a new lease of life, although they have not succeeded in bringing about a sufficiently thoroughgoing renewal in the traditional approach via international law.

New tools of analysis, using the accumulated knowledge and the research methods of many social sciences and natural sciences, have been applied to the analysis of peace, and a new branch of knowledge has grown up around the notions of 'peace research' and 'peace and conflict studies'. This field has opened up new prospects for the study of the social, political and economic dimensions of a lasting peace founded on justice at the level of groups, societies and the world. A great deal of material has been accumulated which now permits the start of a new stage in research founded on the achievements of contemporary scientific methodology and the work of Member States, other international organizations and Unesco itself.

In Member States, most of the efforts to promote peace research have quite rightly been made in the economically developed countries where most modern wars have generally broken out. In the socialist countries of Europe, universities and academies of sciences have carried out research on such themes as the role of international economics, the conditions for peaceful coexistence between countries with different social and economic systems, disarmament, and security and co-operation in Europe. In North America, numerous private or university-affiliated institutes have applied sophisticated research techniques to such problems as conflict resolution. Western Europe has produced numerous studies on the problems of conflict studies. The developing countries, for their part, have continually shown great interest in peace research and have produced excellent researchers in these fields.

The research carried out by the United Nations, in accordance with its peace-keeping functions as laid down in the Charter, has been concerned primarily with specific situations or with the work of the Secretariat in this field. According to Unesco's *International Repertory of Institutions Specializing in Research on Peace and Disarmament,* the United Nations 'as such has done little research into principles or resolving conflicts or keeping the peace'. However, 'while United Nations documentation contains very little straight peace research, a large portion of its content is undoubtedly relevant to peace research'.

A great deal of research was carried out by the United Nations in the 1960s on the social and economic consequences of disarmament. Reports issued since 1970 have dealt with various aspects of disarmament and peace-keeping. In 1971, the General Assembly considered 'it desirable to bring to the notice of the international community the work done in the field of peace research by national and international institutions and to promote, on a permanent basis, in the light of the purposes and principles of the Charter, a recording of the studies devoted to this subject'.[1] Pursuant to this resolution an 'informative report on scientific works produced by national, international, governmental and non-governmental, public and private institutions in the field of peace research' has been produced every other year since 1973.

The statutes of the United Nations Institute for Training and Research (UNITAR), specify its research fields, which include major questions relating to the maintenance of peace and security and the promotion of economic and social development, as well as the techniques and machinery of the United Nations. Of particular interest is a study recently completed and published by UNITAR, entitled *Recent advances in peace and conflict research: a critical survey.* The research programme concentrates on matters relating to the United Nations and provides a liaison between

1. A/RES/2817 (XXVI) adopted on 14 December 1971.

the United Nations and the world academic community. International organizations, peace and security and development and resource problems are the main areas covered by the studies, usually prepared by a single author. The close contacts between Unesco and UNITAR assure the complementary nature of the research programmes of the two Organizations.

After several years of preparatory work done jointly by Unesco and the United Nations, it was decided to establish a United Nations University in the form of a network of research and post-graduate training institutions devoted to action-oriented research into the pressing global problems of human survival. To the extent that the University's work in this field will concern problems of peace, it will offer new possibilities for the development of peace research on an international basis.

Much of the peace research that has been carried out in recent years is the work of non-governmental organizations established either as national or international centres. A detailed description of these institutions is given in the *International Repertory of Institutions for Peace and Conflict Research* published by Unesco in 1973, updating the 1966 edition. Many of them are federated in the International Peace Research Association (IPRA), which has consultative status with Unesco and is affiliated to the International Social Science Council.

Few regional intergovernmental organizations have carried out research on peace-related issues within their frames of reference. Nevertheless, studies relevant to peace research have occasionally been undertaken as part of a programme within a regional organization's field of competence and contribute to the expanding literature in this area.

A programme for the scientific study of tensions and the promotion of international understanding

However basic to Unesco's contribution to peace its statutory role as a meeting place for scientists from different regions and ideologies may be, it also has a special task, recognized early in its history, to promote the scientific study of peace. The second session of the General Conference subscribed to a 'Solemn appeal against the idea that war is inevitable' and voted an ambitious programme of activities on 'Tensions affecting international understanding', which included a number of meetings and publications. The tensions project developed in the mid-1950s into a series of studies on various aspects of racial discrimination and development problems. The twelfth and thirteenth sessions of the General Conference authorized the Director-General to promote research on peace and disarmament and to encourage co-operation with institutions engaged in such research. Accordingly, the *International Repertory of Institutions Specializing in Research on Peace and Disarmament* was published in 1966 and IPRA was established. Further to a resolution of the fifteenth session of the General Conference, the programme was expanded to include the study of the causes of aggression and the determining factors in living peacefully together. Several meetings and publications have dealt with this theme and the related theme of violence. An international expert meeting to advise Unesco in defining its role in developing scientific research on peace problems was held in 1969.

The sixteenth session of the General Conference authorized the Director-General to 'promote and assist the application of the social sciences to the problems of human rights and peace', *inter alia,* 'by stimulating and assisting research and training activities relating to problems of peace'. One of the projects under this programme was an international expert meeting on university teaching and research on problems of peace and conflict resolution, held in Manila in the Philippines, in 1971.

By the time of the seventeenth session of the General Conference Unesco had taken the first steps toward the promotion of peace research institutions. Although some clear plans for far-reaching programmes had been formulated there was as yet no genuinely coherent and *integrated peace research programme* with clearly formulated objectives. Certain specific projects, including a Reader on Peace and Conflict Studies, a meeting on the causes of violence and studies on international organizations were undertaken.

An important project of considerable relevance to the promotion of peace research was undertaken in 1974 under the programme of philosophy. This was the first peace forum on 'peace and convictions'. Although it underlined the difficulties in achieving a common language in speaking about problems of peace, itself a prerequisite to building peace in the minds of men, this first peace forum pointed the way for new and stimulating lines of research.

The promotion of 'peace research' as a scientific discipline and as a field for the application of the social sciences received particular attention at the eighteenth session of the General Conference. Resolution 3.321 authorized the Director-General to promote the construction of peace, *inter alia,* 'by contributing to the development of *peace research* especially and of other relevant disciplines'. The contribution of the social sciences to peace, the study of disarmament and the results of peace research thus all received increased attention.

These initial attempts nevertheless gave results which were necessarily only tentative since the way in which the problems were tackled corresponded to an embryonic stage in the development of peace research. Further peace research must adopt a more sophisticated, complex and systemic approach.

In the years to come, Unesco will make a special contribution towards establishing peace research solidly among the social sciences as understood by the Member States. In that connection the Organization will encourage the creation of national or regional peace research centres and will launch a vast intergovernmental programme on peace research. Unesco will also publish monographs for the general public on priority issues such as violence, sources of tension, the arms race, disarmament and the establishment of a new international economic order.

The general principle guiding this action as a whole is to encourage conceptual, methodological and institutional development of peace research aimed at providing an appropriate response to the social, economic and cultural problems raised by today's dynamic reality.

International law and the challenges of the contemporary world

The establishment of a peaceful world order implies the existence, at the international level, of standards and structures such as will ensure, between States, relations that are based on justice, equity and respect for human rights. International law as a whole provides the bases for a standard-setting order governing not only the relations between States but also the functioning of the institutions born of the collective resolve of those States. Conceived initially as a set of rules applicable in the case of armed conflict, international law was subsequently extended to the most varying aspects of international relations, on becoming changed, especially after the Second World War, into a law of peace. The Charter of the United Nations, which reaffirms the principle of non-recourse to force in the settlement of disputes, constitutes its point of departure. However, while international law derives from several legal traditions, it is still largely European in inspiration.

Legal problems on a world-wide scale

The accession to independence of vast territories has radically changed the physiognomy of the international community, which now finds itself at grips with problems that can only be tackled and solved at world level, concerning as they do armed conflict, economic and social development, the environment, or the distribution of resources. Consequently, international law, which does not possess the same coercive force as domestic law and whose value rests on the adjustment of standards to the reality of international relations and to the aspirations of peoples, has to be fitted to meet the new challenges of the contemporary world.

A similar evolution characterizes the international organizations, which are often the institutional expression of international law and which contribute to its development and codification in their respective fields of competence. Even though the sovereignty of States remains a fundamental principle, awareness of common interests is helping to bring about an appreciable change in the relational aspect of the structures of international society. There is a gradual trend towards a world community in which the general interest of mankind takes precedence over the particular interests of States. The world in which the international organizations operate today is very different from what it was when they were set up. With the massive entry on the world scene of the newly independent States, the composition of the intergovernmental organizations has been radically changed, and the struggle against the various situations of domination or economic and political dependence is reflected in the recent decisions of all these organizations, including Unesco. New forms of action have to be sought so that the said organizations may meet more effectively the new challenges with which they are faced, particularly as regards the establishment of a new international economic order.

A better adjustment of international standards and structures to the new requirements of the contemporary world—which is prerequisite for the establishment of a peaceful world order—is conceivable only on the basis of a thorough reflection on the role played, in their present state, by international law and the international organizations, and on the areas in which an updating process might be applied In this connection, it is for the world community as a whole, but more particularly for the organizations of the United Nations system and for Unesco, to carry out or promote education and research programmes bearing on international relations.

International law and the international organizations are subjects for study included in the scientific disciplines taught at university level throughout the world. On the other hand, research and educational establishments specializing exclusively in international relations are comparatively few in number. According to the *Yearbook* of the Union of International Associations, there are over 330 centres or schools devoted mainly to the study of international relations, to research concerning peace and related questions, but which, although widely accessible to students from the developing countries, are concentrated in a few countries. There are 117 in the United States of America, 26 in the United Kingdom, 22 in the Federal Republic of Germany, 15 in France and 11 in the Union of Soviet Socialist Republics.

Development of law studies and improved distribution of educational institutions

A certain number of institutions which are international in scope play a role of prime importance in the development of the scientific study of international law and international organizations. The Hague Academy of International Law offers to advanced students from all over the world the opportunity of attending summer courses given by the greatest specialists in public and private international law, and of taking part in the activities of its research centre, which it also places at the disposal of legal practitioners. The Institute of International Law, which was established more than a hundred years ago, comprises a small number of distinguished specialists whose task it is to elucidate legal rules in force or in preparation and to propose codifying texts which are often quoted as sources of reference. Another hundred-year-old institution, the International Law Association, which has its headquarters in London, is an international non-governmental organization admitted to information and consultative relations (category B) with Unesco and affiliated to the International Social Science Council. Its aim is 'the study, elucidation and advancement of international law, public and private, the study of comparative law, the making of proposals for the solution of conflicts of law, and for the unification of law....'. It holds a conference every two years attended by members of national branches established in most countries. Other bodies, such as the Carnegie Endowment (United States of America) or the Institute of World Economics and International Relations (Union of Soviet Socialist Republics), conduct, with the assistance of distinguished specialists, research programmes concerning the international organizations. In specific fields of international law, such as human rights and humanitarian law, teaching and research activities are carried out by specialized institutes.

Almost all of the intergovernmental organizations contribute, through their standard-setting work, to the development of international law and certain of them seek to promote the study of international law and of international organizations. In 1966, a programme was launched in the United Nations for the promotion of the teaching, study, dissemination and wider appreciation of international law; it includes the award of fellowships, the provision of advisory services and legal publications, and the holding of seminars. Furthermore, in pursuance of Article 13 of the Charter of the United Nations, the General Assembly entrusted the International Law Commission in 1947 with responsibility for carrying out studies and making recommendations with a view to 'encouraging the progressive development of international law and its codification'; since it was set up, this Commission has examined over twenty international law questions and has drawn up several international conventions. Important decisions relating to international law are also taken by the General Assembly itself, as is shown, for example, by the 'Declaration on Principles of International Law concerning Friendly Relations and Co-operation among States in accordance with the Charter of the United Nations' adopted by it in October 1970, on the occasion of the twenthy-fifth anniversary of the United Nations. The International Court of Justice, established by the Charter of the United Nations as the principal judicial organ of the Organization, and UNITAR, which carries out a programme of fellowships, seminars and publications, also make an invaluable contribution to the achievement of the objectives sought.

It is in this general context, described in broad outline, that Unesco conducts various types of action. In the development of the standard-setting and codification aspects of international law, Unesco is responsible, in its own right, for formulating international norms in the fields of its competence. Twenty-one conventions and other agreements, and sixteen recommendations, have been adopted in this way by the General Conference or by intergovernmental conferences convened by Unesco alone or in conjunction with other international organizations.

The development of standard-setting and of an institutional structure better adapted to the new requirements of the international community

As regards the study proper of international law and of international organizations, Unesco has been participating since 1966 in the United Nations assistance programme referred to above. It has contributed to the promotion of the teaching of international law through the publication of a survey on the importance accorded to international law in higher education in various countries, and through the organization, in Lagos, in December 1971 of a Round Table on the teaching of international law in Africa. Moreover, in 1970, the General Conference invited the Director-General to strengthen Unesco's action for peace through interdisciplinary studies and research in a number of areas, including the role of the United Nations system in the development of peaceful co-operation between nations and the development of the human personality. In conjunction with this project, Unesco has laid the foundations for a long-term study on the role of international organizations in the contemporary world.

In 1974 Unesco organized a symposium for young people with different backgrounds from various regions in the world at which participants expressed their views with regard to the organizations of the United Nations system and formulated recommendations concerning measures that might be taken to ensure that those organizations responded more adequately to their aspirations.

It should be noted that, as part of operational projects carried out in the sphere of international law and international organizations, aid financed both by Unesco and by UNDP is granted to higher education establishments, in Africa and in Asia, so that they may equip themselves for the development of teaching and research in these disciplines. Further, in accordance with the resolutions of the United Nations International Conference on Human Rights (Tehran, 1968) and the Commission on Human Rights, fellowships are awarded to young teachers to enable them to receive specialized training in international law and comparative law in human rights at the International Institute of Human Rights (Strasbourg).

Lastly, Unesco contributes to the study of international law and of international organizations through the issue of scientific publications, more especially in the domain of the social sciences,[1] and through the provision of regular assistance to international non-governmental organizations such as the International Peace Research Association (IPRA) the International Law Association (ILA) and the International Association of Legal Science, which form part of the International Social Science Council.

Unesco's action is designed to foster and supplement the activities of the organizations with specific responsibility for the codification of international law and for education concerning international relations. This action, which is characterized by a global approach in which account is taken of all trends of thought, has a twofold purpose: to encourage, in the world scientific community and in Member States, an effort of reflection calculated to promote a better adjustment of international law and of the international organizations to the new requirements of the contemporary world; and to assist Member States which currently lack such means to equip themselves with the means that will enable them to develop education and research in the sphere of international relations.

In the next few years, Unesco intends to prepare and make available to the universities in Member States new textbooks for education concerning international organizations, so that a better understanding may be gained of the role that these organizations play, and can play, in the establishment of a peaceful world order. Similarly, through the effort of reflection that will be accomplished, particularly through regional meetings bringing together specialists from different geographical and political backgrounds, the new problems of the contemporary world to which international law could help to provide solutions should have been clarified; the authorities responsible for the codification and application of international law should consequently have at their disposal precise data on which to base their appreciation.

1. See, for example, Challenged Paradigms in International Relations, *International Social Science Journal*, Vol. XXVI, No. 1, 1974.

Towards mutual understanding

The General Conference, in resolution 11.1, adopted at its eighteenth session, declared that Unesco should 'intensify its action to preserve peace, achieve *détente* at a still deeper level and strengthen international understanding so as to make this process irreversible'. It is self-evident that education and information can make a significant contribution to this task, since they help to form knowledge, beliefs and ideas concerning the contemporary world and to shape the principles which condition individual and collective behaviour. It is equally evident that education and information can be made to serve antithetical purposes and have often done so with disastrous effect.

In contributing to the reinforcement of peace, education and information will contribute also to the establishment of a new international economic and social order. The two objectives are inseparable and interdependent. Thus education and information aimed at strengthening peace must deal to a large extent not only with the problems specific to that objective but also with those involved in the establishment of such a new order.

Filling gaps, remodelling education and informing the out-of-school public

In this matter, however, there is still a wide gap between aims and achievements. In particular, the presentation of the cultures, values and realities of foreign nations, both in textbooks and teaching aids and by the information media is all too often distorted, giving rise to the transmission and perpetuation of stereotypes and misunderstanding which hamper both the building of peace and the establishment of greater justice in relations between nations.

The full potential of school education, even in the majority of the most advanced countries, is far from being realized. Curricula and the content of courses of study are often ill-adapted to the promotion of peace and international understanding; teachers are inadequately prepared for the task; textbooks and teaching materials are out of date, inaccurate and sometimes even prejudiced;[1] and the school itself operates in isolation from the world beyond its walls. A further problem, even in the best of circumstances, is that of achieving a pedagogy that is truly effective in forming attitudes and patterns of behaviour consonant with the aims of international understanding and peace.

In developing out-of-school programmes a major problem is to find means of access to young people and adults outside the structures of formal or institutionalized education. Considerable numbers can be reached through organizations representing

---

1. For the role of books for the general reader, as distinct from textbooks and teaching materials, in promoting peace and international understanding, see Chapter 3, page 131. Children's books are particularly important in this context.

different groups or interests. However, avenues to the vastly greater numbers of young people and adults who do not belong to organizations and who are not reached by other agencies need to be more fully utilized. Here public information has a major role to play.

In both school and out-of-school programmes an important factor to be taken into account today in determining content, methods and types of activities is the fact that many young people today are more aware of the problem of achieving and maintaining peace, and better equipped to analyse it. This is due to many factors, among them the broader access to education and a certain reorientation of its content, the expansion of the information media, the tendency to bring young people more into the mainstream of community development, currents and exchanges of ideas and campaigns to promote justice, the increasing role of youth movements, etc. In the view of many young people, 'peace can no longer be equated with the absence of wars'.[1]

A trump card: youth

A large proportion of young people appear to be aware that no true peace can be attained so long as there continue to exist vestiges of colonialism, racism, apartheid, neo-colonialism and more generally, the various forms of oppression and domination which are still at work in the world. Many young people include amongst actions for the attainment of lasting peace campaigns for national independence, territorial integrity, equality among nations and the sovereign right of nations to control their national resources and to adopt forms of social organization conducive to the cause of freedom and justice. On a still more general level, there can be little doubt that young people as a whole are particularly sensitive to whatever is entailed by considerations of equity and authenticity. All these factors must be taken into account in education and information programmes.

Educational action at national level . . .

The most recent comprehensive comparative study of education for international understanding was published by Unesco and the International Bureau of Education in 1968.[2] Ministries or other authorities responsible for education in eighty-two countries responded to a detailed questionnaire on the subject. In nearly half these countries laws and decrees concerning education and curricula included specific provisions for education for international understanding. In a much larger number of countries some place was given to such education in school programmes, generally in history, geography and civic education. The importance of out-of-school education was stressed in the majority of replies, with approximately half the total referring to collaboration between the school and out-of-school organizations and, in particular, to the role

1. *Final Report* of the International Seminar, 'Youth, Peace, Education' Gdansk, Poland, 1972 (Unesco, 2460/YD.
2. *Unesco/International Bureau of Education. Education for International Understanding*, Geneva, 1968 (Publication No. 311).

of youth organizations. Other more recent evidence (for example, the surveys of teaching about the United Nations in 1969 and 1974) shows continuing progress in most countries in the development of school and out-of-school programmes aimed at furthering peace and international understanding. The sum total of information available indicates that leadership, stimulus and assistance from the United Nations family of organizations has been significant in strengthening and extending education in this field.

It is impossible in a short space to review the details of action by institutions of the United Nations system to reinforce peace through education and information. Indirectly, by developing public knowledge and understanding of the world problems with which they deal—the solutions of which are fundamental to peace—they have helped to create the climate in which the possibilities for peace can grow. Directly, a number of them have contributed through programmes of education and information on peace issues. They have been joined in these tasks by a broad range of international non-governmental organizations.

Unesco itself has been engaged from the outset in action for the development of programmes of education and information aimed at furthering peace and international understanding. Each of the nineteen sessions of the General Conference has adopted resolutions to that end. The resulting programme of action has been a wide and multi-disciplinary one covering the whole range of education and information, whether for children, adolescents, young people or adults. Methods of work have included colla-boration with non-governmental organizations in a variety of enterprises.

... and at international level through the Associated Schools, the Unesco Clubs and the Voluntary Service

In the course of work in this field, Unesco has devised effective means of furthering on a large scale relevant programmes and activities. It has helped to set up and operate projects which are in effect laboratories for the development of education for peace and international understanding. One example is the Associated Schools Project, launched in 1953, in which more than 1,000 educational institutions in 63 countries take part. Another example is to be found in the rapidly proliferating Unesco Clubs and Associations, at present numbering some 2,000 in 67 countries. In recent years, Unesco Clubs have served increasingly as a link between in-school and out-of-school programmes and activities. At the same time, the establishment of Unesco Associations to enrol adults at all levels of professional activities has been successfully stressed, with a view to bringing about in wider and more differentiated segments of the popula-tion new attitudes and patterns of behaviour aimed at furthering peace and inter-national understanding. A third example is presented by the work of the Unesco-supported Co-ordinating Committee for International Voluntary Services (CCIVS), which promotes national, regional and international service by the movement of thousands of young people each year.

Unesco has also made an important contribution to the establishment of international standards in this field. It participated in the drafting of the United Nations

Declaration on the Promotion among Youth of the Ideals of Peace, Mutual Respect and Understanding between Peoples adopted by the United Nations General Assembly in 1965. The International Conference on Public Education, convened jointly by Unesco and the International Bureau of Education in 1968, adopted a recommendation on Education for International Understanding as an Integral Part of the Curriculum and Life of the School. The General Conference of Unesco at its eighteenth session adopted the Recommendation concerning Education for International Understanding, Co-operation and Peace and Education relating to Human Rights and Fundamental Freedoms. This Recommendation applies to all stages and forms of education. It is an authoritative, comprehensive and detailed statement on what education for peace and international understanding should be and on the steps that Member States should take to further its development. Unesco's proposed future action in this field forms an integral part of its activities in favour of education and information on human rights (see Chapter 1, page 59).

3 Man at the centre of development

In many countries, development was for a long time based on an over-simplified idea that social progress would come about more or less automatically as the result of economic growth.

The theorists whose views were most heeded were of the opinion that growth was a prerequisite for development, with concern for social consequences and social purposes coming at a later stage. In the name of efficiency, or what was taken to be such, it was often thought methodologically sound to plan and proceed with development without taking into account all the factors contributing to an effective improvement of the living standards of individuals and nations, and with even less regard to the requirements of equity in the sharing of effort and the benefits accruing.

The weaknesses of this would-be realistic approach have now been fully shown up by the disappointments encountered and by the critical analysis they have prompted. These weaknesses are: the establishment of self-perpetuating practices, elevating their own aims to the status of absolutes; the unthinking adoption of stereotyped development patterns taken over from a different historical background and ill-suited to the situations and resources of the various societies and to the authentic social and cultural aspirations of the different peoples; the production of imbalances, and an increasingly heavy burden of social expenditure, etc.

Two concepts not to be confused: growth and development

Over the past few decades, the development of all societies has come, irresistibly, to be accepted as a major requirement and an absolute necessity for each and every people and for the international community as a whole. We now have a more accurate and more comprehensive idea of what development processes involve and of the course to which they should be consciously held for the sake of sense as well as of efficiency. Expansion of the economy can no longer be set up as an absolute. It would, of course, be absurd to say that such expansion is not justified, or unnecessary, since it is still an essential prerequisite if the majority of the world's population are to be able to lead a decent life, to develop their potentialities freely and to play their proper part in the concert of nations and the movement of history. For the most deprived countries, it means escape from hopeless stagnation or even real distress. For those which are already industrialized or which have embarked on industrialization, economic expansion is not only a guarantee against collapse, crisis and decline but is the prerequisite for a gradual improvement in the standard of living of the people at large and for the adoption of a foreign policy based on mutual assistance.[1] All the same, although economic growth continues to be unreservedly acknowledged as a necessary prerequisite for development and an essential factor in it, no one nowadays can fail to be aware that it is not the whole of the story; that its justification lies in the social progress which it makes possible; and, above all, that it cannot be *isolated* simply as one *stage* on the way to such progress. Economic development is inconceivable except in conjunction with social development as a whole. It is dependent on the active participation of the whole people, which presupposes both the smooth running of the institutions and agencies of society and the whole-hearted support of individuals and groups.

It is by no means a new idea that development should serve man, but the full significance and impact of this principle have taken time to emerge. In the meantime, the very nature of what we should call 'development' has been found to be increasingly complex or multiform and less and less capable of being circumscribed by a rigid and universally applicable definition. Nevertheless, a few major characteristics seem to have emerged from all the diverse programmes and experiences: first and foremost, the idea of development as a comprehensive, multi-relational process involving all the aspects of the life of a community, its relations with the outside world and its self-awareness.[2] To argue in favour of a process of this kind, it is not enough to say that its

1. However weighty the arguments in favour of 'zero growth', this is an idea which has rightly been criticized and rejected on these grounds.
2. Of particular significance is the development of ideas on the means of ensuring, in each country, that science and technology make an effective contribution to development—the need for which can no longer be questioned. Experience has quickly confirmed (cf. Chapter 4 below) that the transfer of knowledge and the taking over of 'ready-made' solutions are not enough to provide a society with the means of pursuing its own development and carrying it forward independently, according to its own needs and aspirations. Transfers and borrowing are still necessary, but only to complement the generation of knowledge from within, resulting from the society's own scientific and technological research, on which its ability to borrow and assimilate without suffering alienation depends. In turn, however, the acquisition of the means for independent scientific and technological activity cannot be reduced simply to the establishment of a few facilities having little to do with the life of society as a whole. It implies a far-reaching transformation of the life of the community in all its aspects. Genuine appropriation of science and technology is both a basic prerequisite for any progress towards growth, and an integral part of the multi-dimensional development process, linked, through a complex network of interactions, with the other components of that process (economic, political, social and cultural, and involving institutions as much as practice). Implicit in it, above all, is the central reference to man which is the subject of this chapter.

ultimate justification is that man will benefit: the whole process itself, planned by man, must be consciously stamped with humanity. That is the full sense in which the principle that man is, and must be, the centre of development must be understood today. The implications and associations of this line of thought are beginning to emerge fairly clearly, and an attempt might be made to sum them up as follows:

Man: the instrument and ultimate aim of development

To begin with, and in the most obvious way, the 'humanist' principle governs the determination of the *ends* to which development must be directed. Man must *benefit* from it. This fundamental purpose of development must not be limited to providing an external justification for development; it implies that development should not simply be thought of as the materialization of a set of resources and means which may *later* make it possible to put a social policy into effect, but that it should be understood as prompted through and through by the desire to improve the lot of human beings. Only so will it be possible to warrant and secure full acceptance of the renunciations and sacrifices which are, quite clearly, involved for the time being in the long-term undertaking of building up a sound and prosperous economy. For the same reason, development must not merely hold the promise of greater *social justice*: it must, throughout its course, give tangible effect to the principle of equity. This principle must govern the sharing of the social benefits directly attributable to the raising of economic and technological potential, as well as the sharing of effort and sacrifice; it must guide development first towards relieving the direct suffering but also by a continuous process, towards the establishment of social (and international) relations on a juster footing, without undue privileges and unwarrantable exclusions. Lastly, the benefit from development must be of advantage to *man from every point of view*. The raising of the standard of living first of all is, of course, fundamental, but an improvement in material conditions is not enough, by itself, to give people the chance of leading a worth-while life. Development must therefore be aimed at the spiritual, moral and material advancement of the whole human being, both as a member of society and from the point of view of individual fulfilment. It should result in, but also spring from, greater and more enlightened participation by the individual in the life of the community. Far from subjecting people to some form of external discipline, or alienating them by the attraction of foreign ways of life, it should help in emancipating them, enable them to seek their own way, and safeguard their dignity as free and responsible beings. This concern for the human, or in other words the social and cultural purposes of development, must be operative from the outset: to postpone paying attention to higher values until a more propitious future date, for which preparations would be made by exclusively economic efforts, would be to deny the very principle of humanism and would involve the danger of irreversibly damaging the very structures and values that ought to be generally accepted and assisted to flourish at a later date. The humanist character and significance of the development process should be affirmed from the very start.

The humanist principle determines the *paths* of development. While man must be clearly established as the end and the beneficiary of development, he is first of all its *instrument*. Even if it were desired to reduce development to its economic dimensions, it could not result simply from an injection of imported material resources and technology. Its success depends on people. It therefore implies a reinforcement of human potential by way of training suited to the requirements of modernization. At a deeper level, however, it depends on the acceptance, initiative and efforts of individuals within society's structures. In the final analysis, it is based on the smooth running of a community as much as it contributes to it.

Unfortunately, it too often happens that the first result of hurried and disorderly development efforts is to revolutionize the living conditions of whole populations, condemning them for long periods to a state of rootlessness and stagnation and a marginal position, bound to give rise to despair and a breaking of social ties.

To counter these imbalances and maladjustments, the process of development centred on man must therefore necessarily be an *integrated process*, governed by an overall approach giving equal consideration to all sectors of social life, with due regard for the way they interact, and seeking to preserve and consolidate the major balances essential to the smooth running of the community—an approach which pays due heed to the evolution of all the potentialities of the human being and to changes in his place in society; which, in short, makes it possible to consider development, in order to ensure that it redounds to man's advantage, as a complex, interrelational process resulting from the action of many, varied factors on which it, in turn, exerts an influence.

Apart from the harsh material, economic and other limitations to which the process of development is subjected, and the need to meet the elementary needs inherent in human nature, concern for the whole man means that development activities must be directed by reference to the particular aspirations of the various peoples. Even values which are theoretically universal, like those embodied in human rights, are nevertheless differently appreciated and experienced by each nation or even by each social group. Development centred on man cannot mean the imposition of an anonymous pattern; it must be conceived as an *independent* or *self-supporting* process by which a society consciously and freely chooses the pattern to which it intends to conform. It takes shape, for any community, in all the resources and efforts needed to fulfil its special mission at an ever higher level. This kind of development therefore implies, and should at the same time promote, appreciation of these underlying springs of action and consistency in the response to them and the changes they undergo as new problems and new possibilities arise. Only a thorough knowledge of these valuations and aspirations, allied with a clear grasp of development needs and prospects, can usefully help, by continuous investigation of what is appropriate and what incompatible, in matching development to the deepest needs of man without compromising its success.

In addition, the public concerned must be associated in an active and responsible way with the practical definition and effective implementation of particular development projects in order to ensure that development is balanced and harmonious and that it has its full significance and impact from the point of view of man's advancement. An effort to inform and to educate is needed if we are to find means of discovering the authentic aspirations of the public, instead of merely stereotyped or superficial reactions.

The fact that it is impossible to define the concept of development simply and unambiguously may be regrettable from the point of view of logic but it has a positive side. A process of development centred on man can only be an *open process* and must be accepted as such. Determination of the objectives is, of course, an essential prerequisite for guiding and mobilizing community effort but it must not hinder the readjustments which are found to be necessary as work proceeds. The significance of development for most societies cannot be better demonstrated than by considering it in conjunction with what underdevelopment means. Much work in the social sciences has shown that it is impossible to contrast the two in simplified terms, by a straightforward comparison of economic levels, or by reference to a linear or static logic. Seen in this light, development, for a community, is a total adventure on which it launches out, not knowing what changes will occur, an operation which it carries out on itself, and a real labour of self-creation of which its members become the instruments. It therefore calls for complex and flexible planning, constantly subject to revision, with great attention given to changes in attitudes and motivations within the various social groups. At a deeper level, it must engender in the members of the community on whom its achievement depends, a degree of awareness and a capacity for active commitment which will grow as the general conditions of social life are transformed. Hence the importance of a form of education which does not consist simply in handing down and reproducing society but fosters the creativity of the group and its members. Hence, too, the importance of culture as the 'fund' on which a society draws. These principles must be borne in mind in the planning and carrying out of development if it is to be development, not only of things, but of man himself.

A multidimensional, enriching process . . .

Development is not entirely and securely autonomous unless it is at the same time authentic. It must stem from a continually revived awareness of the values by which a community lives, the source of which is its culture, viewed dynamically, just as that culture is the source of the community's identity and of its sense of identity in relations with others. It is with reference to this vital and distinctive capital that concern for the integrity and significance of the environment, pursuit of the 'quality of life' and the promotion of culture, are seen not as superimposed requirements or a kind of luxury but as an integral part of the motivations for development, and become the source of practical policy decisions capable of mobilizing people's energies. The harmony of functions in society, the guaranteeing of a decent and secure existence, the maintenance in a dynamic form of the most important balances of human life, the permanence of profound values as factors making for identity, cohesion and momentum—all these items clearly emerge not only as relating to the ends and ultimate justifications of the development effort but as positive factors and as variables which influence the course of economic, demographic and other phenomena, as well as political phenomena, or even as the prerequisites for the success of that effort, including performance in strictly quantitative terms and from the point of view of economic growth.

There is thus a genuinely dialectical relationship between development processes and the evolution of social and cultural structures. Development strategy should take full account of all these interactions and, on that basis, become an 'operational' discipline in the strictest sense of the term.

It is no less important, if the humanist significance of development is to be brought out, to include consideration of the international context in which it has to be viewed and which, to a large extent, determines its conditions. The notion of underdevelopment—or rather the theory of the obstacles to development—has undergone fundamental revision during recent years. The classic thesis that underdevelopment is simply the result of lagging behind in a preordained pattern of evolution and that all that needs to be considered is how to bring together the necessary ingredients and conditions for a 'take-off' which will make it possible to cross a decisive threshold, is now contested by a series of structurally and historically inspired studies which, based on the notions of domination, unequal trade relations and dependency, show underdevelopment to be the consequence of plunging a society and its economy into a world whose structures condemn them to a subordinate status and stagnation or internal imbalance. These ideas tend to destroy the dream of an 'historical short cut', achieved by a minimum of effort through imitation and mere transfer, and lay stress on the nations' own endeavours in development and on mutual exchange processes. The necessary role of man in assuming responsibility for development is thus thrown into sharp relief.

. . . seen as part of a new international order . . .

But these ideas further demonstrate in striking fashion how national and international factors are interwoven in development and how impossible it is to approach development, to plan it, carry it out and evaluate it, even in an individual country without regard for the international context. Issues such as world poverty or hunger, or over-industrialization—which, on different scores, are nowadays causing so much concern to humanists—can scarcely be regarded from any other standpoint.

From this point of view, the importance of the international community's decision to work in unison for the *establishment of a new economic order* on a world scale cannot be over-emphasized. Engendered by protest against the present inequalities among nations as regards access to wealth and participation in decision-making, this very proper aspiration is directed to bringing about a qualitative change in the system of national life and development, and a far-reaching reform of human relations in the development undertaking.

Over and above the increase—vital in itself—of the resources available to the developing nations, what this new international economic order promises and demands is that each country should be able to make its own decisions and to control its own destiny—which is independence in the profound sense of the term. This represents dignity for the community and for its members. It means, for each country, the promise and the necessity of a recordered, untranmmelled, economic and social life, which will be conducive to greater cohesion and fulfilment of the country's potentialities in a self-directed development effort inspired by freely accepted motivations and aspirations. It is on this account that the new international order should be regarded not simply as an economic order, but as an *order that is both social and ethical as well.*

Lastly, the issues involved in development are of world-wide scope in another sense, for their *impact is universal.* The vital necessity for growth compels recognition even in the most highly developed economies, and the need for a coherent effort to ensure that man takes his rightful place at the centre of the development process is felt in these societies as in others and in terms which, *mutatis mutandis,* show certain matching features.

... and not simply in terms of standards of living

We may go further: what country today, however advanced and even dynamic its economy, however high its standard of living, however splendid its achievements, can call itself fully developed? There is no nation that does not seek, over and above the needs —and the attractions—of growth, to gain mastery of the 'quality of life', to promote higher values, and to achieve justice. All, on this score, can be said to be 'developing', individually and as a group. And there is no ready-made solution for any of them. All can learn from one another.

The problems of development are concerned with the self-fulfilment of man, and the *future story of civilizations,* coming to birth in specific, practical contexts. If man must, as we have seen, be taken to be the *end* of development, it is in the profound sense that he is both its *subject* and its *location.* Development must be designed and determined, even at the humblest level, as a *process ensuring the advancement of man through his own endeavours.* It requires to be governed by thinking that will ensure that attention to specific situations and changing circumstances is combined with awareness of the universal dimensions of this humanizing task, and that the effort to control the always highly complex systems of interactions is associated with reference to the values and the aims that give them their significance.

These principles compel recognition today not only as ethical requirements but, in equal measure, as indicative of the conditions on which the drive and ultimate success of development work depend, both for each nation and for the international community. And yet it must be admitted that development processes are still too often chaotic and irrational, producing imbalances, dysfunctions, suffering and exclusion which, in turn, jeopardize growth; they are insufficiently inspired by regard for human values—or are at least powerless to promote them or even to prevent their deterioration—and, finally, inadequately attuned to the personality of each people and its own creative potential. Practically everywhere it would seem that restrictive processes are operative, rather than the enlightened determination of men and women. Much still remains to be done if principles which are beginning to receive such widespread support are in reality to govern policy decisions and the carrying out of the development effort.

A stimulating critical reflection

Yet resolute action to promote the humanist conception of development and to bring out its practical implications and specific significance has, perhaps, never before had so much likelihood of arousing wide interest and influencing decisions and strategies, for the effectiveness of development strategies is itself being questioned today more radically than it has been before. Concern for qualitative aspects may long have been considered a somewhat Utopian refinement or even a source of hindrance and complications likely to jeopardize the success of the undertaking, but it is now being wondered, even among the technocratically-minded, whether, on the contrary, too summary a conception of the components of development is not largely responsible for the failures and delays that are to be deplored.

What assessment can, in fact, be made of this historic operation of the post-war period, and what principles should be followed in continuing the effort? What promises have been fulfilled? What problems and difficulties have come to light? Positive achievements must, of course, be recognized despite the relatively scanty means available. But the handicaps from which many societies are suffering seem to be renewed and to increase as efforts are made to remedy them; many countries have not yet really crossed the 'take-off' threshold. Hence, despite the hope and determination that continue to be expressed, some confess to a certain lassitude and others to a heightened impression of the immensity of the task, the extent of the sacrifices to be made, and the proliferation of problems. The time has come for critical reflection with a view to adjusting basic thinking and principles of action to a task whose real difficulties are being increasingly appreciated.

The world situation itself tends to give rise to questioning. It is of course, some while since the development 'models' suggested by the cases (in history and at the present day) of the most advanced of the market economies were challenged by certain theorists; but these lately all-conquering models now seem to be revealing their weaknesses; the question of the remedies to be applied to them has at least been raised. The changes that have come about in the distribution of financial resources and in bargaining strength between groups of advanced and developing countries are engendering an atmosphere eminently conducive to questioning. It is not surprising that studies and arguments about the conception of development, the conditions for it, and how to conduct it should have received additional impetus as a result, for development, as a global phenomenon, can be analysed only against the background of the total context in which it is situated. The changes in the system of world trade and relations, and the appeal for greater international equity, are no less important than the problems arising within each national community: they are inseparable from them.

Whether attention be focused on the slow progress of development or on its still too often haphazard character, man's place at the centre of the process is increasingly widely recognized, no longer as a supplementary, indirect determining factor, but as a constituent part, and an eminently positive element of the problem. Social aspects have come to the forefront of governments' concerns, to judge from the exchanges of views berween them in *ad hoc* conferences or in the councils of the United Nations. A very large number of institutions are devoting their efforts to the formulation of a more comprehensive, flexible and constructive doctrine and strategy; official, semi-official and private research institutions, national, regional and international; institutions and organizations in the United Nations system. Among these latter authorities are some that can lay claim to a more fundamental or more general technical competence than that of Unesco. But in the task of elucidation, promotion and implementation that has to be undertaken, an extremely important, irreplaceable and, in many respects, central role falls to our Organization.

Unesco in the service of development:
beyond sectoral action

As a Specialized Agency, Unesco is, first of all, invested with direct responsibility as regards development work in certain specific sectors of social life. Foremost among these are *science and technology* and *education*. But we can see immediately how limited and superficial any overliteral interpretation, giving a strictly 'sectoral' character to these contributions, would be. The extension and improvement of education and the installation of facilities for scientific activity have long since ceased to be regarded as mere social services rendered accessible by the increase of resources due to development, and are unreservedly acknowledged as integral parts of the development process itself, not because they are simply 'sectors', among others, of social life but because they are fundamental factors in the process as a whole. The acquisition and exercise of scientific and technological capabilities are, for a country, the condition on which depends development achieved in independence according to its own particular needs and possibilities. It is education that provides the foundation for building up the human resources necessary to development at every level, and for the active association of all the members of society in the work of development. But scientific and technological activity, as well as education, are linked with other aspects of social life. Their strengthening and gearing to development needs must necessarily be accompanied by a radical change or realignment of the life of the community as a whole. The first need here is for integrated, balanced development, governed by fundamental policy decisions that take account of social needs, possibilities and aspirations. At the same time, the contribution of science and education to development does not mean that they can be regarded simply as technical instruments: as forms of intellectual and spiritual life, they open up the way for man towards an understanding of the world around him and of his own being; they make it possible to master events through thought, and to reach decisions based on a full knowledge of the facts; they are an essential factor in the development of awareness and the winning of freedom. It is, then, at the very heart of its specific task—not to be qualified as 'sectoral' except at the lowest level—that Unesco is brought face to face with the fundamental issue of the conception and application of development centred on man, and in such terms that development itself, in the whole range of its interacting aspects, is thereby affected. In the area of specialized competence indisputably falling to Unesco, development must therefore be thought of in radical terms as the advancement of a community and its members to a more enlightened, freer and more responsible form of existence.

But while science and education afford an outstanding demonstration of the scope of the interrelations between an active intellectual life and the development of man and society, they are not the sole domains in which Unesco, by the very nature of its special competence, finds itself confronted not only with the demands of development but, in fact, with the general issue of its subordination to social aims and its humanist implications. There is, it may be said, no part of this work that does not involve the fundamental concept of development or does not help to show its real significance.

As for *cultural development*, it is no longer simply a higher stage to be reached in development but must be conceived and pursued as an essential part of any comprehensive development. Culture is not a luxury. Not only does it help man to rediscover his own identity in the face of the depersonalization of work, the increasing uniformity of the background to life, the invasion of privacy by the mass media, and the lures of the consumer society; not only can it counter-balance the risks of alienation involved in development which pays too little attention to man; but, in a very positive way, it can help substantially in making individuals willing partners in the development venture, enlisting them as free and responsible beings in the collective undertaking, and strengthening the community's attachment to those values which will ensure its autonomous development as well as its internal harmony and ultimate success. But all this can be done only by a culture based on democracy, which belongs to the people as a whole, a living culture which draws the power to take on new life and adapt to the modern world from loyalty to the spirit rather than the letter of its traditions, a culture, in short, which has sufficient confidence in itself and in its significance to assert its own identity while at the same time assimilating outside elements and entering on a dialogue with other cultures instead of passively submitting to their impact. There is no need for the persistence of certain cultural traditions to be a bar to necessary modernization, and in particular to the assimilation of science and technology; on the contrary, the continuing existence of a flourishing culture which is willing to accept change, while at the same time relying on its own traditions, is coming to be appreciated as the prerequisite for harmonious and dynamic development in which a community can find self-fulfilment. Cultural development, and the people's participation in culture, must be written into the development programme, from the initial stages, as one of the foundations for man-centred development. It is with this in mind that Unesco proposes to serve as a laboratory for the experiments of its Member States, and to provide a forum where they can compare and learn from one another's experience.

Take the question of the *balance* and *harmony of man and nature*. The idea of the *environment* has a central place in the present critical examination of development: wastage of the earth's resources, the despoiling of the natural landscape, the dead-ends revealed by model formulation on a world scale, the deterioration of living conditions, the breaking down of social ties, and the decline in the sense of values, have made the environment issue an epitome of the present uncertainties and difficulties of modern civilization, a particularly sensitive area in the theory of practice of development. Concern for the environment has ceased to be regarded as a negative issue, an artificial, premature brake on the necessary expansion of development: it represents, on the contrary, a very positive summary of the balances that need to be preserved if development is to take place in a harmonious effective and productive way. On the other hand, the more advanced and independent the development of a society, the better equipped it is and the more effective means it has at its command, for the protection and enhancement of its environment. It may, in a sense, be said that concern for the environment simply represents the self-regulation of development, i.e. its subordination to human purposes. What is more, the question of the environment is one of the sensitive aspects of nondependence. In the appeal for a new international economic order, control by each country over its own resources with a view to using them in accordance with its own interests and aspirations, and the ordering by each of the natural, social and cultural background to the life of its citizens, are no less important than the effort to achieve greater equity in the terms of trade. These issues are given pride of place in the demand for autonomy, however, precisely because they are essential to the conduct of development directed to securing the well-being of the population, centred on man and based on active participation by the people involved in it.

As for the *population* problem, emphasis has rightly been laid (particularly at the World Population Conference) on the fact that it can be properly stated only in the context of the level of development of each country, and on the need for a full understanding of the *practical implications* and dynamics of the complex system of interactions existing between demographic variables, economic activity, social and cultural structures and the extension of education.

Again, while the creation of means of *communication between people*, with due regard for the independence and freedom of expression of the different nations, groups and individuals, is dependent on the general achievement of development, it is also one of the basic prerequisites for the considered commitment of human beings to the work of development within the framework of community living. And the free flow of *information*, the access of the specialists and the general public of all countries to the pool of available information, provide the key to each nations's ability to direct its own development in full knowledge of what is involved, for its own purposes and in its own ways, drawing on the human resources to be found within itself.

But the general import on the question of development for Unesco is shown up most clearly in measures which cut across all the different sectors of social life, such as those for the *promotion of human rights and the reinforcement of peace*. It has already been pointed out that conditions will be favourable to development only if there is a general climate of peace conducive to the mobilization of all available resources for the achievement of economic growth and social well-being, and if the dignity of the individual and his place and role within the community are given due recognition by the full observance of human rights. But the converse is equally true: the promotion of human rights and the reinforcement of peace are inconceivable without an improvement in the material living conditions of the population at large, which can only be achieved by development. The necessary implication is, not perhaps that all men must immediately be able to enjoy the fruits of development and of effective equality of circumstances and of opportunity, but at least that a movement to improve the lot of all must be launched, that the most obvious ills must be remedied, that efforts must be made to improve living conditions in accordance with the requirements of justice, that peoples must have a share in decisions concerning the paths to be followed in their development and must themselves work for it, and that new horizons with tangible prospects of improvement must be opened up for them. The active presence of man at the heart of development work, and the demonstration of effective international solidarity, are here of prime importance: development imposed from above may well remedy certain injustices and reduce potential sources of conflict, but it cannot contribute to the promotion of human rights and the strengthening of peace as decisively as development centred on man, and that alone, can do.

A centre for reflection and an instrument of research

In all the areas and at all the levels of its work, Unesco is thus faced with the fundamental problem of development and, in the studies it is carrying out and the operational action it is conducting, it is clarifying the terms of development in relation to the aspects of the life of society with which it is concerned. But it also has to concentrate on the central point at which these multifarious problems can be grasped as a whole, where the mechanisms of development may be laid bare and the conditions defined for a type of development which, in each society, will be centred on man, and in which man will be able to express himself fully and achieve all his potential. It is with this basic research and with the assertion of the properly human implications of development that the present chapter is concerned.

Fundamental research work must be continued in order to clarify and direct Unesco's action on behalf of development in the areas of social life which come within its sphere of competence. But by virtue of its general responsibility for the advancement of knowledge and its use for the benefit of man and society, the Organization also has a broader task to assume—that of bringing the resources of scientific knowledge, particularly in the social and human sciences, to bear in showing up the full implication of the basic problems of development and instigating study and reflection on these problems throughout the world. In doing this, it has no intention of setting itself up in the place of the specialized bodies, particularly those of the United Nations system, which bear responsibility for matters of planning and co-ordination, but seeks only to supplement and extend their action by providing for two-way communication and cross-fertilization between social thought in general and the refinement of development strategies.

Consideration of this crucial and ramifying problem of development centred on man further confirms the principle which has already gained acceptance in connection with other key-problems such as the promotion of human rights and the reinforcement of peace: the competence of an international organization dealing with human affairs through the agency of intellectual life cannot simply be classified as a domain of specialization; the logic of the situation causes it to transcend any neat distribution of responsibilities. Unesco would be failing in its duty if it did not consider both the full implications and the essential principles underlying human problems: this does not mean attributing to itself unlimited technical expertise, but approaching these problems in their true, logical dimensions, which do not permit of any compartmentalization, but rather govern and order all the instrumental and sectoral ways of dealing with them. Among all the United Nations agencies, without making undue claims and without dogmatism, but in a spirit of collaboration showing due regard for the fields of competence assigned, Unesco is fully entitled to take on the task of basic, comprehensive thinking about these problems in the name of man, and of his ultimate purposes and values, seeking not so much to continue particular analytic processes or to bring them to their culmination (and still less to replace them) as to offer a centre, a purpose and a unifying vision for them.

A global interpretation of development

That development should redound to the benefit of man is something that, in principle, few would contest; but this is not the only factor if, as we have just seen, the crucial question remains that of the 'detour', the self-denial and the sacrifices necessitated by the adoption of a certain policy or course of action, and the long-term, in some cases irreversible social consequences to which it leads. Economic growth, though an essential component of development, is by no means everything. Development has sometimes been defined as economic growth accompanied by social change; but it is essential, if development is to be worth anything, that this change should be in a certain direction, for the better, that it should neither condemn man to even harsher conditions nor reduce him to the status of a slave or a robot within a disorganized, soulless community; that, far from constricting man, it should set him free.

The effects of multiple interactions

It is becoming increasingly clear that development is a complex and multidimensional process. It entails, on the scientific and technical, economic, social, educational, cultural and political planes, multiple interactions, the combined effects of which may be either felicitous or disastrous and which, however difficult this may be, must be meticulously co-ordinated in an overall project adapted to social requirements. It is true that development is no longer planned or conducted anywhere by 'sectors', and that efforts are being made to achieve co-ordination by a variety of methods and means. To take merely one example, in Unesco's sphere of activity, virtually all countries nowadays regard the development of education as an integral part of national development. Thus integration is all the fashion. But this is a concept which, though applied in general only to a few quantitative parameters, breaks down or is abandoned in the face of the infinite complexity of interactions and qualitative aspects of the process of development, such as profound changes in men's experience and conceptions of their existence, and radical changes in the structures, form and nature of social life. The vital importance of these factors is becoming increasingly evident, and it is essential that efforts to achieve integration should be more ambitious, better armed for the task and based on fuller information.

It is not enough, either, to direct growth towards the attainment of certain ultimate social goals, expressed in very general terms; or to allocate part of the profits of development to various social services designed to alleviate the people's lot. To make development really efficient, all the goals set must be fitted firmly into the structure and phasing of fairly long-term development plans. Then, at regular intervals, it must be ascertained how far each of these goals has been attained, whether it is appropriate and what indirect results it produces. Such indeed is frequently the intention of the planners, the policy-makers and the organizers. But it must be admitted, at the same time, that there is too little theoretical and practical knowledge available to put these intentions fully into practice and that, with social objectives even more than with economic ones, the planning, execution and assessment of development can only be approximate, for want of knowledge and methodology appropriate to the concrete situation.

This effort to organize development, calculate the cost and produce the best effects on society and individuals must perforce be co-ordinated at the interdisciplinary level. Since manifold and often heterogeneous social factors are involved in development, and since allowance must also be made for their interaction and mobility, development requires the co-operation of all branches of the social sciences including, naturally, the science of economics. Economics, in this context, is not merely a matter of impersonal calculation, but refers also to the behaviour and relations of men, regarded as economic agents—producers, middlemen, consumers, etc.—within a system of multiple social interrelations. It must therefore be regarded not as a separate sovereign discipline, but as one of the social sciences. Sciences and techniques, whose contribution to development is fundamental and in some respects decisive, must participate with their own particular means, but also through practical activities involving a whole series of factors such as human actions and counteractions at individual and group level, and between the human world and the world of matter and figures.

The need for co-operation between engineers and sociologists

It is in regard to the social factors involved in the practical application of scientific and technological theory that scientists, engineers and social science research workers can usefully be called upon to advise, not only on the strategies of science and technology in the service of development, but also on the conditions, the social role and the human significance of scientific knowledge and the technological domination of reality. The organization and humanization of development thus clearly present problems as complex and difficult as they are instructive.

But development also gives rise to social problems at other levels; especially since the process of growth aggravates rather than solves the problem of ensuring fair distribution of the social benefits of development. There tends to be inequality firstly as between different regions of the same country: some of them, for economic or other reasons, are abandoned and left to stagnate whilst others are the scene of mushroom growth with all the social and other miseries such phenomena bring in their train; also inequality—and this has now become the standard pattern—between town and country, giving rise to uncontrolled exoduses, unplanned urbanization, social unrest and so on. No less significant, in that it constitutes a challenge to the very structures of society and their adherence to the principle of equity, is the inequality existing between various social groups and individuals in respect of the benefits of development. It is a question, firstly, of distributing the benefits of growth, such as the provison of better living standards, employment, responsibility, information and knowledge, etc. But it is also a question of sharing out the work involved in development and also, perhaps more important, the social costs of growth. To remedy these injustices, it is not enough to have experienced management personnel with a sound knowledge of the social structure; there must also be political determination on the part of the community, and the willingness to make courageous choices entailing the loss of certain privileges and also, frequently, radical structural changes. But this political determination, where it exists, must be backed by practical knowledge and effective know-how. The first step is for the social sciences to identify and if possible anticipate the most serious problems, and to propose specific measures for solving them. This brings up the scandal both of destitution (which may be defined as the lack of the bare necessities) and also of poverty, a notion which varies with the level and way of life of individual societies, and which cannot be defined by economic parameters alone, since it also comprises social and even cultural elements. The social sciences are expected not merely to diagnose extreme situations but also to identify, in relation to the overall context, phenomena of social stratification and mobility, distribution of duties and responsibilities, earnings and the right to participate in collective decisions, on the basis of an overall survey of social structures and their functioning in existing conditions, in order to improve planning and control. Methods for obtaining these data already exist, but they need adaptation for study of the practical conditions of society, notably in the developing countries, and of the particular character and aspirations of their peoples. Here again, an interdisciplinary approach is essential.

Growth—a double-edged weapon

And lastly, it must be remembered that man, who is, in the last analysis, the agent of development, himself forms part of the fabric of social life; to improve the latter and raise its standards is, therefore, not only an objective which should govern development policy, but is also something which is essential to the success of any development scheme. Development is thus seen to be an organic process involving a number of constantly interacting and overlapping economic, scientific and technical, social and cultural factors. The social effects of growth become in their turn, factors determining the development curve. But not all the processes necessarily converge, and there are social disparities which represent an immediate threat to growth itself, and eventually undermine the whole of society's capacity for effort and progress. Development requires constant adaptation of the forms and structures of social life; and it is essentially a mutation, to be not imposed but deliberately espoused; a complex, innovative process demanding co-ordination of all the manifold, interacting factors. It is incumbent on the social sciences, therefore, by enlisting the co-operation of the other disciplines and developing a concerted body of practical knowledge to support decision and action, and act as adviser both to policy-makers and planners and also to administrators and the public at large.

More and more, development is thought of as an awakening of the very soul of society, a true adventure, enlisting all its creative forces. The lucid determination required of the group, at once rational and instinctive, can only spring from practical, precise interdisciplinary knowledge, adapted to the realities, aspirations and potentialities of the society concerned. To integrate all these diverse and fluctuating elements, the contribution of the humanities must give strong support to that of the social sciences.

Internal and external factors

Another source of complexity is the interpenetration of internal or national with external or international factors in the conditions which engender or perpetuate underdevelopment, or prevail at the time when development activities are being launched or pursued; and these conditions, to ensure success, must be thoroughly analysed. Development almost invariably involves more than just catching up: countries have to establish a new place for themselves on the world scene. There is a call for a multidimensional science wherewith to integrate and control the interaction of all the manifold internal and external factors which intervene, for good or for bad, in the process of development.

Nothing illustrates more clearly the pertinence and urgency of such work than the appeal to the social sciences for systemic, global reflection on the establishment of a new international economic and social order. In order to replace the conflict of interests and the rule of the strong, throughout the world, by a regime based on equity and solidarity, leading to co-ordinated and effective measures generally regarded as both necessary and beneficial, there must be systematic integration, imposed at all levels, and adapted to the evolution of concrete situations. For the reform of the system of purely economic exchanges between all the countries cannot be brought about, essential though this is, simply by setting up a new order: the whole complex series of social factors enters into the picture. Concrete analyses of national development activities must take account, in each instance, of the interaction of fluctuating international and national factors. This opens up a very wide and important field for interdisciplinary work by the social sciences on development problems. Genuinely scientific and impartial surveys should also be made of specific questions such as that of the effects of trans-national corporations, which is also being raised in the United Nations.

At the cross-roads: solutions for avoiding 'off-the-peg' development models

As to the 'Western' model of development, forecasting and the construction of dynamic models have shown that it is not universally applicable. It would be paradoxical at this juncture, when the superindustrialized societies are beginning to wonder whether their own regulative machinery is capable of guaranteeing their harmonious development indefinitely, and are passing through a moral crisis precipitated by their awareness of the deterioration of the values of civilization and the absurdity of becoming slaves of the production-consumer system, if those communities which can still choose their course were to be dazzled or pressured into following the same road blindly and without subordinating their economic growth and social mutations to more genuine ideals. Despite their great and urgent needs, which must be satisfied, there are other roads open to them; and it behoves them, moreover, in the uncertain state of the world, to set a different example. For them as for the 'advanced' societies, the integrated conduct of development should be a means of directing it towards the attainment of far-reaching and freely accepted ends; integration implies reflection, stock-taking and a return to origins. There are grounds for hope that the carrying out of interdisciplinary surveys involving both social science research and the reflection of the humanities and moral sciences will open up new avenues.

Seven aspects of the problem

Development has all too often been accompanied by mistakes and disappointments and given rise to social problems which are sometimes so serious that they represent a threat to the future; but this is a situation too familiar to warrant detailed description here. The explanation lies partly in the urgency of satisfying the immediate needs of deprived communities, but many of these difficulties can be attributed to the failure to take due account of the human factor, or to make a sufficiently sustained or adequately informed effort to co-ordinate all the multiple factors—technological, economic, social, cultural, etc.—whose interaction releases forces which should be harnessed to the attainment of the ultimate aim. These weaknesses form a complex of both theoretical and practical problems, which may be summed up here as follows:

Humanistic principles have become commonplace today, but this does not mean that their implications are always fully understood, much less acted upon.

Too little is known as yet about the aspirations and motivations of societies, their present evolution and their interaction with social changes, as also about the probable reactions of communities and groups to various courses of action and to the implementation of development programmes in general.

Moreover, it is evident that insufficient attention is given to social and cultural factors at the stage of decision-making at which options are defined and programmes planned. The reasons for this weakness seem to be of three kinds: (a) The pressure of the most acute and urgent needs (in particular, economic demands), which must be satisfied, at any price, by emergency measures even if there is a vague hope of attaining a level at which a more sophisticated policy taking fuller account of 'social costs' will really become possible. This applies even to the most advanced countries, since the natural tendency of industrial society is to give absolute priority to expansion at the cost of wasting raw materials and energy, despoiling the environment, upsetting the social equilibrium and sacrificing the quality and authenticity of the cultural life of the community; (b) The defects of the planning (and evaluation) techniques used for the purpose of integrating social parameters proper, particularly those of a qualitative nature into the calculations;[1] (c) At the practical level, the failure to ensure that social science experts who have special knowledge of social conditions or are exponents of cultural values are associated as closely as they should be with the discussion by the planners of development programmes; the lack of contacts, exchanges and effective collaboration between these categories; too little experience of reconciling their attitudes and viewpoints in order to arrive at agreed positions.

The practice of effectively associating the general public with the planning and implementation of development projects concerning a given community is still very rarely followed and the methods in question need to be adaptable to a wide variety of situations.

Many countries still do not possess adequate means for conducting a self-directed review of social realities.

It is common throughout the developing countries to find that there is a shortage of properly trained staff for launching and managing development projects geared to specific situations without falling back on dominant models.

Lastly, the very theory of integrated, harmonized development, to be centred around man, seems to call for further elaboration both in depth and in scope, on the basis of a comparison between the various methods and models of development which different countries in different situations have adopted or are seeking to establish. This would contribute at the same time to the dissemination and wider acceptance of this important concept, by demonstrating its potentialities.

---

1. It is partly due to technical reasons that the role played by social factors is usually confined to providing a general background (or 'climate') or at best a set of danger signals or correctives triggered only by extreme situations or consequences—the 'thresholds' of poverty, disintegration, deprivation, etc., which must not be crossed by specific population categories or by certain limited regions.

In conclusion, it is essential for the harmonization and humanization of development processes that every society should work out a set of co-ordinated measures which must bear its own individual stamp, but it is the duty of the international community to provide guidance, an organizational framework and practical assistance for this task, particularly by promoting interdisciplinary studies focusing on the social sciences, the improvement of their methods and the relations to be established between their findings and operational requirements.

A relative lack of success—evaluation and conclusions

This is not the first time that leading thinkers of the humanistic sciences have embarked upon a searching study of the human aims which should govern growth. The theory and practice of development under national and international conditions, its prospects and significance, have given rise, over the years, to a proliferation of surveys, many of them interdisciplinary, presented in the form of a theory of the 'taking off' or 'catching up' process or as a critical analysis of the international context. The proceedings and recommendations devoted by official research and planning bodies to the analysis of national types of growth or of methods of assistance and co-operation as well as those of intergovernmental co-ordination bodies, afford evidence of an increasingly clear-sighted approach to these problems which has had a positive impact even on the policy adopted by States, at least as regards general concerns and intentions.

At the same time, the history of international action for development and the line of thought to which it has given rise within the United Nations family offers the clearest illustration of the evolution of this problem. It demonstrates in particular the mutual enrichment of theory and practice: it is true, in a way, that where development is concerned, action has never ceased to be experimental nor thinking to be hypothetical, and both are aware that this is so. The implementation of the First Development Decade Programme from 1961 to 1970, its evaluation and the launching of the Second Decade on the basis of an enlarged and updated strategy were the main stages of international action in this field. Unesco naturally played its part in this work, generally in the vanguard, although its counsels were often heeded belatedly and then only partially.

The limited results produced by the First Decade were not attributed solely to the quantitative inadequacy of aid. There was no denying that the guidelines were still rudimentary, that priority was given almost exclusively to insufficiently diversified economic parameters, and that no serious, systematic attention was paid either to the social conditions and dimensions of development or to the role and complexity of human factors.

It was to Unesco's credit that, as early as the 1950s, it was conducting studies on the relations between industrialization and modernization and the evolution of social structures and relations. In 1962, the General Conference had already assigned humanistic aims to development (12C/Resolution 8.1 (c)). And it was in 1968 that the Conference proclaimed the following principle: 'Not only is man at the origin of development, not only is he its instrument and beneficiary, but above all he must be regarded as its justification and its end' (15C/Resolution 8.2.3). But the United Nations, initially, only recognized the importance of the contribution of education and science to development because of their direct impact on economic output.

Half-way through a decade

The adoption of the International Development Strategy for the Second Decade (resolution No. 2626 (XXV)) marked a decisive stage. The Strategy was not content merely to lay emphasis on the social objectives of development. It also stated that social objectives (sustained improvement in the well-being of the individual which might entail 'qualitative and structural changes in the society' are 'both determining factors and end-results of development' and that 'they should therefore be viewed as integrated parts of the same dynamic process and would require a unified approach' (para. 18). On the occasion of the launching of the Second Decade and the programming of Unesco's participation, the General Conference, at its sixteenth session, adopted a series of resolutions (16C/resolutions 9.11 to 9.16) constituting the Organization's contribution to a real doctrine of all-round development in the service of human aims. In addition to outlining a co-ordinated programme which restored the expansion of education, science, culture and information to its rightful place in overall social development, it stressed the importance of social science studies as a means of clarifying the general principles of the effort to promote development and the ways in which it should be adapted to concrete situations.

During the implementation of the Second Decade Programme on this wider basis during the past five years, it has been possible not only to test the practicability of the principles adopted and identify the constraints hampering their application, but also to elaborate the theory in the light of experience. In particular, the work of the competent United Nations bodies (notably UNRISD) on the preparation of a 'Unified Approach to Development Analysis and Planning', which was carried out in two stages up to 1974, investigated ways of eliminating the antagonisms and inequalities engendered or aggravated by the process of development. At the same time, numerous studies were put in hand by the United Nations Regional Economic Commissions and their associated institutes.

The Conference convened in Stockholm in 1972, mindful of the urgent need to preserve the integrity of the environment, drew attention to the manifold and intermeshed social processes accompanying development; concern for the environment was henceforth seen to play a constructive role in maintaining the overall balance which development must be careful to respect. It was not long before there emerged a new concept, that of eco-development. The world conferences on population and food and the decision to study the establishment of a new international economic order have given rise to an increased awareness and a more rigorous conception of the interrelation of national and international factors. Although the purpose of the Declaration and Programme of Action on the Establishment of a New Economic Order, adopted in

May 1974 at a special session of the United Nations General Assembly (resolutions 3201 and 3202 (S-VI)), was to attend to the most pressing matters first by proclaiming, with reference simply to economic relations between States, that there is an urgent need for a more equitable world order, they immediately gave rise to a current of bold and searching reflection within the institutions of the United Nations system. In particular, the General Conference of Unesco took its stand forthwith in 18C/Resolution 12 and the Director-General of the Organization drew the attention of the Economic and Social Council to the far-reaching social implications and ethical significance of that proclamation. What the community of nations, and indeed the whole human race, was being asked to endorse was the adoption of justice and solidarity as the principle and basis of all human relations. This historic step naturally had extremely significant consequences for the theory of development and for the planning and conduct of action taken to promote development. The debate over independence and co-operation was raised to a higher level, and the concept of international task-sharing was seen in a new light. It was gradually becoming apparent that it was necessary, practicable and salutary for countries to rely on themselves and their own resources, devise their own individual models and strategies, remove hindrances to national development and increase reciprocal aid and co-operation between developing countries. All these principles were reflected in the different styles of development.

Towards integrated development

At the same time it was imperative to remedy extreme cases of poverty, distress or deprivation both at international and at national level. The full realization of the ideal of social equity by an entirely new system of development planning could only be a long-term aim, whereas to eliminate poverty and reintegrate and rehabilitate the deprived and the fringe groups left behind by the development process were duties of extreme urgency.

Meanwhile it was becoming increasingly necessary for populations at different levels to play an active and responsible part in the adoption of options and projects relating to development. The successes and failures of the past had also revealed the dangers of allowing the modernization process to clash too violently with the enduring traditions of the different peoples, which are coming to be seen as a potentially constructive factor in the development process. In the search for a form of integrated development centred around man, this sense of the continuity and vitality of traditional values is bound to play an increasingly important role, and Unesco has done much to bring this principle to the fore.

It is, of course, too hazardous and too early to think that the new awareness which has developed within the United Nations family since the launching of the Second Decade has already had the expected effects on national and international activities. However, despite constraints of all kinds and the persistent illusion of the value of short-term benefits, the fact that the international community is gradually coming to realize the dimensions of the problems constitutes a step in the right direction.

As regards Unesco, the surveys which it has regularly carried out or promoted in the field of applied social science over more than twenty years with help from various quarters have contributed to identifying the socio-cultural components of development under changing conditions in specific situations, bringing those components to the attention of the general public and political authorities, and encouraging scientists both to study these problems and apply their findings in practice, while improving the relevant methodology in the light of direct experience. Meetings of experts held in 1970 and 1972 reached provisional conclusions on the subject.

At Unesco: basic studies and concrete projects

The basic studies and practical projects carried out by the Organization in its fields of competence have served to try out methods of promoting ever more extensive integration of the overall socio-cultural context with sectoral operational action, and also to illustrate the resulting gain in significance and effectiveness. Both the general theoretical studies and the operational action devoted by Unesco to the planning and renovation of education in response to social needs are extremely thorough exercises which have made a significant contribution, from the outset, to the integration of development for human ends. Unesco has followed the same lines of approach and the same methods, with the same beneficial results, in planning its policies in regard both to science and to communication. Its programme of cultural studies has enabled many countries to understand better and compare the values which determine their national identity and underlie the attitudes, behaviour patterns and aspirations of their populations, and it has provided a sound foundation for its cultural policy programme, regarded as the core and the culmination of each country's development effort. In recent years, through the deliberations and directives of the General Conference, its programme of studies and practical experiments and its contributions to the work of the United Nations, Unesco has concentrated more and more on analysing and demonstrating the quality of life with its social and cultural dimensions and its significance for the conduct of development.

No less important is the work that Unesco has been steadily carrying on for some twenty-five years in order to equip all countries with more adequate means for social science activities, to promote the training of larger numbers of qualified personnel and to stimulate research furthering the progress of societies and the formulation of appropriate and effective social policies. It is still true that the capacity of the social sciences to contribute constructively to more harmonious and human solutions to the problems of development differs according to regions and countries. But even so, conditions appear to be ripe for a special drive in this direction, which could prove decisive at both the institutional and the practical levels.

In regard to development in general, and more particularly to the conception, planning, conduct and evaluation of development, Unesco is only one partner in a far larger concern—the United Nations system. The first step should therefore be to determine the nature and scope of the Organization's competence in this matter.

At first glance, its competence, being confined to certain spheres of social life—education, science, culture and communication—would appear to be only sectoral. But these spheres pertain precisely to the socio-cultural aspects of development, of which, taken together, they form an essential part.

Then again it is Unesco, as the organization responsible for science, that is entrusted with the theoretical task of enlisting the resources of the social and human sciences for the identification of the major problems facing mankind, including in particular that of development, and ensuring two-way communication between knowledge and action. And similarly, in a more practical way, thanks to its activity in the fields of science and technology and their applications, Unesco provides a context in which the two lines of reflection on development—scientific and technological and socio-cultural—can meet, for their mutual enlightenment and enrichment.

Unesco's role as a mediator between the social sciences and the conduct of development

And lastly Unesco, having very general responsibility for the promotion of spiritual values, is empowered to act as a centre for humanistic and ethical reflection and, transcending purely technical considerations, to view the problems of development in terms of their human significance. In other words, it is incumbent on the Organization, acting on behalf of the United Nations system as a whole, to co-ordinate all efforts in this field.

The central principle underlying the activities to be undertaken may be stated, in very general terms, as follows: to promote the contribution of the social sciences and related disciplines to improved conduct of the overall process of development and to the harmonization of this process with the needs, aspirations and possibilities of societies and the human beings composing them. This, as has been seen, implies the association of a wide range of disciplines and a genuine interdisciplinary approach closely adapted to the dimensions of the problems.

Collaboration with the competent United Nations organizations, notably UNRISD, is now established practice and will be maintained for co-ordinating efforts and making full use of the work already done within the United Nations system.

Nevertheless, Unesco will fulfil its special mission of linking up the work of the social sciences throughout the world with the practical conduct of development. To this end, it will collaborate closely with non-governmental organizations, seek their advice and encourage them to undertake interdisciplinary research on the social problems attendant on the integrated planning and conduct of development.

The Secretariat will carry out, with the appropriate assistance, a selected programme of planned operations on an interdisciplinary basis, making direct use of social science knowledge and methods for solving certain crucial problems of development, drawing inferences useful for policy-makers and practicians, enabling the social sciences to be applied as a matter of course to a large variety of questions and related situations, and contributing to the training of qualified personnel able to use these methods. The choice of where to apply this research will be governed by the latest experience of development activities, the aims pursued and the difficulties encountered; and the projects undertaken will be chosen both for their direct utility in their own field of application, and also for their experimental, exemplary and stimulant value.

In line with its special mission within the United Nations system, Unesco will pay particular attention to the moral significance of the various development options and to the need to take cultural factors into account in the conduct of integrated development.

Efforts will be concentrated on exploring and combining in an overall approach the principles of global development, integrated and harmonized in the service of man, and those of the new international economic and social order, for the attainment of the twofold aim of international equity and social justice.

Whilst investigating the problems of integrated development as a whole, advantage will be taken of such opportunities as may occur to shed light on the significance, within the general framework, of those aspects of development which fall within Unesco's particular field of competence.

Towards endogenous, diversified development

One of the essential characteristics of the present situation in the world is the determination of many States to have regard to the specificity of the social and cultural circumstances of their populations. Development is no longer seen merely as a race to catch up economically with the more favoured nations, which was the idea of it held until recently, but rather as a turning to account of the developing societies' *own* potentialities in addition to a fairer distribution of wealth at national and international level. It is through this twofold action that integrated development will eventuate in the right to express civilizational values deriving from the specific history and social situations of the emerging societies. Without denying the fertile contributions made by other cultural areas, with reference in particular to science and technology and methods of rational organization, cultural identity and certain forms of authenticity are now called for as factors in development.

Transfer of knowledge and cultural identity

Most of the developing countries now consider that national independence, territorial integrity and the abolition of economic domination, while being essential factors, do not in themselves suffice for the establishment of a new international order. To these must be added respect for systems of values and the free choice of 'original styles of development' by populations that are increasingly aware of their cultural and social wealth. Poverty and wealth are no longer conceived solely in terms of money, and some so-called 'poor' countries rightly reject this epithet at a time when certain industrialized countries are having to contend with very precise and disquieting problems of civilization.

Endogenous, diversified development necessitates, in various forms, participation by the population in decision-making and in development projects. The authorities merely give expression to what are often latent motivations, and they are aware of the need for broad popular support to enable original styles of development to emerge and be recognized.

One of the fundamental difficulties encountered in the attempt to create such types of development is due to the need for transfers of knowledge from different cultural areas, without which the economy cannot be modernized. The conditions under which such transfers can be effected while respecting cultural identities need to be studied from different points of view; the results of these studies should make it possible to reconcile aid from foreign sources with the emergence of original styles of development, and thereby to avoid any form of cultural domination based on scientific and techno-logical power.

The relative impoverishment of the least economically advanced countries became even more pronounced following the recent shift in the world economic situation, the ill effects of which are being felt by some countries possessing natural resources just as much as by those whose development is subject to aid and to the hazards of inter-national trade. Moreover, the industrialized countries also come up against the problems of cultural identity and are seeking ways and means of achieving a 'new form of growth' which may comprise the notions of quality of life, preservation of the heritage, and cre-ativity not entailing a harmful break with the past.

Against ethnocentrism and 'cultural arrogance': a new epistemology of development

Due to the changes that are taking place in ideas and attitudes, the ethnocentrism of development studies is being denounced, both in the industrialized countries and in the developing countries. As a result, the all too frequent tendency to have recourse to a few models, which are presented as the only ones possible for development, is called in question; and very often this tendency is accused of masking either a naive idea of cultural evolutionism or a cultural arrogance which is incompatible with respect for what is different. But there is a difficulty of a technical kind which should not, on that account, be overlooked: models are connected with concepts to which recourse is had for measuring the parameters which enter into the planning process. Many research workers and planners therefore attach increased importance to what might be called 'the epistemology of development', progress which would make it possible to put an end to misunderstandings over the various approaches to development, at the level of basic cognitive elements and implicit theories, regardless of the agreements or dis-agreements at the ideological level.

Many specialists and persons in positions of responsibility in every region would like to cast out ethnocentrism from the social sciences, give greater precision to concepts corresponding to realities which have not yet been fully studied and thereby discover not only the material needs but also the social, intellectual and spiritual needs of many populations.

This attitude doubtless stems from a certain disenchantment deriving, for some, from the impossibility of catching up economically with the rich countries and, for others, from the obvious complexity of what constitutes 'quality of life' and calls for another style of growth. It should be noted, however, that it is not a question of a desire to return to an archaic past or to maintain traditional forms of society which would prevent man and society from progressing. Most of the research workers who are sensitive to these problems assert that their conceptions are dynamic in that they are founded on the certainty that there exist ways of attaining development which have not yet been fully explored and which could, thanks to increased support and participation on the part of the population, lead to socio-economic advances which would not entail an increase in economic inequalities, destruction of the human environment or the appearance of baneful cultural consequences.

Against misuse of outside aid—an artificial veneer masking new forms of domination

In the world of today young people are particularly receptive to studies along these lines. They do not hesitate to proclaim their desire for a more forward-looking and more egalitarian society, but at the same time they do not wish to repudiate the past.

In many countries, whether industrialized or developing, groups of research workers and young people, associations and study centres, are already taking part in reflection and action aimed at promoting an endogenous process of development. Although the procedures for participation in development have not yet been made sufficiently clear, many planners consider that in participation lies one of the chances of success open to development plans and projects, even if it were to prove necessary on that account to modify the technical concept originally underlying them.

The ongoing experiments at national level and the existence of multidisciplinary research teams are positive elements which already allow of comparative studies and international co-operation for the purpose of gaining a better knowledge of the various methods used and of stimulating further thought.

Lastly, while the poor countries and the rich countries are aware of the need for increased aid for development, many are uneasy about the consequent adoption of forms of action which may seem like a 'veneer' superimposed on different socio-cultural situations. Some donor countries fear that they will finally be accused of introducing new forms of domination, while the receiving countries themselves are not always in a position to enter into a real dialogue on the inter-cultural significance of the actions to be undertaken in connection with the aid.

A different conception of international co-operation

A need for co-operation is therefore felt, no longer for the sole purpose of integrating and co-ordinating different forms of aid, but also with a view to identifying what may be, in foreign aid, a factor making for creativity and self-directed development founded on the active support of the population. The criteria according to which aid is assigned to development projects already constitute a substantial technical armoury: cost-efficiency and cost-benefit analyses, effects on employment and social mobility, equity, social justice, etc. Many people would like to add to these a criterion to be derived from studies such as those proposed in this section and which might be worded as follows: 'possibility afforded by the project for development in keeping with the population's real needs and deep-rooted aspirations and through its active participation'.

People concerned with the theoretical and practical aspects of development have given definitions of this concept which have varied with time. In the developing countries, during the 1950s, the focus of both thought and action was the problem of decolonization, which was regarded as a precondition for all genuine development founded on the sovereignty and free determination of peoples. The decisive stage of independence was, in each case, followed by a considerable effort to draw up development plans aimed at ensuring economic growth and social well-being. While economic growth continued to be regarded as being of capital importance, emphasis was gradually laid upon social aspects of development. Thus appeared the notions of balanced development and unified approach to development, stemming from a concern for equity and social justice. The different elements of development and the ways in which they interact were then more clearly distinguished, viz.: economic progress, income growth, distribution of wealth, promotion of well-being and development of human resources, in particular through education.

Changing attitudes

The idea that development should be centred on man, on his capacities and creative abilities, led to consideration being given to its repercussions on ways of life, attitudes and systems of values. This sociocultural background was first of all regarded solely as a curb on development which had to be removed, However, the vast scale of the negative phenomena accompanying investments, technological change and the inflow of new products soon made itself felt. Emphasis was then placed on the growing inequalities, the breakdown of social structures, the weakening of family ties, the migration of talent and other effects of the disintegration of societies which had formerly flourished to a remarkable degree. The intellectual élites of many countries felt it particularly incumbent upon them to determine their own identity and to seek ways of attaining a harmonious self-fulfilment. This led to the reinstatement of the systems of values and socio-cultural foundations evidenced by calls for cultural identity and the search for original styles of development. In the various regions these questions were the subject of symposia, articles and books, and, more recently, these ideas have made themselves felt at the level of development policies and plans. Some countries have already firmly committed themselves to original methods of achieving endogenous development. As yet, there is little detailed knowledge available concerning these ventures.

Recently, research centres have been set up to study the components and requirements of endogenous development, one of these being the training of national cadres capable of reinterpreting the accumulated stock of modern technology and science in the light of national socio-cultural conditions. Since the post-colonial period, most leaders have also stressed the need to ensure participation in development by the population, and in many cases positive results have been achieved in this respect.

In the industrialized countries: safeguarding the environment
and the quality of life

In many industrialized countries the notions of 'quality of life' and 'new form of growth' have appeared fairly recently. Sustained efforts have for long been made to improve the standard of living and social well-being, but awareness of the limited character of natural resources, the heightening of the malaise deriving from the accumulation of technological advances the ultimate goal of which does not always appear justified, and the persistence of many forms of inequality, have led of late to the very notion of growth being called in question and given new dimensions. An attempt is being made to find remedies, whether structural or applicable at specific points, for the technological invasion, for pollution, for social isolation and even for the disquiet from which a large number of groups and individuals are suffering. The ever faster pace of day-to-day life has given rise to anxiety and to certain forms of stress which, over and above the difficulties affecting relations between people and between groups, sometimes engender violence. This violence has even begun to reveal itself in a spectacular way—through an increase in acts of banditry, in the taking of hostages, etc.— which often reflects in an extreme and revolting form a more deeply rooted malaise: the breakdown of the sense of values, together with the fascination of material wealth which it is desired to come by without effort. The validity of an economic growth which does not respect ideological and cultural balances is called in question both by governments themselves and by public opinion in a number of countries. While growth is increasingly seen as a means and not as an end in itself, it still remains to define, in many cases, the socio-cultural goals to which it should be subordinated.

Reflection on the ecological aspect, the desire to understand complex situations and to put an end to social isolation, have already led to participation by groups in decision-making, with the agreement and encouragement of the authorities in most cases. In the recent past, these were chiefly community groups entrusted with responsibilities for management and organization; then followed groups of users, consumers and citizens who undertook to see that decisions were taken in full knowledge of what was involved. This participation has necessitated a flow of information from administrations, an effort to engage people's energies and to achieve life-long education, and a concern for a distribution of the benefits of growth centred on the principle of equity and equilibrium between the social, economic and cultural sectors. A broad scientific movement has been initiated by social science research workers, with the object of studying the conditions and procedures for more harmonious growth. The techniques of participation, the structures required for associating the population in decision-making, and the methods of participative planning should nevertheless be improved. The need for co-operation is felt in many countries, so as to afford a broader basis for reflection and to allow of exchanges of experience.

Original styles of development

In 1969, the General Assembly of the United Nations promulgated the Declaration on Social Progress and Development and, since 1970, the action of the United Nations system has been based on the objectives defined in the international strategy for the Second Development Decade.

This unified approach to development is the subject of various studies made by the Economic and Social Council (Ecosoc) and its subsidiary organs, in particular the Committe on Review and Appraisal, the Committee for Development Planning and the regional economic commissions, as well as by various Specialized Agencies, including Unesco, in their different spheres of competence.

For their part, research institutions such as the United Nations Research Institute for Social Development (UNRISD), the International Institute for Labour Studies and the United Nations Institute for Training and Research (UNITAR) are concerning themselves in their work with economic changes and their effects on social policies, social change and labour relations.

Recently, a new aspect of the problem was tackled: at the sixth special session of the General Assembly, in 1974, when the establishment of the new international economic order was being discussed, the notion of the right of States freely to choose their style of development came under consideration. In his report to Ecosoc, the Director-General of Unesco, in March 1975, pointed out more precisely the role of education, science and culture in the definition and practical application of a new international social and economic order.

A new requirement thus emerged: development should be considered not solely as a global phenomenon which cannot be reduced to its purely material aspects but also as a phenomenon which, in every instance, is original and which must be in keeping with the social structures and cultural values of each people. Emphasis is here laid on the *endogenous* character of development.

The United Nations Conference on the Human Environment (Stockholm, 1972), demonstrating the need for the formulation of a concept of eco-development, brought to notice the importance of participation by populations in decision-making concerning their immediate environment, changes in which are seen by them as an infringement of the right to a certain quality of life. That conference also showed that the diversity of development is a necessity deriving from the limits imposed on consumption by the scarcity and the distribution of natural resources.

International action by Unesco

Since it was founded, Unesco has given an important place to research on the diversity of cultures, cultural innovation, international studies and cultural development. The conclusions of the Intergovernmental Conferences on Cultural Policies (Helsinki, 1972; Yogyakarta, 1973; Accra, 1975) reveal the wishes and objectives of the different governments in this respect and therefore constitute valuable elements of appreciation for a reflection on endogenous, diversified development.

At its eighteenth session, the General Conference of Unesco expressed the wish that a research programme be drawn up on the conditions pertaining to the transfer of knowledge (resolution 3.201). This project is closely bound up with the principle of endogenous development and is aimed at preserving the cultural identity, authenticity and dignity of each national group. This concern had already come to light at the time of the exchanges of views on the significance of foreign aid, which took place in connection with different programmes conducted in this sphere by the Organization.

Since Unesco's role is to bring about a universal awareness of the human aspects of development, its programme should clearly show that respect for endogenous and diversified types of development is one of the requirements of our time. The Organization should therefore help to enhance the prestige of the efforts made by the least advanced countries to achieve self-directed development, to define new forms of growth for the most advanced countries and, above all, to ensure that these types of development are respected by the international community and that policies relating to co-operation for development are shaped accordingly.

A number of institutions are bringing their efforts to bear on economic development, but these bodies are not specifically concerned with human factors, which have so far been insufficiently studied and are highly complex. Unesco, while remaining faithful to the proclaimed ideal of the interdependence of development, of the international circulation of knowledge and information, has always paid attention to cultural differences. The new task which falls to it is that of 'revealing' endogenous and specific elements of development, and of promoting the original expression of efforts on the part of populations to achieve development. This is all the more true in that the instruments required for such expression and such participation are precisely those which come within Unesco's fields of competence: education, science, culture and information.

To this end, the research work to be undertaken by the Organization will be based on the following principles: (a) studies on endogenous, diversified development should not be limited, in a changing world, to purely theoretical research; they should be of interest to decision-makers, to development policy-makers and planners, and to specialists in various scientific disciplines; (b) between a narrowly technocratic and economic approach and a reflection on the values of civilization, there is a middle way which fits in particularly with Unesco's mission; (c) special attention should be accorded to the least economically advanced countries, to whose aspirations high priority should be assigned; (d) the countries receiving aid and the donor countries should be associated with this research if a fruitful dialogue is to be achieved; (e) the co-operation should be secured of specialists who, being deep-rooted in their cultural environment, are well acquainted with its values; (f) case studies will be devoted to selected experiments in different geographical, political, social and cultural contexts; they will serve to make national characteristics better known and will contribute to increased mutual respect.

The social sciences:
a means of developing social self-awareness

The social sciences in the contemporary world are a part of the intellectual movement which attempts to grapple with what is styled as modernization development or social change. There is a growing need for fundamental, analytical and bold thinking about development as a systemic and integrated process and about the functioning of societies, and the world at large. It is due to the swift pace of change and the radical and all-embracing character of this change, the gnawing doubts about the relevance of hitherto accepted patterns of culture and structures of civilization, and at the same time, to a sharper awareness of human rights and of a world heritage of human dignity, coupled with more exacting demands for universality and shared destiny.

The social sciences—what for?

It is not easy to delineate the social sciences. They are a group of disciplines which have highly diversified intellectual traditions, methodological foundations and theoretical orientations and which, over the last thirty years, have undergone very considerable modification both in scope and focus. In some countries, the social sciences have emerged from, and are still seen as associated with, philosophical and historical studies, in others their linkages are stronger with the natural sciences or legal studies. In yet others they have been only recently implanted as a distinct branch of study. On the other hand, imbalances exist with regard to the organization, development, the role and the image of various social science disciplines. There are 'developed' and 'underdeveloped' disciplines; there are 'hard' and 'soft' social sciences; there are magnates and paupers amongst them. Apart from the factors which determine the intrinsic growth of and theoretical development of various disciplines, two social factors have a decisive importance here: perception of the need, and the proven competence in dealing with problems of importance. Societies support the social sciences on a substantial scale only when they come to feel a pressing need for the type of knowledge that the social sciences are likely to provide and some conviction that it can be put to practical use. This explains the high status enjoyed by economics in both developed and developing countries, which is not matched by the position of other disciplines. If the social sciences are to perform their legitimate and indispensable function in development as regards both problem-illumination and problem-solving it is necessary to achieve a better balance between disciplines.

A major concern is the development of social science as an intellectual enterprise. The interpretative and instrumental function of social science implies a constant building up of a body of theoretical propositions, developing conceptual frameworks and sets of analytical methods. This applies both to individual disciplines and to social science as a whole. There exists a body of scientific studies of human society which are so closely related that they can be said to possess a real or, at any rate, a focal unity. The social sciences are necessarily interdisciplinary, since social life does not fall neatly into the categories dear to individual disciplines. Hence the need for an integrated approach of the social sciences working together as a whole, so that the tasks and perspectives of different disciplines are synchronized and combined; and the need for creating a universal scientific language and universal principles of a nature to render different propositions translatable and acceptable by the social scientists and the community as a whole.

Too many regions with too few social science researchers

Social sciences in the world nowadays are confronted with conflicting realities. Diversity and unity of mankind are both reflected in their activity. We have now come to realize that social science—much as it is a mode of the pursuit of scientific truth in general, aiming at universal validity, and is concerned with the discovery of regularities of human behaviour and of the functioning of social systems, which obtain validity irrespective of place and time—is not uniform; it is culture-specific or place-bound, it can develop along different lines in different societies, it can emphasize instrumental or interpretative functions differentially, it can select different substantive problems or treat them differently. At the same time, social science is a reflection of the world itself, which although divided into separate nation-States, is increasingly interdependent. However varied ideological and national affiliations of social scientists are, they must confront the larger issues of humanity, which are increasingly global in scale. The problem therefore is twofold: (a) to recognize that the social science is a collective enterprise that, in itself, has no geographic or political boundaries—even though the latter affect the social science because they affect what social scientists do; (b) to conceive a worldwide 'system' of social sciences that would provide both for universalities and cultural and historical specificities.

The development of social sciences throughout the world is very uneven. A cross-national comparison of the number of social scientists engaged in research, imperfect though the data may be, reveals a basic numerical imbalance between the developed and less-developed countries. Europe, North America, and Japan account for about 180,000 social science researchers out of an estimated 202,000, i.e. 89 per cent of the total. Then there are disproportions between and within the developing regions themselves. As a whole, Latin America and Asia are much better endowed with trained social scientists than are Africa and the Arab States. The present situation can be directly attributed to the special historical circumstances in which this branch of knowledge developed and which have led to the considerable dependency of Third World scientists on their developed country counterparts. Various factors contribute to perpetuating this situation in developing countries: (a) the limited number of social scientists trained by the present education systems; (b) the high cost of creating and running modern infrastructures of integrated social sciences research; (c) the concentration in Europe and North America of major academic centres and the channels of publishing and distributing of research findings; (d) the inadaptation of social sciences to the needs of countries, due to the dominant and ethnocentric theories and methodologies in developed countries which still serve as world-wide reference points for research and teaching.

The major issue is therefore to find and promote ways for reducing the imbalances in the international development of social sciences and for creating in each country and region, a critical social science mass in terms of numbers, institutions and standards. Such a critical mass is a condition for the self-directed development of the social sciences, along lines more relevant to the needs and values of each individual society.

Unesco as the agency responsible for the growth and nurture of all the sciences and the only body which provides opportunities to participate in large-scale programmes of intellectual co-operation and thus have access to the world's storehouse of scientific knowledge and information, will logically serve as the focal point and catalyst for this undertaking aimed at both creating social science infrastructures and promoting the development of social science, with national and international, disciplinary and inter-disciplinary components.

A special approach: regional collaboration

The main trend of developments *at the national level* may be mentioned first. In countries of North America (where resources and programmes in the social sciences are particularly important), Western and Eastern Europe and the Far Eastern and Pacific region, as well as in several developing countries, the growth of the social sciences since the Second World War has made decisive steps forward; social sciences have become increasingly institutionalized; the situation varies from one country to another in respect of the speed and intensity of this process; in most countries, however, major if not all social science disciplines are represented in the education system, the governments are the main source of funds and policy-making, and there is a growing involvement of social scientists in national development programmes, public life and public institutions in general. Although this strengthening and institutionalization of the social sciences in the above-mentioned areas have not been matched by quite comparable developments in other, much more numerous, countries of Asia, Africa, Latin America and the Arab region, the efforts that are being made in all countries show their growing concern for the role of social sciences in social development.

One of the characteristics of the development of social sciences in recent years is the growth of *regional collaboration*. This has been fostered, in particular, by the awareness of a basic unity underlying the socio-economic and cultural problems of each of the regions; the desire to collaborate in solving common problems; the felt need to bridge diverse ideological, academic and even administrative traditions; the wish to pool resources in the interest of reducing costs; and the recognition that an international framework ensures a broader base for comparison purposes and a wider application of results.

In *Europe* the most important development has been the creation of the European Co-ordination Centre for Research and Documentation in Social Sciences established in Vienna in 1963. While supervised by the International Social Science Council and assisted by Unesco, the Vienna Centre is the produce of efforts by Eastern and Western European research institutions interested in comparative work. Europe is also abundant in examples of bilateral or sub-regional co-operation, in which national councils or analogous bodies are mainly involved. A realization that development problems are global in nature and that mutual relations between the social science institutions in developed and less-developed countries must be established on an equal partnership basis, was a rationale for the creation of a European Association of Development Research and Training Institutes in 1974. Representing mostly West European institutions, it is making efforts to enlarge its geographical scope and embrace competent bodies in East Europe as well.

In *Latin America*, two regional training and research institutions were created in 1958 with the assistance of Unesco: the Latin American Faculty of Social Sciences (FLACSO) in Santiago and the Latin American Centre for Social Science Research (CENTRO) in Rio de Janeiro. The Latin American Social Science Council (CLACSO), was established in 1967; it comprises 79 research and training institutions of the region, and is concerned with research and post-graduate teaching.

It is the institutionalization of the social sciences at the national level during the last fifteen years that paved the way for the creation of several regional and sub-regional social science associations in *Asia* over the last five years. Among them are the South East Asian Social Science Association, the Asian Association of Development Research and Training Institutes and the Asian Association of Social Science Research Council (AASSREC). It should be noted also that the first international meeting of Asian sociologists was organized in Tokyo in 1973 by the Japanese National Commission for Unesco and with assistance from Unesco.

In *Africa*, efforts to organize regional co-operation in social science are very recent. They started shortly after the accession to independence of the African States south of the Sahara. The first East African initiative was the creation of the East African Social Science Council on a Pan-African scale. A Conference of Directors of Economic and Social Research Institutions in Africa, set up in 1964, has contributed to mobilizing the different national scientific communities around the idea of regional African collaboration, and has led to the constitution of the Council for the Development of Economic and Social Research in Africa, (CODESRIA) in 1973. The Council has now a membership of some 100 African institutions (covering also Arab States in North Africa).

In the *Arab States*, there has been a growing concern for the application of the social sciences to national development efforts and for the elucidation of major socio-economic problems facing the region as a whole. Steps towards regional co-operation of Arab Member States in the field of social sciences were taken among others by the combined efforts of National Commissions for Unesco. At the eighth Regional Conference of Arab National Commissions held in Tunis in 1973, recommendations were adopted urging the development of the social sciences in the region as a means of social development; the Conference chose also several social research themes to be investigated in the Arab States. Equally, regional and/or sub-regional conferences and meetings were organized by national social science institutions and regional bodies, some of them with assistance from foundations, with a view to promoting the development of research and teaching in the area.

Several regional intergovernmental organizations, such as the *Organization for Economic Co-operation and Development* (OECD), the *Council of Europe*, the *Arab Educational, Cultural and Scientific Organization* (ALECSO), the *Organization of African Unity* (OAU) and the *Organization of American States* (OAS) show a marked interest in developing the social sciences. Some of them have programmes in the field of economic and social development and employ the services of social scientists or make use of social science techniques and findings. In certain regions the main emphasis is on economics. Specific efforts have been made by some of these organizations in order to promote social science infrastructures and co-operation within a regional or multinational framework.

Valuable help from 'NGOs' and support from the United Nations

Over the past three decades *non-governmental organizations* (NGOs) have performed invaluable services without which the social science programme of Unesco could never have been executed. These are professional groupings based on national chapters, which promote the development of knowledge in their respective fields through comparative transnational research, publications, organization of world congresses, meetings and conferences, represent the interests of practitioners at the international level and constitute natural links between national scientific communities and the international network of governmental organizations. In 1973, twelve of the NGOs decided to federate within the International Social Science Council, the International Committee for Social Science Information and Documentation remaining an independent body. The new federative structure of ISSC, should create more favourable conditions for promoting the participation by scholars of the Third World in the international life of the social sciences, as well as for the fostering of interdisciplinary work.

The bulk of social science work conducted under United Nations auspices is of the 'applied' variety. Most of the Specialized Agencies, such as FAO, ILO, UNEP, UNICEF, UNIDO, UNFPA, WHO; the Regional Economic Commissions and their specialized Institutes for Economic Development and Planning; bodies like the United Nations Conference on Trade and Development (UNCTAD), the General Agreement on Trade and Tariffs (GATT); the World Bank (IBRD); as well as the United Nations itself with its specialized units in the Secretariat have responsibilities in the socio-economic area and are therefore employers of social scientists, producers of social science and users of expertise. They are, however, not concerned (with the possible exception of UNEP and UNFPA whose aim is also to build up knowledge in their respective fields) with methodology and the development of the disciplines and the disciplines and the profession as such. This role is performed to some extent by the United Nations Research Institute for Social Development (UNRISD) in Geneva (especially in the field of indicators of socio-economic development, regional planning, unified approach to development analysis and planning), and the United Nations Institute for Training and Research (UNITAR) in New York (training of skilled personnel for national and international administrations, research and social aspects of transfer of technology and brain drain).

Special mention must be made of the United Nations Development Programme (UNDP) which, since the late 1950s, has been a continued source of financial assistance to Unesco's efforts to build up social science capabilities in the developing countries. Except in Latin America, however, the UNDP's contribution in this field has been a rather limited one, which reflects Member States' priorities as indicated in their Country Programmes.

Unesco at work: institutional framework and action in the field

Unesco's activities may be roughly divided into four phases. The first period runs from 1946 to about the end of 1952. It is characterized by preoccupations arising from the needs for post-war intellectual and professional reconstruction and out of the then still very imperfect recognition of what the social sciences had to offer as well as the status which social scientists deserved in the world at large. Main effort was directed towards setting up international professional non-governmental organizations, usually in the shape of loose federations of national disciplinary bodies. The World Federation of Mental Health was formed in 1948 and the International Association of Comparative Law mooted in 1949; 1950 saw the foundation of the International Political Science Association, the International Sociological Association, the International Economic Association and the Co-ordinating Committee for Social Science Documentation (later International Committee for Social Science Information and Documentation). The capstone of this structure was the foundation of the International Social Science Council in 1954.

The second phase may be said to open with the first biennial programme, for the years 1953-54, and runs to 1962. It is characterized by increasing decentralization and the development of a field programme. Unesco began to address itself to aiding in the establishment of research and teaching centres in various countries.[1] In addition, several national and regional surveys were prepared in order to assess local needs and identify potentialities for development of social sciences; a survey on social science teaching at university level was started (seventeen volumes published between 1952 and 1973); a quarterly, the *International Social Science Journal* (first called *Bulletin*) was established.

The third phase runs from 1962 to 1972 and is chiefly characterized by an increase of the practical applications of Unesco's programme. The social sciences were called upon to support that side of activities (education, science and technology, mass communications) which touches upon various aspects of development planning. Emphasis was put on field activities (teaching, organizational tasks) in social sciences. At the same time, the interest in training of human resources took on greater importance. Refresher courses and training seminars, which started in the late 1950s, developed considerably in terms of numbers, fields and countries involved.

The fourth period runs from 1972 to the present. It is characterized by the emphasis laid on reinforcing and broadening of co-operation among scholars and institutions within and between major world regions, and on linking the building-up of infrastructures and programmes more closely with development efforts. Unesco is giving support and moral backing to the establishment and operation of regional social science research and documentation centres in those regions which were until now not so well equipped in respect of institution-building. In particular, two social science co-ordination centres were created in 1974, one for Africa south of the Sahara (Kinshasa), the other for the Arab region (Cairo). In addition, an agreement was signed in 1973 between the Lebanese Government and Unesco concerning the establishment of the International Centre for the Humanities and Development at Byblos; the Centre is concerned with interdisciplinary study of the human aspects of development. The twin concern for the regional centres is to help develop the social sciences in the respective regions and to improve their contribution to development efforts. Regional co-operation was given concrete form by the constitution of regional research teams under Unesco's auspices.

Mention should also be made here, in the context of documentation and information in social sciences, of the DARE International Social Science Data Bank, which started its operations in 1975.

---

1. These were: Unesco Institute for Social Science, Cologne (1952); Research Office on Social Implications of Technological Change, Paris (1953); Research Centre on the Social Implications of Industrialization in Southern Asia, an extension of the Unesco Secretariat itself, Calcutta (1956), which moved to Delhi in 1961 to become the Unesco Research Centre on Social and Economic Development in Southern Asia; Department of Sociology at the University of Dacca (1957); Latin American Social Science Faculty, Santiago, Chile (1958); Latin American Centre for Research in the Social Sciences, Rio de Janeiro (1958); Social Science Centre, Athens (1960); Institute for Social Studies and Research at the University of Tehran (1961); Faculty of Sociology at the National University of Colombia (1961); European Co-ordination Centre for Research and Documentation in Social Science (1963); African Training and Research Centre in Administration for Development (1965).

Diversified research strategies and international co-operation

The development of social sciences must be truly endogenous in character. Research strategies and the answers produced by social research should reflect the needs, values and orientations of each community. There is no single correct way of organizing and developing social sciences, as there is no single path to development.

This concern for endogenous and self-directed development of social sciences is the necessary counterpart of the effort to develop social sciences as a global enterprise. A truly international scope cannot be given to social science teaching and research without building up the social sciences in those parts of the world where the social science infrastructure is still inadequate and enabling social scientists from developing countries to take part as full participants in the international life of social science.

The development of social sciences should be promoted within the framework of a clearly defined policy, in order to achieve a well-balanced progress of different sectors of knowledge. This is a prerequisite for interdisciplinary activities in view of problem-clarification and problem-solving functions required by society's developmental needs.

Due attention should be given to the role of educational systems, which must both ensure the training of social scientists to develop national research capabilities and give rising generations of citizens an indispensable social science perspective on problems of general concern.

A key principle in action will be to further strengthen co-operation within and between major world regions. As the costs of setting up and running fully fledged institutions are high, emphasis should be laid on somewhat looser organizational forms of intellectual co-operation, such as co-ordination networks of institutions, co-operative training arrangements and joint research programmes.

The Organization will endeavour, in the whole of this programme, to contribute to the advancement of the social sciences as fields of knowledge, and more especially to the theoretical and methodological progress of these sciences in relation to the most important topical problems of mankind and of the different societies.

The action of Unesco, which should be co-ordinated with the efforts of the United Nations system as a whole, will be deployed through the partnership with non-governmental organizations which represent the international social science community and supported by the regional social science institutions already established with Unesco's assistance in Latin America, Africa, Asia and the Arab region.

The tools of socio-economic analysis

In this century and, especially, in recent decades, rapid scientific and technological progress has had the dual effect of accelerating the pace of development and of increasing man's ability to analyse its trends and to control its direction. There is a growing necessity to understand more fully the implications and consequences of following particular paths towards development. This is true both for developed countries, which are seeking new forms of growth, and for developing countries, which are seeking an endogenous and self-directed development. At the same time, an increasing use of mathematical methods and of computers has brought about considerable progress in the approach of complex socio-economic problems.

Analysis must precede selection and planning

Socio-economic analysis, as its theoretical bases and its applications develop, has become more and more necessary due to the maelstrom of conflicting pressures, and to the increasing amount of data which have to be considered. The accelerating rate of technological change, combined with corresponding changes in the structure of society makes a systematic appraisal and reappraisal of development policies imperative. On a day-to-day basis, decisions need to be taken, in Member States, as to the forms of development desired in the light of the possible consequences of alternative policies. Planners and decision-makers need access to vastly improved sources of information and methods for their utilization in order to formulate policy and planning options more realistically. More information on the complex socio-cultural changes associated with rapid development must be obtained and analysed. More important, tools and methods of analysis to make better use of existing and future information must be made available if we are to better ensure that development is progressive in the broadest sense, that it is directed towards greater social justice and that economic efficiency is not achieved at the expense of important human values. Such tools should permit the taking into account, not only of the direct consequences of a particular policy, but those of the resulting interaction with other policies and trends. Such analysis, therefore, should contribute to the selection of appropriate policies, aiming at the establishment of a new international order—economic, social and cultural.

Quantifying even the qualitative factors

The techniques of policy-making and planning have evolved within sectoral and inter-sectoral frameworks, in the absence of a full understanding of the complex inter-sectoral relationships in society. An integrated approach to development does not imply solely taking account of the various sectors and inter-sectoral links, which has often been the case in the conventional approach to development, but implies, above all, the integration of qualitative factors which are not easily quantifiable. A major effort in elaborating methods permitting the quantification and analytical treatment of these factors is clearly required. The design and implementation of programmes aimed at the achievement of such goals as social justice and the integration of women in the development process require the means of measuring and appraising progress. Such means have been called for by recent resolutions of the United Nations Economic and Social Council and of its subsidiary and related bodies.

The development and application of tools and methods of socio-economic analysis and development planning have evolved in Member States from two distinct sources. The first has been the academic stream from which have flowed the results of academic activities in the fields of methodology and analytical application. The other has been the planning practitioner, both at the enterprise and the governmental level, devising and adapting methods to serve specific planning needs. In more recent times, the need to bring these two sources into closer interaction has been recognized, with academic research becoming more involved in practical problems of development planning and with planners becoming more involved with methodological advances. Such activities as the measurement of social trends through social indicators, the devising of global models to analyse growth projects, the introduction of evaluation procedures in social action programmes of Member States are examples of the interplay between theory and practice.

The United Nations and the need to measure social progress

Of late, increasing amounts of information exchange activities have been formalized in Member States. Newsletters, scholarly journals and governmental publications concerned with methodology and research have come into being, mainly in the developed countries. Especially in the field of social indicators is this evident, with many official and semi-official information bulletins issued. In the developing countries the concern has been on a much more operational level. Task forces within Ministries of Planning and Development, as well as inter-ministerial groups, concerned with methodology and socio-economic analysis have been established to aid in development planning. There is, in fact, a recently established Ministry of General Planning and Socio-Economic Research in one developing country.

Within the United Nations system, there has been a long-standing concern with the need to measure social progress on the international as well as the national and local level. In particular, the United Nations Research Institute for Social Development (UNRISD) was originally involved in indicators for measuring levels of living. From international comparison that work has shifted to the development of indicators for measuring progress at the local level. The United Nations publishes, at regular intervals, a *Compendium of the World Social Situation*. The Commission for Social Development, at its most recent sessions, has stressed the need for social indicators as tools of analysis, planning and evaluation, especially in relation to the integrated approach to planning. The Human Rights Commission has urged the United Nations system to carry out work on social indicators, especially measuring the attainment of human rights and social justice. The United Nations system of Demographic and Social Statistics (SSDS) is made up of sub-systems, some of which relate to certain of the fields of competence of Unesco, and for which indicators are being elaborated, following the guidelines which have been proposed to the United Nations family by the Statistical Office.

At the international level, the efforts of developed countries in the area of social indicators, have also found encouragement in the ongoing work of the OECD for defining social concerns and identifying and suggesting social indicators as measures of progress. Countries belonging to that organization rank amongst the most developed, and both the concerns and the indicators attached to them reveal the high state of development of these countries as well as their aspirations. However, while that work is useful for the less-developed countries, there cannot be identity of social concerns and a common appreciation of the relative values of such concerns for both developed and less-developed countries.

The concern for socio-economic progress cannot be considered in isolation in a perspective of unlimited, uncontrolled growth in a world of interdependencies. In order to deal with these problems, there have been major efforts at constructing world models and using them to analyse world-wide development possibilities and constraints underlying the dynamic interactions between major sub-systems such as natural resources and their utilization, environmental deterioration, demographic growth, etc. Such models as 'World Dynamics' (MIT-Club of Rome), 'Latin American World Model' (Bariloche-Club of Rome) and the ILO 'BACHUE-2' inter-sectoral world employment model are illustrations of some of the activities of scholars in Member States and the United Nations system. The International Social Science Council is active in promoting international exchanges of information and training in the field of world modelling.

Social indicators, simulation and evaluation

Recent efforts of Unesco in adapting and applying methods of socio-economic analysis and development planning have concentrated upon social indicators, simulation models and evaluation techniques. In the present biennium, activities concerned with social indicators refer to three areas. The first relates to the identification of key indicators of social and economic change with such systems used for appraising the socio-economic progress of countries towards the objectives of the United Nations Second Development Decade. This work comprises participation in the work on social indicators attendant upon the development of SSDS, both on the theoretical issues related to construction of social indicators, and on proposing indicators for sub-systems relating to education, culture, etc. The efforts of Unesco, complementing the work which is being carried out by the OECD on social indicators, are directed mainly to the requirements of developing countries, not only on the definition of concerns and the identification of indicators for descriptive purposes, but on applying indicators as an input in the development planning process of these countries. The second project relates to the use of socio-economic indicators in development planning in Member States. Such indicators are more suitable than highly aggregated indicators tailored for international comparison, since they permit analysis of the distribution of social development within countries. The third area relates to indicators of the quality of life and of the environment. The common concern of these projects is the methodology of indicator identification, selection and analysis, taking into account work in this field carried out by other organizations and institutions.

Early efforts in simulation models were concerned with tools of sectoral planning, namely education and scientific manpower. The Unesco Educational Simulation Mode (ESM) has been used as a tool of educational planning in over twenty Member States, by the World Bank, the ILO and is used for the educational sub-system of the ILO inter-sectoral employment model (BACHUE-2). In the present biennium, emphasis is laid upon training national planners in the use of ESM, the application of models linking education with migration and initiating a new programme on integrated modelling and dynamic systems analysis. This effort is devoted towards promoting the use of integrated modelling as a method of development planning and as a tool for development planners.

Unesco's involvement with techniques of evaluation is not recent. A manual on evaluation techniques intended for operational projects was first issued in 1959 and revised in 1966. In the present biennium, a new manual has been planned, based on the rich experience gained in the interim, as identified in surveys, studies and international exchanges of experience.

Basic methodological development in these areas often comes from academic research institutions and is founded upon disciplines, frequently of a very high level of technical complexity. Unesco is neither an academic research institution, nor a government planning agency, but it deals with both. Its concern is to promote both the basic methodological development and its applicability in the field of policy-making and development planning.

Unesco's programmes in this area, while remaining responsive to new methodological developments, cannot be all-encompassing. Some concentration is necessary and a selection made of those tools which will best serve in analysis (dynamic systems analysis, modelling, socio-economic indicators) and in efficient planning (evaluation techniques, indicators of change and development) and are within the particular social science interdisciplinary competence of Unesco.

Methods of socio-economic analysis, planning and evaluation, necessary as they are, as such, are not to be seen in isolation, but rather as an intrinsic necessary component of many other specific objectives of Unesco and as a means of providing Member States with useful assistance in development planning.

Cultural policy and participation

Participation in cultural life and its corollary, the development of endogenous cultural activities, are a general requirement of our times. They are linked with the acceleration of the forces at work in society and with technological progress, which have made works of the mind and cultural values more widely accessible.

Opportunities of this kind have become more frequent either because the policies followed within the limits of traditional cultural activity have led to an enlargement of the public for forms of culture that have hitherto been the preserve of an élite, or because education has brought about profound changes in cultural and artistic training and aroused people's curiosity, or again, because the range of the information media has been enormously extended by progress in communication techniques and the advent of 'cultural products' offered to individuals at reasonable prices.

Access and participation

But genuine participation by the majority in cultural life is still often no more than theoretical. In many cases—and this is paradoxical only in appearance—easy accessibility has hampered participation, whereas this is spontaneous in traditional communities so far preserved from the disequilibrium of modern urban life in industrialized countries.

Furthermore, in many cases, the creative process and the works to which it gives rise have become more complex and are hence more difficult to approach. The fact that many people do not make the necessary effort to penetrate into certain particularly difficult areas of artistic creation and culture in no way signifies that they are impervious to such aspirations. The abilities that remain dormant within a number of them could emerge if the people concerned were put in a position where they could overcome the social, economic and educational restraints to which they are generally subject or the psychological obstructions that curb their initiative.

Consequently, securing majority participation in the cultural life of society does not consist solely of creating economic and social conditions such as will facilitate free democratic access to culture but also of associating this potential public, at all levels, with the preparation and implementation of a cultural action comprised in a global policy relating to the quality of life.

It follows that cultural action cannot be restricted to the mere spread of culture, neither can access to culture be reduced to access to cultural works. For, while access to culture implies that the individual has resources, it also implies on his part an ideological or psychological intellectual investment which itself requires, in many cases, the performance of that liberating act which consists in asserting one's personality in the search for cultural identity. What is expressed through majority participation is first and foremost a feeling of belonging to a culture and to the society from which it emanates. Even when this culture is related to others, it evinces a specificity which is a reflection of its identity. This is true of all countries, and is more obvious still in cases where cultural identity is asserting itself with particular force as the expression of the dignity of peoples that until recently were subject to foreign political and cultural domination. It is in this way that access becomes participation.

Where individuals are concerned, access and participation may be factors making for creation and innovation, the exploration and free expression of oneself, and may therefore lead to new and as yet unsuspected forms of art.

The culture of the élite and the culture of the masses

The problem of participation is not only a matter for the individual; it calls for the search for collective solutions. Where the 'people at large' are concerned, and not only the traditionally privileged social categories, participation in culture implies, in addition to the definition of national objectives, the use of means which could not be provided by any private action; and this means a *cultural policy*. The promotion of participation in cultural life is thus, strictly speaking, dependent upon a social project—in other words, upon fundamental political options. This is why cultural activity is one of the priority duties of States.

At this point two questions must be asked. Access, and facilitation of access, to what culture? Participation, and facilitation of participation, in the cultural life of what society? The ideas of freedom and democracy implied in these questions accentuate their complexity while making their true dimension clearer. They implicitly set the major problems which, in varying degrees, every cultural policy has to face: culture of an élite and mass culture; dominant cultures and minority cultures; official culture and counter-culture; multicultural societies and freedom of expression, etc. They also indicate the interactions of cultural policy with social policy, educational policy, communication policy, etc.

An effective participation by the population at large in cultural life requires, on the one hand, the implementation of key policies integrating cultural activities and the various kinds of action which, in other sectors, contribute to the achievement of the desired objective; and, on the other, the use of special techniques.

The key policies touch on three sectors, namely: education, communication and book promotion, in which action by the public authorities may encourage an activity in depth whose effects will be felt particularly in the medium and long term.

Towards a coherent cultural policy: three key sectors . . .

Education

There is a reciprocal influence between cultural policy and educational policy, considered not only within the limits of education in school, but in the broader context of life-long education, including the school, vocational training, continuous training and general cultural activities, extending to all the stages of life.

The adoption of strategies linking cultural projects with educational projects is, moreover, logical. If the majority's means of access to culture are identical with its means of access to knowledge, a community cultural project will have no meaning and no chance of succeeding except in so far as it is linked with a project for enabling people at large to have access to knowledge. Education must be open both to the contemporary cultural situation and to life in general. Teaching methods and even the content of education will have to be adapted, so as to allow not only for 'real life', but also for 'the life of the imagination'. For this purpose, education needs to undergo a transformation from within, affecting both its content and its spirit. In addition, it must awaken in the pupils an awareness that they are rooted in their cultural traditions, so as to establish unifying ties in time and space which will determine the distinctive nature of the culture they have inherited.

Lastly, the content of education and of cultural activity will cover the arts, leisure activities, and science and technology, so as to make of them realities which are known, accessible to all, whose effects on daily life it must be possible to explain and discuss.

Communication

If a policy of *laissez-faire* is followed, urban expansion is increasingly accompanied by a mass consumption of audio-visual products, while other media, such as the press and the cinema avoid decline only by submitting more and more to the most questionable commercial and ideological pressures. Cultural development and cultural participation call for the support of the threatened activities and for the definition of a code of ethics for audio-visual products.

It is not clear that communities subjected to the phenomenon of mass culture become amorphous masses as easily as some people may think; resistance to the assaults of consumer culture is, in fact, far from being negligible. It is none the less true that the traditional mass media should receive appropriate aid in order to provide a better quality production and a bigger range of choice according to subject-matter and to aesthetic or ideological preferences; and that the use of the mass media should be defined and applied with the utmost strictness so as to minimize the risk of the proliferation of a purely consumer sub-culture.

It seems essential, however, to pose the problem in terms of international co-operation, having regard to the size of the investments to be made, the vastness of the areas covered by broadcasts and the strong impact of the messages. The preparation of a code of ethics and the use of powerful educational resources obviously form part of the tasks of the international community. The technical, legal and administrative problems entailed by the use of these resources at international level will have to be studied in depth so that appropriate solutions may be found and suitable programmes may perhaps be drawn up.

Book promotion

Books constitute an indispensable factor in the implementation of cultural, educational and communication policies. However, their writing and manufacture, their distribution and use, give rise to special and closely interrelated problems which require an overall and specific approach, as was shown particularly during International Book Year in 1972. In an annex to this section, a synoptic review is consequently given of the promotion of books and the reading habit.

. . . and three techniques

Wider participation in cultural life calls for measures of decentralization, concerted action and promotion.

Cultural *decentralization* concerns both activities and the elaboration of the public decisions which give rise to them. In countries with a complex administrative structure and a high consumption of mass cultural products, it implies the mobility of central activities, the creation of regional activities and the development of small local centres. In other countries, decentralization of activities implies mobile action and equipment and the broadcasting of central programmes of activities by radio and, where appropriate, by television. Stress will be laid on the national heritage of the respective countries, but this will also be set against the background of the world cultural heritage.

This geographical decentralization will acquire its full meaning only if it is accompanied by a decentralization of decision-making going hand in hand with the possibility of genuine local or regional initiative. This will be achieved by handing over the powers and means of action, particularly financial ones, to the appropriate decision-making bodies, and by a genuine sharing of decision-making power among those politically or administratively responsible and the other participants in the cultural dialogue.

Without a policy of *concerted action* and co-operation, with regard both to activities and to decision-making, a policy of decentralization remains a dead letter.

To begin with, non-institutional and non-professional activities require particular attention, at least in the industrialized countries. Although some rich countries practise a policy of contact between professional and non-professional creative art, in order to encourage the latter, this policy is still insufficiently widespread. In countries where traditional cultures are still very strongly rooted, the problem is simply to maintain their spontaneity and their originality.

Concerned action in regard to decision-making can be achieved by establishing advisory structures at local, regional and national level, both for the determination of the aims, ways and means of the cultural policy and for the supervision of its implementation and participation in any necessary adjustments.

This process of participation creates a need to learn, which is met by *promotion*. The latter is rather an attitude than a strictly defined subject; it helps to create the conditions which enable individual persons or a social group to discover for themselves their problems and to face up to them, so as to secure their own advancement. Seen in this light, promotion consists of arousing within the community a feeling of belonging and of active fellowship. It serves the furtherance of information, communication and expression, by putting individuals in touch with each other and by acting as an intermediary between the various sectors of the public, creative artists and their works. This activity, which at the same time possesses the features of an education, a technique and an art, in *the many forms which it may take*, leads gradually to a taking of initiative and a sharing in responsibility on the part of the members of the community, to the development of their creative abilities and, as part of joint projets, to their active contribution to the cultural life of society.

Among the obstacles : the complacency of the élite, cultural imperialism, abuse of the mass media

The foregoing proposals fit in with activities which have already been undertaken in some countries or to situations which are spontaneous or which have been fairly long established in the way of life of other countries. It is, however, necessary to acknowledge the obstacles which still stand in the way of participation.

First, there is the *persistence of various forms of inequality* : the material inequality between social categories and between peoples, which is a source of obstruction that keeps many persons in ignorance of their own culture; the persistence of 'cultures of the élite', in which a minority of initiates takes pleasure while the great majority remains unaware of the refinements of such cultures; the complacency of this élite, which sees the democratization of culture as the spread of the bourgeois practice thereof; the persistence of the cultural domination of some peoples over others; and lastly, the inequality between generations, resulting from the progress made in the education of young people and the difficulties experienced by the elderly. The problem of the various kinds of inequality must be linked with that of reinvigorating regional or local cultures in certain countries, and with the problem of freedom of expression in countries where the fate of cultural freedom reflects the fate of freedom pure and simple, which is in jeopardy there.

Similarly, the *use of the mass media*, if it is insufficiently controlled, represents in many cases (due to standardization of content, poor quality of messages, undue proportion of commercial and political propaganda)—particularly if account is taken of the powerful impact that these media can have—the chief means by which the culture of the general public is destroyed. Above all, however, the indiscriminate use of the new mass media leads to a diminution of sociability and of creative power, on the part both of individuals and of communities.

The ill-effects of the persistence of forms of inequality and the unsuitable use of the mass media are aggravated by a *shortage of material and human resources*. In the rich countries, following on an initial stage when traditional cultural policies were relatively successful and when the 'natural public' for culture—that is to say, the educated sector of the population—took advantage of the activities offered in considerable numbers, it has been realized that, because of lack of equipment, of funds and, in some cases, of qualified staff, a whole marginal sector of the potential public has not only remained apart from new cultural currents but has been unable to devise cultural practices of its own. In the case of the poor countries, a shortage of means of action, both material and human, has meant that they have been unable to develop a systematic policy to cope with the invasion of poor quality products, the deterioration of local cultural heritages, and the need to be firmly incorporated in the process of contemporary cultural development.

The impact of intergovernmental conferences on cultural policies

Concern for the promotion of a wider participation in cultural life is to be found in a series of statements and recommendations adopted at intergovernmental conferences on cultural policies (Venice, 1970; Helsinki, 1972; Yogyakarta, 1973; Accra, 1975). These testify to the growing importance attached to cultural policies by Member States and also to the recent development of the concept of the right to culture.

In the same spirit, the General Assembly of the United Nations at its 28th session (1973), urged governments to give particular attention to 'involvement of the population in the elaboration and implementation of measures ensuring preservation and further development of cultural and moral values'. This resolution also recommended that the Director-General of Unesco should 'analyse the role of the mass media in the preservation and further development of cultural values, in particular with respect to integration of the mass media into national cultural policies'.

These decisions reveal a growing awareness in Member States of the overall nature of development and of the cultural dimension that is inherent in it. They show that the true cause of the disequilibrium by which the world is confronted at the present time is as much a crisis of values as an economic crisis; that, more than to comfort, more than to enjoyment, man aspires to new values; that this seeking after values is a cultural process whereby man manifests his essential dignity, his equality with everyone in the world, by communicating, creating, fashioning himself, by giving to life a certain meaning and a certain substantiality which stem as much—if not more—from 'being' as from 'having'.

States have also realized that, whatever their kind of social and political organization, the assertion of cultural identity and its corollary, the promotion of cultural values, necessitate the establishment by the authorities of mechanisms for encouragement, compensation, assistance and support, as well as for correction. Otherwise, the natural course of events would run counter to cultural life. Very few countries, however, have resolutely chosen to carry out a policy of this kind.

For Unesco—five principles of action

Unesco's action in this field is based on the following principles:
Cultural action should be set in the overall context of the multidimensional development of nations.

The components of cultural action should be analysed with due regard to the diversity of situations: dominant or minority culture, established or dissident culture, culture of an élite or mass culture, one single culture or several cultures, etc.

The methods to be used in cultural action should be based on a strict and objective appreciation of the results of these approaches and the three basic instrumental principles should be constantly borne in mind, namely: decentralization (which is the basis of regional or local initiative), concerted action (which paves the way for genuine participation by the general public) and promotion.

Cultural action which plays a part in the endogenous and harmonious development of each nation should, through a balanced exchange of experience and knowledge, lead to a convergent effort by the international community.

Member States should be assisted in the elaboration of their cultural policies through intergovernmental conferences held at regional level, thereby establishing ways and means of international co-operation in respect of cultural action.

Books and reading

On account of the spectacular advance of audio-visual techniques, books can no longer be separated from other forms of communication. They still have specific characteristics, however, in that the decoding of the message they contain demands active participation on the part of the receiver—the reader—who has to make a creative effort to reconstruct the message and integrate it into his own thought pattern, but who has the advantage, unlike the cinema or television viewer, of being able to regulate at will the rate at which the different sequences are presented to him and to return to earlier passages if necessary. This possibility of reinterpretation and retrospective criticism makes reading a dialogue.

As the simplest, most diversified, most easily handled and least costly vehicle of thought, books are a privileged instrument of knowledge, reflection and expression, as well as the essential tool for lifelong education; they thus constitute a powerful factor in participation in cultural life in the widest sense of the term. If books are to play this part to the full, they must not only be made available to the greatest possible number of people but must also correspond to the needs and aspirations of all. Yet they are still far from occupying a place in the life of everyone, everywhere, and much remains to be done to improve book production, distribution and use.

Eight billion books per year, but the developing countries produce only one in five

Thanks to the post-war revolution in book production and distribution techniques, it is now possible to put on the market large numbers of good quality, inexpensive books. Pocket books are sold at prices which the general public can afford and distributed through a network of sales outlets which have nothing in common with the traditional bookshop. Between 1950 and 1970, world book production doubled, as regards numbers of titles sold, and tripled as regards numbers of copies. Over 550,000 titles and about 8 billion copies per year are now on the market. But distribution remains very unequal.

Although the developing countries represent about 70 per cent of the world population, they produce scarcely a fifth of the books published in the world, the rest of the production being concentrated in about 30 industrialized countries. They therefore suffer, in varying degrees, from a serious shortage (sometimes amounting to a dearth) of books, and this slows up considerably their economic, social and cultural progress. The chief obstacles to the development of local production are the cost of intellectual production (authors' fees, acquisition of copyrights, financing of translation), and the cost of manufacture, in which the two main items are machinery and paper but which also includes professional training. Until they are able to cater for their own needs, the developing countries are obliged to meet their home demand—which is increasing with the spread of education and the advance of literacy—by recourse to outside sources of supply. This involves them in expenditures which are all the heavier in that high transport costs have to be added to the price of the books themselves and that payment has to be made in foreign currency. Moreover, the imported books are by no means always suited to the aspirations of their peoples, whereas their national authors, who are often forced to publish their works abroad because they are not included in the local publishing economic circuit, would be in a position to meet most of their needs. Outside supplies can therefore only be temporary palliatives and not real remedies for the book shortage. Whether they are commercial or whether they are in the nature of bilateral or multilateral assistance, international exchanges should be regarded as a form of co-operation and not as a form of economic and cultural domination which would in the long run hinder or stifle local production.

Problems of distribution are as great as those of production

The problems of distribution are as important as those of contribution. They arise both within and beyond frontiers. Within countries, distribution points are often too few in number or situated in such a way that they are not accessible to all potential readers. There should be distribution points wherever people meet, particularly near their places of work, and one major difficulty is to ensure a continuous and ever-renewed supply of books even in the remotest areas and the small, poor communities. Arrangements such as distribution co-operatives, book clubs with a chain of depots from which subscribers can obtain books, direct sales by correspondence when postal communications make this possible, door-to-door selling, the inclusion of youth centres and cultural centres in the distribution networks, are aimed at strengthening the traditional role of the bookshop. Efforts are also being made to extend the network of traditional libraries by setting up libraries in firms or by supplying rural areas through bookmobiles or book boxes, often transported by animals, so that all sections of the population can have access to library services which, because they cost little or nothing, often constitute the most effective means of distributing books. Going beyond frontiers, book distribution is also aimed at increasing printings and thus reducing the cost price per book, as well as ensuring the spread of national cultures. Book distribution is hindered by material and economic obstacles (difficulties and cost of transport) or by legislative obstacles (quota systems, import duties and taxes) which can only be overcome if the countries concerned establish a concerted policy, for the most part regional in scope.

Too many non-readers, even where books are available

The promotion of reading cannot be dissociated from the efforts undertaken in book production and distribution. Although the reading public has perceptibly doubled over the past twenty-five years and the number of potential readers continues to grow, on account of the population explosion and the general advance of education, several concordant surveys have shown that, even in countries with a flourishing publishing industry, the percentage of the non-readers of books is often high, sometimes exceeding 50 per cent. The causes of this phenomenon, which has been the subject of many studies, are all the more difficult to determine because there is not one kind but many kinds of reading, and because reading habits vary considerably according to age group, level of education, socio-cultural background, and motivations. The reasons most often given are lack of time, material living conditions, the cost of books; but there is also a feeling, prevalent in certain sections of the population, that culture is reserved for others and that books, written in a language not always easily understandable to them, deal with questions outside their sphere of interest. On the other hand, competition from the audio-visual media does not seem to be a determining factor. Using as a basis surveys relating to readers' tastes, reading habits and purchasing power, research is now being carried out to determine what techniques should be used to promote reading, both in and out of school. Special efforts must be made on behalf of those adolescents who are totally deprived, on leaving school, of the framework provided by the education system, and on behalf of newly literate adults, who may rapidly lose the knowledge they have gained if they have no access to reading matter specially fitted to their needs.

The impact of the International Book Year

International Book Year, 1972, marked an important stage in the implementation of the activities of the world community for the promotion of books. Not only did it impart new vigour and impetus to the programme which was launched half-way through the First United Nations Development Decade to stimulate the production and distribution of books in developing countries; it also provided an occasion for the

realization by all Member States of the need to rationalize and integrate the endeavours made in the various spheres of activity connected with book promotion, which
led to the adoption of a whole series of practical measures, many of them designed to
fit into a long-term plan of action. The same concern for harmonization and dovetailing
of programmes was shown by the international organizations, both governmental
and non-governmental.

The results of the International Book Year provided the General Conference
with the basis for a long-term plan of action under the heading 'Books for All', which
it approved unanimously at its seventeenth session and which was focused on four
main objectives: (a) use of books in the service of education, international understanding and peaceful co-operation; (b) encouragement of authorship and translation,
with due regard to copyright; (c) production and distribution of books, including
the development of libraries; (d) promotion of the reading habit.

Towards a world network for book promotion:
national councils and regional centres

A rational implementation of these various types of activities, which are closely interconnected, requires a global approach, and Member States are gradually establishing
national mechanisms for co-ordination. An instance of this is provided by the *national
councils for book promotion* which were set up on the recommendation of the General
Conference and which are instruments for concerted action, within which representatives
of public authorities and of the reading public (those responsible for youth movements, trade unions, cultural associations and parent-teacher associations) collaborate
to compare and apply national book policies integrated in general development plans.
They have a particularly important part to play in the developing countries, where
their tasks are principally: to contribute to the establishment of national publishing
industries which are capable of meeting the needs of endogenous development, quantitatively and in financially viable conditions; to serve as co-ordinating mechanisms
for programmes of bilateral or multilateral co-operation; to supply the regional centres
for book promotion with the necessary framework for the implementation of their
activities. At present, relatively few councils have reached the operational stage (eight in
Asia, five in Latin America, three in Africa, one in the Arab States), but about twenty
others are being established.

Despite the diversity of national situations, many problems affecting books
are common to all the countries in a given region and can only be properly tackled
and solved by means of joint action. This has led the developing countries to set up
intra-regional co-operation centres, of which the main purpose is to encourage local
publishing activities and to adapt the market so as to provide wider outlets for national
production. To this end, they collect and distribute statistical information, publish
bibliographies, carry out research and surveys, organize vocational training courses
for the various branches of book production, and launch joint publishing programmes,
among which joint publications of childrens' books occupy an important place. Two

centres have already been in operation for several years, one in Tokyo (Japan) for Asia—working in close co-operation with the Unesco Regional Centre in Karachi (Pakistan)—and the other in Bogotá (Colombia) for Latin America. More recently, national centres to work at regional level have been established in Yaoundé (Cameroon) for Sub-Saharan Africa and in Cairo (Egypt) for the Arab countries. Their activities will gradually cover all the countries in the two regions concerned. There is no European centre, but the participating States at the Helsinki Conference on Security and Co-operation in Europe formulated a whole series of suggestions for the strengthening of the role of books in this part of the world.

Paper shortage

At the international level, several organizations of the United Nations system contribute, directly or indirectly, to the implementation of the book promotion programme. UNCTAD, UPU and GATT are associated in Unesco's action to facilitate the acquisition and distribution of certain materials of an educational, scientific and cultural character, including, in particular, books and publications. UNIDO is particularly interested in promoting technical books and periodicals to assist the integration of young people, especially those in developing countries, in their industrial environment. Traditionally, FAO has always helped the developing countries to set up national paper and wood pulp industries; in association with the World Bank, UNCTAD, UNIDO, UNEP and Unesco, it is now studying ways and means of combating systematically the serious consequences, particularly as regards educational, scientific and cultural progress in developing countries, of the recurrent difficulties arising from paper shortage. UNDP is at present contributing to the financing of four national book development projects, for which Unesco is the executing agency; its assistance could be requested for the regionalization of the activities of the Yaoundé and Cairo centres.

The Economic and Social Council of the United Nations adopted, in July 1974, a resolution inviting Member States and United Nations organs and bodies and all other interested international organizations to give their support to the Unesco programme for the promotion of books.

Even when book promotion and reading do not constitute one of their primary objectives, a number of *international non-governmental organizations* carry out activities in which books play a part, and they thus contribute more or less closely to the implementation of Unesco's programme. Apart from the surveys and studies which they publish on questions relating to books, they are able, through their vast network of national committees throughout the world, to assist national programmes. Those which group together the associations of authors, publishers, translators, librarians and booksellers, set up in 1973 an International Book Committee which was joined later by the representatives of associations for reading and for children's books. This Committee, of which the composition reflects the diversity of geographical, political and cultural areas in the world, is at present the only channel through which those people who are professionally concerned with books can combine to place their experience and their co-operation at the service of Unesco's action. In particular, an International Book Prize was established to be awarded each year for eminent services to the cause of books by a person or an institution.

'Books for all'

Unesco's programme for book promotion is designed to stimulate, harmonize and support activities conducted within the international community, with the object of making available to as many people as possible books likely to encourage the full cultural self-fulfilment of the individual and national development in all its aspects. In order to achieve this aim, the Member States and professional organizations are making efforts to conduct simultaneously in the closely interdependent spheres of book production, distribution and use, actions requiring a global approach.

Unesco's essential role is to promote these actions and this approach by contributing to the establishment, operation and development of mechanisms for the preparation and implementation of concerted policies for book development, at national, regional and international level.

This role comprises responsibilities for information, guidance and assistance, which lead Unesco: to provide Member States and organizations with regular information on their respective activities and experiments, with a view to the mutual enrichment of their programmes, and to make a comparison between the needs of some and the assistance potential of others; to undertake or instigate study, research and meetings of experts, and to make their conclusions available to the international community, so as to enable the action to be undertaken with a clearer understanding of what is involved; to afford assistance and advice to countries and bodies at their request, and to mobilize, under the bilateral or multilateral co-operation programmes, the resources needed for the implementation of projects undertaken in the developing countries.

Stimulation of artistic and intellectual activity

While artistic creation is now readily recognized as a response to deep needs and as a form of active participation in the harmonious overall development of any community, it must be admitted that its function in the field of socially-oriented activities raises specific problems. Artistic creativity does not easily fit into the usual framework for determining the relative usefulness of functions and material goods. For this reason, art and artists were long dependent on religious, political or social institutions which regarded the stimulation of artistic creativity as only an incidental effect of their efforts to achieve their major objectives. But the increasingly pronounced specificity of man's aesthetic inclinations and needs raises the problem of the status of art and the artist.

The artist in the community: radical changes

The situation of the artist varies, of course, according to his disciplines, the cultural tradition to which he belongs and the social organization of the country in which he lives. Several solutions have been proposed at different periods and in different regions. At present they are all going through a difficult process of adaptation and redefinition.

In traditional societies, the artist was an active element in social life and, as such, was harmoniously integrated with his community. His role was recognized and institutionalized. His productions satisfied the real needs of his people. But the introduction of modern ways into these types of society brought about radical changes which inevitably affected the artist's situation.

The increasingly intensive organization of the developing countries as a necessary result of the process of modernization, may well disturb the former status of the artist which integrated him, in a functional and harmonious manner, with the needs of his society, but there is no certainty that this will be replaced immediately by a new status corresponding exactly to the complex requirements of the new situation. On the other hand, the rate of development of strictly artistic activities seems to be accelerating as new forms, new techniques and new languages are invented. This acceleration is not without problems for the artist grappling with his work. The new communication media and the invention of new techniques make it necessary for creative talent to be continually adapted to their demands. The artist is constantly obliged to adjust his position in order to maintain the equilibrium between traditional values and innovatory techniques, between continuity and a clean break with the past, between faithful representation and innovation, between authenticity and receptivity. This raises the problem of exchanges between the arts of different cultural traditions, with reference to the points of contact which it is necessary to establish between the different forms of artistic creativity, by such means as will guarantee reciprocal enrichment while avoiding harmful acculturation processes.

Liberalism or State support: advantages and disadvantages of two rival statutes

In other types of society, the artist is situated at the crossroads between the professions, the wage-earning occupations and trade. He belongs to none of the categories established to classify the immediately productive activities of society. His rights are only partially protected. The taxation system usually works against him and many countries find it difficult to integrate the artist into their social security scheme. For a long time the system of patronage existed, which, although helping the artist, made him subservient to the wishes—or even, in some cases, to the whims—of a generous donor who was responsible to no legal or institutional authority. The liberalism of the market for works of art finally has the effect of placing the artist and his production at the mercy of speculative commercial transactions and the uncertainties of supply and demand. Even though a positive tendency is emerging among municipal, regional or national authorities to give more financial support to artistic creativity, this is not sufficient to solve all the problems experienced by the artist in these types of society.

Lastly, in other types of society, the collectivization of the means of production and the socialization of property and functions prevent artistic production from being treated like a mere market commodity and thus confer upon the artist a status which is integrated into the general condition of workers in these societies. However, the fact that the public authorities are accepting the responsibility for the financing of artistic work does not remove the problem of the delicate balance which must be established between the institutionalization of the artist's status and the need to preserve his freedom to create and to develop his talent in his own way. But, beyond all differences of situation and status, it is in the social role of the artist, in his commitment to serve the needs of his people, that there lies the most important source of encouragement for artistic and intellectual creativity. This is why the necessity and importance of the adequate training and deep motivation of the artist and his public seem to be gaining wider recognition.

Creativity and participation

This training should be provided as early in life as possible, both in school and out of school, using methods appropriate to each situation. It is not a question of training, on the one hand, producers possessing the highest possible degree of technical skill and, on the other hand, knowledgeable consumers capable of appreciating such and such a refinement. The aim is rather, at a deeper level, to make the artist fully aware of his role in society and his responsibilities towards his people and, on the other hand, to make the public *participate* in the various stages of the creative process. In this way the stimulation of artistic and intellectual creativity will produce its best results and will be integrated into the various activities contributing to the multi-dimensional development of a society.

But if that is to be achieved, priority should be given to making good the lack of precise and detailed information in the field of artistic and intellectual creativity, this information being difficult to obtain and use owing to the very nature of this activity. Conceptual machinery—definitions, categories, typology, etc.—is also lacking, and the most urgent task seems to be to set it up.

The stimulus of the non-governmental organizations

The stimulation of artistic and intellectual activity has often held the attention of public authorities in so far as they have seen in it a not insignificant factor of social cohesion and development. But apart from these internal considerations, the international community has become aware of the importance of *exchange* in the field of creation.

For instance, after the First World War it was suggested that an institutional framework might be established for the efforts made to establish and strengthen international exchanges in the field of creation. The International Institute of Intellectual Co-operation attached to the League of Nations represents the first attempt at international action, in the modern sense of the term, to promote artistic and intellectual creativity.

Besides this governmental effort, the non-governmental action which developed at the same time played an important role. Institutes for co-operation were set up from the beginning of the century in various fields: literature, theatre, music. However, it was due to Unesco's work that this action took on a new dimension and that the non-governmental organizations were able to expand and create a wide network of links between countries and regions. From its inception, Unesco founded or gave support to the foundation of the International Theatre Institute, the International Music Council and the International Association of Art. These *non-governmental organizations* have not only benefited from subventions and from the network of exchanges established by Unesco, but have also been closely associated with the Organization's programme. Their action has therefore been directed along the lines of the principles laid down in the Constitution of Unesco and the United Nations Charter. The non-governmental organizations have mobilized artists and their disciplines for the furtherance of these principles. The purpose of such associations and contacts with the contemporary world was to encourage creativity. Above all, exchanges, symposia and joint studies were able to contribute to the creation of an environment which would be conducive to the development of talent and creativity.

Unesco: a centre for the promotion of artistic activity and the exchange of experience

Apart from its aid to non-governmental organizations, Unesco conducts its own activity. Thus, starting from the session of the General Conference held in Beirut in 1948, Unesco has endeavoured to associate artists closely with its work. A resolution requested the Director-General to institute an examination of the contributions which creative artists could make towards Unesco's purposes and the means whereby the working conditions of the artist could be improved and his freedom assured. New impetus was given to this work by the intergovernmental conferences on cultural policy held in Venice (1970), Helsinki (1972), Yogyakarta (1973) and Accra (1975), which adopted a series of recommendations relating to the arts and popular traditions, to the role of audio-visual media, to copyright, artistic co-operation, etc. It was recommended in particular that an International Symposium be convened on the role and place of the artist in contemporary life. This symposium, held in July 1974, concluded with a series of recommendations which reviewed, updated and developed the previous programmes and objectives.

Among Unesco's most important activities in the field of stimulation of artistic creativity may be mentioned: the translations programme which is intended to increase knowledge at the international level of works written in languages that are not widely spoken (from 1950 to 1975: 500 literary works): programmes of records divided into three series (about 100 records), to establish an inventory of the principal little-known musical cultures and to promote new works; and forums of composers and young performers organized at regular intervals. Unesco has also made an effort to promote festivals and exchanges of artistic groups and to spread knowledge of the arts of Member States through a series of travelling exhibitions, particularly under the East-West Major Project. In addition to a series of films produced under this Major Project, Unesco has encouraged production, or has itself produced, a set of prototypes of audio-visual recordings of traditional artistic events. It has organized a series of symposia, forums and studies concerning cinematographic art, television, the new media known as light-weight video and the constitution of cinematographic archives. By setting up multi-purpose workshops Unesco has tried to develop inter-disciplinarity in art, encouraging exchanges and experiments. It has sought to promote the mass media as an autonomous form of creation and to make artists in the traditional disciplines familiar with the new audio-visual techniques. It has begun a large-scale inventory of existing films on ethnography, films on painting and sculpture, on theatre and mime, on the performing arts, and on music and opera. With regard to art education in or out of school, Unesco has produced a series of films, slides and television programmes and published four books. A pilot project on the training of African film producers was launched in Upper Volta. Finally, as regards oral traditions, it is to be noted that a ten-year plan was adopted in 1972 for research encouragement of existing centres, opening of new centres, dissemination, publication and adaptation.

Protection without constraint

Unesco's action in this sphere is based on the following principles:

Creativity is a complex process which depends at once on the latent creativity of the socio-cultural environment and on the concerted action of artists, public authorities, the public itself and international exchanges in this sphere.

The protection of traditional artistic values must be ensured so as to stimulate creation and collective and popular forms of permanent creativity.

The artist should be able to rely on increased material protection as well as on the guaranteeing of his freedom to create.

Artistic and intellectual creativity can and should be stimulated both by government action at the level of ministries of culture, by the action of international non-governmental organizations and by public and private action at the national level, benefiting from the aid and advice of Unesco.

Training activities are necessary in order to ensure the integration of new techniques and traditional disciplines, and also to enable the artist as well as the public to adapt themselves to new languages, so as to promote true *participation* and the communication which is essential for the maintenance of harmonious relations between groups and countries in the dynamic reality of the contemporary world.

The international vocation of art demands that special attention and encouragement be given to comparative research which, by bringing out the major, abiding themes, over and above the different national and cultural ways of treating them, makes it possible to discern, in the concrete work of art, the unity of man's design.

4 Man and the horizons of science and technology

Since the industrial revolution in the nineteenth century, in which they played a decisive role, science and technology have profoundly marked the development of the most advanced societies. To a certain extent, however, they have done this independently one of the other. Science provides abstract and increasingly precise representations of reality, which bear upon ever broader categories of phenomena: first, matter, then life itself, and, since the expansion of the social sciences, society. Technology provides processes and procedures, in an increasingly generalizable and transmissible form, which enable men to act upon these same phenomena. This relative separation of the two fields is now, however, a thing of the past.

A major feature of the twentieth century: the integration of science and technology

A major feature of the twentieth century is, and will continue to be, the increasing integration of science and technology. Technology is no longer developed empirically, but rooted in science. As regards science, which develops according to its own inner logic, as though its sole aim were to erect a system of knowledge, its advancement depends in many experimental fields upon the use of advanced technologies devised for purposes other than scientific. This integration of the two lines of development, that of knowledge and that of know-how, has at all times marked the intellectual processes of certain major scientific innovators, from Pasteur to Fermi. Today, the speed and efficacity with which information is exchanged has helped to generalize this trend.

Its consequences are many: scientific and technical activities which are rooted on the one hand in science and on the other in technology can no longer be treated distinctly. Their scale and complexity are such that it has become imperative to ponder their ultimate purposes, to guide them in the desired direction and marshal their resources, in particular by planning the development of the relevant institutions. It is from this standpoint that the application of science and technology for man and society is viewed in this chapter.

The problem must therefore be considered in the light of Unesco's general mission, which is to promote the development of scientific knowledge, because it has an intrinsic value. If science and technology are to be applied with an eye to the future, taking account of the way knowledge evolves, it is vital that the source of what may tomorrow prove essential should not be allowed to dry up. It follows that the development of the basic sciences must be fostered on a world-wide basis.

Can scientific development be guided?

However, the profound impact that science exercises on the life of societies through technology raises a crucial question: to what extent can scientific development be guided or directed? If it is to be directed, it is first necessary to anticipate what results can be expected of research. Such anticipation presents certain difficulties. Account must be taken of the different stages in, and the complexity of, the process which leads from basic research, by way of applied research and technical development operations, to practical achievements; of the need to ensure interdisciplinary convergence in order to obtain results; and of the time required to disseminate such results. If the problem in question is a major one, there may be a lengthy interval between the formulation of a hypothesis and the achievement of results. In any case, it is difficult to forecast how lengthy this interval will be, since research presupposes the taking of risks, which are likely to be all the greater the more innovatory the research. Accordingly, long-term forecasts play an essential role in guiding the advance of knowledge as well as in the planning of scientific and technological development.

Moreover, in its applications to economic and social development, modern science implies that each specialist must take account in his work of the findings most recently made in his particular discipline. Except in certain extreme cases, it is no longer possible for the investigator to work in isolation. Thus in order to guide or direct the course of scientific development it is necessary to have an exchange of information, which in turn calls for international co-operation. In anticipating science's impact and planning its development, the essential elements to take into account are the universality of science and its international character.

Science, mankind's common heritage

In point of fact, in its innermost reality, scientific evolution is international because that reality is the work of scientists, engineers and technicians who recognize one another as members of a world community made up of a large number of associations, organizations or networks of informal relationships bringing together the specialists in each branch of knowledge. The barriers which become established in certain areas of technology, in particular as a result of the exercise of copyright on intellectual property, of commercial competition or the obligations of secrecy, may have considerable practical importance. It is none the less true that science is acknowledged to be mankind's common heritage by those very persons who develop it.

The key to the application of science for man and society thus remains international scientific co-operation. Moreover, if the problem of guiding or directing science in the best interests of man and society is to be mastered, such co-operation must be backed by the participation of scientists themselves in the complex procedures which, at national, regional and international levels alike, ultimately lead to the decisions taken by the political authorities with regard to the human and material resources to be made available to science and technology.

The political dimension of science and the unequal distribution of scientific activity

The political dimension of science is now, in fact, quite patent; it stems from the power that knowledge confers upon the individuals, groups and countries which possess it. The magnitude of the resources which must be deployed is such as to necessitate direct action by governments and even, in certain cases, the joining of efforts by countries which individually do not possess sufficient resources to cope with the common problems which arise. However, the political dimension of science does not result solely from its material impact. It is also the product of certain socio-cultural factors whose importance has only recently been perceived.

It is a characteristic feature of the present-day world situation that some nations have an infinitely greater share than others in the activities which contribute to the advance of knowledge. What is known as modern science is the product of the work of a relatively small number of teams of scientists working in a limited number of countries. It is now recognized that the interplay of motives and value systems has been a predominant factor in directing the intellectual efforts which, by processes we do not yet understand very well, have led to the present level of scientific knowledge and its assimilation. To be sure, scientific developments cannot be regarded as being simply a series of conscious responses to specific social needs. On the contrary, they frequently trigger off new aspirations or create an awareness of new needs. However, the questions which the scientific innovator asks himself, in the fundamental sciences, reflect, as do the practical problems which the engineer must tackle in the field of technology, the particular culture of the society in which they live. The widely differing extent of the contributions made by the different societies to the development of science and technology has resulted in the existing corpus of scientific knowledge being in some measure irrelevant to the problems facing the world today. New ways must therefore be explored to reorient science and its applications in the best interests of the world community if the needs of all the societies which compose it are to be taken into account in endeavouring to institute a new international order.

The promotion of endogenous scientific and technological development

Over and beyond this necessary reorientation, the basic objective which must be pursued consists in promoting the endogenous scientific and technological development of each nation. From this standpoint, the application of science and technology for man and society calls for a twofold line of action. On the one hand, existing knowledge must be used to solve present-day problems in agriculture, industry, communications and the other sectors of economic life; such action is focused on a horizon the remoteness of which can be determined only by reference to the urgency of the problems to be dealt with, and the major problem here is that of the 'transfer' of knowledge. On the other hand, the necessary capabilities must be developed to enable all countries to take part, in the longer term, in the world-wide progress of science and to cope with their indigenous problems as equal partners of those countries which are most advanced in regard to the scientific and technical knowledge required. In both these cases, action must always be undertaken within the political and socio-cultural context of each particular country.

The United Nations system is endeavouring, through the medium of the Specialized Agencies, to conduct its action on both these levels. Some of the short-term problems relate to sectors that fall within the competence of other Specialized Agencies, and are outside Unesco's terms of reference. In consideration of its particular mission within the United Nations system and of the general lines of action that have just been defined, Unesco itself concentrates its activities on promoting endogenous scientific development which, in most of the developing countries, involves looking farther ahead. A general four-point strategy has been adopted: (a) to promote scientific education throughout the population; (b) to assist in the training of specialized personnel and in the setting up and operation of institutions engaged in higher education, research and the provision of services in the scientific and technological field; (c) to promote the formulation of scientific and technological development policies; (d) to develop a better understanding of the impact of scientific and technological progress upon society.

Science and society

The image of science: for some, a tangible reality; for others a remote entity

To the men of today science and the role of science mean very different things according to the society to which they belong. In the most industrialized countries—those where modern science has taken shape and where it has achieved its most outstanding successes—scientific research, the means which it brings to bear and the advances which it has made possible are tangible realities for the majority of citizens; everyone knows that many of the sophisticated objects used in daily life turn to account the applications of scientific discoveries and that the level of general well-being and security enjoyed in respect of health, living conditions and leisure activities is the result of countless scientific activities which are constantly being developed along new lines. This is not true for the great bulk of the population of the rest of the world. For the peasants, often illiterate, in the far-flung corners of the developing countries, but also for all those who live in traditional civilizations or who, in the urban centres, have a very low income and educational level, science is a remote entity, alien to the world which surrounds them and of which they are unable to imagine either the purpose or the effect.

The different conceptions of science reflect not only differences in the levels of material civilization—by nature scientific and technological—attained by the various societies, but also—and perhaps above all—deep-seated and essentially cultural differences in attitudes to the physical world and to nature. Science is built upon rationality; however, rational explanation, from the standpoint of certain beliefs or metaphysical systems, is but one form of explanation among others: even in those societies which are most pervaded by science and technology, the age-old debate on the relative merits of the various forms of explanation possible is still going on. In addition, the modern development of science and its applications, which has led to the present state of knowledge and technology, has been significantly influenced by the evolution of Western societies which have set great store on a particular type of acquisitive and competitive spirit—in a word, by a particular system of values which is probably in no way universal and which is very far removed from that accepted in other regions of the world. This system of values has thus affected the historical emergence of discoveries and the march of science.

Science and culture: a relationship not to be disregarded

The relationship between science as an established body of universal knowledge and societies as they actually exist in the contemporary world cannot therefore be reduced to a single pattern nor in every case present comparable problems: as it is indisputable that the developing countries must, on the one hand, avail themselves of the results already achieved by science in order to ensure their economic growth and raise the standard of living of their populations and, on the other, develop their own potential whereby to elaborate the new scientific and technological knowledge they require, it is a matter of great urgency that the human aspects of science and technology peculiar to them be studied. What are the effects of science on traditional forms of culture and how can it be assimilated by them? What are the effects of culture on the development and utilization of science and technology? What is the place of scientific creativity among the highly individualized forms of creativity which characterize civilizations in their diversity? A further reason for attempting to throw light on these questions is that their importance for the success of an endogenous scientific development policy in the developing countries has hitherto been somewhat disregarded.

But the relationship between science and society also presents problems in those countries where, since the industrial revolution of the nineteenth century, modern science has taken shape. Prior to the expansion of production which characterizes that period, industrial and agricultural techniques were, for the most part, of empirical origin and, in the case of the mechanical arts, the fruit of individual invention. The social impact of the major scientific theories and experiments was small, as was the interest shown in them by governments. The position of science in society changed when pure and applied scientific research appeared as a key to technological progress; growing importance was attached to research and to scientists, and a belief in the limitless advance of science for the good of mankind—'scientism'—emerged. Science and technology came to be indissolubly linked. Consequently, during the last three decades, the relations between science and society have become truly institutionalized as evidenced by the place occupied by science and technology policy in national policies.

Science, ethics and politics: a many-sided problem

The misgivings—and, on the part of certain scientists themselves, the disapproval—to which the use of technology for the purpose of war, domination, prestige or profit has always given rise have become increasingly frequent in recent years and have rebounded against science. Certain signs of disenchantment appeared in the sixties when it emerged that a substantial proportion of the national resources allocated for scientific and technological research was being used for the development of nuclear weapons, the very existence of which could place the future of mankind in jeopardy and give rise to absolutely irreversible forms of pollution. In 1967, the percentage allocated to the military sector in the budgets of five of the major world powers, although smaller than what it had been, represented between 30 and 50 per cent of the resources earmarked for research and development. At the same time, the growth of major technological research programmes relating to the conquest of space mobilized such substantial financial and human resources that some governments were led to reconsider their economic and social consequences under the pressure of public opinion in their countries. Furthermore, the possibilities afforded by science and technology in spheres directly affecting men's lives—health, housing, etc.—were more clearly recognized and the relative meagreness of the research resources assigned to these spheres was criticized. It was in this connection that the objectives of the science policies adopted by States and the use made of the findings of science were contested, far more than science itself. However, questions were raised in regard to the directions in which science is moving.

It is obvious that the same techniques can be used for ends which are beneficial to mankind or for dangerous ends—or again, that they may lead to a spectacular

saving in human labour or threaten individual freedom and the harmonious development of society: an example of the first case is provided by atomic energy and of the
second by information science. But this does not mean that the idea that science is
neutral can be unreservedly accepted. Scientists, and particularly physicists during
the period when vast progress was achieved in the nuclear sciences, discussed this
problem at length.

In this connection, different cases need to be distinguished. When what is
involved is a misuse of science and technology as they have already been developed,
the measures to be taken to protect society are not, strictly speaking, a matter for
science. They are the concern of the political authorities, and it is especially important
to bring nations to understand that what is involved here is a vast area in which it is
technically and practically possible for them to co-ordinate their efforts. In the case
of a recent discovery which may lend itself to various applications, considerable
research and development work, entailing the mobilization of substantial resources,
will be necessary before processes or products of practical use can be derived from
this discovery. It would be worth while considering the repercussions of these processes
or products on the society of tomorrow before embarking upon such applied research.
If the dangers involved were to be weighed in advance, which is generally possible
by drawing on expert opinion, this would provide useful guidance for those responsible
for taking decisions. Lastly, in the extreme and most critical case, the very nature of
the research undertaken leads scientists to make known their feelings concerning
the danger involved in merely venturing into the area concerned; indeed, the implications of some forms of fundamental research are so great that the person engaged
in them assumes the part of an 'apprentice sorcerer', to use a familiar image, and is
incapable of controlling the consequences of his discoveries. This is the kind of case
to which world opinion was alerted by those scientists who were themselves engaged
in experiments involving manipulation of the genetic code.

As things stand at present, awareness and an objective analysis of the situation of modern science in respect of these three types of difficulty could help to clarify
the prospects for the long-term development of science, not only in the most developed
countries but for the whole of the world community.

Science and society: controlling technological progress

A postulate implicit in many traditional approaches to the problem of studying the
relationship between science and society is that knowledge advances by virtue as it
were of an autonomous process and that science, regardless of the technological
resources available to it, possesses its own specific and ineluctable logic of growth.
This standpoint no longer seems acceptable. It is increasingly evident that science
is a social institution subject to trends which reflect those of the society of which it
forms a part. Its role is no longer simply to ensure that man has increasing power
over nature or to solve the technical problems with which it is faced in the different
spheres of interest to man: standard of living, health, welfare. It now has another

major goal—that of moulding economic, social and cultural systems and transforming them, according to the objectives which each society sets itself.

One of the major problems of our time is to reconcile the two aspects of science, namely its universality when it seeks to explain the laws of nature and its specificity when it assumes particular social functions. The exchange of ideas and experience relating to this problem will make it possible to explore new methods of framing and formulating national science policies (cf. pages 153-64). Indeed, it is increasingly obvious that in order to define a nation's research objectives it is necessary to take into account the real complexity of the economic, social and cultural situation specific to it and the possible repercussions, for good or ill, that any technological innovation or advance in a particular field—health, housing, the production of consumer goods—may have for other fields. What is therefore needed is to identify ways and means of progressing such that a globally optimal future situation can be achieved, in conformity with the system of values which has been chosen, rather than to seek outstanding results in particular fields. Undoubtedly, in order to achieve this, new methods of 'mastering progress' must be found; this problem exists both in the most industrialized countries, when what are involved are advanced technologies which may be feared to have a dehumanizing effect upon society, and in the developing countries which are seeking appropriate technologies in line with both their material and cultural aspirations. To solve this problem it will be necessary to have recourse to new conceptual approaches in regard to interdisciplinary research, as well as to the social sciences, which need to be vigorously stimulated (cf. Chapter 3, pages 113-21.

The prospects opening up before mankind in respect of the benefits to be drawn from the application of science are undoubtedly bright; however, they are not without dangers. Investigation of the interactions between science, technology and society is of key importance for the international community to be able to establish a hierarchy of research objectives, reflecting an acceptance of common and universal values as to what the ultimate aims of science should be. Such an investigation should also, in the long run, lay the foundations for new types of relationship between those who develop science and those responsible for the policy decisions on which, within each government, depends the use made of scientific results. Lastly, it should afford a means for reflecting on how the application of science can be better adapted to the various social and cultural situations which exist in the world.

The advancement of pure research or the practical application of science?

The conceptions which have prevailed in Member States with regard to the ultimate aims of science have been reflected on the one hand in national science policies and, on the other, in the views expressed by certain major scientific bodies serving governments in an advisory capacity (academies of sciences, consultative committees for science and technology) in the reports by means of which they justify scientific development plans or propose the distribution of budgetary resources among the major national institutions responsible for the financing of research. The significant fact is that the proportion of national resources devoted to military research and development and to major aerospatial or nuclear programmes has appreciably decreased since 1967 in the budgets of most of the major world powers which exercise supremacy in the field of advanced technology, and that this decrease has been to the advantage of research of social interest in the civil sector (health, housing, land use). At the same time, the percentage of the national product devoted to all research and experimental development activities in these countries tended—with very few exceptions—to peak at around 2 or 2½ per cent or even to decrease. The debate concerning the technological gap between the United States and Europe, which started up between Western countries as a result of the fact that the conditions for technological innovation seemed to be more favourable in the United States than in other countries with market economies, led the governments of some of these countries to lay stress for a number of years on encouraging industry to put the results of science to practical use rather than on stimulating new discoveries. These tendencies bear witness to the uncertainty which has recently appeared with regard to the interactions between science and society in some of the most industrialized countries.

In most of the developing countries, the growth rate of the resources allocated to science, though scarcely one-tenth of that in the industrialized countries, has been steadily increasing in relative value. It is often higher than that of the resources allocated to education and this growth, achieved under sometimes difficult economic conditions, bears witness to the hopes that these countries set on the development of science and of its applications.

Scientific research is, of course, not neutral

As for studies directly concerning the interactions between science and society, they have been very many and carried out primarily by universities through the agency of their social science institutes. Private groups of scientists or specialists in long-term forecasting who have concerned themselves with 'futurology' or futures studies have been led to devote a large part of their work to anticipating the possible consequences of foreseeable scientific progress between now and the end of the century, for the different societies and for the world as a whole. The hypotheses formulated for instance by the Club of Rome, although challenged since, have prompted many countries to give more searching consideration to the direction in which science should be encouraged to move and the problem of the relations between science and society.

The socio-economic aspect of the problem has been the subject of regional or sub-regional consultations, organized in particular by the OECD, the EIRMA (European Industrial Research Management Association) and the Council for Mutual Economic Assistance. At the level of the world scientific community as a whole and in regard to the ethical and cultural aspects of the problem, the work of the Pugwash Movement has been of particular significance. In January 1975 this movement held its 22nd meeting on science and ethics and the participants, in a statement that was destined to arouse great interest, agreed to 'reject the notion that science is something "value-free", carrying with it no ethical commitments'.

Good use of research: a subject for reflection and study

In the United Nations system, the Advisory Committee on the Application of Science and Technology to Development was led to draw up the World Plan of Action for the Application of Science and Technology to Development on the basis of the most generally accepted conceptions in regard to the relationship between science and society, particularly in the countries concerned, during the nineteen-sixties. Unesco had previously noted certain aspects of the problem when the study on 'Current Trends in Scientific Research' was being prepared, but an individualized programme, provided with significant resources, was established only from 1973. In 1974 the General Conference adopted guidelines concerning a programme of studies on the human implications of scientific advance, including the misuse of science, and the United Nations General Assembly requested the Specialized Agencies, including Unesco, to go into greater detail in the studies which they are pursuing in this sphere. WHO, FAO and the IAEA are specially concerned with the social and human implications of specialized scientific research coming within their fields of competence.

An example—the case of the geneticians

Of recent events which have been of particular importance in this connection, mention should be made of the upsurge of public opinion which followed the decision taken by specialists in human genetics meeting at Asilomar (California, United States of America) in February 1975 to halt experiments and research in a branch of research considered to be particularly dangerous for mankind. The related ethical problems were discussed at Varna in the framework of a meeting organized by Unesco, and mention was made of the positive role which could be played by research in molecular biology in solving them. At the present time, these questions relating to the utilization of certain recent discoveries or certain spectacular technological advances in the fields of therapy, telecommunication, information science and chemistry are in a state of ferment. Although not dealing directly with the problem of the interactions between science, technology and society, the United Nations Conference on the Human Environment (Stockholm, 1972) played a very important role in promoting awareness of the world-wide dangers which certain scientific applications may represent for the whole of mankind, in the long term, particularly as a result of pollution. The notable development of the ecological sciences over the last decade has indeed resulted in a mounting accumulation of data bearing on the analysis of the possible implications for the planet as a whole of the uncontrolled development of certain types of utilization of natural resources. It cannot be denied, however, that the conclusions which have been drawn from this by insufficiently scientific minds have sometimes triggered attitudes on the part of the public which constitute a downright denial of science.

Informing the general public and increasing awareness

In the interactions of science, technology and society, the importance of sound understanding by the public of the objective realities involved is in fact considerable. There is obviously a danger that a lack of information on this subject and an inadequate understanding of science may, as has already occurred in certain areas of public opinion, lead to a resurgence of irrational forms of approach to the problems of nature and the future of mankind. Periodicals devoted to the popularization of science which are published in the most developed countries, by raising the public's level of scientific culture, help to check such a tendency. Since 1950 Unesco has been publishing *Impact*, a journal specially designed to acquaint relatively informed readers with the possible implications for the development of societies of recent scientific discoveries in specific technical fields.

Unesco will stimulate reflection on present trends in science and technology in relation to society, on the cultural and moral problems posed by scientific progress and on those human aspects of science and technology which are specific to the developing countries. Through studies and publications such as the journal *Impact*, Unesco will seek to facilitate public understanding of the socio-cultural effects likely to be produced by the different scientific disciplines and their technological applications. In close collaboration with the major international non-governmental organizations in the field of science, Unesco will seek to make scientific research workers even more aware of their special responsibilities in this connection and of the ethical problems confronting them. Particular attention will be given to young people who, whether they be scientists or not, are directly interested in the future of science and technology. Lastly the Organization will encourage regional co-operation for the study of philosophy and modern scientific methods in relation to the different cultures.

Science and technology policies

During the last forty years or so, the spectacular progress of science and technology, the source of economic and military power, has led many countries to invest an increasingly large proportion of their physical and intellectual resources in research projects and scientific and technological training programmes. The amount of national resources allocated to the financing of research has thus multiplied in a few decades. The developed countries are now spending from 0.5 to 4 per cent of their gross national product on such research. Concurrently, higher education and technological training systems have undergone great changes affecting their nature as well as their scope in order to provide the qualified personnel required in these countries.

Why State action?

Research and training activities, reflecting the effort to ensure the renewal and transmission of knowledge, have gone hand-in-hand with the widening of the applications of science and technology to all areas of economic and social life. The resulting process of technological innovation is playing its own significant role, alongside capital and labour, and as an independent factor, in economic growth. It is also bringing about considerable changes in ways of life which are disrupted to an unprecedented extent by the introduction of new technologies. These technologies are being increasingly developed today on the basis of a scientific analysis of the phenomena involved, rather than in an empirical way as hitherto.

The far-reaching consequences of scientific and technological activities for society and the magnitude of the resources they demand have therefore led States to study the whole range of problems connected with the development of science and technology and to influence the course of this development; this is the object of science and technology policy. It bears, in particular, on the organization of the means required for the production and use of scientific and technological knowledge and on the allocation of the resources devoted to those purposes.

The development of science and technology within a society is primarily governed by the degree to which there is an acute awareness of the need to advance the state of knowledge and use it as a basis for action, whether in the general national interest or to promote production or to improve the living conditions of communities. The demand for science and technology expressed by certain social groups—the country as a whole, production sectors, different communities—is addressed to one particular group, namely, that consisting of research workers, engineers and technicians. The extent of the demand depends on social, economic and cultural factors and involves motivations and scales of values; its importance is decisive. A certain idea of the relations which should be established between science and society is reflected, then, in all science policy. The magnitude and nature of the efforts which will be devoted by the community to science and technology depends on this idea. (cf. pages 146-53).

Decompartmentalizing disciplines and creating favourable conditions for research

Policy in science and technology concerns first of all research, the source of innovation; it also concerns the practical application of its findings. To be effective, the range of activities covering the execution of research projects and the utilization of the improved techniques derived from such work demands, in addition to an infrastructure of services, many different types of specialized personnel, training in the use of the techniques in the sectors in which research findings can be applied and, lastly, an adequate level of general scientific education among people working in this field. Unless all these conditions are fulfilled, science policy cannot have any real impact on the development of science and technology as a whole. Accordingly, it is also concerned with activities relating to science teaching and extension work, the training of technicians and engineers and higher education, as well as with services such as scientific and technical information and documentation, metrology, scientific instruments and the various surveys and studies connected with the environment (cartography, meteorology, hydrology, etc.). Science extension services (agricultural, industrial, medical) are vital linchpins in the sectors of application and must also be taken into account.

The complexity of these elements is such that a high level of organization and the convergence of many different lines of action are required. What is more, the compartmentalization of disciplines that has long held sway in the field of research has given way to interdisciplinarity in the study of practical problems which do not lend themselves to analysis by methods determined on the basis of the traditional categories of knowledge. For example, in order to plan new public health systems it is necessary to draw upon knowledge in the fields of medicine and sociology and even of economics. Similarly, it is becoming more and more apparent that compartmentalization is a brake on scientific advance; links must be established between universities and industry, institutions engaged in theoretical research and laboratories for technical development and, where necessary, between the State and business firms, so as to work out functional programmes.

A further difficulty stems from the fact that scientific and technological development is affected to a marked degree by the question of scale. The conception and development of certain techniques or prototypes and the scientific work on which they depend are not within the reach of every country simply because of the great number of highly specialized disciplines involved and the sheer size of the installations required. This makes it necessary for countries to join forces whenever large-scale projects are tackled and underlines the vital importance of international co-operation in scientific development.

Lastly, the specific conditions governing scientific work, and more especially research, play a decisive role: it is a well-established fact that research cannot thrive in no matter what environment or working conditions. A measure of freedom is necessary for creative activity, just as much in the realm of pure science as in the field of its applications. The legitimate aspirations of those who make their professional career in research, industrial development and innovation cannot be disregarded by a science and technology policy which cares for individual values.

The essentials of science policy: selectivity, forecasting and international co-operation

A science and technology policy serves a real purpose only in so far as it proves capable in the light of its review of all the problems involved in scientific and technological development, of guiding the relevant activities towards the general aims of national development. To achieve this, a necessary preliminary is to express these general aims in terms of scientific and technological objectives. Under the highly complex conditions obtaining today in modern societies, there is a very large number of such objectives, distributed throughout the various economic and social sectors. Science policy aims primarily to establish their relative priorities. It must fix them first for scientific and technological research itself, in other words, for programmes generating new knowledge, but bearing in mind that the substantive content of part of these programmes is not amenable to any plans other than those relating to the allocation of resources, since the moment of discovery cannot be predetermined. But science policies must also fix priorities for the application of science and technology to development. Choices have to be made and guidelines laid down with regard to the modernization of production infrastructures, the introduction of modern techniques into key sectors, the development of techniques appropriate to the country, the use of new techniques better adapted to the natural or social environment. This second aspect of science policy is indissolubly linked with other questions of national importance such as: agricultural development, industrial development, land management, urban development, trade policy, employment policy.

Policy-making in science and technology presents certain specific difficulties which are not found to the same degree in other aspects of national development policy. In the first place, it must plan for long periods ahead since the results of scientific and technological activity will only become apparent in the long run. It is difficult to work out a policy in the absence of forward-looking assumptions regarding future trends in the country's production system and even, generally speaking, in the absence of a sort of preconceived model of the economic and social structures that it is hoped to achieve. In the second place, policy-making is almost inevitably selective in the majority of countries: it is, indeed, practically impossible for all nations to be in the vanguard of progress along the whole front of science and technology because of the limitations imposed by the huge scale on which it is necessary to establish national scientific communities, and infrastructures for research and experimental development work. The conditions of modern science make complementarity between nations obligatory in advanced fields. If science policy has to be linked with educational policy, employment policy and sectoral policies in the fields of application, then it must also tie up with national foreign policy so as to identify the areas in which national efforts and international co-operation support each other.

Overwhelming differences in scientific and technological potential

While the task of formulating a science policy is governed by the same principles in all countries because of the universal character of science and the process that leads from a new discovery to its application, the ways in which it will have to be actually applied in the various countries differ considerably according to the nature and level of the scientific and technological development reached by each country. The first point to bear in mind is that the greater part of modern science and technology, as we know them today, has been built up in the developed region of the world whose needs and aspirations they reflect. The overwhelming majority of research projects (95 per cent) is still being carried out today in the twenty-five countries that are the most developed in economic terms, regardless, moreover, of what their science policy may be. If we consider, in the most powerful of these countries, the research fields to which the greatest resources have been allocated, we find that these relate, in the first place, to military aims or large-scale programmes combining prestige motives with the pursuit of industrial power (nuclear energy, space programmes) and, in the second place, to economic objectives (computer science, electronics, aeronautics). These countries generally possess a number of scientists and engineers which is of the order of 100 to 300 per 10,000 inhabitants, a developed industrial sector, a diversified economy and a high urban development rate. In some of these countries, the resources allocated to scientific and technological development, which had steadily increased up to the end of the last decade, have tended to diminish in relation to the national product. At the same time, more emphasis has been laid on social objectives (environment, health, land management) which will probably bring about a change in research priorities in the coming years. This shows that the science policy of these countries has been strongly influenced by the recent trend in thinking about the relations between science and society.

At the other end of the scale, as regards the size of resources devoted to science and its prospects of development, we find the thirty or so countries classified among the least developed. In these countries, whose economies are more often than not predominantly agricultural, the scientific and technical personnel strength does not generally exceed a few hundred scientists and engineers per million inhabitants; illiteracy is still rife and there is relatively little demand for science. For these countries the road to development necessarily lies through the application of the findings of science as it has been organized by the efforts of other countries, and through the rapid implantation of technologies which are appropriate to their own very special conditions. It will inevitably take a long time to build up a sufficiently vigorous scientific community and establish the network of institutions which are essential to endogenous scientific growth. Education, and higher scientific and technological education in particular, are the first priorities in this area. It is essential to concentrate all the slender resources available and devote them to a small number of carefully selected key problems in the fields which are most vital to medium-term development—land and water management, agriculture, inexpensive forms of energy—and the science policy of these countries consists mainly in making strictly determined choices. It must be linked with the regional or international co-operation programmes that are being currently prepared in order to help them to advance beyond the point before which self-supporting scientific and technological development is clearly impossible. It should be noted that in these countries the social sciences, which make it possible to base the technological progress of society on a thorough knowledge of cultural data, have an important role to play.

In the other countries (fewer than a hundred) the number of scientists and engineers ranges from 10 to 100 per 10,000 inhabitants. The contributions to development that can be expected from technological progress in the industrial and agricultural sectors and advanced research are extremely varied, as are the problems involved in the improvement of the quality of life as regards hygiene, housing and environment. No matter what order of priority for research fields may be decided on by the governments when setting the objectives for their science and technology policy, these countries must take three factors into consideration: the scale of national research capabilities, the production system's power to use these capabilities, and the level of scientific education among the people at large.

A country's research capabilities are measured by the manpower employed in research and technological development and by the number, size and quality of laboratories and research institutes. Their efficiency depends largely on the organization of institutions and the co-ordination that enables their activities to converge; it conditions, in its turn, the range and scale of the technological projects that the country can undertake with some chance of succeeding. A country with a large population —even if the relative density of its scientific and technical manpower is low—is able to set up teams in many different disciplines and so to venture upon more ambitious projects than a small country with a higher level of research potential in only a few disciplines. The scale and quality of scientific and technological capabilities ultimately determine the range of subjects that a country can cover on the science and technology front and guide the choice of research priorities. Only if a country has adequate capabilities can sizeable resources be allocated to long-term research with all the serious risks this implies.

At the crossroads of research and its applications: government action

The impact that national research capabilities, when used to the best advantage, can have on the country's development in the various sectors of economic and social life depends on the liaison established between research and the production system. The problem is presented in a different light according to whether the great majority of applied research and experimental development projects are being carried out in production enterprises themselves or, on the contrary, in institutions, such as universities, which are relatively independent of the production system. However, the process by which the findings of research work reach the stage of their practical application almost always calls for government intervention to a varying degree. Science and technology policy must deal with the means of stimulating and financing research and, possibly, with the legislation, which are calculated to promote contacts between study and research institutions and establishments responsible for introducing innovations and radical changes into production methods.

The level of scientific education of the population as a whole determines both the country's research capabilities and the extent to which the production system can absorb technological innovations. The ratio between the specialized manpower having benefited from higher education in scientific and technological disciplines and the size of the population gives a fairly accurate idea of the extent to which a general education in science and technology is prevalent throughout the country, because of the science teaching infrastructure which it implies 'upstream' and the utilization in the production system which it implies 'downstream'. A major objective of science and technology policy in countries with a low scientific potential will therefore be to increase the capacity of scientific and technological training facilities, whereas in countries with a higher manpower ratio in this field emphasis will be laid on the need to employ the available personnel more effectively.

Implementation: problems of structures and training

As regards its implementation, science and technology policy involves carrying out certain essential functions relating to the *planning, co-ordination and stimulation* of scientific and technological activities. The performance of these functions raises specific problems concerning institutional structures, decision-making procedures, information and the analysis of basic data, as well as the legal instruments (legislation on patents and licences and the importing of technology) or financial means (research funds) which are needed in order to influence the course of scientific and technological development.

Most modern States, and the majority of developing countries, are now equipped with appropriate governmental structures for the formulation of their science and technology policy. But almost all of the thirty or so least developed countries referred to above still lack such structures. As for decision-making bodies—such as those which define objectives or draw up major national programmes for concerted research work—they are still finding it difficult, in certain countries, to carry out their tasks because of the lack of adequate analytical methods or statistics on the national and international situation in the field of science and technology. Furthermore, the legal or financial instruments which could be expected to give a decisive impetus to the course of scientific and technological development—because, for example, they are designed to increase the funds from various sources devoted to science and technology, or to promote the demand for science and technology—are still lacking in many countries. According to the situation prevailing in each country, there is still a need, therefore, to establish or improve one or other of the components of the machinery enabling the government to control national scientific and technological development in such a way as to attain the objectives of its policy.

Lastly, the performance of the functions involved in the implementation of science and technology policy calls for a new generation of specialists who are not numerous enough or adequately trained as yet. Because of the relatively small number of institutions in a position to provide this training, international action to promote exchanges and the organization of specialized courses is the most effective means of enabling the present nucleus of specialists to contribute to the dissemination of the indispensable knowledge and methods. At the same time, there is a great need for comparative analyses, both quantitative and qualitative, of the scientific and technological capabilities of the various countries and their experience in the planning, co-ordination and encouragement of scientific and technological activities. As a research subject, science and technology policy is a relatively new field of studies and does not yet have the advantage of having its own well-tried analytical methods. There is good reason, therefore, to continue to strive for international co-operation in conducting the studies and research which are needed in order to arrive at a better understanding of the determining factors in scientific and technological development in various situations, work out the techniques used in planning, determine priorities, and establish forecasts in this field.

Policy-making machinery throughout the world

The universal character of science and the importance of scientific exchanges between countries have always given the world scientific community cause to reflect upon the prospects that science and technology open up for the future of the nations. It is only during the last decade, however, that the concept of a world science policy has gradually taken shape, a policy that would tackle the problems raised by imbalances in the localization of research and the great inequality of national capabilities, and their implications for long-term trends in the distribution of wealth and power among the nations. The search for a new international economic order is leading the community of nations to attach increasing importance to such a world policy. No matter what roads it may follow, this policy must be founded, first, on an increasingly accurate picture of national situations in all their diversity and secondly on more detailed knowledge, drawn from the countries' common experience, of the possibilities and repercussions of science policy.

The efforts of countries in setting up distinct policy-making machinery in science and technology have generally gone hand in hand with the size and complexity of the scientific enterprise. In the group of least developed countries, where the scientific infrastructure is minimal, the economy based on the exploitation and export of primary products and the import of almost all manufactured goods and equipment, there is very seldom any form of governmental machinery for the formulation of national science and technology policy nor any readily identifiable scientific and technological component in their overall development plan. Although science and technology have been relegated to the realm of lesser priority areas, because of more pressing and basic needs, most of these countries have, however, been sensitized to the potential long-range benefits of their capability build-up in science and technology, and in several of them, some form of advisory function in scientific and/or technological matters has been entrusted to a governmental department dealing generally with education, or natural resources or industry. In many instances, early investigation has been made on possible policy-making machinery, and it can be expected that the need for establishing such machinery will become more acute in the coming years.

Different stages of development: from embryonic co-ordination to ministerial structures

In the other developing countries, which are in early or intermediate phases of industrialization and which aim chiefly at import substitution for common consumer goods and some intermediate products, industrial technology is for the most part imported from abroad. In these countries, technological innovation and the supporting research and development programmes are designed primarily so as to adapt foreign techniques to the local environment. These countries have established over the years a small core of research institutions, generally relating to agriculture, mining, health or industry, with some measure of basic research carried out in the universities. They have engaged in significant science education programmes and have devoted particular attention to developing their scientific and technical manpower. Most of these countries have evolved wide varieties of policy-making and/or co-ordination mechanisms for research and related activities, tailored to their particular needs, and ranging from a single research council with a co-ordination function in a particular area of scientific endeavour (agricultural, medical, industrial research councils) to a full blown government department with policy-making and administrative responsibilities over all aspects of the national scientific and technological development. In several of them, priorities have been formulated, and distinct science and technology plans have been prepared and included in the national development plan.

Valuable efforts have been made for surveying the scientific and technological potential in a number of countries, although the surveys often proved highly inadequate for decision-making purposes, because of a lack of sufficiently reliable, comprehensive or detailed information, both qualitative and quantitative. Concern has grown among developing countries in the past few years about the adequacy of foreign technology (i.e. imported from advanced countries) to meet their needs, and the search for alternative technologies has now become a major policy issue in several of them. Institutional arrangements for addressing this problem may be expected to constitute an important policy objective in the coming years.

The institutionalization of science and technology in the industrialized countries

In industrialized countries there are generally fully pledged government organs for science and technology policy. These have often undergone spectacular reforms at the apex of the governmental decision-making structures. Strong links exist with the educational, industrial, agricultural, health, environmental and foreign policies, as well as with the overall socio-economic planning organizations and with the State budget. Parliamentary control over the science and technology policies of governments has often been exercised through parliamentary committees. Sectorial research bodies such as research councils, academies of science and science foundations have been set up to bring together, in a purposeful national R&D system, a scattered network comprising thousands of research units and laboratories.

In the more advanced of the industrialized countries, in which the main emphasis is gradually shifting from the production of goods and services to the management of the complex systems governing society's functioning and development, science and technology have become a basic institutional necessity of society. This raises crucial questions, as ethical, political and juridical considerations have to be weighed against scientific and technical ones. It can be foreseen that one of the key problems of such societies will be the organization of science and technology: and the creation, dissemination and application of new knowledge.

Regional and world co-operation

At the regional level, a number of intergovernmental organizations have in the recent past devoted considerable attention to policy issues relating to the scientific and technological development of their member countries, and have evolved policy guidelines for co-operation among these countries. The organizations which have carried out the most extensive work are the Organization for Economic Co-operation and Development, the European Economic Community, the Committee for Mutual Economic Assistance, and the Organization of American States. The Organization for African Unity has recently set up a special unit dealing with scientific and technological co-operation. There are also a number of smaller regional groupings (South-East Asian countries, Andean countries, etc.) where the co-ordination of research policies and programmes is being promoted.

At the international level, most of the organizations of the United Nations system have been dealing with one aspect or another of the application of science and technology. Since the pioneering United Nations Conference on the Application of Science and Technology to Development (UNCSTD, Geneva 1963), the United Nations system as a whole has been committed to the strengthening and co-ordination of its activities in this field. The three principal policy-making and monitoring instruments of a co-ordinated approach in the United Nations are: (a) the Ecosoc governmental Committee on Science and Technology for Development (CSTD); (b) the Sub-Committee on Science and Technology of the United Nations Administrative Committee on Co-ordination (ACC); and (c) the United Nations Advisory Committee on the Application of Science and Technology to Development (UNACAST) which also acts as Unesco's advisory committee on matters relating to scientific and technological development. The Economic and Social Council, as well as the General Assembly of the United Nations have recently requested that 'the planning of activities in the field of science and technology in the various organizations of the United Nations system should be harmonized and gradually integrated into a *United Nations science and technology policy*'. In response to this request, the Executive Board of Unesco decided in 1973 that the Organization should play an important role in such an integrated approach to science and technology within the United Nations system. In this connection, Unesco is already inserting its action in a broader framework elaborated with the co-operation of, and adhered to by, the United Nations family of organizations as a whole. This framework was set out for the first time in the *World Plan of Action for the Application of Science and Technology to Development* published by the United Nations in 1971.

Since 1961, the Organization has assisted Member States at their request in establishing, strengthening or operating their national science policy-making bodies.

In such matters, Unesco's action has not only been guided by the United Nations World Plan of Action and by the Regional Plans which constitute annexes thereof, but also by its own experience gained through the granting of assistance to individual Member States and through the organization of a series of governmental expert meetings and of four regional ministerial conferences held respectively in Latin America (CASTALA, 1965), Asia (CASTASIA, 1968), Europe (MINESPOL, 1970) and Africa (CASTAFRICA, 1974). A fifth such ministerial conference was prepared for the Arab States (CASTARAB, 1976). This experience has been further expanded in the Organization's publications entitled 'Science Policy Studies and Documents'. It has also been synthetized in a book called *Science for Development*, available in English, French, Spanish and Portuguese.

Although there exists neither a standard pattern for the formulation of science and technology policies nor a standard layout for research institutions and scientific services, certain general guiding principles can nowadays be formulated concerning questions such as planning techniques or the functions to be performed by various scientific and technological institutions so as to tie in with one another and thus constitute an organized and truly operational network. A great diversity of situations has been encountered by the Organization in its assistance to Member States. More than sixty Member States have been advised by Unesco during the past fifteen years on the setting up or strengthening of science and technology policy-making bodies and in twenty-two of these countries Unesco's support has led to the adoption of new legislation.

In most instances assistance was granted to specific institutions, such as governmental or semi-governmental institutions entrusted with planning and decision-making on a comprehensive national scale. In certain instances these bodies were also responsible for inter-ministerial co-ordination of the national R&D activities, of the related scientific services, and of the major technological innovation operations (including key activities related to the transfer of technology). Such entities normally take concrete form as a separate ministry of science and technology and/or a special national council closely linked to the highest State offices (Prime Minister or President of Republic).

It might finally be mentioned that, at the request of the United Nations Advisory Committee on the Application of Science and Technology to Development, detailed surveys have been carried out in a number of developing countries, with a view to determining the nature and extent of national institutional needs in science and technology. These surveys are designed to help Member States in the preparation of National Development Plans and may also serve as a basis for UNDP 'country programming' operations in the field of science and technology. These activities constitute an organic link between Unesco's science and technology policy programme, and its operational programmes, (cf. pages 164-80), which aim *inter alia* at building up the institutional infrastructure of science and technology of the developing countries.

Unesco will continue its efforts to bring about a fundamental reorientation of world research towards peaceful ends, the wider circulation of scientific and technological information and an increase in the countries' capacity to ensure their own scientific and technological development according to their needs and with their own resources.

With a view to assisting Member States to develop science and technology policies, Unesco will provide advisory services to Member States at their request; will conduct studies and research on questions related to the planning of science and technology development and to budgeting techniques in this field; will organize symposia and publish studies and reports including the series 'Science Policy Studies and Documents'. The training of planners and research managers will be furthered by the organization of training courses and seminars and the award of study grants. Exchanges of information will be promoted. Unesco will organize regional conferences of ministers and sub-regional meetings and seminars and will set up an operational management of an international fund for the promotion of research and experimental development in Africa (and possibly also in the Arab States).

Lastly, the Organization will participate in the formulation of an overall science and technology policy for the United Nations system, particularly by assisting in the preparation of the Second United Nations Conference on the Application of Science and Technology to Development, scheduled for 1979.

The encouragement of research and the establishment of new foundations for science and technology

Research today: organization, complexity, scope

Historically, science has expanded at an ever-increasing pace, but it is only recently, in face of the vast upheavals wrought by science and technology in fields which are critical for the survival of mankind (war, economic competition, food, health, etc.), that this has become a subject of concern.

This expansion has been accompanied by far-reaching changes in the mode of production of scientific research, its institutions and its complexity. Formerly, advances in science were due essentially to individual efforts, often made somewhat at random. But in recent decades the development of research has increasingly involved synergistic action, such as the setting up of teams of research workers, and also a change in scale, necessitated in particular by the fact that huge and costly facilities and equipment are indispensable in order to carry research over to the next level of complexity and depth (for instance, in elementary particle physics, astronomy, oceanography, medicine, information processing, natural resources surveying, etc.). Nowadays, major advances in knowledge are generally the result of systematic research undertakings involving many high-level specialists assisted by a large body of technical and administrative staff, thus requiring an entirely new type of organization.

Research institutions have also evolved. Over the years, the increasingly systematic adoption of a scientific approach to solution of the concrete problems which arise in all fields of human activity has led to the setting up of research and development laboratories administratively and financially attached to the establishments destined to benefit from the results of their work (industrial enterprises, government departments, etc.). The research infrastructure has thus been considerably enlarged, the major part of basic research (expanding in absolute terms, but representing an increasingly small fraction of the national research effort) remaining in the universities, while the rest was transferred to new types of specialized research institutions, where virtually all applied research and development work was carried out.

Thousands of specializations

The diversification of scientific knowledge is also increasing immeasurably as more and more aspects of the material universe and more and more forms of human activity are being investigated in greater and greater depth, within the framework of increasingly rigorous theory building. Fields of specialization (pure and applied sciences, natural and social sciences) now number in the order of a thousand and gone are the days when it was possible to be simply a physicist or a biologist. Interdisciplinarity thus becomes a highly complex process involving a very large number of specialists from essentially different disciplines, and this complexity accentuates the difficult problem of communication which is thus posed. The fragmentation inherent in the growth process will increasingly affect our ability to tackle development problems, for the solution of which we will require an entirely new type of scientist, trained in the methods of global analysis and able to identify the problems and to select techniques whereby they can be solved.

This growth process and the attendant qualitative changes constitute determining factors for the future development of science and scientific communities and for the future participation of these communities in the development efforts of their countries.

Regional disparities : the 'map' of Nobel prize winners

But the growth of science has not been of nearly the same magnitude in all regions of the world and examples of disparities are legion. There are indications that any given country's share in the world production of knowledge in the basic sciences (number of scientific papers in physics or chemistry published in international journals), for instance, may be in direct proportion to national wealth (gross national product). It is possible, then, on the basis of their relative share in the world GNP in 1972, to form an idea of the relative contribution of the different regions of the world to the advance of knowledge: North America, 35 per cent; Europe, 40 per cent (of which U.S.S.R. 10 per cent); Asia,

16 per cent (of which Japan 7 per cent); Latin America, 5 per cent; and Africa, 2.5 per cent. The profile may be different in other disciplines, but probably not radically. Regional disparities are even more pronounced when one considers advanced research and looks at where breakthroughs are taking place—for instance the countries where Nobel prize winners work.

The fact that scientific progress originates from some countries rather than others can only have the effect of creating an imbalance in its content and consequently of making it lose its relevance to the whole of mankind. For while the universal character of scientific method cannot be questioned, it is probable that the choice of research themes is influenced by individual or collective concerns, that is to say, in the end, by the concerns of specific societies. If this is so, the lines of development of science are determined by the general socio-cultural context of a given country and reflect its values, problems and aspirations.

However, there is nothing fatal about the present situation. The history of science in the past 150 years or so is one of constant emergence of new scientific communities on the world scientific scene, with the United States first forging its way through to the forefront of science towards the end of the last century by the side of France, Germany and Great Britain, soon followed by the U.S.S.R. and Japan. This broad profile keeps on evolving, with important scientific communities now emerging in a number of developing countries.

Furthermore, the question arises as to whether science can continue to expand at the fast pace referred to above. There seems to be a limit to the number of scientific research workers that a society can sustain, however advanced the society may be, and also a limit to the rate at which these research workers can obtain results. There are signs that certain saturation effects are beginning to make themselves felt in the scientifically developed countries.

Organizing co-operation, guiding research, improving the distribution of training facilities

Therefore, the problem at hand is one of organizing international co-operation to make room for the newcomers, of helping them build up their capacity, and at the same time of reorienting science towards the concrete development problems of the majority of the world.

As science and technology develop, both in extent and diversity, so do their potential applications. But there is a significant difference in the degree to which countries are able to make effective use of the potential of science and technology towards their national developments. Many of them do not yet possess the critical elements of trained manpower, institutional infrastructure and other resources and capabilities that are necessary to exploit the existing heritage of science and technology, let alone the research capabilities for problem-solving and technological innovation appropriate to their needs. Overall, developing countries are spending twenty times less than industrialized countries on research and development.

As regards the education and training of scientists and engineers, the developing countries are similarly disadvantaged. The average number of science degrees per 100,000 population (in 1970) was 37 for North America, 13 for Europe, but only 3 for the Arab States, 2 for Asia (including Japan), 1.4 for Latin America and 0.2 for Africa. The industrialized world as a whole is estimated to possess ten times as much (i.e. 90 per cent) of the total stock of world scientists and engineers as the developing world, an imbalance which might take as long as a century to be reduced, at present respective rates of growth.

The sharp differences in the relative shares of various groups of countries in the overall growth of science and in the overall financial and human resources devoted to it in the world set the background against which the development of scientific and technological research and training should be analysed. For the purpose of this discussion, this is taken to lead to four areas of endeavour: international co-operation among scientists, adequacy of current science and technology to the needs of developing countries, the world situation in higher education and training, and the building up by countries of national capacities for generating their own technologies and adapting foreign ones.

A favourable factor in international research: the traditional co-operation of scientists

The universality of the laws of nature has made the conduct of science an international co-operative undertaking almost from its historic beginnings. Scientists have always had a tendency to congregate according to their discipline, beyond the borders of their particular background or of their social or national origin, and the international scientific community is recognized today as a precious channel for better world understanding, co-operation and development, a role which the Unesco General Conference formally emphasized in 1974.

To any practical extent, the machinery for international scientific co-operation is essentially based upon international non-governmental organizations, such as the many scientific unions affiliated with the International Council of Scientific Unions (ICSU), Union des Associations Techniques Internationales/Union of International Engineering Organizations (UATI), World Federation of Scientific Workers (WFSW), and numerous other professional regional and international organizations. There also exists a growing number of international and regional institutions which contribute significantly to achieving co-operation in research and training and make it possible to utilize more efficiently common resources and promote rapid communication of research results. These centres often possess expensive equipment which is used by international teams with a research programme at a scale that no single country could afford.

But the rising complexity and costs of collective undertakings in both basic and applied fields of scientific endeavour (sub-nuclear physics, nuclear energy, space exploration, computer development, environmental research, ocean research) as well as their far-reaching economic and political implications, have increasingly forced governments to step in, in developed and developing countries alike. Therefore, the machinery for international scientific co-operation is also very much dependent on intergovernmental agreements.

The general problems of international scientific co-operation will require the active involvement of intergovernmental organizations, such as Unesco, in many ways. The working out of intergovernmental agreements on scientific co-operation programmes on a world scale or on an inter-regional scale will rest upon the good offices of Unesco to provide the mechanisms for effective government support. On the other hand, at a global level, Unesco is the natural channel for bringing to the attention of governments the assessments made by the international scientific community on the future prospects and implications of scientific and technological advances. Finally, Unesco remains the major organization where arrangements can be made among Member States for the formulation of world priorities in the coherent utilization of resources for the advancement of science and technology.

In spite of several major efforts, there remains a serious imbalance in the opportunities for participation and communication with the world scientific community on the part of scientists from developing countries. Considerably more resources must be provided and greater attention must be given to this aspect of co-operation if their potential is to be fulfilled, and arrangements will have to be found in the years to come to link weak and isolated national scientific communities to the world network.

Can research concentrated in the most developed countries cater to the needs of the less developed societies?

Furthermore, the constant evolution on the research front leads to new interdisciplinary approaches, and the birth of new disciplines that help us tackle new classes of problems often requires the support of international machinery to bring together specialists from different horizons and provide them with the necessary channels of communication. Cases in point can be seen in the areas of energy, information processing, system analysis, future researches, etc.

In view of the fact that advances in science and technology are achieved primarily in the most developed countries, mounting doubts have been expressed in the past decade or so as to whether these advances really cater to the needs of the developing societies.

The inequality in scientific and technical development has contributed to the increasing dependence of developing countries upon the industrialized countries and the solution of this problem carries great priority in the programmes aimed at the establishment of a new international economic order. In this connection, the United Nations General Assembly stated explicitly that one of the main principles of this new economic order should be 'to give to the developing countries access to the achievements of modern science and technology, and to promote the transfer of technology and the creation of indigenous technology for the benefit of the developing countries in forms and in accordance with procedures which are suited to their economies'.

This question immediately leads to two complementary questions: whether and how to use the existing pool of knowledge, i.e. to transfer technology, and how to develop alternative technologies, i.e. technologies out of the mainstream of current technological trends observed in advanced countries.

Implications and limits of technology transfer

Technology transfer raises many issues of a political, social and economic nature which go beyond the scope of this discussion. In purely scientific terms, the adoption of a foreign technology will practically always require further research and development work to adapt it to a social and natural environment different from the one for which it was conceived. International co-operation among countries with similar environments can help reduce the costs and risks associated with the transfer process. The problem of information is also seen to be paramount, and the creation of new information networks, or the expansion of those already existing, on the economic and technical characteristics of technologies of potential interest for developing countries will probably be among the major tasks of international co-operation in the years to come.

Technology transfer, however, has its own limits and, economic and related considerations apart, the development of tailor-made technologies to suit the problems at hand is ideally a better solution. In developing countries, the economic and social conditions will often require the design of technologies with a totally different set of characteristics (labour-intensiveness, energy requirements, use of raw materials) than those of currently available ones. To any practical extent, this will amount to the development *ab initio* of so-called 'alternative' technologies rather than to adaptation work, with full resort being made to modern science, as required, involving even sometimes basic research in conventional areas. Such a drastic reorientation in approach cannot be expected to take place overnight among the scientific establishments. There is a need to constitute a number of nuclei research groups, in addition to the few which already exist in the world (developed as well as developing). Here again international co-operation is an important mechanism for linking scattered research groups, providing them with the necessary means for consolidating their knowledge and experience, and disseminating their results.

Higher education and the training of engineers and technicians: the effects of the integration of science and technology

Higher science education, which traditionally trains secondary school teachers in the different disciplines together with scientific research personnel, has not always, in all educational systems, been established in sufficiently close relationship with training for engineers or higher technicians.

The recent change in conceptions concerning science and technology policies (cf. pages 153-64), pointing in the direction of the integrated development of science and of technology, has been accompanied by a progressive coupling of the two corresponding types of education and by a broadening of the function of universities to include training for engineers in countries where previously the principle of 'engineering faculties' had not been accepted.

This change in university institutions reflects the urgent need to link together knowledge and action, as part of the general tendency to develop the applications of science to development. However, except in some groups of countries which have founded their education on the principle of the integration of basic science, applied science and engineering, the present structures are still inadequately suited to meet this need. From the point of view of systems and structures, what is involved is a strictly educational problem (cf. Chapter 5, pages 207-12). But this problem will be solved only in so far as the contents and methods of science and education and of engineering training are subject to reforms, and to a large extent convergent reforms.

Such must be the prime purpose of the reorganization of higher science and technology education which is to be undertaken in many developing countries. At the same time, steps must be taken to guard against that academic and formalistic conception of the process of transmission of knowledge which persists in many countries, where long-established models are applied to higher science education, at the cost of effectiveness. Great progress may be looked for in this connection from the widespread introduction of modern audio-visual aids, of which, unfortunately, singularly little use has so far been made in universities.

In the developing countries science and technology students will, in the course of their careers, have to exercise direct or indirect responsibilities in the scientific and technological development of their countries. An equally important approach here will therefore consist in training them to take into account the interactions between science and society (cf. pages 146-53) and between technology and the environment (cf. Chapter 7, pages 304 ff.). In addition to the practical need to provide all engineers with basic management skills, in preparation for their future role in societies in the process of industrialization, it is consequently necessary to link higher science education to adequate social science education and, in those branches of technology in which human activities directly impinge upon the natural environment, to ensure that all science education incorporates the findings of modern environmental research.

The remodelling of education should not be limited to educational content and methods, but also relate to the organization of education. The general renewal of higher education required in order better to meet the needs of society is in fact particularly necessary in the field of science and technology. There must be reforms to enable higher science education to satisfy qualitative and quantitative manpower needs more effectively, to be more open to the world of work and to recruit experienced engineers as teachers, at least on a part-time basis. Such reforms (see Chapter 5, pages 230-6) necessarily call for measures specific to the situation of the country concerned and presuppose the drawing up of increasingly varied models. Regional co-operation can provide a powerful contribution to the identification of new lines of approach.

Similarly, technical and vocational education needs continuing reform so as to be better co-ordinated with national manpower needs, and avoid unemployment of school leavers. Its content must become less theoretical, better adapted to the local environment and oriented towards employment. In this regard, Unesco has an important role to play in setting standards, and in helping in training activities at all levels and for all types of technical and vocational education.

The foregoing considerations hold good for all levels of education. In the case of the highest levels, other problems, common to higher science education in every country, arise. They are the consequences of the speeding-up of the advance of knowledge and the incessant accumulation of research findings. Higher science and technology education must in fact satisfy a set of contradictory conditions. It must prepare the student to exercise his creativity in his particular discipline in the course of his professional career, which calls for a thorough grounding in research in advanced fields, and a precise specialization. But it must at the same time enable him to acquire, in a fairly broad range of disciplines, the basic skills without which he would not subsequently be able to increase his knowledge or take his bearings in new fields, or to tackle the interdisciplinary branches which are likely to emerge as a result of the evolution of science. Ways and means must be found of providing training which reconciles these needs. They have been found in a number of advanced centres, generally established in countries with long-standing scientific traditions. There the student can acquire not only the most up-to-date knowledge but also irreplaceable experience in respect of the organization of research, documentation and education.

The efforts already made within the framework of international co-operation to ensure participation, for limited periods of time or on the occasion of special courses, by students from all regions of the world in the activities of centres selected for their excellence at world level, should be continued. One of the resulting advantages is that the establishment of a network of personal relations among specialists concerned with the same problem is thereby facilitated and also, when what is involved is the application of science or technology to development, the groundwork is laid for the efforts of all to be able to converge upon the problems of a few. The choice of disciplines is of major importance since it is binding on the future in that the young scientists or engineers whose training is thereby determined are called upon to play a promotional role in their respective countries. This choice should be founded on the current world situation in science and technology, which provides pointers as to the directions in which major innovative breakthroughs may be achieved, and also on priorities in regard to the application of science and technology to development, as they have been recognized by the international community.

A balanced network of research and training institutions

An important factor in the development of a national capacity in science and technology is the establishment of an array of institutions with research and/or training functions. The comprehensiveness and balance of the institutional network are important features in the build-up process.

Critical choices have to be made as to areas of specialization to be developed, especially in countries with a small pool of qualified manpower. A certain balance must be reached between fundamental and applied disciplines failing which the country may find itself unable either to tackle fundamental problems or to transform the results of basic research into useful applications. Social and natural sciences must be developed in harmony so as to allow comprehensive approaches to the solving of practical problems in all their aspects, technical, economic, social, etc. . . . The balance among different levels of qualification is also an important aspect of manpower development, and a problem common to many developing countries is the lack of technicians to support the work of high-level specialists in research and production.

The design of research institutions, both basic and applied, is a question which has not been satisfactorily resolved yet, in most developing countries as well as in many developed countries. The major difficulty resides in striking a balance between two conflicting requirements. On the one hand, there is the need to work above the critical mass of resources necessary for research work to be effective, in terms of manpower, facilities and equipment, leading to a concentration of activities in a single institution; on the other hand, there is a need for the research scientists and engineers to be close to the terrain where practical problems arise, whether it be the village, the small industrial enterprise, etc., a requirement which leads to a dispersion of the research performers with their tools away from a central institution, either physically or organizationally. Alternative technologies might mean not only new technical processes, but also require new institutional set-ups for their conception, and developing countries might well face a major problem in the years to come in designing 'alternative' institutions better suited for bringing science- and technology-based innovations to where the mass of the people live, the villages and the rural areas.

The application of science and technology in the various sectors of national activity will require not only research and training institutions, but also a number of service institutions, related to metrology and standards, scientific and technical information, scientific apparatus, natural resources surveys and so on. Such institutions often are a prerequisite to the conduct of research in the country, or the application of research results, or the transfer of technology from abroad.

Circumspect recourse to outside aid

The development of the institutional infrastructure is partly conditioned by objective requirements of efficiency and critical mass, and of balance and linkage among its several components, and partly determined by policy decisions as to direction and pace. The selective distribution by disciplines or technical areas depends on the natural and human resources available, but also on development policy related to defence, foreign relations, trade, finance, as well as the specific policies in agriculture and industry. The pace of development is likewise limited by objective constraints (there is a ceiling for instance to sustainable growth rate in manpower development), but is also subject to broad policy directions. Resort to outside assistance is one such major policy issue. In cases of very small infrastructures, in absolute terms, assistance would appear indispensable. In other cases, the pace of development can generally be accelerated by increasing the level and strength of exchanges with the outside world, at the cost, however, of submitting the society directly or indirectly to the impact of foreign modes of thinking and value systems, and therefore at the risk of making the development process less endogenous. The measure of tolerable exposure is currently a matter of heated debate among policy-makers in all parts of the world.

The extent to which alternatives exist to national research undertakings depends very much on the subject area. In developing the institutional infrastructure of research and training establishments, a major policy question usually arises as to the respective priorities to be allotted to the different components of the institutional base, by fields of training or research. There is a category of research problems which can be handled by outsiders working in outside establishments, on behalf of the country, as for instance certain types of industrial processes, testing operations, instrumentation, etc., where the results are in principle transferable. Another category of research problem concerns the living and natural environment of the country and these problems can be handled by outsiders, but preferably working *in situ* because of the country-specific nature of the object of investigation, for instance, agricultural, medical, natural resources research. A last category of problem cannot possibly be dealt with otherwise than by nationals working *in situ*, i.e. problems involving the social and human environment, where even the particular approach or method can be dependent on the economic, social and cultural determinants of the society concerned. This broad categorization has direct implications as regards the profile of the manpower development programme, of the institutional development programme for research and training, and of the technical assistance policy.

The scientist—torn between the attraction of the frontier disciplines and the needs of national development

In improving national capacities for a self-sustained process of scientific and technological development, proper consideration must be given to the complex interactions between science and technology on the one hand, and technology and society on the other, specifically as regards the appropriate character of the technology.

The debate concerning the relationships between science and technology is widespread and all nations are seeking to strengthen the coupling. Thus those countries with a highly developed scientific research base are seeking institutional, intellectual and financial stimulants for improving productivity, modernity, efficiency and competitiveness of their technology. Developing countries, possessing little indigenous capabilities, are advised first to develop the infrastructure for science which would provide the basic knowledge to be later transferred into technological applications in a so-called vertical transfer process. But in addition to the enormous investments and time delays inherent in this process, there have often been disappointments in developing countries when their scientific staff is drained away internally or externally by greater affinity to the frontier and often esoteric disciplines outside their countries than to the internal development issues and national needs. Furthermore, the lack of coupling between the developmental sectors in these States and the higher education and research sector often prevents the effective utilization of scientific personnel in these endeavours even when the spirit exists. Clearly, the 'pull' of the economic market place and societal needs must be coupled with the 'push' of the scientific and technological base for effective meshing between these elements. Otherwise the frustrations of the 'educated unemployed' and continuing inability to build a technological society above a scientific foundation will persist.

But the problems of effective technological transfer are still more complex. For example, many of the issues concerning the transfer of technology from developed to developing countries (the so-called horizontal transfer process) involve economic, government and policy questions, sometimes tied to multi-national structures beyond the scope of this discussion. Furthermore the questions of 'appropriateness' open up entirely new dimensions. By this is meant that the technology should be designed so as to take into account the constraints imposed by a host of factors, such as the environment, the culture, the labour situation, etc. While this might imply simplicity in design and operation and require an 'intermediate technology' approach, one should not exclude *a priori* the application of modern principles or high technology which might under certain circumstances truly be the most appropriate and enable the developing countries to 'leap frog' other development deficiencies. The use of communication satellites, for example, might be considered when ground communication links and infrastructure are lacking.

Importing wisely

Furthermore, there has been an increasing recognition that technology cannot merely be imported and used effectively, but that in most instances it needs to be adapted to suit the new environment, different economic situations or other governmental or community policies as well as different social and cultural factors. Coupled with this has been a growing recognition that help in finding solutions to development problems cannot necessarily be found by looking towards technologically advanced countries, but that in many instances tapping the more appropriate experience of nearby countries in the same region and facing similar problems may be more fruitful. In any case, a national pool of scientific and technical trained manpower of an adequate size and with a broad range of qualifications is a prerequisite for the development of a technology appropriate to local conditions.

It is still an open debate among sociologists, psychologists and epistemologists whether science and technology evolve according to their own built-in dynamics or in response to a particular quest by human beings and under their full control. Whatever the case, the development of science and technology as seen in a broad historical perspective, seems in the last resort to be based on man's capacity to master two

classes of phenomena: energy and information. Close study of the various manifestations of what we call scientific and technological progress, without ever stopping
to define it, will inevitably bring us back to these two basic concepts. On the one
hand, the mastery of energy has enabled man over the centuries to minimize his efforts
in obtaining a given result, that is, to enhance the material value of his action. On the
other hand, the mastery of information has enabled him, also over the centuries (for
before the data-processing revolution, there was the invention of writing, then of
alphabets, etc.) to develop his intellectual potential, that is, to reach a higher stage
of evolution in terms of mental adaptability or freedom, comparable to the stage
reached in terms of physical freedom.

Two keys to progress: the control of energy and information

The fundamental nature of these two determinants is currently being illustrated with
eloquence by the world energy crisis and by the problem of the information explosion.
In both cases, major political and economic interests are at stake, which affect the
balance of power in the world. There are signs that the development status of nations
will increasingly depend in the future on their resources, capability and know-how
in these two areas.

Rational organization of resources and the achievement of a world-wide
consensus on ethical, social and technical standards to be applied in the utilization
of energy and information, are major international tasks. As regards information,
this has been identified as one of the ten problems on which Unesco will focus its
programme (see Chapter 10, pages 355 and 360). But there is also an obvious need to
devote significant efforts to advancing our basic knowledge and our technological
proficiency in these two fields of energy and information, which would seem to be
among the very first world priorities in science and technology. The scale of effort
required in both areas seems to suggest the need for a global attack. But, at present,
international co-operation in these areas is only in its early stage, and could easily
afford to be expanded and accelerated. These two fields of science and technology are
of such importance that they have been dealt with under separate headings later in
this chapter (see below, pages 180-9).

Research and development, transfer of technology and the international economic system

In the majority of the most industrialized countries, the increase in the resources
allocated to research and development (R&D) over the last ten years has been accompanied by a parallel increase in the number of staff employed in these activities, and
by an expansion of the research institutions and groups devoted to them. The proportion of persons employed in R&D as compared with the total number of workers has
exceeded 15 per 1,000 in some countries, and during the period under consideration,
increased by between 20 and 25 per cent for the European countries as a whole. However,

in some countries with market economies, the rate of growth of resources has been appreciably lower than that of staff; the percentage of the national product devoted to R&D has not increased and has even decreased, in two countries: the United Kingdom and the United States.

The efforts made by the developing countries during the last decade have been considerable in all regions, and in many of them the growth rate of public spending on R&D has been distinctly higher than that of public spending on education. The number of staff employed in R&D has often increased fivefold. The imbalance between the scientific and technological capability of the most industrialized countries and that of the developing countries is therefore apparently on the decrease; however, the gap was so great at the beginning that the disparities remain of the same order of magnitude. As regards the results of research in the field of technology, the gap is even continuing to widen, as is shown, for instance, by trends in the number of patents for inventions registered or held in the developing countries by foreigners originating from the most industrialized countries or by multinational corporations: the number of such patents is constantly increasing as compared with the number of patents taken out by nationals. This is one aspect of the general process of the transfer of technology, the importance of which is constantly growing.

As regards the 'transfer of technology' to the developing world, the attempt through aid programmes and multi-national corporations' sales to provide the same forms and identical technologies to developing countries so that they might follow in the footsteps of the industrialized countries has, to say the least, not been totally successful. The increasing 'technological gap' and dependency which have been a part of this attempt have led to greater frustration on the part of all concerned. This is not to say that the increasing availability of modern wonders of medical immunization and pharmaceuticals, miracle grains and efficient synthetic fertilizers and the increased capabilities for finding and exploiting natural resources have not had an important impact on developing countries, but rather that the continuing injustices in the international economic system, together with the difficulties developing countries encounter in choosing and mastering their technology, have penalized them.

The contribution of the international organizations

The United Nations system, bilateral aid programmes, and donor foundations as well as NGOs, have all played a role in attempting to solve these problems over the last twenty years.

To any practical extent, the Specialized Agencies in the United Nations system all contribute in one way or another to the application of science and technology to development at national level, and to the build-up of national capacities in research and training. The IAEA is in fact the main United Nations institutional instrument for the advancement and co-ordination of research in all the basic sciences related to atomic energy. WHO likewise deals with human biology and epidemiology; WMO with climatology; FAO with agricultural sciences, ecology, biological sciences related to food and nutrition; ITU with communications technology; IMCO with marine pollution; UNIDO with the entire spectrum of engineering and technological disciplines coming under the broad umbrella of industrial research; the United Nations with research on transport, energy, mining. Finally, UNCTAD has been involved with the specific issues of technology transfer, and WIPO with those of licences. This list is not meant to be exhaustive, but to show simply the wide range of technical subjects covered on the whole by the various agencies.

UNDP, on the other hand, has come to take an increasing responsibility for financial assistance to developing countries in the development of their infrastructures for scientific and technological education. Institutional support (for which Unesco has often served as the executive agency) has included the provision of experts and specialists for short and long terms, scientific and technical equipment and essential instruments for demonstration and research, as well as fellowships to enable indigenous staff eventually to take over from the experts.

At the global policy-making level, policy matters have been vetted and a host of recommendations made by Ecosoc, most particularly on the role of science and technology in the development of nations, on arid zones research, on the World Plan of Action for the Application of Science and Technology to Development, on technology transfer and appropriate technology, on application of computer science and technology to development and on the brain drain. All these recommendations have provided the necessary policy guidance to agencies of the United Nations system on priorities, orientation and co-ordination of programmes aimed at applying science and technology to development and at setting up the necessary national infrastructure for this purpose.

A privileged field of action for Unesco

Unesco's interest in overall basic scientific research and training has been sustained from its inception. Over the intervening years other United Nations agencies have undertaken major programmes related to their specialized interests, but, Unesco is unique in the breadth and depth of its interests in science and its consequences for mankind. Thus, Unesco is responsible, within the United Nations system, for the development of fundamental programmes in scientific and technological research and training as well as for the promotion of international and regional co-operation in these fields and its role has often been stressed in United Nations documents and resolutions (e.g. World Plan of Action, etc.). More recently, an important role has evolved in connection with assistance in the development of endogenous capacities for science and technology, in particular as they relate to the adaptation and development of appropriate technologies. This role has taken greater priority in conjunction with the increased attention to science and technology policies, especially through ministerial conferences, and as the issues of development became of increasing concern to the United Nations system (cf. pages 153-64).

Unesco's relevant activities can be described under three headings, although their interdependence is obvious: (a) general programmes for research and training;

(b) special assistance to developing countries; (c) promotion of international co-operation.

In connection with research and training, strong co-operative links have been established with the appropriate scientific and professional international communities, especially in the life sciences (cell research, microbiology, brain research) and in chemistry, mathematics and computer sciences. The organization of post-graduate training courses has allowed a large number of scientists to upgrade their technical skills and become acquainted with the latest findings, techniques and equipment. More recently, emphasis has been put on the use of systems analysis and global mathematical modelling for tackling problems related to the environment, energy and natural resources. Another area of concern in this programme, is the coupling of the university and research communities so as to enable them to handle jointly the complex issues of technology transfer, industry, government and management.

Since 1968, a coherent programme involving international and regional co-operation has aimed at evolving methods for improving the education of engineers and technicians through revision of curricula, industry-education co-operation as well as continuing education. The environmental aspects of the training of engineers are now receiving increased attention and, in co-operation with UNEP, a coherent international programme has been developed in this area and it will provide useful elements for future Unesco programmes.

Concerning technical and vocational training, many developing and industrialized countries have recently carried out far-reaching reforms of their training systems to make them better suited to their socio-economic development aims. The 1962 Recommendation on Technical and Vocational Training, was revised and elaborated in co-operation with ILO, and was adopted by the General Conference in 1974. This is an international instrument of major importance, and for the years to come it will serve as a basis for the action of the Organization and as a guide for Member States who wish to improve their systems and institutions for technical and vocational education.

The programmes for developing countries originally concentrated on support for the building of institutional infrastructure and on technological research and higher education and were aimed at assisting Member States to train their own scientists, engineers and technicians for development and to strengthen their applied research capacities. These activities have been financed mainly from extra-budgetary sources.

In connection with the promotion of international co-operation, Unesco has worked closely with non-governmental professional organizations, often providing a mechanism for the establishment of new organizations as new fields or areas of concern for co-operation developed, so that today Unesco finds itself at the hub of an elaborate but potentially enormously powerful world co-operative network to assist in intellectual as well as action-oriented tasks.

Furthermore, Unesco has acted as an organizer for international and regional co-ordinated research programmes where the problems exceed national capabilities or approaches. Special mention should be made of the International Centre for Theoretical Physics (Trieste), created in 1963 by the IAEA, which from 1970 has been partly financed by Unesco and by a substantial contribution from the Italian Government. ICTP has planned extended high-level seminars, associate schemes and federation agreements, in general countering the isolation normally associated with scientists in developing countries and enabling them to make significant contributions to the world scientific community.

Unesco is also supporting the work of other centres such as that for Theoretical Mechanics (Udine) and the Centre for Heat and Mass Transfer (Belgrade). As early as 1960 Unesco recognized the significance of computer sciences in establishing the International Computation Centre in Rome which, now expanded in line with new developments in this field, is called the Intergovernmental Bureau for Informatics.

Consonant with the growing utility of regional co-operation for the sharing of resources and facilities, a number of regional centres have been established and supported for training and exchange of information, such as those in Physics, Chemistry, Biology and Mathematics in Latin America. Networks of co-operating training and research institutions and research workers are also being developed in different regions and a regional concern for curriculum improvement in science and engineering has also been initiated in Africa (CEEMA, Sciences Faculties) and Asia.

During the next few years, Unesco will give special attention to the fostering of improved research co-operative systems between individuals, institutions and governments through the establishing or strengthening of appropriate co-operation networks; the scientific and technical aspects of the process of technology transfer and of the development of alternative technologies; the promotion of scientific and technological higher education and the training of engineers and technicians with a view to increasing national capacities for endogenous scientific and technical development in developing countries; and the support of institutional development operations of direct relevance to the countries' development needs.

Co-ordination with other organizations in the United Nations system is ensured by means of the distribution of responsibilities according to the fields of application of research institutions: Unesco is responsible for research in all the basic sciences, as well as in the applied sciences (especially environmental sciences) and engineering sciences, while the other United Nations agencies take care of mission-oriented research institutions in technical areas of the various application sectors (e.g. agriculture, medicine, industry, communications, transport, atomic energy applications, etc.).

The Unesco programme is further based on the principle that maximum use has to be made of the country's own resources, first and foremost its human resources. Emphasis is therefore laid on upgrading the qualifications of the country's manpower, and in so doing, to resort as far as possible to training institutions within the country, or otherwise within the region.

Many countries with a small scientific and technological potential cannot afford significant research or training programmes in all fields of science and technology relevant to their development needs. Unesco advocates the pooling of resources on a regional or sub-regional basis, and relies on international and regional centres for the training of national manpower.

A key factor in development: energy

Since energy is required for any kind of material change, physical or biological, it is essential to the material progress of the world. Together with knowledge (more precisely, information) it is one of the fundamental ingredients in the development of societies. The harnessing of energy in all its forms (fossil, hydro, solar, etc.) has considerably affected the nature of civilizations, not the least our own industrial civilizations, and the world of tomorrow will be shaped irreversibly by the particular energy systems used (including sources, and production and distribution schemes).

Per capita energy consumption rates can vary between one and a thousand

The world-wide trend in energy consumption shows a constant increase, both overall and on a per capita basis, for which growth rates are currently of the order of 5 per cent and 2½ per cent respectively. There are however large regional differences in the level of energy requirements and the rates of growth. For instance, energy consumption per capita in 1973 was 11,888 kilograms (coal equivalent) in North America, but only 516 in Asia (excepting the Middle East) and 377 in Africa. When one considers consumption levels in specific countries, the differences appear even greater. In most of the least developing countries, the level of per capita energy consumption is in the order of tens of kilograms (coal equivalent), i.e. 11 in Burundi, 12 in Upper Volta, 13 in Yemen, 21 in Chad, etc. while in advanced industrial countries, it is in the order of thousands, e.g. 6,694 in Czechoslovakia and 11,237 in Canada. In those societies where energy consumption is the highest, the per capita consumption rate is around 1,000 times that of the lowest consumers.

The problem of the availability of energy resources on a world-wide scale did not really arise until the 1950s, when long-term development plans began to point to the possibility of a shortage. Later inventories of resources potentially available to mankind showed however that in the long range, the limiting factor on energy production and utilization would not be so much the availability of resources as the pressure on the environment.

The 1973 oil crisis: world interdependence in the field of energy

The 1973 oil crisis marked the end of an era during which the cost of energy was relatively small; it showed to what extent there were differences in national situations in respect of energy, but it also revealed, through the magnitude of its effects on the world economy and financial resources, the extent to which countries were interdependent in the energy field and the common problems which it is important to solve. A large number of non-petroleum-producing countries suddenly found themselves in a situation of shortage; one of the immediate consequences of the crisis was a vigorous relaunching of scientific and technological research for the purpose of breaking free from their dependence on a particular source of energy which had become too costly. At the same time, the fragility of industrial and agricultural structures of production based upon the utilization of insufficiently diversified energy resources was recognized, not only at national level, but also at regional and world level.

Consequently, a complex set of scientific and technological problems calling for a multidisciplinary approach was given leading importance in the science policies of all the industrialized countries as well as those in the process of industrialization: the exploration and evaluation of fossil sources of energy—coal, natural gases, tars; the transformation of these resources by pollution-free processes and their utilization by means of conversion—e.g. the gasification of coal; study of the entire energy cycle—production, conversion, storage and transportation—for each of them as a prerequisite to their effective utilization; the constitution of genuine 'energy systems' founded on a wide range of energy sources; and lastly, the interaction of these systems with the economy and the environment, particularly in the case of nuclear energy.

By and large, the placing of limits on energy consumption emerged as an important element in any long-term energy policy, even if this entailed reviewing industrial production systems and undertaking new research on energy-saving processes. Thus, the crisis led not only to a global reconsideration of the future development of the planet's energy resources, but also to the definition of new R & D objectives of interest to the whole of the world community.

The developing countries: energy resources, industrialization, agricultural economy

For the developing countries, some of the technological problems by which they are confronted are of the same nature as those met with by the industrialized countries. The ongoing survey of fossil fuel resources must be continued in the light of the new situation resulting from the economic interest attaching to resources that have hitherto been neglected, such as oil shales or low-grade coals, which are fairly plentiful in the earth's crust (cf. Chapter 7, pages 267-9). There is also a need to develop technologies with a view to using these resources for industrialization purposes, to develop economic means of transporting energy over long distances and to envisage the possibility of using nuclear energy, taking into account not only the effects and cost of the different technologies, but also the relationship between energy and the structure of production systems and, more generally, of society itself. In these areas, the developing countries have to turn technologies developed by the industrialized countries to account in the framework of strategies by means of which they can gradually acquire a certain measure of independence in respect of energy, without which there can be no economic independence. They should give priority attention to working out these strategies, basing them on thorough knowledge of the possibilities afforded by the different processes of energy production and on their having the necessary capability to use these processes in their particular economic and social circumstances. In the short term, the limited scientific capability of some of these countries probably does not not allow them to create *ab initio* new technologies for all the forms of energy which may be of interest to them; however, regional or subregional co-operation among countries with common economic interests and comparable resources may provide them with a means of tackling with a good chance of success the improvement and adaptation—which may consist in a simplification—of some of the most important technologies.

However, in the developing countries with predominantly agricultural economies, the energy crisis, which led to a dramatic increase in poverty, highlighted particular energy problems. For it is essential for their development that the energy requirements of rural areas be met since any increase in agricultural production calls for an increase in the amount of energy available, be it a question of simple agricultural practices such as irrigation, the modernization of farming through the use of machines or fertilizers, or lastly the transportation of produce for marketing. The same is true where raising the rural population's standard of living is concerned. The drop in food production which followed the oil crisis in certain developing countries is a consequence of these countries' technological dependence as regards the energy used in rural areas, the cost price of oil products having become prohibitive. New technological solutions must be found for the production and distribution of energy in these areas and, in general, in areas with scant resources.

Unconventional and non-polluting energy sources

Unconventional sources of energy, such as solar energy, geothermal energy and wind power, are particularly well fitted for the local and limited use which would be dictated by the requirements of these regions. They do not have the disadvantage of requiring substantial investments or complex mechanized and automated equipment. Over the last decade, outstanding advances have been made in studying them. Processes and appliances have been developed that can be used for pumping irrigation water, for refrigeration or to meet the power requirements of small agricultural communities. However, their large-scale utilization in practice still requires far-ranging study and the combined efforts of many specialists. For solar energy, a number of widely differing questions remain to be settled, involving precise knowledge of climatic factors governing isolation, exact determination of required network capacity and density, examination of the measures to be taken to ensure local participation in installation and maintenance, etc. In most cases the time has not yet come for making the final choice of processes and equipment, based on studies relating to the profitability of manufacture and utilization, which depend on industrial policy. The situation is comparable with regard to most other unconventional energy sources. It is indispensable that wide-ranging and concerted research programmes be carried out.

In 1972 the General Conference of Unesco decided that international co-operation should be fostered in selected fields where breakthroughs in research would make it possible to develop pollution-free sources of energy. The Unesco Secretariat started preparatory activities through contacts with non-governmental organizations working in the energy field, i.e. the World Energy Conference, the International Centre for Heat and Mass Transfer, the International Solar Energy Society. These organizations visualized the role of Unesco as a promoter of world-wide scientific and educational activities related to fundamental energy problems, and they concurred with the general orientations of the programme towards the study of future energy sources, such as nuclear fission and fusion, solar and geothermal energy and ocean tides and thermal gradients.

In 1973-74 Unesco co-sponsored, and participated in, the international scientific congress 'The Sun in the Service of Mankind' and several scientific seminars and summer schools in the field of heat and mass transfer. A feasibility study was undertaken on the promotion of Asian regional research programmes in the field of heat and mass transfer with application to solar energy and wind power. A symposium on solar energy was held in 1976 in co-operation with the World Meteorological Organization. This symposium was devoted to discussing the co-ordination of the work of scientific organizations in Member States on such aspects as comparable radiation data, direct radiation on other than horizontal surfaces, the influence of the spectral composition of solar rays and solar energy applications in various regions of the world.

An international forum on fundamental scientific and technological energy problems took place from 8 to 12 December 1975 at Unesco Headquarters in Paris. The forum, through discussion based on the latest and best-reputed predictions on growth in energy consumption, potential of global non-renewable energy resources and predictions on the possibility of matching up energy resources with consumption, drew up a list of the most important scientific and technological problems crucial to energy development and requiring international co-operation for their solution. Furthermore, this forum re-examined the general area where United Nations organizations might concentrate their efforts.

Interest in world energy problems has been shown in one way or another and to varying extent, by various institutions in the United Nations system—more particularly the International Atomic Energy Agency, the United Nations Institute for Training and Research, the Food and Agriculture Organization of the United Nations, the United Nations Secretariat and Regional Economic Commissions and Unesco.

The United Nations Secretariat, through its Department of Economic and Social Affairs and its Regional Economic Commissions, has long been involved in many aspects of energy, research, from exploration to planning, with regard, among others, to geothermal energy. The Food and Agriculture Organization of the United Nations (FAO) has become active in work on use of agricultural by-products, wood fuel and animal manure. The United Nations Industrial Development Organization (UNIDO) has been studying the industrial aspects of energy utilization, the manufacture of equipment for generating and using energy. The United Nations Conference on Trade and Development (UNCTAD) has been dealing with foreign trade including energy products as well as the shipment of energy, the International Labour Organization (ILO) with employment and safety in coal mines and oil fields, the World Meteorological Organization (WMO) with wind and solar energy and the International Bank for Reconstruction and Development (IBRD), which in the past was mainly concerned with the financing of energy investments, has broadened its activities to a considerable extent, including studies on the financial effect of oil price fluctuations. The United Nations Development Programme (UNDP) has continued to finance activities relating to energy in accordance with priorities established in co-operation with its Resident Representatives in each individual country.

The orderly development of energy resources: national policies, international co-ordination

The orderly development of energy resources over the coming decades to meet the needs of all countries, and to reduce the imbalance between poor and rich countries energy-wise, will require a global approach and a closely co-ordinated action on the part of international organizations, among which the United Nations system should play a major role in bringing individual countries or groups of countries to harmonize their policies. These policies need to be future-oriented, and recognize the importance of energy research and development in support of bold and unconventional approaches needed to alter the present predicament. In this context, Unesco can best contribute to an overall effort in focusing its action on stimulating countries to formulate energy R & D policies and on arranging for international co-operation in critical fields of energy R & D.

The implementation of energy R & D policies at national level will rest on upgrading capabilities in research and training in this field, and on developing the institutional infrastructure, along the same principles as those applied in the development of the national scientific and technological potential.

As concerns international co-operation, two main lines of action will be pursued. First, action will be taken to promote programmes of research and training aimed at studying fundamental scientific and technological problems related to energy, or advancing the state of practical knowledge. Secondly, regional co-operation will be promoted among countries having similar energy resources problems, from the economic and environmental points of view, for the pooling of their resources in applying and adapting existing technologies to their own context.

A feasibility study will be undertaken on the creation of an International Energy Institute within the United Nations system, which would be responsible for assisting developing countries in research and exploration in the field of energy resources.

At the crossroads of science and technology: informatics

The place occupied in the world today by informatics is the result of a series of factors which, since the 1960s, have given the then nascent computer industry, and processes in which these new machines are used, an ever-growing economic and even social importance. Of these factors, science and technology have played a very great role, for the development of informatics has benefited from the convergent efforts of a large number of disciplines; but their role is far from being exclusive. If there is a field in which the interactions between the most abstract type of basic science, the most advanced technological inventions and applications, industrial potential and the economic and social conditions pertaining to the organization of production are at once the most manifest and the most complex, it is undoubtedly that of computer science.

The computer: a new potentate

Now the increase in the number of computers, in their capabilities and their fields of application, the economic concentration which results in their manufacture being placed in the hands of very few producers, in very few countries, and lastly the fact that other essential tools of production are increasingly dependent on computer science, pose problems which affect the developed and developing nations alike.

In 1968, the United Nations General Assembly recognized the importance of the phenomenon and called for the preparation of a comprehensive report on the problem. In 1974 it decided 'that the Committee on Science and Technology for Development shall act as a focal point for activities concerning the application of computer science and technology for the benefit of the development of all countries and particularly that of the developing countries, in view of their specific problems, and that, to assist it in this work, it should rely principally on the expert services provided by an existing United Nations body or bodies, such as the United Nations Educational, Scientific and Cultural Organization or the Advisory Committee on the Application of Science and Technology to Development, or by other competent intergovernmental organizations, such as the Intergovernmental Bureau for Informatics'.

To what extent can policies concerning science and technology and their applications on the one hand, and the development of scientific and technological capabilities and infrastructures on the other, play a role in the future evolution of the world situation in respect of computer science? It is necessary to tackle these questions both from the angle of research and development on, and the production of, hardware, software and systems and from that of the utilization of computer science for the socio-economic development of the developing countries.

An almost total monopoly

With regard to the first of these aspects, a first remark needs to be made: at present 90 per cent of the total turnover of the data processing industry (by virtue of which this industry is the third major industry in the world) is in the hands of a small number of multinational corporations, one of which accounts by itself for two-thirds of the world markets. It is a fact that, as a whole, the developing countries are having to abandon for the time being all idea of playing any role, even a small one, in the production of computers; a number of developed countries are themselves having to make do with operating under licences. Many countries consequently have no choice but to accept, passively, the new hardware distributed by the manufacturers and to abandon any attempt to control the changes likely to be produced, in the economic, social and cultural context peculiar to them, by the specific directions for the use of this hardware. It is obvious that, if a new world order is to be established, steps should be taken to prevent this leading to a one-sided predominance about which nothing could be done.

In these circumstances, scientific and technological research, which constitutes the basis for all new developments in respect of both software and hardware, is principally geared to the interests of the few manufacturers and it is a direct result of this that generations of increasingly sophisticated computers have succeeded each other. Gradually, however, the tendency towards the hypertrophy and increasing complexity of such equipment has ceased to appear ineluctable (in consequence, it may be said, of 'technological spin-offs' from advances achieved in connection with other areas of advanced research, space research in particular). The equipment has become diversified. It is now recognized that mini-computers and increasingly 'intelligent' (to use the accepted term) peripheral units could meet the needs of countries in certain regions as well if not better. Thus the problem of the future evolution of hardware has been raised, but this is not so much a question of science policy as of industrial policy, a field in which an international agency such as UNIDO—to mention only intergovernmental organizations—is particularly competent.

Nevertheless, all countries, provided they are sufficiently equipped scientifically, can participate in the development of software and services. For such development does not require substantial investments; it is enough for there to be suitably qualified personnel as well as a certain capacity for organization. As the expansion of software and services may in many circumstances hamper the expansion of informatics as a whole, mastery of this field may also influence future developments throughout this sector in the interest of the world community.

Informatics in the lives of nations

It is also necessary that the political, economic and social role played by informatics in the lives of nations should be fully understood by the decision-making bodies of the various countries concerned. Unesco was the first to endeavour to foster this awareness by assisting in the establishment in 1960 of the ICC (International Computation Centre) which became the Intergovernmental Bureau for Informatics (IBI). In particular, the IBI makes representations to government officials in various regions to convince them of the need for an overall and precise view of the implications of informatics. It has contributed to its being accepted that informatics should constitute one of the principal elements in national science and technology policies. Moreover, certain developing countries in Africa and South America have already established national machinery for supervising the introduction of computer science on their territories and have embarked upon studies relating to software and services.

From the point of view of the utilization of computer science for the socio-economic development of the developing countries—which is the second element to be considered in the context of the problem as a whole—it can be stated that the dissemination of computer science is a prerequisite for the development process. In the first place, it constitutes an essential tool for economic and social planning, making it possible to process a large number of data, construct models and keep track of the implementation of programmes and projects. In the second place, it provides a means of improving the conditions pertaining to the management of enterprises and administrations of all kinds in countries where the very lack of trained personnel and the absence of sufficient experience in respect of organization often stand in the way of modernization. Lastly, it considerably increases the developing countries' chances of successfully moulding systems of production which, while helping them to meet their own needs, also enable them to compete on world markets. It is therefore in the greatest interest of the developing countries to accord a growing place in their science and technology policies to computer science, both to protect their economies against outside domination and to place in the service of their development objectives an instrument of unparalleled effectiveness.

In order for there to be rapid progress in computer science in these countries, there must be a substantial increase in the number and qualifications of the relevant personnel. In contradistinction to other branches of modern science, what is involved is not merely establishing the necessary education programmes and making available to universities computers adapted to real needs, but also familiarizing all students with their use since they are proving to be necessary in virtually all branches of science, technology and economics. In the field of general education, a certain measure of success has already been obtained in providing secondary-school pupils with a grounding in the utilization of the relevant scientific concepts concerning computers. As for computer techniques, they are well known and disseminating them presents no major problems: in this connection, it is not, by nature, more difficult to train this category of staff than staff in other specialized disciplines. However, computer science is a field which is very rapidly changing, and the intensive exchange of knowledge and experience among specialists is indispensable in order to guard against the premature obsolescence of related education programmes. The IFIP (International Federation for Information Processing) is concerned with the professional aspects of computer science, while UNISIST, a world science information programme, is according a growing place to it (cf. Chapter 10, pages 355 ff.).

The international scientific community has, for its part, to consider also two major problems of a general character. The first concerns the implications of computer science for development. There is not yet nearly enough knowledge concerning the processes whereby informatics may be integrated into societies which are ill-prepared to receive it on account of their socio-economic and cultural characteristics. There is a need for studies drawing on the social sciences in regard to both general aspects and particular cases, in order for the developing countries to be able, with knowledge of what is involved, to reach a decision concerning the transfer of this particular technology and its adaptation to very different circumstances from those in which it saw the day. The second concerns the basic principles of informatics research, i.e. those on which the construction of new and increasingly specialized or diversified hardware will be grounded, or which will lead to existing hardware being used for entirely new purposes. Informatics is at present one of the key areas of science and, as such, one in which international co-operation may make it possible both to make better use of acquired knowledge for the good of mankind and to slant new research towards fields from which the majority of men can benefit.

The computer in the service of regional and national objectives

To counteract the present disparity between countries where informatics is concerned —a disparity which should not be measured solely by the number of computers possessed by each country, but also by a country's ability to use informatics for the attainment of its national objectives—it is important that, at government level, there be developed greater awareness of the concrete implications of computer science. Such awareness is a prerequisite for priorities and strategies to be the subject of progressively more precise national policies and concerted efforts at regional and world level. Unesco, in conjunction with the Intergovernmental Bureau for Informatics, will therefore continue to provide in these spheres the stimulation and encouragement which characterized its action at the meetings held at regional level in 1975 and 1976.

With regard to scientific and technological research, carried on in its countless facets by a multiplicity of institutions of every size, distributed through all countries of the world, selectivity is highly desirable in regard to the areas on which international co-operation should be focused. It is important to concentrate particularly on new fields of basic research which may, in the long run, open up entirely novel vistas for the development of computer science. On account of the interdisciplinary character of such research, Unesco's action in this direction will be carried out through specialized scientific institutions, but also through the scientific community in general.

The future development of the informatics infrastructure in the developing countries will obviously hinge on the training of teachers and research workers. The general thrust of this training, the different levels at which it should be dispensed and the occupational requirements for which it should cater pose problems no less important than that of its content. Regional co-operation seems to provide the best means whereby the different countries may define their own objectives, in the light of an examination of common problems.

The organization of training facilities could also be to a large extent regional. However, one should not underestimate the fact that a student who wishes to train for a career in informatics—be it for research in the field of software, development applications or the use of computers in management—must have prior scientific training which is not of a fairly high level but which also presents certain particular features. It is therefore important that this be taken into account in the establishment of science education programmes on the one hand—e.g. in mathematics—and in that of research and education infrastructures on the other. It is consequently important that the development of computer science be integrated in policies relating to the development of national scientific and technological potential.

Towards a better understanding of the nature and scope of science and technology

Few of the peoples of the world are so isolated as to be beyond the range of the increasingly numerous and radical changes which are occurring nearly everywhere today. A large part of such changes have their roots in science and technology, resulting either from a quantitative expansion of the organized body of knowledge or from its application to the solution of practical problems through creative decision-making efforts.

Lack of knowledge of the benefits and hazards of science

In spite of the pervasive influence of science and technology, their respective natures and roles are little understood by the average citizen, even in countries with high literacy rates and where the majority of students complete secondary education. This lack of understanding has very practical consequences inasmuch as it is difficult for a society and a culture to harness science and technology for national development if they do not form an integral part of the culture they are intended to serve, and if the public does not understand both the potential benefits and hazards involved. But there are also behavioural and social consequences. When the members of a society feel caught up in a frightening torrent of change which they believe to be not only uncontrollable but even incomprehensible, the conditions exist for seeking recourse through various forms of irrational behaviour. Consequently, if broad consensus exists at the international, national, and personal levels in respect to the promotion of development and peace, few areas are more deserving of priority than efforts to help to develop a world-wide understanding of the nature of science and technology and of the roles they play in the modern world.

The need for thoroughgoing reform of curricula and methods

Certain problems confront these efforts within the formal education system. Those of a structural nature, which of necessity affect the whole system of science and technology education, have already been mentioned in the introduction above. There are, in addition, others of a more pedagogical nature.

These problems relate to both contents and methods which, in the case of scientific education, are extremely closely linked. The aim of such education, indeed, is not only to impart knowledge as such, but also to teach about the use of concepts and promote powers of observation, analysis and reasoning; and the methods used are themselves such as to develop the student's abilities. In former days, too much memory-work was used in the teaching of the natural sciences and this in itself, since it called for the repetition of verbal formulae without any exercise of the critical faculty, prevented development of the capacity for observation and concrete analysis essential in scientific work.

The reasons why contents and methods are still in many cases unsatisfactory are manifold. Some of them are purely material: in many of the poorer developing countries, teaching materials and aids are in short supply, out of date or not kept in proper repair. Others relate more to the terms in which the objectives of scientific education are defined and the curricula by means of which it is hoped these objectives can be attained. As long as elementary scientific education was based exclusively on the use of textbooks, which were inevitably specialized, it tended to take forms reflecting a transient state of knowledge, a particular stage in the development of education theory and, above all, the nature of the environment—usually that of certain industrialized countries—where it was elaborated. Despite the considerable progress made during the past decade, the education of today is still to some extent tradition-bound. In many developing countries, science is still taught by people without specialized training or belonging to generations not versed in modern teaching methods. The methods used in scientific education for continuous assessment, examinations and the evaluation of school performance for purposes of vocational guidance also require considerable improvement.

What is needed, in many countries, is a thoroughgoing reform of curricula and methods. This should usually be accompanied by an increase in the time devoted to science and technology in primary and secondary schools and a complete overhaul of learning sequences, so that the pupil is led to acquire progressively fuller knowledge and understanding, as a basis for university specialization in some particular branch of science or technology. Increasing importance should be attached to integrated scientific education, designed to train alert minds, capable of grasping the full complexity of the problems.

Experience has proved that no educational reform can be successful unless there is broad teacher participation in planning it or if it fails to take into account certain regional characteristics. The elaboration of new objectives and curricula for science teaching is therefore a major undertaking comprising a diversity of operations impinging on the educational system of each country concerned.

Greater use of the mass media in non-formal education

As regards non-formal education, an enormous gulf exists between the level of activity that is needed and that which is actually being undertaken in any deliberate way. This can be appreciated by the extremely limited use made of mass media, the poor quality of the little that is done in this matter, the scarcity of reading materials for young people and adults, the little support given to science and technology clubs as a means of promoting interest in these fields. Little of what is done is publicized, rare are the efforts designed as measurable learning experiences, i.e., in terms of objectives to be achieved, methodologies and materials to be employed, means of assessing the results achieved, etc. In short, the present world situation in this area of non-formal education is largely one of inadequate and ill-designed activities.

The scientific education of the general public, which does not involve the same degree of active participation on its part as non-formal education properly speaking, has an important role to play in the dissemination of general scientific culture. The popular press in most developed countries makes a valuable contribution by publishing regular science columns commenting on and explaining, in non-technical language, current events in the field of science and technology; and scientific journalists or columnists are now an accepted category of information personnel. The fact remains that along with scientific material, the mass media put out messages which are completely at variance with the rational character of science, so that scientists feel increasingly that it behoves them to help to give the general public information about the nature and scope of scientific discoveries and the explanations science offers for phenomena all too commonly regarded as mysterious. As regards those countries whose information networks are still inadequate, a vast amount needs to be done to ensure that, as they develop, these networks will promote the dissemination of elementary scientific and technical information appropriate to the social and cultural milieu. This is essential if the developing countries' science policies are to succed.

A recovery which must be sustained

Some of the problems identified above have been the target of various types and levels of actions undertaken by Member States, by Unesco and other United Nations Specialized Agencies, and by interested non-governmental organizations. As concerns school programmes in science education, reforms have been made in school science programmes in response to the need to include the process of scientific inquiry in science courses and to modernize their content so as to reflect the rapid advances in modern scientific knowledge. The initiators adopted a completely new strategy in the form of what came to be known as science curriculum projects.

These projects placed much emphasis on organizing course content around important unifying concepts revealed through a process of inquiry and investigation; in addition, new materials were developed which were designed to give students the opportunity to 'learn by doing', an approach considered to be a fundamental component of all scientific inquiry. The first science curriculum projects were concerned with mathematics, physics, chemistry and biology, at the upper level of secondary education. They were subsequently extended to both the primary and the tertiary levels, as well as to other forms of secondary-level education. More recently, this expansion has taken in various aspects of non-formal education.

Unesco was involved with some of the pioneering efforts to improve science education in developing countries. In 1963, it began a series of pilot projects in the basic science disciplines at the secondary level, which were intended to give teams of selected individuals from developing countries opportunities to design innovative approaches to science education which would be appropriate to the conditions into which they would be introduced. Subsequent projects were started aimed at the primary and lower secondary levels. A flexible approach is now being used by which support can be given both to local groups which are designing and testing new content, methods, and materials, and to national and regional institutions which are already at the stage of implementing tested innovations.

Unesco has co-operated with various organizations (international and regional; inter- and non-governmental), and especially with the education commissions of the various international scientific unions, in convening international and regional meetings and workshops and in preparing various publications, among which is the series 'Teaching of the Basic Sciences' and the well-known *Source Book for Science Teaching*. Assistance has also been obtained from various multilateral and bilateral funding agencies in promoting educational reform efforts which have included science education.

Some Member States have developed a polytechnical component of general education which is intended to help the learner understand and cope with the man-made world, just as the science component helps him understand the world of nature. This approach has two purposes: to orient general education to prepare pupils better for their working life, and to introduce the fundamentals of applied technology for subsequent production purposes.

Extending technological education, in the face of strong prejudice

A major obstacle to the extension of technology education in many developing countries has been the resistance on the part of pupils and their parents to courses in manual and technical work which are considered inferior to more academic studies. Education for girls in this field has also lagged behind that available to boys in many countries. Some Member States are now overcoming this resistance, partly by carefully prepared campaigns through the mass media leading to legislation in which technology education has become compulsory.

Unesco's action in this sphere has consisted in organizing sub-regional meetings and undertaking case studies on technology in general education. Furthermore, under a programme initially labelled 'integrated *science* teaching', several national groups have been formed which are adopting also a 'technological' approach.

Promoting out-of-school activities

Efforts outside the context of the formal education system to promote science and technology are scattered. In some Member States, there are national bodies whose activities clearly constitute a type of non-formal education. They include museums of science and technology, science clubs for youths and adults, science fairs and Olympiads for youths, popular science journals, special radio and television programmes, articles in daily or weekly news publications, travelling exhibits. In many countries, however, no national policy has been formulated.

Unesco, for its part, has encouraged Member States to establish their own national policies and infrastructures for public education and information in science and technology, and to assisting in the creation and functioning of the International Co-ordinating Committee for the Presentation of Science and the Development of Out-of-School Scientific Activities (ICC). The ICC and its affiliated national organizations undertake various activities, including regional science fairs, training courses for national leaders of out-of-school activities for science and technology, and the publication in four languages of an international journal—*Out-of-School Scientific and Technical Education*. Unesco itself has published various reports and bibliographies on out-of-school science activities. It has also organized a regional seminar for leaders of youth science activities in Asia and published a handbook on the subject for use in Latin America.

Unesco's role as a catalyst

Unesco's overall policy is to promote the qualitative improvement, modernization and adaptation to local environmental conditions of science and technology education. Its role is that of a catalyst. It will seek to facilitate the acquisition, storage, retrieval, analysis and dissemination of ideas and information on science and technology education, through the establishment of networks for this purpose, through meetings and the publication of teaching materials. It will promote studies and educational research through competent local groups and through other organizations, particularly non-governmental organizations; assist national groups with a view to promoting innovation and experimentation and provide study grants to nationals from developing countries to enable them to become familiar with scientific and technological methods.

5 Educational action

While there can be no question of considering education in isolation from science, technology, culture and information, as a social practice that may involve all the members of society in one way or another, education has its own characteristics which call for specific forms and actions, the establishment and development of special structures and institutions, the constant improvement and renewal of its content, methods and forms, the enrichment and updating of its concepts, and indeed, the elaboration of new concepts.

Education and society

While education is determined by society, it none the less exerts a great influence itself on the way in which society evolves. The lines of force and the scope of that influence depend upon the role which a given society attributes to education, on the percentage of the population which enjoys its benefits, and on its objectives, content and methods.

The post-war period in most countries was marked by a very high rate of growth in enrolments in the various levels, types and forms of education. Some countries carried out reforms—often major ones—of their education systems. In a good many Member States, the competent authorities and public opinion are coming out more and more strongly in favour of thoroughgoing changes in their education systems because they consider that those systems do not correspond to modern conditions or requirements, or meet their development needs. Member States are thus concerned both to pursue, or even accelerate, the expansion that has already been begun, and to emphasize a much-needed qualitative reform. With this in view, Unesco has undertaken to clarify the concept of lifelong education, the generalization of which seems to be one of the essential prerequisites to ensuring that education is suited to the modern requirements of social progress. The clarification of this concept, its enrichment on the basis of the experience of Member States, and the promotion of its application constitute a task of paramount importance for the Organization in the field of education.

This task embraces the various fields of policy, structures, methods and training of staff personnel in education, both formal and non-formal, at all levels, and it affects Unesco's entire programme. That programme thus aims to satisfy the desire of Member States that the international community should contribute to a genuine democratization of education. Democratization not only means providing equal opportunity and treatment in education, but also entails qualitative changes —often very radical ones—in the lines of emphasis and functioning of existing systems. In many cases it takes full effect only if it is carried out within the context of major social and economic changes.

Education and development

These objectives are part of the current of ideas about education which relate it closely to development. It is evident that a great deal of effort still needs to be made before democratic, lifelong education becomes a reality in all countries. Particularly in the developing countries, a high proportion of the population still do not have the basic minimum of knowledge, skills and culture, and it has been observed that very often education does not seem to fulfil all the hopes that were placed in it during previous decades as a factor of development and an instrument of social, cultural and ethical progress. Speaking generally, it is becoming obvious that educational activities should, in a more clear-cut and more innovative way, make for social advancement through better use of a community's own human and natural resources, and foster the fullest development of all members of the community without exception.

This being the case, the Organization's main lines of action in the field of education are laid down within the context of the two-way relationship between society and education, taking into account the polyvalent, polymorphous and integrated character of the latter: education is linked with the national setting, it is designed with a view to the objectives particular to each society and sets out to develop a creative spirit that will enable its citizens to acquire the will to contribute to the development of that society and the means of doing so.

An essential role is also played by activities which have a direct impact on the national educational situations and which are aimed at strengthening the ability of Member States to make a critical study of their own education systems with a view to formulating an appropriate education policy.

The renewal of education in keeping with the aspirations of individuals and the needs of development in all its forms indeed implies first of all a fundamental task, namely the definition of national education policies that are sufficiently precise to be able to help in the making of decisions and the allocation of funds.

Work on all fronts, in the context of lifelong education

A growing number of States are giving priority to educational planning and the definition of comprehensive strategies which embrace all types and levels of education, in their quantitative and qualitative aspects, and integrate the educational system with other systems of economic, social and cultural objectives. In many cases, such strategies may imply options affecting education at the first and second levels as well as higher and adult education, together with all aspects of informal education.

Higher education is being increasingly required to play a central role in these strategies. Indeed, it is expanding everywhere, and needs to be democratized, as well as renewed, diversified and integrated into society, putting aside any élitist conceptions. Co-operation is being intensified at the higher education level, particularly between institutions and also on a regional scale. The social as well as geographical mobility of people engaged in post-secondary education also deserves particular attention because it is becoming increasingly widespread, and the Organization has begun long-term action in this regard.

The organization of life-long education should also link up with the education provided for adults (objectives, structures, content and methods). The extension of adult education constitutes one of the characteristic problems of education in the contemporary world and should take account of the growing body of knowledge and its rapid obsolescence, the need for more and more frequent occupational updating, the development of the media, and the need to make use of leisure time. It should also remain as flexible as necessary in its various approaches and endeavours, and thus play an innovating role for the entire education system.

In its efforts to promote the formulation of educational policies, which is of course the sovereign privilege of each State, the Organization has to promote national activities concerned with devising a type of education that will effectively contribute to development from within as well as to the improvement of methods and techniques used in the planning, administration and management of education systems.

Qualitative aspects

In these efforts, Member States of the Organization find that they have to devote increasing attention to the qualitative aspects of educational development, particularly all the factors relating to structures, content and methods. Lifelong education is an ongoing process which should ensure the genuine democratization of formal and non-formal education. Within this context there appears to be an increasing need in Member States to define, within the education system, structures that are complete, coherent and at the same time flexible and diversified, structures which allow the educational process to be adapted to all the ages of man and to all the objectives of social, economic and cultural development. There is likewise a noticeable trend in a number of countries towards making greater efforts to supplement the formal system with educational activities geared to specific objectives such as community education, literacy training, refresher courses, etc.

Unesco has made a considerable contribution to the elaboration of the concept of life-long education and will continue to collaborate in this regard with other international organizations and primarily those of the United Nations system. The International Conference on Education, the biennial meetings of which are organized by the International Bureau of Education, likewise provides an opportunity to develop this concept as it relates to the structures and content of education, taking into account economic, scientific, technological and cultural changes. In this connection, the increasingly close relationship between so-called general education and technical education constitutes an important subject for consideration and experimentation in the international community. Initial and in-service vocational training is not a component to be isolated from other objectives of education; it must be related to the improvement of general education, and cultural, economic and political education because of the many-sided, interrelated nature of the entire educational process.

Changes in content should be closely associated with the modification of methods and means. The interdisciplinary approach and the new possibilities opened up by educational technology and the mass media make a renewed effort at research and experimentation mandatory. Unesco should increase its contribution to that effort so that appropriate educational technologies may be developed on an international scale with a view to a more rational and more systematic use of human and technical resources that will make countries technologically independent and self-sufficient.

Lastly, the renewal of educational systems calls for the training of full-time or part-time staff engaged in research and experimentation and in education itself. Educators are the principal agents of reform and innovation, and various social and cultural factors, as well as changes in content and methods, help to bring about profound changes in the conditions under which teachers exercise their profession. The educator should be increasingly alert to the life of the community around him and to individual and collective aspirations. Furthermore, quantitative problems of a scale which has still not been properly measured are and will continue to be encountered in the developing countries, whose needs for teaching staff will be considerable in the forthcoming decades. Lastly, representatives of other professions and other members of the community are participating, or should participate, along with teachers, in the educational process. These needs and changes necessitate a renewal of the curricula and methods used in training all these teachers and educationists.

A major responsibility for Unesco

Thus, in the field of education, Unesco has a major responsibility to pursue the various objectives thrust upon it by life-long education. Those objectives are closely interrelated and the Organization must encourage pursuit of them within the international community, as it has already done, especially by convening regional conferences of

Ministers of Education, the International Conferences on Education of the IBE, meetings of the senior education officials of the twenty-five least developed countries, the International Commission on the Development of Education, and also by means of its publications and international exchanges of experience.

The 1977-82 period should constitute a new stage in this effort, making it possible to offer Member States a large-scale contribution to the progress of education in its relations with the knowledge, work and systems of values which form the warp and woof of societies. This programme also sets out to confirm the importance of education in solving problems related to the development of man and society and the balance between man and nature. More than ever before, education is in a dialectical relationship with the factors affecting the harmonious economic, social and cultural future of each individual and each nation, and it is in this spirit that the various sections in this chapter have been conceived.

Educational policies and planning

Educational policies and strategies in the world today are strongly influenced by the scientific technological revolution and by the fact that the majority of countries throughout the world are rejecting 'élitist' education systems in favour of those designed to provide greater social justice. The emergence of a programme of action for the New International Economic Order adds another dimension to educational development; awareness that beyond the problems confronting States are those confronting mankind as a whole, and that education must contribute to finding and applying the solutions.

The demands of democratization

As a result, the major problem for educational policy-makers is, without abandoning the need for expansion of education, thoroughly to reappraise its conceptual underpinning, its objectives, structures and priorities. The renewal of educational systems is increasingly seen as a condition which is essential to both democratization of education and its relevance to social, economic and cultural requirements of societies.

Educational policies are obviously a sovereign right of each country. At the same time, there is a growing tendency to consider educational policy as a major factor in achieving a synthesis of different cultural traditions with modern scientific discoveries as well as in ensuring the democratization of education and in improving its internal and external efficiency. To be effective, then, educational policy and strategies must ensure a constant interaction between the educational process and the socio-economic environment in which it occurs, making adjustments as and where appropriate.

As part of the evolution of the concept of educational policy, there is also a noticeable trend towards the broadening of its content. Educational policies tend to deal not only with minor improvements in existing systems, but with broadening the field of educational action. Educational systems are increasingly becoming systems of life-long education containing formal and non-formal, in-school and out-of-school elements, which are mutually complementary.

A new perspective—learning is no longer confined to the school

In this new perspective, the formal school is no longer the sole repository of knowledge: resources, personnel and learning content are increasingly being drawn from the entire social matrix. In particular, the production activities of a society can become important sources of education.

Educational policy implies making fundamental choices; it cannot however be limited to the proclamation of a few overall guiding principles. Rather it must seek to articulate specific social, economic and cultural goals through educational objectives. Educational policy thus serves as the framework of action for the entire spectrum of education both formal and non-formal: reforms and innovations in structures, curricula, methods; literacy campaigns; environmental education, etc.

Educational planning is the process of transcribing policy goals into operational strategies and targets on the basis of a careful diagnosis of the existing educational system; together with educational administration and management, concerned with the mechanisms in achieving those targets (see pages 203-7, below), it is a tool for implementing educational policy.

As educational policies evolve, the notion of educational planning must also adapt itself to new situations. The diagnosis of present shortcomings of educational systems, the concern for qualitative aspects of educational development are becoming increasingly important elements in the planning process. Regional, local and institutional planning are in many countries in the process of becoming important complementary processes to planning at the national level, and planners themselves are beginning to pay more attention not only to the design of educational plans but also to their implementation and evaluation, underlining the links between policy, planning, financing, administration and management. Educational innovations, such as the introduction of various schemes of non-formal education, raise formidable new planning problems in terms of both overcoming the constraints of existing educational arrangements and of intensifying and diversifying the use of resources. It is in the area of educational financing where the need for an exchange of experiences about the mobilization and distribution of resources as well as the reduction of unit costs is particularly important. Similarly, planning the optimal format and location of educational facilities becomes a pressing task especially in rural areas and among the lower socio-economic groups of society.

Successful planning of educational development and innovation depends on a thorough understanding of the dynamics of educational systems and of the economic, social and political factors influencing them both from within and from outside the national environment. It is towards this understanding that a major effort of action-oriented research is to be directed. In this effort, Unesco has a major role to play both in initiating research and in establishing and sustaining means of communication whereby existing research results can be better exchanged and utilized.

Linear expansion is no longer adequate

The concept, content, methodology and practice of educational policy and planning have developed originally as a branch of general socio-economic policy and planning. They have been for several decades an important feature of the development of education in countries with centrally planned economies. More recently some form of educational policy formulation and educational planning has been adopted by almost all Member States. Its content, methodology and effectiveness, however, differ widely from country to country depending on their social, economic, political and cultural goals. As outlined above, there are however general trends in the evolution and practice of both educational policy and planning. Educational policies, originally confined to a few general guiding principles, are more and more taking the form of a systematic and comprehensive structure of goals integrated with the socio-economic and cultural environment. Educational planning was seen essentially as an exercise predicated on models of linear expansion of existing educational systems. In many countries, educational planning was synonymous with forecasting the requirements of qualified man-power, and the scope of planning was largely limited to higher, specialized and second-ary education and to vocational training, i.e. to the modern sector of the economy. In the late 1960s, educational policy-makers and planners gradually became aware of the multiplicity of internal and external economic and social factors which intervene as constraints in the effort to plan and develop educational systems, and began to develop a more global approach to educational planning. This approach embraces the formal school system and the whole spectrum of out-of-school activities, and takes into account manpower and employment requirements as well as the social demand for education. Particular attention is given to the rural areas, where the majority of the world's population is concentrated. In short, educational planning is called upon today to play a critical role not just in the expansion of educational systems, but in their renewal, thus responding to the world-wide demand for making educational systems—in and out of school—more responsive to the needs of all people.

Several international forums have helped to promote the exchange of national experiences in this field: the United Nations Conference on Human Environment, Stockholm 1972; the United Nations World Population Conference, Bucharest 1974 and the Conference on Security and Co-operation in Europe, Helsinki 1975.

Unesco and the development of educational policies and planning

Unesco has played a major role in the evolution of concepts of educational policy and planning. The earlier period of scattered activities was succeeded by a definition of clearer organizational goals in the field of educational policy and planning, guided by a view of education as an integral part of the overall socio-economic development process. Unesco sponsored the introduction of a new method: fixing goals for expansion by representative regional conferences followed by a periodic assessment of progress made. Various international and regional organizations have been associated with these conferences. A special effort has been made to demystify foreign educational aid and to emphasize the need for formulating national educational policies based on the principles of self-reliance.

In its 1961-62 Budget, Unesco devoted some $400,000 to training, consultative services and technical assistance for educational planning. By 1975-76, the Budget for educational planning activities including educational facilities had grown to $15,850,000. A growing number of Member States now have their own personnel trained in planning and management, thanks to the training programmes at the International Institute for Educational Planning and Unesco's Regional Offices. This explains the shift to more requests by Member States for high-level consultants and mobile teams of specialists to collaborate with national authorities and specialists on well-defined tasks.

At Headquarters, the activities of the planning sections have continued to expand. Between 1961 and 1965, the Organization established Regional Centres for Educational Planning and Administration in Beirut, New Delhi, Santiago and Dakar; similar centres for educational facilities were also established in Khartoum, Mexico City, and Bangkok. They were subsequently incorporated into the four Regional Offices for Education, which continue to offer the same specialized services to Member States. In 1963, Unesco established the International Institute for Educational Planning (IIEP) in Paris, to help improve educational planning in Member States through a programme of research, advanced training and dissemination of information. In 1972 several senior posts of regional advisers in educational policy and planning were established.

Unesco's activities to promote educational policy formulation and planning must henceforth be carried out in the context of development strategy of the United Nations and in the perspective of the establishment of a new international economic order.

Educational development is to be considered as endogenous. International co-operation, however, has an essential role to play in order to help countries clarify policies, achieve a better understanding of the dynamics of educational systems and of concepts such as democratization or lifelong education, and improve planning tools.

Exchange of experience and information, advisory services and research

Unesco will seek to strengthen the existing national capacity of Member States to define, implement and evaluate, their own education policies and plans. There are three main ways in which it proposes to provide this reinforcement.

The first is the systematic and regular exchange of experience and information on new developments, particularly about new trends in educational policies and strategies, which are locally developed and based on local resources. The exchanges will take place mainly within the context of symposia and seminars, of biennial sessions of the International Conference on Education (organized by the International Bureau of Education) and of regional conferences. The latter attended by the ministers of education of a given region, will deal with international co-operation for educational development and will provide the basic elements of a vast programme for the preparation and implementation of educational innovations.

The second consists mainly of a series of advisory services (missions to the different countries, carried out mostly by the regional offices) and training services (training courses and programmes at various levels and on various aspects of educational policy and planning). The aim is to develop increasing capacity in Member States to undertake critical appraisals and the renewal of their education systems and to formulate plans and projects to expand and improve education, with special emphasis on the needs of the least developed countries.

Lastly, a programme of research (conducted mainly through the International Institute for Educational Planning) and information will make it possible to extend the data base required for the design and implementation of educational plans. In addition to the publications (the bulletins of the International Institute for Educational Planning and of the International Bureau of Education, case studies of particularly interesting new experiences in planning and policy-making, results of international and regional symposia on research), the programme includes six major research projects dealing with questions such as the role of educational planning and administration in enhancing equality of educational opportunity; the relationship between education, employment and work; the planning of education at levels other than the national level (regional, local, institutional) and the relationships between administrative structures and the planning processes at these different levels; the special problems confronting educational planning and administration in rural and particularly poor areas, etc.

Educational administration

Evidence of the rapid expansion of education in many countries over the last ten years is seen by the high percentages of national budgets devoted to the education sector: a figure of 25 per cent is common and some Member States are devoting over 30 per cent to education. Yet in spite of these enormous efforts, particularly keenly felt in countries for which this level of investment represents a considerable sacrifice, the results are often not living up to reasonable expectations. In many countries, only around 20 per cent of the formal school-age cohort is actually benefiting from this expenditure; the rest either drop out early or are never enrolled in the first place.

Record education budgets but galloping inflation in recurrent costs

A number of factors which explain this situation have been cited in the previous section, perhaps the most important being the reliance on a system built on the principle of linear expansion. But there are organizational shortcomings as well. An education system, whatever its conceptual strengths and weaknesses, can only be as good as the national capacity to make it function. This capacity is embodied in the infrastructure of educational administration.

The major consideration in designing and operating a system to meet national education needs is not so much the capital cost aspect as it is the recurrent costs. Noting that the recurrent cost requirements in an expanded education system are not only not being met but are expanding at a much faster rate than capital costs, analysts of the present difficulties in Member States are examining the problems arising in educational administration in hopes of finding solutions to the ills of the system as a whole.

Compartmentalization of decision-making and shortage of qualified personnel. . .

Several problems have been identified and found to be widely shared. The first is that decision-making responsibilities at the government level on matters relating to education and training are frequently divided up between several ministries mandated to run operational programmes in these areas: education, labour, agriculture, health, social welfare, youth, etc. Programmes tend to be developed in isolation and on the basis of different, often diametrically opposed notions of the best way to design and administer the learning process. This lack of horizontal communication between ministries can also be found vertically between decision-makers at the top and those who, at the district or local level, are expected to operationalize the decisions taken. Thus, excessively centralized structures have been identified as the cause of many difficulties. If all administrative responsibility is centralized at the top, the result tends to be a degree of disinterest, sometimes even apathy, at the local level arising in large part from the failure to involve the local population in meeting their own education needs. This situation complicates the already difficult task of trying to develop new delivery systems to cater to the new dimension of lifelong education and particularly to administer non-formal education programmes.

Finally, at all levels but especially at the middle, there is a serious shortage of qualified administrative personnel. Efforts have been made to combat this shortage but management and administration skills are in such great demand not only throughout the public sector but even in the private sector where material rewards are frequently greater, that even the few who have received specific training in educational administration, whether locally or abroad, are frequently lured away into other jobs.

... main obstacles to a new approach

Educational administration was having difficulties satisfying the demands placed on it even when the problem was comparatively simple and the strategy for resolving it could be and often was summed up in the concept of meeting the demand for 'more and better'. Now, administrators, like planners, are faced with more than a simple question of aggregation and extension: an entirely new approach is called for if administration is to play a role not in maintaining or expanding existing systems, but in bringing about and sustaining major educational reforms, including the opening up of the possibilities of non-formal education.

Research, experimentation, information exchange and training are the bases upon which any strategy for the development of such an approach must be built. By virtue of its situation, its mandate, and long experience, Unesco is uniquely placed to take an active role in promoting the development of this approach.

The concern of governments over the question of the administration and management of education is not new. Governments have studied the problem and attempted to reorganize ministries and departments of education and institutions as far as governments' regulations and practices will allow. Most faculties of education and advanced teacher-training institutions now offer courses in the management of education. Senior government officials are being trained in public administration and management, often through bilateral assistance. However, in the case of developing countries, much of the training is done in industrialized countries and the types of situations and case studies used may bear little relation to the problems in these countries.

Towards scientific education management systems
adapted to specific national needs

With the advent of the modern management sciences, a number of countries have transformed their education management systems by making use of computers for scheduling and time-tabling, for inventories, payroll, financial accounting and statistical data storage, analysis and retrieval. More recently, techniques like Programme and Performance Budgeting (PPBS), Programme Evaluation and Research Technique (PERT), operations research and various systems analysis and control methods have been adopted. The use of these modern approaches, however, is by no means universal and in many cases little is known about the results obtained, good or bad, in the instances where they have been used.

The search to find ways of expanding the educational system has typically led to the use of facilities on multiple shifts, to sacrificing maintenance programmes for investment in new facilities and, failing all else, to looking abroad for capital assistance. In recent years, as Member States have begun to make progress in adapting their education systems to their development aims, they have begun to identify ways in which facilities can also be tied to national goals. On the one hand foreign exchange costs are being reduced through greater reliance on locally available resources, both material and human, while on the other, design concepts are being developed around the educational needs of each country.

Training and information

During the last fifteen years, Unesco, largely through the IIEP and Regional Training Centres or Regional Offices for Education, has provided training for high- and middle-level personnel. On-the-job training has been provided by long-term experts financed by UNDP, while the United Nations Office of Technical Co-operation has provided assistance to governments to improve their administration, though not necessarily to serve the education sector. In fact, a high percentage of persons trained in this field are lost to industry and commerce, as mentioned earlier.

Unesco has developed regional units which undertake studies on problems faced by Member States in planning and building educational facilities. Initially these units were autonomous institutes, but during the 1973-1974 biennium, their functions were transferred to the Regional Offices for Education.

Unesco's activities in the field of administration and management of education form an integral part of educational policy and planning. It is the responsibility of educational administration and management to consolidate scattered initiatives and direct them toward the renewal of the educational system. Particularly important in this process is an increased awareness of the need to see administration as a link in the overall chain of designing, implementing and evaluating plans for the development of education.

To undertake a critical examination of their own situation, Member States must have access to information on various models or structures of administration and management (including management of facilities) and to others' experiences in the application of modern management techniques to educational systems, particularly as regards reform initiatives taken by Member States with similar problems. With this in view, Unesco will publish in the next few years abstracts of research in educational administration, management and facilities and will promote joint research programmes and information exchanges. Symposia will also be organized and their results published; case studies will be published on a number of topics such as budgeting of education, decentralisation, involvement of the public in educational management, etc.

To overcome the problems facing them and to benefit from an increased access to information, it will be necessary for Member States to undertake massive training of their administrative personnel. Unesco's action will be geared toward helping Member States to carry out these training programmes, bearing in mind that generally speaking, the most effective and relevant training is best given on the job. Training will be decentralized as much as possible to the Regional Offices for Education to form the first links in a chain of institutions co-operating together and with the IIEP to improve the administration and management of educational systems at the regional level.

These information and training activities will be complemented by advisory services designed specifically to help the least developed countries to develop their own industry and management procedures for establishing educational facilities.

Educational structures

Any in-depth reform of education is first and foremost a structural reform. The structure of an education system is probably the best possible pointer to a government's educational policy and discloses most about the policy's aims. The growth of the education systems in many countries was for long the result of initiatives, often private initiatives, taken one after another and in no logical order. Except for fairly rare periods of educational renewal, the education which these systems aimed to provide was, generally speaking, a reproduction of existing models. Its principal objective was to transmit knowledge and values which were considered to be stable and which were necessary for turning out a certain kind of person who constituted the acknowledged end-product of education. The functions of education were few and simple: a small number of parallel streams existed, providing an education designed for each of the broad categories of which society was constituted. The idea of a type of education common to all had not yet taken shape. Access to education was restricted to a small number of individuals.

The need for common educational experience

As a result of changes which have occurred with considerably increasing speed over the last few decades, the problem now appears in a radically different light. Education is seen both as a factor of development and progress and as a fundamental right of human beings, who are the agents and final aim of development. These two concepts converge, encouraging governments to make access to education generally available and to increase the volume of education offered.

Broader access to education is nevertheless not the only condition necessary for its democratization. Equality of opportunities of success must also be achieved, and this implies the adaptation of education to the characteristics of the various groups, to their needs and to their motivations. The resulting diversification matches the diversification needed for education to be able to discharge extremely varied functions in order to prepare the individual for his different responsibilities and different tasks in an increasingly complex society. While the diversification of types of education is growing, the need for an educational experience common to all, and in any case for an education of equal quality for all, is seen as an indispensable condition for democracy. Specialization is being carried further and further but should not occur until everyone has received a solid grounding of general knowledge, common to all, enabling them to make the necessary choices and take the necessary retraining in good time. Some States have already established education systems based on an approach of this kind.

Lifelong education and continuity of the educational process

The greater demand for education is coupled with the increasing length of the educational process, itself associated with the continual growth in the volume of knowledge and its rapid obsolescence. There can, however, be no question of prolonging schooling or university education indefinitely. The concept of lifelong education implies that the adult, at different times in his life and within the framework of his various experiences, makes use of all the educational opportunities offered to him. In addition, as knowledge is more and more frequently acquired outside school, even if school continues to play a central role, new forms of education which are able to mobilize complementary resources are being added to the traditional structures. This gives rise to the problem of ensuring coherence between these various elements in the education system, which ties up with the need to link together the various levels, stages and types of education created by successive additions for different kinds of student and with dissimilar concerns in mind. The vertical and horizontal linkage of the systems of education, conceived of as a single whole, is becoming a matter of necessity. The search for conceptual coherence in any case goes hand in hand here with a parallel concern for economic viability. To improve the cost benefit performance of education, which is frequently the biggest item of public expenditure, it is vital to apply the criterion of greater efficiency in distributing tasks among the various educational agents involved. Schools are required to provide knowledge and skills, inculcate values and shape the attitudes and aptitudes for which they are particularly responsible, leaving to non-formal education the responsibility of providing a more flexible, more empirical or more specific training.

Non-formal education is ceasing to be considered as a mere palliative for the inadequacy of initial education. Adult education ties in with school and university education which prepare the individual for the subsequent stages of learning. The same desire for efficiency which leads to the establishment of more rational forms of organization, also leads to improvements in the way they function. Together with the idea of continuity between the formerly strictly separate levels of education and between the various rigidly separated streams, the need for greater mobility is also making itself felt. This implies more flexible procedures for promotion, a new view of examinations and pupil assessment and of the recognition of educational experiments, all of which will lower the excessively high level of educational wastage associated in particular with grade repetition, and will make it easier to transfer from one type of education to another. The reduction in unit costs thus obtained will permit savings to be made, enabling funds to be provided for new activities. Structural reform thus seems to go hand in hand with educational planning.

The establishment of coherent structures is also a response to the desire to reconcile, in the organization of the education system, the various aims of education and the sometimes contradictory obligations which these impose on each of its component parts. Thus, for example, the terminal nature of each educational level or type of education, which has, as far as possible, to provide practical knowledge, has to be reconciled with its function of preparing for the acquisition of knowledge at subsequent stages; young people must be enabled to find a useful job quickly and to assume adult responsibilities without prejudice to their chances of supplementing their initial education later on; steps must be taken to ensure the necessary continuity between theoretical education at school and university, and practical and specialist training in the productive sector. The necessary continuity between the different elements of training is thus not restricted to the education system proper but must ensure a better interpenetration of school and community. Through the reform of structures and the reform of curricula and content, education is seeking for a relevance which will enable it more fully to satisfy the aspirations of the individual and the needs of society.

Replacing empirically juxtaposed systems by complete, diversified and flexible structures

It is impossible to give an exhaustive list of the action taken and reforms carried out by Member States in this connection, but their number and variety are a sufficient demonstration of the importance which Member States attach to the restructuring of education systems.

These reforms have generally been actuated by two related concerns, first to round off the structures of education which, generally speaking, began with the primary level and were then extended to the subsequent levels, and secondly to link together and to harmonize the various elements which had been superimposed or juxtaposed in an empirical way over the centuries without really constituting systems.

A large number of countries thus began by developing the types of education required to meet the unsatisfied needs of various groups such as adults, the illiterate, young people with various handicaps, children of pre-school age or migrants. The existing system was in some cases filled out by adding those missing parts which could contribute to the solution of a problem, e.g. practical pre-vocational or vocational post-primary or out-of-school programmes for unemployed school-leavers. Other reforms have rearranged the years of study, ending the traditional division into levels, as in those cases where a course of basic education has been introduced which may be either longer or shorter than primary education and may be organized outside school for young people or adults with little or no schooling. This rearrangement of years of study has occasionally led to the introduction of systems of recurrent education or educational credits which make it possible to ensure the vital interpenetration of study and productive work. Some reforms have been actuated by the aim of delaying the age of specialization in order to provide all pupils with a common basic syllabus of sound general instruction. This concern with democracy is found again in the conception of the comprehensive schools which have been introduced in various countries in order to bring a larger number of different streams of education together in one and the same school. Structural reforms have also frequently aimed at eliminating the rigid separations between one stream and another and between general and technical education, and at facilitating transfer from one to another. This same concern for mobility underlies many of the steps which have been taken to introduce more flexibility into the procedures for pupil assessment and promotion; some countries have tried to get rid of examination systems based on purely academic criteria and to recognize a wider range of experiences and give the student a 'second chance', thus reducing the drop-out rate at the same time. In a growing number of countries, schools have made contact with the working world (the 'polytechnical school', 'the school-in-the-countryside') and, on an increasingly broad scale, with the community. Schools have often been transformed into community education centres for both adults and children where the traditional distinction between formal and non-formal education disappears.

It has been possible to observe a similar reorganization in higher education, which has become diversified through the addition of new kinds of institution (institutes of technology, short courses of higher education, the open university, the university of the air) intended to meet the needs of new kinds of students and to play new roles in the community. In a smaller number of cases, the whole of the education system has been reorganized around a basic unit ('educational nucleus') the characteristics of which have been expressly defined in relation to the concept of life-long education.

It should be added that the many steps which have been taken in recent years to reorganize education systems have gone hand in hand with the generalization of educational planning. Among other things, these measures correspond to the concern to distribute the different educational roles among the various agents and institutions concerned following a criterion of greater efficiency for a given task, and the concern to redistribute resources to achieve a better cost-benefit ratio, making the funds thus saved available for new activities.

The reorganization of education systems is obviously affected by the conclusions reached about agricultural and vocational training or in the context of the world employment programme by certain organizations of the United Nations system such as the Food and Agriculture Organization (FAO) and the International Labour Office (ILO).

Unesco and the restructuring of the education systems

Unesco's previous activities in this respect have been threefold. First, it has tried to help Member States in developing certain component parts of their education systems which were either lacking or which did not receive sufficient attention, such as literacy (see pages 240-5), adult education (see pages 224-30), special education, or pre-primary education, in which field it for a long time delegated a large share of its responsibilities to the World Organization for Early Childhood Education. Unesco has also contributed to the development of higher education in keeping with its new tasks (see pages 230-6).

Secondly, Unesco has made a considerable contribution to the elaboration of the concept of lifelong education, in which interest has been shown, although in somewhat different ways, by other organizations of the United Nations system, the International Labour Office, for instance, showing particular interest in recurrent education or by other intergovernmental organizations such as the Council of Europe and OECD. Unesco's activities in the field of lifelong education have taken the form of publications, expert meetings and an effort to organize and co-ordinate the activities of certain groups of teachers and non-governmental organizations.

Thirdly, in recent years, Unesco has begun to study certain specific problems related to the reorganization of education systems. Mention can be made in this connection of the 32nd session of the International Conference on Education which discussed the effectiveness of education systems and wastage through repetition and dropping out, and the 34th session on the relationships between education, training and employment, with particular reference to secondary education. There have also been expert meetings on the psychological development of the child from birth to the age of six and its effects on the educational process; on the basic course of education; and on relationships between education and the working world. A current study on the rigidity of structures as a factor in wastage and another study on examinations may be cited in this connection, as well as two Unesco-Unicef regional seminars on basic education in East Africa. Unesco's activities in the field of higher education have mainly taken the form of studies on certain major problems, assistance to Member States for the development of institutions, the concerting of international efforts within the framework of two conferences of European Ministers held in Vienna in 1967 and Bucharest in 1973, and action to implement the resolutions of the General Assembly of the United Nations concerning the establishment of the United Nations University. Finally, Unesco has undertaken conceptual activities at regional level to achieve comparability and international recognition of studies, degrees and diplomas.

Overall approach and specific tasks

The considerable achievements in these various fields must now be integrated into a comprehensive whole and supplemented both by the study of fields not previously considered and by the use of new forms of action.

The introduction of educational structures suitable for promoting lifelong education raises the fundamental problem, requiring further study, of how to link together the various formal and non-formal components of education systems, in order, both to ensure the coherence of these systems and to mobilize and make effective use of all available resources for the development of education.

Apart from the traditional components corresponding to the various levels or types of education, greater importance must be given to educational activities or programmes of an innovative kind adapted to the needs of different countries and groups and suitable for meeting new or current requirements: the introduction in those Member States where it proves necessary, of a basic course of education which, whether formal or non-formal, will improve the first phase of the initial training given to all, whether children or adults; programmes for young unemployed school leavers; programmes for young workers.

It also seems necessary to place greater emphasis on forms of education which have not always received attention commensurate with their importance: pre-primary education, which should be generalized, using methods that take account of the human and financial resources of each society and its social and cultural characteristics; special education for mentally and physically handicapped or socially maladjusted young people.

Lastly, it is vital to create conditions for the more flexible functioning of education systems, eliminating the rigid divisions between streams and adopting procedures for assessment, promotion and guidance such as will increase vertical and horizontal mobility within these systems, especially through increased opportunities for going back into the education system after periods of employment.

Educational content, methods and techniques

Within educational systems, educational content and methods give rise to problems which are specific and at the same time related to the evolution of policies and to the transformation of structures. To a large extent, the lack of relevance of content and methods is responsible, because directly perceived by pupils and students, for the feeling of dissatisfaction frequently experienced by them during their studies. The concern to renew content and methods lies at the heart of the universal desire to ensure that education meets the requirements of our time.

The educational act in the strict sense of the term—the act of teaching and learning—is defined by content and methods. This act is a complex process affected by many different factors: the needs and values of societies evolve at the same time as their educational requirements; the widely observed increase in attendance number has led at various levels to whole changes of scale; the development of the mass media is transforming the conditions and methods of acquiring knowledge and attitudes; the educational function of the community and the family is being transformed; lastly, the human sciences, such as psychology and sociology, shed light on the complexity of the educational act and the need to base it on a whole multidisciplinary background of knowledge, practice and techniques in the field of communication and organization that should gradually become a real 'educational technology'.

Transformation of the field of knowledge and evolution of societies

In the preparation and application of content and methods a number of different problems have to be taken into account:

Within this general context, the preparation and application of content and methods are hindered by difficulties which are peculiar to them.

The most obvious of these is the transformation of the field of knowledge caused by the progress of science and technology. The methods and content offered by traditional curricula must be reviewed in the light of these radical changes, for example in the field of applied linguistics, modern mathematics or historical method.

Secondly, and more generally, the tasks henceforth assigned to education by a world affected by technical, social (and doubtless moral) change are linked to the emergence of new ultimate aims, in particular the search for a new world order, embracing the economic, social and cultural aspects of life, for which the peoples of the world are calling more and more urgently. The new interest that is being shown everywhere in the problems raised by the natural and social environment, including, in particular, population growth, the need for new food resources, the protection of the natural heritage, the strengthening of community bonds and of structures conducive to sociability, individual creativity, the creation or re-creation of authentic folk cultures, should lead, to a greater or lesser extent according to the country, to a doubtless gradual, but probably fundamental revision of the content and methods of educational systems.

Thirdly, the users of educational systems expect content and methods to be less theoretical and better adapted to the social environment, and more deeply rooted in national languages or mother tongues. More important still, they expect education to be more resolutely oriented towards life and capable of helping children, young people and adults to understand the world in which they live or are going to live, and to transform it. School textbooks must no longer be based on content relating to cultural and ethnic values (or indeed to natural and social conditions) other than those of the country in which the child or adolescent is living, so as to facilitate the learning process and the individual's adaptation to his family and social environment. In particular, content and methods designed in terms of lifelong education should relate the educational institution more closely with the working world and should effectively equip pupils for socially useful activities and enable them to acquire the basic knowledge, skills and attitudes which will help them to take their place in working life, whether the emphasis is laid on training them for their future role as productive workers or on moulding cultured, alert-minded and socially well-adapted citizens. One of the possible ways of overcoming the difficulties encountered is to get young students to take part in work-related activities. In any case, it is necessary to put an end to the present antinomy between 'manual work' and 'intellectual activity', and to bring so-called general education and 'technical' education closer together.

Lastly, there are the added difficulties encountered by those countries that have recently acceded to independence: content, methods and materials are still all too often those left over from the educational systems of the former colonial power (and sometimes even out of date in their metropolitan country of origin). In order to improve educational methods, content and techniques in this case, it is necessary to make a special effort, in a resolutely forward-looking spirit, to achieve a synthesis integrating the cultural heritage and modernity. In this context, the aim should be to develop and promote original methods and techniques geared to the educational needs, economic and technological conditions and cultural characteristics of the developing countries.

Renewal strategies

Thus there is an obvious need for new strategies for the renewal of education. However, these will not gain acceptance unless they are all part of an overall design. All too often, it seems hitherto to have been thought sufficient to subordinate decisions concerning content to planning, while at the same time modelling methods on content (for example, decisions to construct educational buildings are still all too often taken before the nature and forms of education to be provided therein have been determined). Coherent and concerted change must replace runaway innovation.

Planning, structures, content and methods must be considered as equally important and interdependent elements of one and the same system. For example, the transformation of content calls for the modification of the forms and instruments by which this content is expressed. It is apparent today that the transformation of the relationship between teachers and taught (resulting from social changes), the development of informal education, a field pre-eminently suited to self-instruction, and doubtless also the emergence of new methods of disseminating and storing knowledge, all lead to an emphasis on the pupil's or student's independence and to placing the learner at the centre of the educational process and to involving him more closely than previously in the planning of his own course of studies and the assessment of his own progress.

Systematic research into, and integrated development of, content and techniques, based on an interdisciplinary approach and a rational use of organization and communication techniques should make it possible gradually to work out valid alternatives to traditional educational configurations capable of satisfying the present or future needs of Member States more rapidly.

The fact cannot, however, be disguised that this line of action, aimed at establishing a new, integrated approach keyed to the requirements of life-long education, is still far from having been accepted as the guiding principle for the activities of educational authorities: in 1973, most of the educational systems of Member States still devoted between 2 and 6 per cent of their operating budgets to the elaboration of content and methods and the financing of textbooks, to educational equipment and materials, and to the promotion of the educational sciences (between U.S.\$2 and U.S.\$40 per annum and per student).

Preparing curricula in terms of an overall educational process

Innumerable activities have been undertaken by governments and educators with regard to the reform of curricula, the renewal of methods, and educational technology. Unesco's action, which has been linked up with that of Member States and of groups and specialists in order to strengthen it, has grown out of 'pinpoint' or partial projects, and has gradually developed into a programme reflecting on overall view of the educational process.

It is a well-known fact that attempts at curriculum reform, which have been so numerous in the majority of countries, have for long focused only on one particular discipline and have not often affected more than one stage of education; similarly, Unesco devoted its initial activities in this field to certain selected disciplines or to the content of curricula corresponding to one specific objective, such as education for international understanding or science education.

Then, as the importance of the role assigned to education in the development and building of the national community became more and more apparent and as its new functions became more clearly defined, a growing interest was taken in Member States in overall curriculum reform. This led to many studies and meetings organized, in particular, with the support or on the initiative of regional organizations. It was on a proposal by Unesco, which had convened a meeting of experts on primary and general secondary curricula in Moscow in 1968, that a seminar was organized at Gränna (Sweden) in 1969 by the International Association for the Evaluation of Educational Achievement. This meeting was the point of departure for a joint study and training programme adopted by the International Institute for Educational Planning and the International Curriculum Organization (ICO). In 1974, meetings of experts on the design or evaluation of curricula were organized by Unesco as part of the activities of its four Regional Offices for Education. In 1975-76, Unesco was engaged in assessing the effects of the concept of overall lifelong education on content and on the methodology of the design and evaluation of curricula, and several meetings of experts have recently been convened to deal with these subjects in 1975-76. The Unesco Institute for Education (Hamburg) has realigned its research activities so as to focus them on school curricula and their evaluation within the context of lifelong education.

From audio-visual methods to full educational technology

A similar trend has emerged in the field of educational materials, methods and techniques. Emphasis was initially laid on the use of audio-visual aids; the field of interest subsequently widened to take in the application of educational psychology, of the theory of the learning process and of new methods of programmed instruction, group dynamics and microteaching. The Organization collaborated with groups of specialists, provided assistance to Member States and conducted experimental projects. It cooperated for this purpose with international organizations such as the ILO International Centre for Advanced Technical and Vocational Training, Turin, and gave its support to such institutions as the Latin American Institute for Educational Communication.

It has become increasingly clear in recent years that the application of new methods and the use of new technologies should be sustained by a general conception of education which itself reflects an overall view of the educational process and its ultimate objectives. Unesco helped to foster this growing awareness by organizing a meeting in Geneva in 1971 on the use of systems analysis in the organization of the learning process, a topic on which a handbook has since been produced in several languages for the developing countries. Since then, curriculum reform and the use of new methods and technologies have come to be considered as part and parcel of a general effort to renew educational systems. This was the background against which Unesco, in 1972, established an Asian Programme of Educational Innovation for Development (APEID), which is supporting the efforts of national institutions for research and innovation and particularly those relating to curricula and methods. Another main theme of Unesco's programme derives from conclusions reached as a result of operational action: in the case of educational technology just as in that of educational concepts, the process of transfer pure and simple must usually be replaced by a policy of adaptation, and Unesco is endeavouring, while pursuing its study of advanced technologies, to promote the development of appropriate or suitably adapted technologies.

The points of view of the 'teacher' and the 'learner'

The Organization's action must be conducted in the light of the demands of lifelong education and with reference to self-instruction as the basis of any sustained effort to make progress. Emphasis should be laid on the individualization of education, the act of learning rather than that of teaching, on a strategy which seeks, as regards curriculum content, to determine the minimum requirements of the learning process as well as the material that is appropriate to the later stages of education, and, as regards methods, to provide the maximum opportunities for learning and advancing, to develop the critical faculties and increase freedom of choice.

Towards comprehensive reform

A special effort will be made to encourage comprehensive and decentralized renewal strategies aiming to harmonize the development of content, means and techniques, in preference to fragmentary, piecemeal actions, which are unlikely to make an effective contribution to the improvement of educational systems.

The very conception of the reforms undertaken to date—usually with respect to the various subjects and levels of education—should be replaced by the concept of an overall reform of content embracing the educational process as a whole.

The Organization should also strive to conteract the tendency of each subject to develop its specific methods in isolation: methodology must be based on the needs of the different target groups just as much as on content, in accordance with a consistent and truly interdisciplinary approach.

More emphasis on culture and national languages

Efforts should be made to reconcile the often divergent demands of disinterested acquisition of knowledge and cultural advance, on the one hand, and of preparation for occupational activity and employment on the other; to facilitate the establishment of curricula which give expression to the aims of national policies, and more especially to give greater importance to national cultures and languages; and to give greater weight to science and technology, and to recast curricula on interdisciplinary lines so as to focus them on a better understanding of contemporary world problems.

Networks for innovation

The actual flow of information on educational experimentation and innovation among Member States should be strengthened and systematized. Particular attention should be paid to the systematic utilization of results which have already been obtained, often in fields other than that of formal education, when the methods in question can be applied immediately. Encouragement will be given to preliminary studies, which bring to light areas of resistance and factors conducive to the success of innovations (for lack of which so many reforms have failed), as well as the development of methods of critical analysis and evaluation designed to improve innovative action at all stages.

The programme will help to develop a world system for the exchange of education information based upon national institutions, which will be strengthened accordingly, and an articulated complex of regional and sub-regional co-operative networks designed to facilitate the practice of educational innovation for development and embracing the majority of interested Member States by 1982.

In this connection it is planned to set up, now that the Asian Programme (APEID) has become operational, networks for Africa (NEIDA), the Caribbean region and South East Europe, the Arab States and Latin America.

Production of educational materials and development of educational research

The achievements of science and technology should make it possible to use a wide and varied range of materials and facilities, including the new mass media, in the service of a renewed concept of the educational process, and to develop an appropriate technology for education so as to eliminate technological dependence and to ensure better adaptation of methods to the social environment.

In this connection it is intended to contribute to the strengthening of national capacities for producing and distributing purpose-designed educational materials which are adapted to local resources. An international aid programme to promote the development and expansion of sub-regional industrial capacities should be sponsored.

It is particularly important to create conditions for the gradual and continuous strengthening of national research and development capacities in the greatest possible number of Member States so as to enrich national experience and to stimulate and intensify international thinking in the field of the design, application and evaluation of curricula and educational methods in the light of the requirements of lifelong education, and to develop an increasing number of formulae for improving the application of the findings of the educational sciences to the educational process at all its levels; to establish criteria and recommendations for the selection and organization of curriculum content and to develop a general methodology for the evaluation of content.

Lastly, looking to the future, scientific research must help to determine (in the light of the present trends and the probable evolution of the situation) how educational establishments can train individuals capable of adapting to the changes which will occur in the societies of the future and of making effective use of the progress achieved by science and technology to promote the development of education in a rapidly changing world.

Training of educational personnel

The raising of the school leaving age in some countries, population increases and efforts to make school enrolment general in others are having various effects on the demand for teachers and on teachers' functions. In addition, the changing role of teachers and other educational personnel, which is the result both of changes in society and in the systems, curricula and methods of education in the context of lifelong education, has implications for the pre-service and in-service training of the various categories of teachers and for their status and conditions of work. All these factors make it necessary to prepare proper policies for the initial and continuing training of educational personnel, taking quantitative and qualitative considerations into account.

Horizon for 1982 : 5 million teachers to be trained?

Although in some countries the number of applicants for employment in education exceeds the number of jobs available, in the vast majority of cases there remains a considerable demand for teachers, despite the efforts that have already been made during the last decade. The provision of universal primary education in 1985 in the three regions of Asia, Africa and Latin America would call for over 12 million teachers, which is 3 million more than in 1977. Bearing in mind all potential world needs, the number of primary school teachers to be trained during the six-year period 1977-82 may be estimated at over 4 million, the majority of whom would be for the least developed countries.

The problem is equally serious in secondary education since, during the same period, the annual average rates of increase for teaching staff should be 3.9 per cent in

Asia, 6.1 per cent in Latin America and 6.4 per cent in Africa, on the basis of the present rate of growth in secondary school enrolments. In these three regions, training would thus have to be provided for 542,000, for 352,000 and for 125,000 teachers respectively. Nevertheless, the real need will probably be greater still in view of the growth in primary school enrolments and the increased number of children entering secondary school after completing their primary education.

In coming years, therefore, one must expect to see the recruitment crisis, still acute in many developing countries, continue or even get worse in those countries where population growth and the rapid expansion of enrolments in primary education will lead to an increased need for staff throughout the educational system. In those same countries, however, the qualifications of serving primary and secondary school teachers still leave something to be desired, despite the unquestionable improvement which has occurred over the last ten years in the level of training of newly recruited teachers. Training methods, particularly methods for the professional training of teachers, which have shown their worth over the last ten years will thus have to be generally applied and refresher training for large numbers of serving teachers will have to be continued. Since the establishment of teacher-training systems does not place an excessive financial burden on governments, the task of steering a sufficient number of secondary pupils into teaching and establishing a network of interconnected institutions pursuing common educational aims within each country will certainly remain a major concern over the next six-year period in some of the countries of Africa, Asia and Latin America, whatever the scope of the future reforms envisaged in the education systems of these regions.

The response to the different problems at present posed by teacher training must take account, in the context of the differing national situations, both of immediate needs and long-term prospects. If the most urgent needs are neglected, there is a danger of situations being allowed to continue in which education, and particularly primary education, which concerns the bulk of the population, betrays the most serious short-comings. If no attention is given in training prospective teachers to the profound trans-formations which will gradually affect all education systems in the coming decades, there is a danger that essential developments will be compromised.

The adults of the twenty-first century

The adaptation of the role of teachers to changes in society and in education systems themselves calls for great foresight. The training teachers receive is reflected in the education they give, and the effects of this education extend into the working life of the pupils these teachers have themselves taught. The adults of the early twenty-first century will have passed through the hands of teachers and other educational specialists trained in the next few years. This shows the importance of forward economic, sociological, technological and cultural planning in the elaboration of policies for the training of teachers able to help their pupils to adapt to the society of the future. This is a problem common to all Member States. Present training and further training systems and plans still prepare teachers only imperfectly for the responsibilities which they will have to shoulder as a result of the profound changes which will occur in the structure of educational institutions in the content of education and in teaching methods in the context of life-long education, the need for and the aims and forms of which were amply defined by the International Commission on the Development of Education in 1972.

Whatever changes are envisaged in education systems, teachers will be required to co-operate closely in the preparation and implementation of these reforms and innovations. Their contribution to, and acceptance of these changes in the education system are the essential precondition for their dissemination and their effectiveness. It has become clearer that teacher training should have more precise and better organized links with educational research, curriculum design and the production of teaching materials and aids, so that teachers can play an active part throughout their careers in the complex process by which educational innovations can come into being (even at a modest practical teaching level) and spread.

Even now in some countries, developments in educational policies have led to profound changes in education systems with regard to content, teaching methods and teacher-pupil relationships. The emergence of new kinds of educational technology, particularly audio-visual media, has played an important part in this change and the teacher is now required to use new educational tools against a background of new surroundings, new ways of using educational facilities and new timetables. The content of the initial training given to prospective teachers in the strictly professional field of the science of education has already been subject to revision in many countries and will probably be so in all countries in the near future, considering the speed with which the new educational principles employed spread. In these circumstances, the continuous training of teachers becomes quite indispensable.

Broadening the range of skills required and diversifying the teaching profession

Teacher training must, furthermore, take into consideration the need to strengthen and improve preparation for the teacher's working life and scientific and technical training, seen not only as enabling the numbers of specialists required in the various subjects to be trained but also as giving each individual a better understanding of his environment and the world in which he lives. One of the consequences of this idea is the trend towards the integration of technical and vocational training with general education, a trend the importance of which is stressed in the Revised Recommendation concerning Technical and Vocational Education, adopted in 1974 by the General Conference of Unesco.

Another characteristic of the changes currently taking place is that one can see the emergence of education systems which employ the services not just of one single type of teacher but of various kinds of specialist teachers. First of all, side by side with the full-time teachers, part-time educational personnel are employed in these systems to pass on knowledge or develop skills which call for practical experience of production or management. This is one of the trends in education's growing responsiveness towards society. Secondly, the use of particular technical media like radio, television and the various, sometimes very elaborate, systems combining audio-visual media makes it necessary to call on the skills of technicians and even engineers who thus contribute their know-how to the work of education. Finally, educational research, curriculum design and the production of teaching materials call for ever more numerous and more specialized personnel and are also moving towards a growing participation by teachers at all levels. Education can therefore not escape the diversification which is characteristic of the changes occurring in all professions today. The broadening of the range of skills of personnel and the variety of professional requirements, make it necessary to envisage new types of training or further training institutions, involving staff with increasingly diverse forms of initial training either full time or part time in education. It is vital for these personnel to be fixed by the same spirit and have a common outlook based on training suited to the objectives in view.

The social responsibilities of multi-skilled teachers

Two complementary trends appear in the context of lifelong education. To begin with, all the social forces involved are required increasingly to co-operate in defining the aims and methods of education, and consequently in defining the functions of teachers and the training they receive. In addition, every nation and group is moving towards a mobilization of all the human resources able to contribute to education. Secondly, in a growing number of countries it is being found necessary to make more use of teachers from the formal system to develop non-formal education for young people and adults. The concept of the teacher with a variety of skills is thus the subject of investigation and experiment, and in some countries even of methodical applications in response to national education policies and plans.

As regards educational personnel needs, qualitative aspects are inseparably linked with quantitative ones. All the predictions usually made are based on relatively modest assumptions regarding changes in the structures of education systems. These predictions are valid in the short term, seeing how slowly these structures alter, but they are probably not valid in the long term. The teacher or educator will certainly always play a central part in the educational process but the changes occurring in this process will be accompanied by changes in the teacher's functions which will have important repercussions on the way quantitative needs develop.

In all countries, even the poorest, the teaching profession at the present time accounts for a considerable proportion of the wage-earners among the active population. This means that the problem also has a social and economic dimension. In certain national communities, particularly in rural communities, teachers play an important social role which goes well beyond their educational function through the simple fact that they sometimes represent the few really educated people in the community. This is an aspect of their social role which cannot be ignored, and it should not be forgotten in the specific analysis of each national situation which is essential in order to bring teacher training into line with the national education policy.

Initial training, continuous training and the development of the role of the teacher

All Member States, and particularly the developing countries, have made considerable efforts to train more teachers in order to respond to the growth in population and, in many countries, to deal with the backlog in school enrolments. Between 1965 and 1970 in the developed regions, the average annual rate of increase in the number of teachers was thus 1.8 per cent for primary education and 4.1 per cent for secondary education. The figures were much higher for developing countries, being 4.8 per cent and 7.7 per cent respectively, and in Africa were as high as 5.2 per cent and 8.6 per cent. Considerable funds have been devoted to teacher training in the various regions, although not enough to satisfy the needs which would arise if education were to be provided for all. The role of teachers is changing qualitatively in many Member States and considerable changes have occurred with regard to their practical activities and traditional role, leading to changes in their training.

Until recently, Member States and Unesco concentrated a major portion of their efforts on pre-service training. Gradually, particularly as a result of plans for reform and the introduction of innovations, the need became apparent for providing serving teachers with further and even continuous training enabling them to put new curricula, methods and techniques into practice.

The shortage of qualified staff led the 1960 Montreal Conference on Adult Education to recommend that teachers from the formal system should be initiated into the methods of adult education. A few countries have followed this recommendation either experimentally, taking advantage of certain teacher-training projects in which Unesco is playing a part in Africa, or more systematically (Asia, Latin America and, in a few cases, in Africa too). This new concept of teachers with varied skills is still far from being generally applied.

The training and status of educational personnel: areas for priority action

As a result of the teacher shortage, Unesco was obliged to consider the problem of making optimum use of the teachers available and the problem of their functions and qualifications in the context of society as a whole so that society could benefit from their work, the rigid compartmentalization into formal and non-formal, school and out-of-school education no longer being applied.

The specific problems of training teachers for technical education were, in addition, dealt with at seminars and in publications under the Organization's programme and in the Revised Recommendation concerning Technical and Vocational Education (1974). This states, in particular, that arbitrary distinctions between teachers in various categories of schools (technical schools and general schools) should be done away with and that this, furthermore, should contribute to abolishing barriers between the levels and areas of education, especially through a better integration of technical and vocational education with general education.

The Organization has also done standard-setting work on the status of teachers as a whole (preparation and implementation of the ILO/Unesco Recommendation concerning the Status of Teachers; part of the Revised Recommendation concerning Technical and Vocational Education also deals with the status of teachers in this branch of education and their training). Unesco has also carried out an international survey on the professional freedom of teachers.

This standard-setting work is conducted in co-operation with non-governmental teachers' organizations which collaborate regularly with Unesco in deciding how these recommendations will be applied. They also play a very useful part in the study of all matters relating to the changes at present taking place in the roles and functions of teachers and to their pre-service and in-service training.

Unesco has furthermore made an important contribution to the training of teachers in developing countries, particularly those which have become independent since 1960. In co-operation with UNDP and the Member States concerned, the Organization participated, between 1960 and 1974, in the initial and further training of 31,000 secondary teachers, 10,000 teachers for technical education and nearly 300,000 primary teachers. Various pre-service or in-service training activities have also been organized in co-operation with Unicef involving almost 70,000 teachers.

The Organization's work has also extended to the training of lecturers for training colleges and of inspectors, categories of staff who have a decisive role to play in the introduction of change and innovation. All these operational activities have also frequently provided a response to the need for the renewal of curricula and methods, not only for the training and further training of teachers but also for primary and secondary education itself. The Organization has thus been associated with Member States in the reform of educational systems.

Over the last ten years. Unesco has carried out studies on trends and methods in the training and further training of personnel which have enabled the international community to exchange a considerable amount of information on innovations by Member States in this field. On the basis of these studies, guides and publications have been produced and meetings of experts held, providing an opportunity to make known the results of national experiments in the training of teachers, inspectors and educational administrators and to clarify the role of teachers in non-formal education. The 35th session of the International Conference on Education (1975) in particular, enabled all Member States to review the changing role of teachers and the effects of this change on pre-service and in-service teacher training.

The activities which Unesco proposes to carry out in the next few years—mainly in the form of meetings, seminars, studies, surveys and the circulation of documentation—are based on a number of principles which are worth mentioning.

The first principle is that the training of educational personnel must play a significant role in educational innovation. Teacher-training institutions must themselves be the spearhead of any educational reform and must be in the vanguard of innovation and creation. The teachers and specialists they train must be the agents of reform, which is a continuous process of change and which presupposes teachers' support and participation.

A second principle is clearly laid down by the Recommendation of the 35th International Conference on Education: pre-service training is now seen as nothing more than the first stage in a process of continuous training. Unesco will thus promote the formulation of integrated policies and plans of continuous training for all categories of educational personnel, having regard to the new roles and requirements emerging in the context of lifelong education as a result of economic, technological, social and cultural change, to the changes which they impose on education systems and to developments in educational technology.

Bearing in mind these two principles, Unesco will carry out activities to identify and encourage innovations in training schemes for educational personnel. Lastly it will pursue its standard-setting activities, particularly through efforts to further the implementation of the Recommendation concerning the status of teachers and to prepare the extension of the Recommendation to other categories of teachers.

The last principle to be followed is that of integrating as closely as possible such conceptual and standard-setting activities with practical ('operational') field co-operation with Member States, through the setting up or strengthening of national institutions for the training or further training of teachers and educational supporting staff, exchanges of experience and of persons between such institutions, regional meetings of national specialists in training, etc.

Adult education

Access by adults to a type of education that is linked with all aspects of life, that is provided in different forms and spread over a period of time constitutes a fundamental dimension of the right to education and an essential factor in effective participation in social and cultural life. There seems to be unanimity on this point and there is, at the present time, a broad agreement of principle in the different countries on the need to promote adult education using procedures consonant with the diversity of situations.

In many cases, however, the human and material resources allocated to adult education are not in keeping with its acknowledged importance: while a few governments of both industrialized and developing countries devote 10-15 per cent of their education budget to the education of adults, many ministries of education allocate to it less than one per cent of their resources.

Towards education adapted to all ages and linked to all aspects of life

Besides the increased demand for education, various factors combine to produce a need for the development, more especially, of adult education. We might mention in this respect the ever-increasing volume of knowledge and the greater and greater rapidity with which it becomes obsolete; accelerated technological evolution and changes of an economic kind which make vocational refresher training and retraining necessary; the growing complexity of social phenomena and inter-group relations; the development of the information media; the extension of leisure time.

In countries where the school component of the education system is not adequately developed and where it cannot meet alone the urgent need for generalized basic education in the near future because of the heavy financial burden involved, adult education can make an effective contribution by responding directly to the practical needs of economic, social and cultural development, since it is aimed primarily at the economically active sectors of the population.

Adult education becomes an intrinsic part of educational systems designed with lifelong education in mind. By educating parents and parents-to-be, it creates a favourable environment for the education of children and is seen, then, to be complementary to it. Promotion of adult education is thus an important factor in the general promotion of education.

It differs from other sectors of education not by level or content—necessarily very varied—nor by the nature of the institutions which provide it—for it may be formal or non-formal—but by its target audience and, to a certain extent, by the methods it calls for.

Emphasis needs to be placed on the important role that it can play in relation to educational innovation, to the benefit of the educational system as a whole. Less bound by traditions or the constraints imposed by institutions, curricula and examinations than other elements in the system, adult education can be a testing ground for the formulation and development of innovatory approaches capable of being extended to other types of educational action.

The objectives: individual fulfilment, the struggle against illiteracy, refresher training and civic training

Adult education may be regarded as a set of activities corresponding to a series of objectives, of which the most important are: (a) the extension of general knowledge within the context of lifelong education, individual fulfilment and access to culture; (b) the intensification of the struggle against illiteracy; (c) the enhancement of occupational efficiency by means of initial and refresher training and retraining with a view to greater occupational mobility and advancement; (d) the understanding of the major problems faced by the national and international community, and active participation in civic, political and international life; (e) the acquisition of practical knowledge in areas such as health, nutrition, upbringing of children, consumer affairs, etc. Adult education thus covers the whole range of skills and knowledge which contribute to the harmonious development of the personality, the roles of individuals in society, and the knowledge or attitudes that are implied by such roles.

The links between adult education and working life, which are of special importance for development, involve, at the present time, a number of specific problems: the role of vocational training, in the widest sense of the term, at the different stages of life, having special regard to the rapidity of scientific and technological development and the need for occupational mobility or advancement: ways of involving workers in the drawing up and organization of education programmes; finding the most appropriate status for organizations concerned with training; finding ways whereby adult education, while being organized on a more systematic basis, can retain its characteristic features of spontaneity, diversity and the voluntary participation of those involved.

These issues arise in the urban milieu just as they do in the rural environment. In the latter case they assume considerable importance, as adult education is the main avenue whereby, in the short term, the community may achieve the technical progress which is vital to the improvement of its standard of living and organize itself for participation in national economic and social life. Only in so far as they are addressed to a community in which adults have become aware of the possibility of changing their situation can extension courses in agricultural production, health and public hygiene and attempts to organize rural institutions have any impact. Adult education is one of the essential elements of any integrated rural development policy (Chapter 6, pages 245-53).

From the social vocation of popular movements to the educational responsibility of economic enterprises: an increasing variety of responsible bodies

Because adult learning needs and interests are so varied, and because the educational offer must meet the adult learner in the situation where he actually is, and must be highly relevant to his needs as he perceives them, it has been—and often is—a feature of adult education that it is scattered, fragmented and of an *ad hoc* nature.

In some countries the most important providers of adult education are popular and social movements, to which people have chosen to adhere; in other countries the main provision is made by economic enterprises, either directly, or through agencies appointed by them, and in yet other countries the public education system has extended the provision initially made for children and the young to cater for all age-groups of the population on a part-time basis.

Governments wishing to promote adult education must then find ways of channelling support to a multitude of agencies, and special efforts are needed to ensure the spread of innovations from one area of adult education to another, to ensure the wider application of results of research, and even to secure availability of appropriate teaching/learning materials.

Although the diversity of forms of adult education and of the agents involved may pose certain problems, it also has a positive aspect because of the resulting variety of inputs. Furthermore it may be expected, within the context of a learning society, to go on increasing. What is required, however, is adequate co-ordination and communication at the various levels.

In this respect, experience shows that marked progress has been made in the countries where the multitude of agencies in adult education have formed networks of mutual aid and co-operation, and have set up *service agencies*, whose primary function is not to teach adults, but to provide services to those who do in fields like information, research, training of personnel of various kinds, development of teaching materials, loan of materials and equipment, etc. Such servicing agencies take various forms: institutes, councils, boards etc. They are governmental or voluntary in nature but usually supported by public funds. In addition to their national functions they usually form the link for international contacts and exchanges.

Ad hoc activities and systematic action

Whereas the very wide range of adult education activities now embraces all levels of the educational system, from pre-literacy to post-graduate studies, the earliest ventures in adult education—which go back quite a long way—took the form of *ad hoc* activities designed to offset the consequences of restricted access by large sectors of the population to formal education and to satisfy certain occupational or cultural needs. These activities were carried out in a number of ways, within an institutional framework or outside it, with the use of conventional teaching methods or innovatory practices, and by a wide variety of agencies: public services, non-governmental agencies, voluntary movements, social or religious, private enterprises and, more recently, international organizations, both intergovernmental and non-governmental.

It should be noted, however, that, since the 1960s, adult education has made unprecedented progress, both quantitatively and qualitatively, in response to the needs arising more especially from the scientific and technical revolution and the accession of a great many countries to national independence.

Several organizations of the United Nations system have made significant contributions to the education of adults. In addition to its work in the field of vocational and professional training and in connection with its World Employment Programme, ILO has promoted and developed workers' education especially in the context of workers' participation in the affairs of society through their membership of trade unions. ILO has also undertaken important normative action especially with regard to paid study leave. FAO has been active in agricultural extension work, nutrition education and co-operative education. Both organizations have co-operated with Unesco in the experimental literacy projects. WHO has increased its activities in health education, and Unicef has found that caring for children necessitates not only parental involvement, but parents' education. More recently the World Population Fund and the United Nations Environmental Programme have made specialized contributions in their particular spheres.

While most of the other agencies have adopted either a subject-centred approach or limited themselves to particular target audiences, it has been incumbent on Unesco to promote the development of the general institutional frameworks, structures and organizational patterns that can best meet the varied and changing educational needs, both of the Member States and of the international community.

The promotion of adult education has been one of the Organization's objectives since its creation. The three successive international conferences convened for this purpose (Elsinore, 1949; Montreal, 1960; and Tokyo, 1972) have been the main milestones in its action.

The Tokyo Conference

In the years following the Montreal Conference and more specifically after the World Congress on the Eradication of Illiteracy (Tehran, 1965) Unesco has given priority to action in the field of literacy. In the late 1960s, however, it became apparent that the time had come to move on a wider front. The preparations for the Tokyo Conference revealed that significant developments in various directions had taken place in a large number of Member States. A universal desire became manifest for an overall development of adult education seen as an essential prerequisite for economic, social and cultural development as well as for the implementation of policies for lifelong learning.

From the discussions which took place at the Tokyo Conference it emerged that adult education might be regarded as: (a) an instrument for promoting awareness, an instrument for socialization and sweeping social change (it aims to create a society conscious of the value of a sense of community and mobilizes energies: self-education and educating others is the duty, as it is within the power, of all); (b) an instrument whereby the whole man (including man at work and man at play, man in his civic and family roles) can achieve fulfilment, by helping to develop his physical, moral and intellectual qualities; (c) an instrument for preparing the individual for productive activity and for participation in management; (d) an instrument with which to combat economic and cultural alienation and prepare the way for the emergence of a liberating, genuine national culture.

The Tokyo Conference, which had before it the conclusions of the Intergovernmental Conferences on Cultural Policies (Venice, 1970 and Helsinki, 1972), also expressed the view that, as an essential component of both lifelong education and cultural development, adult education helped to bind them together as the two inseparable facets of one and the same process.

Lastly, the Tokyo Conference considered that the elaboration and adoption of an international instrument bearing on the quantitative and qualitative development of adult education was an important objective for the 1970s.

The medium-term period: the establishment of national networks in the service of endogenous educational development

For the medium-term period 1977-82 the promotion and intensification of adult education and further training has a double meaning. It is an objective in itself, but on the other hand, it is an important means of action for attaining many other objectives. It appears to be both an important aspect of the right to education and a prerequisite of the contribution of education to economic, social and cultural development.

Unesco's action should be shaped in accordance with the characteristics observed in adult education in the different countries and which form its specificity: the indispensable and considerable variety of objectives, approaches, methods, target audiences, agents and resources involved and the flexibility that must be maintained in the diversity of undertakings and approaches.

Adult education is in essence a multidisciplinary activity. The promotion of a particular programme, whether concerned with rural development, population problems, improvement of the environment, active participation in the life of the society, to mention but a few, demands combined application of: (a) knowledge of the characteristics of the particular target audience and individual learners; (b) knowledge of the subject-matter; (c) organizational and promotional skills; (d) relevant educational methods and techniques.

In practice most programmes suffer from inadequacies in one or more of these fields. The measures to take to bring about an improvement will differ, but shortcomings can best be identified and adjustments made where there are *networks* in adult education that enable a lively communication to take place, horizontally between agencies engaged in various kinds of adult education, and vertically between grass-roots activities and the national centres of policy-making and decision-making.

It thus becomes a principle of action to help countries to develop networks that best suit their particular circumstances and to build up the basic services needed for a comprehensive endogenous development of adult education.

Unesco must also continue to contribute to the *development of international exchanges of information*, ideas, experiences and of persons and collaborate with international and regional governmental and non-governmental organizations active in this area.

In addition, Unesco's action which, during recent years, has been focused more especially on the institutional development of adult education and the intensification of international co-operation in this domain, should lay more stress on the *qualitative improvement* of adult education. It will, accordingly, be extended to deal with the problems involved in: the formulation of programme content and methods adapted to the characteristics of adult education; the training of personnel; the dissemination of information to the agencies involved as well as to the different target audiences; co-ordination at three levels—between governmental agencies, between these agencies and non-governmental organizations, and between the two preceding categories and information organs and services.

Lastly, the development of adult education in a manner suited to its acknowledged importance in the implementation of lifelong education policies would seem to require the adoption of legislative and administrative measures so that its action may be consolidated and developed without being affected by short-term economic fluctuations, as is still often the case. *Standard-setting action* will, accordingly, be pursued—if Member States deem it desirable—by the preparation of instruments dealing in depth with certain specific aspects of adult education, from the standpoint of the needs of different categories of persons as well as from that of the means to be employed.

Higher education and the community

Higher education is assuming an increasingly important role in the educational system and in the life of nations, as it is expected to respond to the new demands arising from the rapid transformation of societies and to the aspirations of individuals for economic, cultural and intellectual improvement.

In addition to the traditional functions of higher education, teaching, training and research, as a means for the transmission and advancement of knowledge and for the provision of qualified manpower, new emphasis is laid now on the obligation to adapt the higher education system to the society in which it operates, and to the many needs of that society. As centres of reflection and research, the system also serves the international community. These are convergent and complementary objectives.

Poor cousins: the rural areas

Established chiefly in urban areas and aimed at training an élite, institutions of higher education have helped to maintain and emphasize, in the majority of countries, a cleavage between urban and rural populations on the one hand, and between intellectual and manual workers on the other. These gaps have by no means totally disappeared, even in the most industrialized countries, not to mention the countries which imported models from old colonial powers. The gravity of the problems can be seen from the fact that 61.2 per cent of the total world population dwells in rural areas, and in several developing countries the percentage reaches more than 75 per cent. The way to integrated rural development would be much easier if higher education were made accessible to and relevant for rural populations. This is a particularly striking illustration of two demands which must be met by higher education and which must determine its development: democratization, and integration in the community in which it must contribute to development.

Extending the mission of higher education to the whole community . . .

On a more general level, higher education should be more widely involved with society, from which it is all to often isolated. Its institutions should cease to be passive repositories of knowledge and should take an active interest in the problems of development. This would imply, in particular, that higher education, in addition to its traditional, discipline-oriented approach, should adopt an interdisciplinary approach. This is particularly important in developing countries, where scientific, technological and cultural talent tends to concentrate in the higher education institutions, especially the universities. Yet the university people suffer from intellectual isolation and are deprived of the facilities necessary for advanced research. Action-oriented research is only beginning to develop.

Only too often are brilliant research workers from developing countries engaged abroad in projects with little relevance to the development plans of their home countries.

... and its diversification in relation to the labour market

The contribution of higher education to development requires firstly the establishment of closer links with the demands and conditions of employment.

In the developing and developed countries alike, the output of higher education institutions in the various disciplines is not sufficiently well geared to the quantitative needs of society, except in cases where the economic and social system provides for the planned use of human resources in the service of development. Unemployment and underemployment are prevalent among certain categories of graduates whereas in other sectors there is a shortage of highly qualified personnel. The question, in qualitative terms, is whether the content and performance of higher education systems are able to meet the needs of society and the new and changing methods of production, particularly in the labour market.

Building a bridge between the university and the working world, slowing up the brain drain to other countries and to private industry

Higher education is too often non-existent in rural development. In addition to this its relationship with industry is not close enough. The relationship between the university and industry should lead to the adoption of practice-oriented programmes at the university and enable industry to absorb university graduates without much waste of time and effort. Moreover, a much higher degree of interpenetration between higher education and the working world should be achieved by increasing the number of administrators, doctors, lawyers, technicians, artists and representatives of various other sectors of society, who combine their normal professional activities with teaching in higher education institutions. The generalization of this practice would help to adapt educational content to the demands and characteristics of society, would facilitate student guidance and contribute to bringing the university out of isolation. Moreover, while academics are often remote from practical affairs, practitioners may underestimate the value of independent study of the issues with which they are dealing. Closer collaboration between the university, industry and the social administrations would be mutually beneficial. On the other hand, it must not be forgotten that high-level scholars are often tempted by the higher salaries and better working facilities offered by private industry, at home or abroad, or by foreign universities. Suitable incentives should be provided to induce them to accept and remain in teaching posts in national universities. As a first step, a status of university professors providing some minimum guarantees should be clearly agreed upon.

An increasingly urgent requirement: mobility in its three aspects— transnational, interdisciplinary and social

Among the long-term problems raised by the expansion of higher education systems in a manner conducive to the endogenous development of communities, the problem of the mobility of personnel—students, teachers, research workers and professionals—is becoming increasingly significant. Its implications are manifold for it is not possible to confine the problem merely to its international aspects. It is also necessary to give consideration to social mobility as an essential factor contributing to democratization.

The main reasons for the increase in international mobility are well known; a desire and need for mobility is increasingly making itself felt in all countries. This need is felt all the more in developing countries because, for some time to come, it will be essential for them to send their future doctors, engineers, teachers, technicians and so forth, to gain their qualifications abroad, or at least to acquire a further specialization. There are similar movements also between industrialized countries. But that is only one side of this problem: it is also necessary to take into consideration the trainees' reintegration in their home community, for every government is concerned to make use of its citizens who have been trained abroad within the shortest possible time. Moreover, mobility should not take place only between nations. Higher education must also contribute to social mobility: new categories of students should therefore have wider access to post-secondary courses as lifelong education progressively becomes a reality.

Encouraging exchanges and retraining, establishing new criteria for the recognition of degrees and diplomas

It must be acknowledged that mobility, viewed as a whole, has not generally been sufficiently clearly understood. Hence the desirability of adapting movements of persons more adequately to the new factors affecting the changing conditions of society—economic, social, historic and legal—upon which mobility depends. With regard to those factors which are within the competence of the Organization, it would thus seem to be a matter of urgent necessity to pave the way for improving such exchanges. Action should be taken, in particular to promote a fuller evaluation of training so that when trainees are about to begin or continue their studies, or embark on occupational activities, or when they apply for further training or to be retrained for other employment, they can be guided into paths which are better suited to the development needs of the societies to which they belong and also to the requirements of their own personal fulfilment. The purpose of the Organization's long-term action is to contribute, for the benefit of those who are responsible for assessing training, to the preparation of new instruments of evaluation (whether legal or institutional), units of measurement which are better suited to the circumstances, fuller information, and methods and techniques which provide a means of attaining the end in view. This is also the purpose of the action which is being taken to promote the comparability and recognition of studies, diplomas and degrees which replaces the traditional evaluation criteria by more flexible criteria based less on the school and university career than on personal experience, education acquired by various different methods and the notion of training in stages.

Towards a reconversion of international co-operation in terms of development needs

International action for co-operation among universities and other institutions of higher education requires some serious thinking. The purpose of inter-institutional co-operation, particularly in the developing countries, should no longer be to establish new institutions of traditional kinds or to develop those already existing, but rather to assist in the establishment of new types of institutions suited to the needs of the society or the individuals which they are supposed to serve. Twinning or bilateral co-operative arrangements among institutions exist already, but they have often resulted in institution-building, with 'co-operation', which can only be a two-way process, being in fact reduced to one-way traffic or 'assistance'. Inter-university co-operation should be reoriented to take into account the requirements of development and the need for international understanding, mutual appreciation of cultures and international communication. Arrangements should be made for co-operation among institutions in: research, by identifying institutional, national and sub-regional needs in specific fields; teaching and training of academic personnel in their own country, with some short periods of training abroad only if needed for purposes of national development; and administration, by providing training for administrative personnel at various levels. Inter-university co-operation can also be achieved through setting up university consortiums and centres of excellence on the basis of common disciplinary or problem concerns or of geographical proximity of institutions, in order to pool resources and maximize their use.

The intensification of co-operation between higher education institutions at regional level, which in no way excludes co-operation with the rest of the world, can thus be seen as a means of fostering communication between different cultures in the same region, of strengthening awareness of cultural identity and of contributing to the endogenous development sought after by so many countries.

Lastly, it seems increasingly necessary that the international university community should devote a larger part of its work and reflection to the study of the major problems with which man is now faced and which have a determining influence on his destiny.

Recent trends in higher education: increase in enrolment numbers, changes in methods and curricula

In the last few years, those concerned with the improvement of higher education have given it serious thought on account of increased demand and still greater expectation that it should be made relevant to contemporary society. While growth in the number of students enrolled was more rapid during the 1960-65 period, growth rates declined from 1965 onwards, especially in Europe, but also in Africa and Oceania. In Asia the slowing is less marked. Table 1 shows the average annual rates of growth (as percentages):

Table 1

	1960-70	1960-65	1965-70
World total	8.8	9.6	7.9
Africa	10.7	12.9	8.6
Latin America	11.0	9.9	12.1
North America	9.2	9.3	9.2
Asia	10.0	10.2	9.8
Europe	7.3	9.5	5.2
Oceania	8.0	8.8	7.1
Developed countries	8.3	9.3	7.2
Developing countries	10.7	10.9	10.6

Qualitatively, remarkable changes have occurred in the higher education system in terms of emphasis being laid on the use of new methods and techniques, broadening of curricula to suit undergraduates' needs and wishes, greater student participation in administration, improvement of staff-student ratios (noticeably in developed countries), introduction of new subject-matters, and new types of institutions (comprehensive higher schools, open university, problem-oriented multidisciplinary universities), as well as on consideration of the international dimension of higher education. Principles of financial assistance to students are becoming more flexible and generous. The relationship between manpower requirements and higher education is getting increasingly complex, particularly in some developed countries; while there is a tendency to offer a large number of career-oriented courses, there is growing evidence that a higher education provides no guarantee of finding suitable employment.

These concerns are evident in the various efforts made by Member States to rethink or reform higher education—some inspired by student unrest, others to avoid it, and still others to make higher education more accessible, relevant, and productive.

Inter-institutional relations have helped universities in the developing countries build up new departments, train their staff for teaching and research and obtain academic personnel and equipment from abroad. International and regional co-operation has been developed by non-governmental organizations and through rectors' conferences; and seminars and supporting activities for training of specialists in various fields including university documentalists and librarians have built up substantial links between institutions and individuals because of common concerns.

Unesco at work on all continents

Intergovernmental conferences on Education, the Application of Science and Technology to Development and on Cultural Policies, and meetings of experts organized by Unesco have all emphasized the need for intellectual co-operation through institutions of higher education. The Second Conference of Ministers of Education of European Member States (Bucharest, 1973), for instance, made recommendations to Unesco and Member States in connection with (a) changes in structure, curricula and methods of higher education in view of its increasing enrolment and its changing functions, and of the shift of emphasis in educational systems towards lifelong education; and (b) objectives, ways and means of European co-operation in the field of higher education. The Final Act of the Helsinki Conference on Security and Co-operation in Europe (1975) also contains proposals for university co-operation and exchange in the fields of education, culture, economics, science, technology and environment. Efforts are being made by Unesco to assist Member States in implementing the recommendations. Moreover, Unesco has undertaken studies and issued publications on the development of higher education, international comparability and recognition of studies and degrees, alternative university structures and innovations in higher education and lifelong education.

Precisely in order to foster European co-operation in higher education, Unesco established the European Centre for Higher Education in Bucharest in 1972. An advisory committee helps in drawing up the programmes for research and studies and, especially, for collection and circulation of information. A similar effort is being made to establish a centre to serve Latin America and the Caribbean.

The Regional Institute for Higher Education and Development in Asia, established in Singapore in 1970 as a result of the Joint Unesco-International Association of Universities study, has examined the role of universities in planning development and conducted courses for governmental officials and young academics. Unesco provided assistance to a project on Higher Education and Development in Africa and aided the Arab Educational, Cultural and Scientific Organization (ALECSO) and the Association of Arab Universities in drawing up a plan for an Arab Regional Institute for the Development of Higher Education. A network of centres like those mentioned above could, through their research, training and information services, help Member States develop their higher education system.

As regards the need for the contribution of higher education to planning and development and data collection, useful work has been initiated by the International Institute of Educational Planning and the International Bureau of Education.

Finally, the establishment in 1972 of the United Nations University under the joint sponsorship of the United Nations and Unesco constitutes an important landmark. Conceived as an 'international community of scholars engaged in research, postgraduate training and dissemination of knowledge', the United Nations University will have the task of studying, from an interdisciplinary standpoint, the urgent problems concerning the survival, development and welfare of mankind. Besides offering opportunities for throwing light on these problems through the combined intellectual efforts by the most distinguished institutions and individuals of the international community, the United Nations University will also help to strengthen the solidarity of this community and stimulate the flow of ideas by endeavouring to alleviate the intellectual isolation of academic and scientific communities in the developing countries. As the three programme priority areas have been identified, as World Hunger, Natural Resources, and Human and Social Development, it is to be hoped that close collaboration between Unesco and the University, by bringing to bear a common approach to the study of problems, will produce significant results.

Future lines of action

During the next few years, Unesco will follow three main lines of action. First, the Organization will take steps to promote the awareness of higher education as a community development factor. Meetings, studies and publications (complemented by advisory services, financial aid and fellowships) will be devoted to higher education as a community development factor, the democratization of higher education and the relationship between higher education and lifelong education. The latter will also be the theme of a preparatory meeting for the third Conference of Ministers of Education of European Member States, scheduled for 1979-80.

Secondly, Unesco proposes to intensify inter-university co-operation by: (a) strengthening regional co-operation between universities; (b) encouraging world-wide exchange of information on innovation in higher education through co-operation with international governmental and non-governemental organizations, (in particular with the International Association of Universities); (c) stimulating the participation of universities in development efforts and in the promotion of international objectives. The Organization will also co-operate in the activities of the United Nations University.

Lastly, Unesco will help to improve the mobility of students and teachers and to promote the international comparability and recognition of studies, diplomas and degrees. Action will be aimed at establishing standards: the preparation of multilateral regional conventions will be accompanied by measures to establish procedures and machinery to provide for the effective application of the principles set forth in the international legal instruments. Studies and surveys will be carried out on the problems of mobility and of international recognition of degrees and the results widely published.

6 Participation

The levels of development vary considerably, not only between one country and another but also between different geographical zones and population groups within individual countries. History shows that, if action for development is not inspired by principles of equity, it is liable to perpetuate and even accentuate such inequalities. These inequalities make for tension and social unrest, for they set the groups that benefit from development against those which, be they a majority or a minority, do not benefit from it or derive inadequate benefit from it.

Unesco's action in favour of disadvantaged groups

By studying existing situations and suggesting corrective measures to Member States, Unesco can and should play an important part in eliminating such inequalities. This is necessary for various important reasons, the first of which, a moral one, is that if man is to be both the agent and the beneficiary of development it is absolutely essential that the community as a whole should join in the effort required and reap the benefit. What is more, if most of the population does not benefit from development, tension is likely to build up among groups and States and is bound to jeopardize both national order and world peace. A development policy offering advantages to only a part of the population compromises the strengthening of national identity and unity and results in wastage of that most precious of resources: human potential.

Unesco gives special attention in its programme to various population groups regarded in many countries as disadvantaged. The problems of some of these groups have already been mentioned in connection with Chapter 1, inasmuch as their condition is connected with one form or another of respect for human rights.

In this chapter the approach is complementary. What is needed is to ensure the individual and collective advancement of certain categories of persons, who, in general, should themselves play an active and leading role in their own progress. This difference in approach explains the wide range of situations dealt with in this chapter, which are related to a great variety of social and cultural factors and do not imply that any particular category of persons is totally, or permanently, or in regard to all aspects of its life, to be included among the disadvantaged groups.

The different sections of the present chapter concern:[1]

Illiterates who, lacking the essential means of access to knowledge and human communication, are seriously restricted in their capacity for self-fulfilment and active participation in the life of the community. Illiteracy is rightly considered a major obstacle to political, economic, social and cultural progress.

Rural communities which, especially in the developing countries, lack social services, modern infrastructures and educational and training facilities, and are therefore not always able to reach more than very low levels of productivity. Since in many cases they do not manage to provide for their basic needs in the region they live in, they are seldom able to avoid drifting ever more rapidly to the towns.

Young people, some categories of whom, having no job opportunities and no prospect of being given political, economic or social responsibility, are vulnerable groups within each community. The young are often quite unable to assert themselves and to play the important part in society that their potential—in terms of talent, drive and spirit of innovation—warrants.

Other categories of persons, whose situation is such that they are occasionally or constantly out of step with society, present the community with more or less serious individual and social problems. In some societies, this applies to old people, in others, to persons whose drug-taking or violence is evidence of the difficulties with which they are confronted.

Illiteracy from the country to the city outskirts: a dangerous source of dissatisfaction and disillusionment in young people

Each of these categories has its special features, but they all have many characteristics in common, so that overall action can be taken to deal with them. Thus, illiteracy is worst in country areas. Likewise, when solutions are being sought to the problems facing various groups who are disadvantaged as regards education, vocational training and social responsibility, if work with young people is combined with such efforts, the proposals made may be concerned with the reforms required to reduce inequality rather than with makeshift and palliative measures. The problems involved in the situations

---

1. Women and girls still suffer from various forms of discrimination, on account of social and economic structures and certain cultural factors in particular. Such inequalities prevent them from fulfilling themselves as individuals and playing their part adequately in the family, at work, in civil life and in the community in general. This problem and its possible solutions are dealt with in Chapter 1, pages 42-9.

mentioned on pages 260-4 are obviously more serious in areas without the necessary social facilities, where conflicts are liable to persist.

Much of Unesco's programme concerning these objectives should be designed to help Member States improve the condition and hasten the development of certain population groups in the poorer parts of country areas or the outskirts of cities whose relative size varies considerably from one country to another. In general, these groups are, characteristically, chronically short of basic necessities, and for lack of organization among their members they are unable to express their desires forcefully enough to improve their situation. Another feature of their situation is that they take little or no part in the life of the community.

This vicious circle cannot be broken from outside, by the influence of international action alone, for it is primarily the task of Member States themselves to define appropriate policies, which should reflect the national will to attain a level of balanced development while preserving the special features which make of each people an original and unique entity. At the same time, emphasis must also be placed on the role of international co-operation. It is Unesco's duty to contribute to this effort in its various fields of competence, through study and interpretation of the phenomenon of underdevelopment and of its human implications, giving at least as much importance to the qualitative and moral aspects of the development of human groups as to the quantitative aspects, which are often more noticeable.

National policies, like external co-operation programmes, should be planned in relation to the overall context. The idea of 'integrated' development, which is being increasingly widely accepted, should be given practical expression through joint local and national action by a variety of disciplines and services and, within the United Nations system, through co-ordinated activities. However, such efforts towards integration should be extended and intensified. For there can be no real social change to help disadvantaged groups until policies for the introduction of the necessary changes in the overall social context have been drawn up and applied.

In most cases, aggravation of these problems would have disastrous effects upon the peoples directly concerned and would be evidence of an imbalance within the community as a whole. The following strategic implications stem from these facts. Illiteracy cannot be eradicated unless the people concerned and organizations which serve the public make an effort to do so; the integrated development of country areas cannot be planned without taking account of regional and national development, including that of urban centres; the status of women cannot be changed so long as the causes and factors that determine it persist; lastly, overall development with a view to eliminating such disparities cannot be achieved unless the various groups of young people are actively associated with the dynamics of social, educational and cultural action.

In short, activities must not be confined to any particular group regarded as disadvantaged; they must help to modify the conditions and social structures which give rise to the problems of these groups. This way of tackling problems together opens up great possibilities for interdisciplinary work in Member States, in Unesco and in the United Nations system.

Eliminating illiteracy

Calculation of the number of illiterates has always proved difficult, either because census methods are not always reliable, or because in countries where the illiteracy rate is high, figures are often incomplete or do not even exist. It frequently happens, in addition, that the data are not comparable because of different definitions of 'illiteracy'. Estimates give grounds for affirming, however, that in this last quarter of the twentieth century the world is still far from having achieved universal literacy.

Eight hundred million illiterates still, even if 'relative illiteracy' is decreasing

Although illiteracy at the world level dropped, proportionately, from 44.3 per cent in 1950 to 39.3 per cent in 1960 and 34.2 per cent in 1970, the number of illiterates throughout the world still stands at some eight hundred million. Whereas illiteracy is decreasing in relative terms, as a result of the action taken in many countries, the population explosion and the inadequacy of educational systems are encouraging its growth in absolute figures.

In 1970 Africa and the Arab States showed the highest illiteracy rates among their adult population, followed by Asia and Latin America. Illiteracy rates in these four regions dropped by between 7 and 9 per cent during the 1960-70 decade. But whereas in 1970 the illiteracy rate stood at 24 per cent in Latin America, in Africa and in the Arab States it exceeded 70 per cent, and was nearly 50 per cent in Asia.

The illiteracy problem is not restricted to the developing countries. Two major industrial countries recently announced national programmes for their illiterate population sectors, which are numbered in millions. These are not *ad hoc* measures, but programmes designed on a long-term basis since traditional primary education cannot, in its present state, solve the problem of 'drop-outs' who swell the number of semi-literates or illiterates.

Whereas the practical efforts and far-sighted policies of certain governments in Africa, Latin America and Asia have succeeded in considerably reducing illiteracy in several countries, in other instances the lack of adequate resources and absence of political determination have prevented any effective action. At the same time, external aid programmes have not been focused sufficiently on the elimination of illiteracy and have not always been designed in such a way as to foster the formulation of policies and projects in keeping with the practical conditions obtaining in the recipient countries.

Illiteracy and poverty go hand in hand

Illiteracy and poverty go hand in hand. In the twenty-five least-developed countries, where per capita income is less than $100 per annum, illiteracy rates rise to over 80 per cent. What is more, the proportion of women among illiterates continues to increase: 58 per cent in 1960, 60 per cent in 1970. The number of men and women illiterates was, during this period, appreciably higher in rural zones than in urban areas. Despite the progress achieved by primary education, many children still do not attend school or fail to complete the full course of studies. If the trends of the last two decades continue in the twenty-five least-developed countries until 1985, fewer than 30 per cent of children in the 6 to 11 age-group will attend school and new generations of illiterates will join the ranks of adult illiterates.

There is a further aspect involved in the illiteracy problem: it is the consequence of political and social inequalities, and is even a factor of inequality in itself. Following the inequities born of the colonial system, the socio-economic situation still presents features (subsistence economy or barter trade, social exclusion, etc.) which give no incentive for literacy. Delay in the adoption or application of agrarian reforms as well as other factors restricting popular participation in development have weakened the motivation of adult illiterates and have made it difficult to enlist the support of society, as is vital to every literacy operation. At times literacy campaigns seem hardly capable of advancing beyond the pilot, or even symbolic stage. There are also literacy programmes which, although reaching fairly considerable sectors of the illiterate population, appear to have been developed with a view to the immediate need for training semi-skilled labour rather than regard for the social factors without which development is only partial.

The two keys to lasting literacy: the motivation of those concerned and the political resolve of governments

Even where programmes exist, obstacles often appear to be insurmountable—lack of human and material resources; élitist social structures favouring minorities; inadequate communication transport; multilingualism, lack of written material, etc. But the main obstacle is probably the absence of a 'literate environment'. In face of the persistence of certain ways of living or inter-group relations it must appear questionable whether literacy is the key to better communication.

At the same time it should be noted that despite constant efforts and the progress recorded during recent years, a considerable number of problems still have to be solved as regards methodology, particularly in the formulation and use of teaching methods consonant with the situation, needs and aspirations of adult illiterates in the Third World.

The problem of illiteracy is thus seen to be an alarming and complex one, closely bound up with the overall development situation and operations. It calls for political solutions reflected in practical measures not only of an educational kind, but economic, social and cultural as well. These measures must be adopted by the governments of Member States in full awareness of the grounds for them, and their consequences. The problem is, however, virtually world-wide in its scope and it is also at a world-wide level that it must be studied and dealt with, through a multitude of projects involving international co-operation.

The recent history of literacy action is marked by campaigns or programmes carried out in many countries, either by the public authorities themselves or by semi-governmental or non-governmental organizations or, again, on the initiative of private individuals. Whether these programmes (differing widely as regards duration and scope) have been based on an overall strategy catering for illiterates without any distinction as to category, or on more selective criteria, the results achieved—which it is in any case difficult to assess in a scientific manner—range, according to the country and individual judgement, from complete success to out-and-out failure.

Certain governments have undoubtedly achieved successful results by organizing adult literacy action in the form of mass campaigns supported by firm political determination and designed as part of far-reaching social transformations carried out with the well-organized participation of the population. In most cases high priority has been assigned to the school enrolment of children, while adult literacy action has been relegated to a secondary place. In instances where primary education is virtually universal, the allotting of a negligible part of the budget to adult literacy work, the greater part being reserved for the formal education of children and adolescents, has resulted in a considerable widening of the gap between the literacy rates of the two categories, and has slowed down short-term development, which obviously involves primarily the working population. In certain countries, literacy action has recently been linked with the struggle for national independence and the assertion of cultural identity.

Tehran 1965—a historic turning-point—and the lessons of the Experimental World Literacy Programme

Unesco's duty to associate itself with the struggle against illiteracy was proclaimed as far back as the first General Conference (1946). Recommendations and resolutions adopted at numerous international conferences and meetings have endorsed this mission and acknowledged Unesco's competence in this field. From a conception of literacy action associated with basic education, there has been a move towards a functional conception linking literacy action with economic development; this evolution shows that the part played by Unesco has changed as ideas and attitudes have developed within the international community. The World Conference of Ministers of Education on the Eradication of Illiteracy held at Tehran in 1965 marks this historic turning-point.

The Experimental World Literacy Programme (EWLP) which emerged from it was carried out from 1966 to 1973, a period during which, under the auspices of Unesco and in co-operation with UNDP and other organizations in the United Nations system, special importance was attached to the implementation of intensive, selective projects in eleven of the twenty countries taking part in it. A critical evaluation of the Programme—completed in 1975 in co-operation with UNDP and published in the form of a global report at the beginning of 1976—made it possible to draw a great many lessons in regard to organization, financing, methodology, results and international co-operation in literacy action.

In this connection the evaluation stresses, for example the need; (a) to link literacy work with overall, concerted action for development which will include, besides economic growth, far-reaching social changes; (b) to view, in consequence, the 'functionality' of literacy action in its widest sense—cultural, social and political as much as occupational and economic; and (c) to determine the nature of and procedures for international assistance assigned to literacy action on the basis of national priorities and conceptions, a standpoint that implies diversified strategies and conceptions of international co-operation in this area.

Unesco's literacy action has, from very early on, been moving towards decentralization. Mention should be made more especially of the part played by the Regional Centre for Functional Literacy in Rural Areas for the Arab States (ASFEC), Sirs-el-Layyan, Egypt, and the Regional Centre for Adult Education and Functional Literacy for Latin America (CREFAL), Patzcuaro, Mexico. These two centres have been contributing for a quarter of a century to the training of personnel and have provided technical assistance to the Arab States and in Latin America. Since 1968 the International Institute for Adult Literacy Methods in Tehran has been fostering the exchange of information and documentation between literacy projects in different regions of the world.

Integrated with endogenous development and based on lifelong education . . .

Literacy is at once a right of every individual, a factor making for development and a component of lifelong education. All literacy action is based on the universal right to education without which there can be no equality of access to the possibilities of participation in economic, social, cultural and political life, and on the fact that the objective transformations wrought by any development process cannot come about as long as one is exclusively confined to oral communication; such communication, although functional in static contexts, does not allow sufficient accumulation and use of knowledge in changing societies. Lastly, literacy action is but one stage in the educational process and literacy has no purpose until it leads to further activities and the fulfilment of potential along one or other of the numerous lines connoted by the principles of lifelong education. Unesco's activities should be planned and conducted in full awareness of these ethical, socio-economic and educational dimensions of literacy action. The standpoint of literacy action is, in fact, not dissimilar from that of lifelong education in that such action tends to be an integral part of educational structures and policies, while as regards integration of the various services involved in community development, it fits into a broader framework, for example that of modernization of the rural environment.

Literacy programmes must be adapted to local conditions. The way in which the literacy problem presents itself differs considerably from one country to another and varies even within national frontiers. It is on the basis of these specific conditions that each Member State must decide its own literacy policy, which should be tailor-made to match the endogenous development effort. Hence the need to give concrete expression to international co-operation through a diversity of conceptions, strategies, contents

and methods, attaching special importance to socio-cultural features such as local traditions and languages which must be taken into consideration in the planning of literacy
campaigns. This diversified approach to the problem should be encouraged by Unesco
through the intensive exchange of experience between all countries.

As far as literacy work is concerned the concept of functionality is to be understood in the widest possible sense—economic, social, cultural and political—as denoting
the way in which the literacy process attempts to meet the need to learn the rudiments
of written communication and arithmetic and the other needs felt by every adult as an
individual and as a member of the community. To enable these different needs to be
satisfied there are types of integrated programmes designed to strengthen the learning
process and make literacy action a process of change that is both produced by, and
productive of other changes. This relation must not, however, be confined solely to the
objective of strictly economic development; it must imbue every area, whether economic, social, cultural or political, in accordance with the needs and motivations of adults
themselves and the general context in which the literacy process is taking place. This
functional link between literacy action and the life of the men and women towards
whom it is directed must be reflected in the conception of programmes, the choice of
institutions taking part and the nature of the relationship between learners and teachers.

. . . literacy implies the active involvement of society and the mobilization of world resources . . .

Literacy programmes imply the active, constant involvement of society. The elimination
of illiteracy demands, first and foremost, a clearly expressed political resolve that is
carried out in practice. Literacy programmes call, then, for the convergent, systematic
efforts of national authorities, planners and technicians, in active liaison with representative sectors of the community, and, more especially, grass-root organizations and illiterates themselves. In countries where the problem is most acute and where resources
are in shortest supply, general mobilization of this kind is vital to success and implies
extensive sacrifices that can only be made if there is clear understanding of the role that
the literacy process can play in social change and development. The role of young people
is essential, mainly in the organization of voluntary assistance. Adoption of a single
national literacy policy must go hand in hand with a large number of methods, means
and types of action at the various levels of its implementation.

Literacy action demands the world-wide harnessing of moral and material
factors. The eradication of illiteracy before the end of this century is possible in theory
if account is taken of the resources at mankind's disposal. For this aim to become a
reality depends mainly on the determination of governments, the depth of their commitment vis-à-vis the problem and the extent to which they will mobilize their human
and material resources. Support by the world community can be a determining factor in
the successful culmination of national efforts. Within the United Nations system the
major share of international responsibility falls on Unesco. Its action, if it is to be fully
effective, will have to be linked with that of the United Nations, the other Specialized

Agencies, multilateral or bilateral financing sources and non-governmental organizations. International aid to literacy operations, far from replacing national efforts in intellectual or material terms, must be increasingly designed in relation to endogenous development.

. . . according to a strategy adapted to a wide variety of situations

In the next six years Unesco will seek to achieve the following: that Member States in which the level of illiteracy is alarmingly high should assign high priority to literacy action in their national development plans and in their national budgets, that the present trend in Member States towards illiteracy (in absolute terms) should be reversed, that literacy activities should be more effectively integrated with development, and that international co-operation in this field should be considerably strengthened.

The Organization will therefore carry out studies and research with a view to obtaining a clearer picture of the problem of world literacy, establish and promote the exchange of information, develop awareness in world public opinion, assist Member States at their request to formulate strategies, organize or encourage various training activities and strengthen co-operation with international or bilateral aid institutions and with international non-governmental organizations which are concerned with literacy work—always bearing in mind the immense diversity of circumstances in Member States and the differing stages reached by them in literacy work.

Integrated rural development

By 1975 the population of the world had risen to 3,988 million inhabitants,[1] of whom 61.2 per cent, or 2,439 million, lived in rural areas. Corresponding percentages were 32.6 (370 million) for the developed countries and 72.5 (2,070 million) for the developing countries. The living conditions of this major part of the world's population are characterized in most countries by the predominance of a vicious circle of poverty, hunger and ignorance. Despite the extent of the flight from the land, which has given rise to further serious problems, it is estimated that by the year 2000 half the world's population (3,215 million persons) will still be living outside the towns.

---

1. United Nations, *Concise Report on the World Population Situation in 1970-1975 and its Long-Range Implication*, New York, 1974.

Poverty and ignorance: a vicious circle

In many cases, the economic structures peculiar to the rural world are often ill-adapted and constitute a source of injustice. On the one hand, owing to the lack of sufficiently effective agrarian policies, the all-too-frequent abandonment of food crops in favour of industrial crops, underemployment, inadequate technical training for farmers and the low productivity of a good many farms make country-dwellers an underprivileged stratum of the population; on the other hand, farm products whether intended for export or for the national market suffer the effects of the deterioration in the terms of trade, and this dooms farmers to gradual impoverishment.

According to some estimates, out of 560 million persons who had in 1969 an annual income lower than the equivalent of U.S.$50, 480 million were living in rural areas. In 1970, 400 million people in the world, mostly living in the countryside, were suffering from serious malnutrition and sixty-one out of ninety-seven developing countries had a food deficit. It is estimated that that same year, the developing countries— 70 per cent of the world population—produced and consumed only 40 per cent of the food produced throughout the world. In those same countries, food production per inhabitant increased by only 0.5 per cent per year on the average between 1960 and 1970. Approximately 80 per cent of the world's rural population are without health services: in sixteen of the least developed countries, there are more than 20,000 inhabitants per doctor. As for community and transport facilities, these are insufficient or even non-existent.

Problems of no less importance arise in Unesco's fields of competence. As regards education, most of the 130 million children between the ages of 6 and 11 who do not attend school, and most of the 800 million illiterate adults, are rural inhabitants. Besides the quantitative lack of educational services there is often a qualitative incongruity: the explicit or implicit objectives of the education given to men, women and children in rural areas frequently reflect a concept of education geared to the needs and values of urban society. An education of this type not only does not satisfy the needs of country-dwellers but may actually encourage migration towards the towns.

The low level of their training all too often prevents rural populations from enjoying the benefits of progress in science and technology, increasing their productivity and bettering their living conditions. Furthermore, the needs of these populations do not have a very high priority in scientific and technological circles. Partly at least because of the cost of research, the developing countries, which account for two-thirds of the world's farmers, were in 1965 employing only 17 per cent of all agricultural research workers, devoting 0.26 per cent of the value of agricultural production to research, as compared with 0.87 per cent in the developed countries.

Two types of equally unacceptable consequences follow from this state of affairs. On the one hand, since they are not guided by even the most rudimentary scientific information, farmers often make irrational use of soil, water and vegetation, which may result in the breakdown of ecosystems, a fall in productivity and the exhaustion and possible abandonment of the land. On the other hand, the introduction of technologies that are advanced but insufficiently suited to local conditions may also contribute to undermining the physical bases of rural life. It is therefore important to find ways and means of placing at the disposal of rural populations know-how and techniques that can contribute to the solution of everyday problems without causing a break with the pattern of the physical and social environment.

Isolated and ill-informed

The isolation of the rural world because of distance and the lack of transport facilities is compounded by the paucity of the information media. For example, in the twenty-five least developed countries, where 90 per cent of the population lives in rural areas, the annual newsprint consumption does not exceed 0.1 kilogram per inhabitant, and in two-thirds of them there is not even one radio receiver for every forty persons. Communication is often limited merely to the family and the village, its essential instrument being the spoken word enriched by the traditions which ensure cultural continuity.

Rural populations have both a more limited access to communication media than town dwellers and a narrower range of choice. The transistor set is often the only possible link but very often the messages which it disseminates are broadcast by urban producers and are of an essentially commercial nature. In this connection, one of the problems that arises is accordingly to see to it that the information media become increasingly instrumental in bringing about positive changes in living conditions, without impairing cultural authenticity. This point is extremely important since many rural societies are the heirs and repositories of rich cultural traditions, the manifestations of which reveal a remarkable creativeness that often contrasts with the poverty of expression of their material lives.

In many cases the rural environment is characterized by inequality and injustice in other sectors as well. This means that country-dwellers are more vulnerable to exploitation, and this in turn leads to a process whereby a larger proportion of the population is relegated to the fringes of society. Thus rural communities are often noted for the weakness of their institutions, and the rural population, which is frequently illiterate, unorganized, impoverished and sometimes ignorant of the language used for administrative purposes, is handicapped when it comes to solving its problems within the framework of social structures which it does not understand or which even reject it. This being the case, the rural environment may tend to turn in on itself and sometimes to resist change.

Integrated rural development—a global, diversified approach devised in terms of local conditions and the human context

From the foregoing it emerges that rural development poses many vast and complex problems. It is clear today that its various aspects are interdependent and there is reason to believe that a number of failures observed in the past were due, in part, to the fact that the programmes launched concentrated on some particular aspect of the problem, to the exclusion of others. Then, too, some programmes undoubtedly did not take sufficient account of a number of particular features in the environment considered: the facts prove that the diversity of rural situations is such that the methods used must be highly flexible and suited to the local environment, especially the human context. Hence emphasis is increasingly being placed upon a concept that is both comprehensive and diversified, namely that of integrated rural development.

Experience has shown that rural populations can mobilize their latent productivity for the sake of their own development, especially when they see some advantage to themselves in so doing. The men and women who are the goal of development must also be its agents. In view of this, it seems more and more obvious that rural community leaders and representatives must play a principal role in rural development.

It is within the framework of these general guidelines that the various components which may go to make up rural development strategies are to be sought.

The implementation of a rural development policy calls for resources that may come either from the State, from the rural communities themselves or more usually from both. It is thus important that rural development generate sufficient resources to be self-sustaining, and these resources will come primarily from agriculture. Traditional forms of agriculture, however, which are the fruit of the experience of many generations, often make optimum use of the factors of production within the context of the existing social organization and technology. Their productivity can only increase substantially if that balance is changed, usually as the result of outside influences such as an agrarian reform, more advanced technology, or some new form of production. In order to achieve any progress, these new influences must be adapted to the physical, biological and human environment in which the production takes place, and which is already subject to the influence of a large number of variable, interdependent factors.

Rural development cannot consist merely in spreading improved techniques from the advanced countries in an environment where they are unknown. It is advisable first of all to develop agricultural, ecological and socio-economic research at the national and regional levels, and in particular to try to devise suitable methods and techniques for development. This would seem to be a prior requisite in all rural development action, and a great effort is needed in this respect.

It is important that policies in the fields of science and technology (Chapter 4, pages 153-64) should take into account the specific needs of rural environments, with a view to contributing to a balanced development as between town and country. Research in the fields of agriculture, ecology (Chapter 7, page 274), hydrology (Chapter 7, page 285) and the devising of suitable techniques for the development of small industries in rural areas are some of the priorities.

The task of disseminating new methods and techniques falls to extension, vocational training and agricultural credit services, co-operatives, etc.

The impact of sociological and economic research may be particularly significant at this level because it can help to clarify the conditions governing the introduction of innovations designed to enable rural communities to raise their standard of living. Such research should be an integral part of any rural development project so that its progress may be evaluated continuously.

Education as a component in development: essential and complex . . .

Education stands out as an essential component in any development programme. It must first of all provide rural populations with the instruction that will enable them to make their voice heard and participate fully in the political, economic and social life of the nation. Next it should give them both the general knowledge and the elementary scientific and technical information needed to increase their productivity and improve their living conditions. In other words, it should be adapted to the conditions and needs of the rural environment, within the context of lifelong education and equality of opportunity. Education in rural areas cannot be considered separately from the national education system. While different lines of emphasis may be followed in rural and urban environments, a division into 'rural education' and 'urban education' will undoubtedly not be very helpful in enabling country-dwellers to reach a standard of living equivalent to that of townsfolk, or in satisfying the dictates of social justice and national unity. In the present situation of most societies, where wage scales and social prestige are proportionate to education, educational systems should offer young countryfolk the same opportunities as their city cousins. The development of education in the rural environment should therefore be based on the principle of equality of opportunity. It is specially important that the quality and output of education in the rural environment should be gradually brought up to a level equivalent to that of urban education, which is far from being the case at present. In particular, too many rural primary schools offer only an incomplete course without any possibility of pursuing further studies.

This does not mean that the development of any form of education in a rural environment does not raise specific problems, for instance because of the dispersion of the rural population as compared with the concentration of urban populations, and because of the discrimination suffered by rural areas with respect to social and economic investments. The solution of these problems often calls for considerable effort in the way of specific educational projects for the development of education in the countryside (see Chapter 5, pages 201-3). In order to encourage the rural population's participation in development, the school authorities might call on families to share part of their responsibilities (Chapter 5, pages 203-7). In some countries this movement has led to the rural primary school taking over other educational needs of the community, such as adult education.

It is desirable that primary and secondary education curricula should take account of the local environment: special techniques must then be developed for rural areas as well as for the towns. Forms of scientific, technical and economic training linked to work have special significance in rural surroundings where children generally have a pre-scientific familiarity with nature and agriculture (See Chapter 5, page 213). Since the vast majority of illiterates throughout the world are country-dwellers, rural areas are the first to be concerned by literacy training. Experience acquired in connection with the world experimental programme has shown that the concept of functional literacy should be expanded beyond the purely technical dimensions and embrace considerations of a social, economic and cultural order. Speaking more generally, the backwardness of rural areas in the field of education and their development needs make it necessary to expand out-of-school education, including the training of farm workers and craftsmen, out-of-school programmes for women and young people (see below, pages 254 ff), and educational television and radio broadcasts. Non-academic methods are particularly suited to the training of agricultural workers, as experience shows that such training is not effective unless it is based upon practice (Chapter 4, page 180, and Chapter 5, page 224).

The training of senior staff is an important part of rural development. In general, agricultural higher education institutions should have closer relations with the rural environment and take an active part in its development. The practical training of students, especially through courses that form part of the curriculum, should be developed along with economic and liberal studies, particularly extension work, rural education studies and farm management, and the training of specialists in the planning of integrated rural development (see Chapter 5, page 230). The training of technicians and other middle-level agricultural staff raises similar problems.

An essential condition of progress in education for rural development is undoubtedly the training of qualified teachers and instructors in sufficient numbers. It is highly desirable for such staff to be thoroughly familiar with the rural environment in order to be better able to adapt their teaching to the public and develop close links with the rural families and communities concerned (Chapter 5, page 218).

Despite the spread of transistor radios and, to a certain extent, the circulation of newspapers, a great deal still remains to be done to develop communication in rural environments. Radio and television can play an essential role as a channel for communication between farmers and the public authorities. A rural press, dealing with questions of interest to countryfolk and providing them with useful information, likewise needs to be developed so that new literates do not lose the skills they have acquired. It may also help to rehabilitate national languages as vehicles of culture.

The mirage of the 'green revolution'

These are the various elements that may constitute an integrated rural development programme. It should be noted however that such a programme will come up against numerous difficulties. Owing to the many factors involved it is necessary to choose from which angle a given situation can best be tackled in the hope of achieving progress. In practice, even supposing that the means were available, it is impossible simultaneously to make the material investments, to introduce the institutional changes and to mobilize the human resources which would enable a rural community to set its feet firmly on the path of self-sustaining development. The problem is to define a strategy that is valid in time, taking into account the most obvious restriction that weighs upon the rural world, namely the relatively long period required for any improvement in agricultural productivity. It would therefore seem desirable to treat certain national efforts to develop particular rural areas as real pilot experiments, to be planned and evaluated with the greatest care, and to learn from comparative studies of these experiments. At the same time, progress should be made in devising a precise methodology for the purpose of actually defining the objectives of rural development in each particular situation.

It is evident that the major objective, common to all situations, is the struggle against poverty, but past experience has amply demonstrated how difficult it is—for instance by means of technical innovations—to raise the standard of living of the whole population simultaneously without neglecting, and even sometimes sacrificing, the most underprivileged. A well-known example is to be found in the consequences brought about in certain areas by the introduction of new high-yield varieties, 'the green revolution', which had the effect of disturbing agrarian structures, pushing smallholders into debt and ultimately increasing social inequalities. Conversely, there have also been cases in which the improvement in health and hygiene conditions of the poorest sections of the population was only momentary and, whatever the beneficial effects, did not suffice to raise the standards of living of the entire community. However far-reaching the measures designed to enable rural communities to emerge rapidly from the impasse in which many of them find themselves, it is therefore essential not to neglect a more systematic approach to the problem of rural development in its long-term aspects, and to study in depth the ways and means of bringing about integrated rural development, which in many cases necessitates a radical overhaul of prevailing socio-economic structures.

In regard to the problems of the rural world, Member States differ in their policies and in their experience. In some developed countries, inhabitants of rural areas, who now represent only a minority of the total population, take an active part in economic decisions, and the essential role which they play in feeding the entire population has been recognized. Governments have made considerable efforts to extend to them progressively better services in the way of education, health and community supplies and facilities (drinking water, electricity, communications). Steps have also been taken to increase their income by means of price maintenance, subsidies, transfers, etc.

Growth of the modern sector or balanced development of urban and rural areas?

In the developing countries, stress has often been laid on the growth of the modern sector. It was thought that this would produce sufficient indirect effects to overcome bit by bit the poverty of the rural world, but in many cases those effects were not so general as expected. Some countries have long been following a development policy that strikes a balance between town and country, between the modern and the traditional sectors. This example tends to be increasingly followed today and in some cases rural regions have already undergone major transformations. Recent development plans have often given greater priority than previously to investment in rural areas. Thus data gathered by FAO show that in the national plans of thirty-seven developing countries, an average of 20 per cent of their investments are devoted to agriculture. It also happens however that the priority placed on rural development in statements and plans is not sufficiently reflected in practice: institutions are less well integrated than in theory, the methods employed do not give sufficient encouragement to popular participation, and the programmes are too short and too uncertain to make a radical transformation of existing conditions possible. There is, however, a growing awareness on all these scores, and the development policy of many countries is now going through a transitional phase.

The efforts made by Member States to develop education, science, culture and communication have, generally speaking, reflected the above-mentioned trends. In those countries which have followed a policy of balanced development, education has spread in rural areas, whether in the form of primary schooling, literacy campaigns or the training of technicians. Agricultural research, surveys of natural resources, the development of manufacturing processes which make it possible to increase rural employment, the provision of water for agriculture and other rural needs, etc., have all been given their due. Cultural policies have sought to preserve and develop rural traditions while at the same time promoting the modernization of the countryside and developing its information facilities.

The conceptual and operational options of the United Nations and Unesco . . .

During the 1960s, the United Nations laid stress on the growth of the gross national product of the developing countries through industrialization and the development of infrastructures, and helped to attain these objectives by offering the assistance of their Specialized Agencies. While this policy did bring about a relatively high average rate of economic growth in some developing countries, assessment of the First Development Decade showed that it had scarcely benefited the most underprivileged, particularly the least advanced countries and the disadvantaged rural populations. The studies and observations made on that occasion brought to light the insufficiency of economic growth as the sole objective of development and the need in future to attach greater importance to the distribution of income and to the standards of living of the most deprived with respect to nutrition, health, living quarters, education and culture. For this reason the agencies of the United Nations system now consider that rural development programmes should have a more integrated character and are endeavouring to co-operate more closely than ever in this field. FAO, Unesco and ILO have been co-operating since 1970 in the field of agricultural education and in 1974 the Administrative Committee on Coordination decided to undertake the inter-agency planning of rural development activities. The World Bank Group's hard and soft loans for agriculture and rural development rose from 18 per cent of its total financing operations in 1967-68 to 34 per cent in 1974-75. Lastly, recent meetings that have been held within the framework of the United Nations system, particularly the World Population Conference and the World Food Conference, both held in 1974, stressed the priority that should be placed on rural development and the importance of the integrated approach.

Since its inception Unesco has been concerned with the educational aspects of rural development. The 1950s were marked by the promotion of 'fundamental education', a multipurpose type of adult training which Unesco tried to develop in the rural communities of all the developing regions. From 1965 on, the world-wide functional literacy programme mainly benefited rural areas. For the last ten years Unesco has helped many Member States to train primary school teachers for rural areas. Activities designed to bring about equal access to education, especially for girls and women, have largely concentrated on rural areas which are the most disadvantaged in this regard. In the field of educational planning, Unesco has in recent years worked for the democratization and regeneration of education, paying particular attention to the needs of rural areas. More specifically, under its 'education for rural development' programme, Unesco has helped Member States, on the one hand, to train agricultural specialists, technicians and instructors and, on the other hand, to adapt the curricula and structures of primary education to the needs of rural communities. Other activities have related to the development of the mass media in rural areas, particularly the radio and rural press. Lastly, the programme on man and the biosphere, the programme concerning the preservation and development of cultures, particularly oral traditions, and the research programme in applied social science all bear on important aspects of rural development.

Unesco has thus advanced in the direction of conceptual and operational integration with a view to rural development—internally, by broadening the number of disciplines on which it draws in this connection, and externally, by contributing to bring about, within the United Nations system, a broad consensus regarding the role which a truly integrated rural development can play in the establishment of a new international order.

. . . leading to multidisciplinary integration and concerted planning

Unesco proposes to intensify its action in favour of rural development by promoting a multidisciplinary, integrated approach which neglects none of the essential aspects of the question; by basing its action on the principle that human relations should be established on a just and equitable footing; by associating the public as closely as possible in all action for rural development; by refusing the mere transfer of existing models— policies and programmes should be adapted to suit the specific characteristics of each situation.

Unesco should therefore take steps to ensure, by means of studies, meetings and publications, that there is full recognition of the importance, function and complementary nature of the various factors involved in integrated rural development, the interaction between these factors, the effects of changes and the need to take them into account in programme planning. Within its fields of competence, Unesco will assist Member States, at their request, to establish and implement integrated rural development programmes. It will promote the production of documentation and audio-visual materials, the organization of exchanges of views and experience, and the training of personnel. The introduction of innovations, especially through experimental projects, will be encouraged.

The place and role of young people in society

Youth: how to define the term?

There is no generally accepted definition of 'youth'; criteria of age, level of socialization or level of social or cultural expression do not adequately account for a situation which is inherently variable from one country or social context to another. Nevertheless, youth constitutes a group which is identifiable as such by every society, and which, as a rule, corresponds to the 15-24 age-group.

On average, this age-group represents between 7 and 10 per cent of the population as a whole, with departures from this figure in certain areas or social categories. It includes schoolchildren, students and, in most countries, a majority of young workers. In all regions, the latter make up a growing proportion of the working population, with the result that young people's preoccupations and reactions are not the monopoly of the schools or the universities: their effects are making themselves felt in the world of work and production.

This group, then, is far from homogeneous; the situation of young people varies both from one country to another and according to their socio-economic background. It is more accurate to talk of groups of young people, whose specific situation, place and role in the society of their country should be analysed in relation to the experience, socio-economic conditions and social system peculiar to the country in question. Furthermore, to whatever social group they belong, young people may or may not be organized. This distinction is necessary if one wishes to grasp the meaning of young people's various forms of expression; the level of organization to be found among young people may provide useful indications to their social and cultural status in the various countries.

The outcasts of the education system

In many countries, especially in developing regions, one of the principal problems is that of access to education and equality of opportunity. Despite the efforts being made by all States to reform their educational systems, the rate of educational wastage too often remains excessively high. In some developing countries it is as much as 40 per cent in primary education, which means that many children find themselves pushed out of an educational system with no possibility of re-entering it. This wastage merely grows worse at the secondary level, and is even more serious in higher education, to which only a small minority of young people gain access—the proportion is sometimes lower than one student per thousand inhabitants. This phenomenon, which is not found on the same scale in all countries and all social categories, affects all groups of young people in all developing regions.

Social situation and working life

In these circumstances, the preparation of young people for a working life, and hence for the social and cultural life of the nation, encounters tremendous difficulties. Faced with the large number of adolescents who have never gone to school or have received no more than rudimentary education, vocational training establishments can play only an extremely limited, compensatory role, and are themselves in danger of upsetting the balance even further.

The rural areas are the home of the most disadvantaged groups. In most cases, the opportunities open to them (training possibilities, level of employment and living conditions in general) are much more limited than in urban areas, which are the focal points for industrial development: in consequence, young people in rural areas suffer from a feeling of isolation and frustration and are tempted to leave the countryside for the towns.

In industrialized countries too, the situation and social role of young people varies according to the socio-economic conditions. In some countries, young people have been playing an increasingly important part in social life for quite some time. This is notably apparent in a particularly high level of organization, which may reach 80 per cent, taking all forms of association or grouping into account. These various organizations play a role, recognized by society, in preparing young people for social, cultural and economic life, at both local and national levels.

In countries that are currently in the throes of economic difficulties, the growth of unemployment, which particularly affects young people who are looking for a first job, or who have recently started work, and the difficulties of a social or psychological nature (marginality, delinquency, a feeling of uselessness) due to prolonged insecurity combine to heighten the tensions which usually exist between youth, eager for change, and the rest of society, more anxious for stability. The unease felt by young people about economic machinery over which they have no control pushes them into forms of activity that are attributable to their social status (young workers, students, etc.), much more than to the fact that they are young.

Overestimating youthful contestation

Somewhat hasty extrapolation of conclusions drawn from the events which occurred in some developed regions during the sixties, and which made a deep impression on the life of certain industrialized societies, has given rise to a number of errors of perspective; the importance and influence which these phenomena have had in other regions has been overestimated, and an attempt has been made, wrongly, to use them as a basis for proposing diagnoses and remedies applicable indiscriminately to all countries and all situations. The tendencies actually manifested by the various groups of young people have not borne out the validity of a number of studies, and even activities, which were undertaken on these assumptions and flawed by a form of ethnocentrism.

Since young people are affected by factors and conditions influencing the whole of the society to which they belong, it is important, in the various national situations, to seek out concrete data concerning participation of the various groups of young people in the life of society in the variety of fields in which such participation may be observed (educational system, machinery of production, cultural facilities, etc.).

Youth: an asset for development

The studies begun during the First United Nations Development Decade, and which are still continuing, show that, generally speaking, insufficient use is made of young people as a reservoir of human resources. The fact is that the attempt to mobilize young people for the work of nation-building can succeed only if it rests on precise knowledge of young people's real situation in society. Despite the large number of projects implemented, sometimes with the assistance of international organizations, such mobilization has fallen a long way short of its full desired effect because, in many cases, the forms of activity proposed were alien to the situation of the countries concerned.

New forms of activity must be found which will enable young people to be associated in development strategies, bearing in mind each country's specific tendencies and taking due account of socio-cultural differences. Admittedly, the immediate purpose of any programme thus proposed must be to achieve concrete results but, in planning such a programme, account should be taken of the fact that many groups of young people in all regions, with their keen awareness of the problems of social justice, show marked interest in the qualitative implications of development. Over and above their involvement in the social realities of their country, many young people, on world issues such as peace, international understanding, human rights and the struggle against colonialism and racism, express opinions and convictions which show that there are shared fields of concern among groups belonging to different countries and socio-cultural backgrounds. In many respects, these preoccupations coincide with the efforts currently being made by the international community to establish a new world economic and social order.

Through their willingness to commit themselves on such matters, and through the examples of serious thinking and action set by their organizations, young people show that their participation in the life of the community cannot be confined to carrying out orders: they aspire to a say in decision-making.

The part played by the associations, movements, etc., which young people form, for purposes which are usually educational, social or cultural, varies according to the country and the socio-cultural conditions. The percentage of young people who are members of such organizations in relation to the age-group as a whole ranges from under 5 per cent in some countries to 80 per cent in others. It is certain that, in many developing countries, youth has embarked on an organizational phase which denotes a growing awareness of the need to mobilize as many young people as possible in the service of development.

The integration of young people in the life of society

It is therefore evident that the questions which arise in regard to youth are to a very large extent connected with educational, social and cultural activities. This is the triple field of action towards which converge, on the one hand, the efforts of Member States, through schooling, vocational training, out-of-school education, cultural activities and the organization of leisure activities and, on the other, the initiatives of young people and their various organizations. The problems encountered by youth-directed activities go beyond the strictly technical institutional framework. They often arise from the indiscriminate application of analyses and solutions which do not stem from national circumstances or from young people themselves. The tendency which seems to be emerging in a great many Member States to attempt to involve young people more closely in society and to acknowledge the importance of their social role is proof of the interest taken by all societies in young people's concerns and in the search for new solutions to the problems which they raise.

Youth-directed activities have undergone a considerable change in the past few years, both in Member States and in the organizations of the United Nations system and non-governmental youth organizations themselves. The development observed varies according to country and socio-cultural context, but it is possible to pick out some of its essential characteristics by region and type of organization.

The changing attitude of the public authorities: updating the status of young people

In the developing countries, the action taken by public authorities bears witness to society's increasingly broad recognition of the role which youth can play in the task of development. The mobilization of young people for tasks of nation building has often been the cornerstone on which appropriate structures have gradually been erected. In a great many of these countries, young people have taken a major part in the struggle for decolonization, and their participation in development has been a natural and indispensable consequence.

In a number of industrialized countries, young people's participation in social and cultural life has increased appreciably in the past few years, as is borne out notably by the change in the social and legal status of young people—in particular the lowering of the voting age and the greater responsibilities now given to youth organizations, some of which are empowered to present proposals to the national authorities concerning normative action to improve the situation of various categories of young people. In other industrialized countries, although the general level of organization of young people is still relatively low, the events of the 1960s have led the public authorities to propose certain measures designed to modernize the educational system and the socio-educational or cultural establishments catering for young people. Thus, machinery for participation and joint administration now exists to give young people a say in certain decision structures.

For the past ten years or so, youth questions have loomed increasingly large in the concerns of international bodies, and especially the organizations of the United Nations system. The General Assembly, the Economic and Social Council and the governing bodies of various Specialized Agencies (in particular FAO, ILO, Unicef and Unesco) have discussed the education of young people for peace, international understanding and respect for human rights, youth participation in national and international development and forms of communication linking young people, their organizations and the United Nations system. In the past few years, and in particular at the World Assembly of Youth (New York, 1970) and on the occasion of the United Nations Conference on the Human Environment (Stockholm, 1972) and the World Population Conference (Bucharest, 1974) young people have been able to voice their analyses and proposals to the organizations of the United Nations system. Machinery for consultation has been set up in the form of groups of young people responsible for advising various organizations (United Nations, FAO and Unesco in particular) concerning their youth programmes and the participation of young people and youth organizations in the framing and implementation of their programmes.

From expression to participation

It is, indeed, through their organizations that young people have been able, at both national and international levels, to express their points of view most clearly and to achieve concrete results. Although at certain times in the past and in certain societies young people have shown disappointment with the work done by their organizations and with their unsatisfactory structures, it seems that for some years now, motivated by the interest which they take in social problems, they have been working to strengthen those organizations and to direct their activities into fields which appear to them to correspond to certain very broadly shared aspirations: development, the environment and active defence of human rights are the issues which motivate large groups of young people in the various regions.

In its initial stages, Unesco's action consisted mainly of *ad hoc* activities whose principal aim was the promotion of out-of-school education. The co-operation established from the outset with Member States and non-governmental organizations led to the organization of the first large-scale international conference on youth (Grenoble, France, 1964), at which Member States expressed their desire to see Unesco take up a more active role in this field. Thanks to the establishment of closer working relations with non-governmental youth organizations and National Commissions, the scope of the programme was accordingly widened to include questions of young people's participation in national development and in international co-operation. The various forms of consultation with young people established by the Secretariat, as regards both preparation of the programme and its implementation, made youth a genuine partner of the Organization and not merely the recipient of the action undertaken. Unesco was also led to analyse the various aspects of the crises which occurred in several countries towards the end of the 1960s, and which brought certain sectors of youth into the limelight.

These analyses were conducive to more serious thinking on the specific problems of youth, to the extent that they revealed both the shared motives underlying young people's activity and the diversity of situations in the various regions and countries. More recently, indeed, these analyses have led to a new attempt to diversify approaches in order to mobilize broad sectors of youth around issues of concern to society as a whole, such as peace, development, the practical uses of science, the renewal of education and the environment. Thus, in the past few years, the programme has made it possible for young people to participate in projects simultaneously affecting all Unesco's fields of competence. This interdisciplinary approach has been beneficial to the whole Secretariat, through the fresh contribution it has brought, as well as to the youth programme itself, which is at present in the process of being progressively refashioned, along lines that have met with a favourable response in both Member States and youth organizations.

At Unesco: three aspects of the programme for youth

Unesco will continue to conduct its activities in close collaboration with Member States and youth organizations and also to strive to make contact with young people who are not covered by organizations. It will collect and disseminate data, making it possible to keep under review and predict trends in phenomena concerning youth, looking upon young people not merely as subjects for study but first and foremost as active subjects, who are capable of participating fully in the development of the society in which they live.

Taking into account the interest shown by young people in major world problems such as development, the strengthening of peace, the struggle to combat colonialism, racism and apartheid and the establishment of a new international economic order, Unesco will seek to provide young people with opportunities for effective action, for example, by encouraging voluntary service organizations or by co-operating with national liberation movements.

Lastly, close attention will be paid to disadvantaged young people (young people in rural areas, young people who are unemployed and young people who have never been to school or who have received only rudimentary education). In collaboration with the public authorities and non-governmental organizations, therefore, new and original procedures and particularly flexible formulae must be found for addressing such young people, drawing considerably on the human, technical and cultural resources of the countries concerned.

Forms of artificial paradise and social disharmony

There are few countries in which situations compromising the full realization of the potential of individuals and of society are not actually experienced or felt to exist by greater or lesser sections of the population. In most cases, these are forms of social disharmony manifesting themselves as unbalanced relationships between certain categories of people and society as a whole. Analysis shows that it is possible to draw a kind of structural distinction between peripheral or disadvantaged groups (country-dwellers, women, etc.) and categories of an essentially fluctuating composition consisting of people whose common characteristic is that they are, at a particular moment, in conflict with the whole of society or excluded to a more or less marked degree from the material or moral advantages which society can and must normally confer on its members. We shall consider some of these categories—drug users, social misfits and old people.

'Structural' handicaps and situational disharmony

What these various phenomena have in common is that they result from situations in which the individual is seen to be different from the group taken as the norm. The difference may be either a physical one, as in the case of the elderly, or intellectual or mental, or it may result from conduct considered to be reprehensible. If the social structure provides no place for such an individual, or ceases to provide one, the result will be both fear and exclusion.

These situations characterized by disharmony are not new, but the problems they raise are particularly acute today. But they vary considerably in importance from society to society: manifestations of violence are more frequent in some States and the use of drugs is seen as constituting a greater danger in others, whilst the idea of old age is relative, and attitudes towards the elderly vary in different societies. Although it is not within the power of education, cultural activities, the social sciences and the information media to bring about any radical change in the facts underlying these problems, they can make some contributions towards doing so, in two ways: firstly, by enabling those who are in these situations to understand them and to face them in a more effective and more constructive way, and, secondly, by encouraging society at large to adopt a more rational attitude towards them, particularly through a better knowledge of the causes, nature and evolution of these problems.

Excesses which have wide repercussions

The use or abuse of a number of substances considered as either licit or illicit leads to difficulties of which the authorities in many countries seem to be becoming increasingly aware. Today, however, public opinion and the authorities frequently consider the consumption of these products not as an offence which must be punished, but as a social problem and as the symptom of a crisis, of unrest or of a shortcoming. Many societies, whether industrialized or not, are consuming greater quantities of substances traditionally used or of certain products used for therapeutic purposes but often to excess, or else to satisfy a desire to escape, to avoid the issue or to challenge the established society and culture. One industrialized country estimates that the abuse of alcohol costs industry 1 million dollars each working day, or 250 million dollars a year. A Latin American State estimates that there are 5 per cent of alcoholics and 15 per cent of excessive drinkers among its population aged 15 and over. In 1969-70 one Asian country distributed 2,423 kilograms of opium to its 87,945 officially registered drug addicts. It therefore seems necessary firstly to identify the reasons for this state of affairs, which will differ from country to country and even from region to region, and secondly to seek to remedy the situation by making constructive suggestions as to compensatory activities for those experiencing difficulties which lead them to make use of these drugs.

States are becoming increasingly aware that an educational policy is needed in this field and that it is urgently necessary to provide training and information for instructors and those in authority. They are carrying out experiments and commissioning research. Solutions have been sought in many directions, such as education, medicine, psychology, sociology and other disciplines, in the reorganization of certain social structures, legislation and so on. However, there is too little exchange of information among those in charge of this work in the countries concerned. Some countries are turning to international organizations or bilateral aid in their search for solutions.

From the United Nations Commission on Narcotic Drugs to the regional conferences of Unesco

The organizations of the United Nations system carry out activities and programmes to deal with problems connected with the use of drugs and there is also a specialized intergovernmental body, the United Nations Commission on Narcotic Drugs. In pursuance of resolution 1.202, adopted by the General Conference at its sixteenth session in 1970, Unesco has studied this problem from the point of view of education, the mass media and social science research. Unesco's role has been clearly defined in relation to the role of the United Nations, which is principally concerned with international regulations, control of the production of certain drugs and trafficking in them,[1] the role of WHO, which concentrates its attention on epidemiological, biological and medical research and on the problems of treating drug users, the role of FAO, which contributes to the study and implementation of projects for replacing the growing of certain drugs derived from plants, and the role of ILO, which co-operates in the vocational training of former drug users or their rehabilitation in the working world. At the end of 1972, the United Nations established UNFDAC (United Nations Fund for Drug Abuse Control)

---

1. The 1961 Single Convention on Narcotic Drugs, at present in force with 106 ratifications, and the 1971 Convention on Psychotropic Substances, which has not yet come into force.

with a view to integrating all these activities, and in 1973 a permanent co-ordinating body, the Inter-Agency Advisory Committee on Drug Abuse Control, was established.

Unesco's main task was prevention; its aim was to modify the demand for drugs, thus supplementing the measures which had been taken against production, trafficking in drugs and their supply. The Organization's activities, which began in 1971, were directed at the developed countries in the first instance. Emphasis was laid, first, on young people and the use of drugs in industrialized countries and, second, on a study in depth of the various cultural situations, by organizing sub-regional meetings on the education of teachers and parents, and by undertaking country studies.

During 1975-76 the programme was extended to the less industrialized areas such as Latin America and the Caribbean, Africa and Asia. Efforts are being made to get teachers and parents to discuss the matter without emotion and to approach the problem from a psychological and sociological point of view, without considering any specific substance. At the present time this seems to be the most effective policy for preventive education.

The Organization will continue to clarify problems associated with the use of drugs and to formulate suitable educational policies, mainly through regional meetings, the circulation of information on research and the publication of studies and experiments carried out in the developed countries, Latin America and Asia.

Knowledge of the economic, social and cultural factors involved in the use of drugs will be developed through comparative studies on drug consumption, the publication of a newsletter to disseminate the findings of social science research and training courses for social science specialists in fields relating to the used of drugs. The more general problem of social maladjustment will also be studied and possible remedies proposed.

Violence: the fruit of maladjustment

No region of the world seems to be escaping the rising tide of individual or collective violence. In some countries, the authorities are concerned about the increase in armed attacks, in others, about acts of vandalism. Violence is even found in schools and universities. Here, too, solutions are being sought sometimes by strengthening institutions with authority and sometimes by encouraging increased participation by individuals in community responsibilities.

The number of young people and adults showing signs of social maladjustment continues to increase in many countries, although there seem to be no apparent physical or mental handicaps which can explain this. This social maladjustment manifests itself sometimes by the exclusion of groups or individuals, who thus find themselves pushed to the background, and sometimes by a reaction on the part of the maladjusted, who themselves leave the 'system' through delinquency or by adopting ways of life which society frequently finds it difficult to tolerate. Some States are concerned about this problem. Having already undertaken research on it, they are attempting, by making innovations in lifelong education and by using methods some of which are profoundly imaginative, to find new solutions to problems which have suddenly become much more acute.

To deal with violence, or at least with some of its aspects, was one of the responsibilities Unesco assumed at its foundation. In the early stages, attention was concentrated on the effects of international tensions, and from 1947 to 1956 a programme was carried out on the study of international tensions as they affected international understanding. In this context, the appearance and persistence of attitudes leading to aggressive behaviour were analysed.

Study on: tensions and aggressivity, their connection with racism; the role of the mass media

The study of such aggressive behaviour and its philosophical, social and cultural aspects received fresh impetus when the principle of a long-term plan of integrated activities for the establishment of peace was adopted by the General Conference at its fifteenth session, in 1968. This plan included, for example, a study of the effects that recent scientific research will have on our understanding of human aggressivity. A symposium was held on the reduction of aggressivity through the organization of contacts between social groups, and on the analysis of the scientific aspects of the problem (the hormonal and neuro-physiological bases of aggression, environmental causes, etc.). Another symposium was held in 1970 on violence and the mass media.

The many activities undertaken in connection with these questions also included a study of the specific problems associated with certain aspects of violence in social structures related to colonialism, racism and apartheid. More recently, meetings, studies and publications have been devoted to the concept of non-violence.

In an endeavour to discover the causes of violence, the Organization has undertaken a comprehensive study based on the considerable amount of research already carried out in various fields, particularly the social sciences. In November 1975, an interdisciplinary meeting to study the causes of violence identified certain trends in current research which demonstrate the complexity of the social problems associated with the phenomenon.

In the next few years Unesco will make comparative studies on: violence and the processes of socialization and desocialization, the relations between the structures of violence and the victims of violence, manifestations of violence in schools, the situational contexts of violence, the perception of violence by the public and the role of the mass media.

The frustrations of old age

Although problems concerning the elderly are of a very different kind, they are none the less a form of social disharmony in a number of countries. This is a relatively new phenomenon, for at certain periods the elderly have been considered—and still are, in some societies—to be the repositories of wisdom and experience, and this has given them an important status as advisers worth listening to, persons of consequence and, in private life, the unchallenged heads of their families. In an increasing number of countries, however, owing to an increase in the life-span, often accompanied by the weakening of traditional family and social structures, and the effects of the fact that new age-groups are entering upon a working life, the problem of the exclusions and frustrations to which the elderly are exposed in certain kinds of society is becoming acute.

In the United Nations system the problem of the elderly has been dealt with primarily by WHO, with regard to the medical aspect, and by ILO, with respect to matters of employment. The United Nations itself dealt first with problems of social security, before tackling the matter at a general level. Although much has been accomplished, a great deal certainly remains to be done to prepare people for the circumstances of old age and to plan ways of integrating the elderly more effectively into the life of society. This would be an entirely new kind of activity for Unesco and a field in which it might be called upon to play a pioneering role.

Steps will therefore be taken gradually to elaborate and define the framework for the Organization's action, and the main directions it should take, in co-operation with the other organizations of the United Nations system and the appropriate international non-governmental organizations. A list of priority activities will be established on the basis of recent research.

It is important that the Organization should tackle each of these problems within the context of an overall social dynamic and not merely as isolated symptoms. Owing to the links which exist between some aspects of the problems, approaches should be complementary and comparative studies and exchanges of experience undertaken. There is an obvious need for close interdisciplinary co-operation and for collaboration with the other agencies of the United Nations system and competent intergovernmental and non-governmental organizations.

7 Man and his environment

The spectacular and practically universal development of technology, combined with constantly increasing urbanization, has obviously led to far-reaching changes in traditional ways of life, first of all in the industrialized countries and then, more and more, in the developing countries. In consequence of these changes, whole sectors of the population have been cut off from the close contacts they had so far maintained with the natural environment. This has been described as a divorce between man and nature, brought about by the victory of technology, but leading little by little to greater weakness in a civilization which neglects the very bases on which its development must be founded. Paradoxically, this movement away from natural processes and balances was taking place at the very time when the population explosion, combined with the desire for better living conditions and greater consumption of material goods, was placing an unprecedented strain on the considerable but nevertheless limited resources that nature offers us.

The 'environment crisis' and the 'crisis of civilization'

Imperfect understanding of the natural systems and mechanisms which make possible the maintenance of life on earth; disregard of the unintentional effects of technology, in particular the various forms of pollution; poor management of the soil, forests and water; unbridled consumption of fossil fuels; uncontrolled urbanization; the relegation of the rural population to a marginal position; destruction of the existing background to life; and the crushing of traditional cultures—these are the most obvious and most frequent disadvantages of the change that is taking place in the relations between man and his environment. While these changes are not recent—and while, in particular, the concerns to which they give rise have been reflected in Unesco's programmes from the very beginning—it is none the less true that the collective awareness of what are commonly being called environmental problems, and the international action being taken as a result, represent a phenomenon that is new both in its scope and in its consequences: the Unesco conference on the rational use and conservation of the resources of the biosphere in 1968, and the United Nations Conference on the Human Environment in 1972, mark stages in this growth of awareness on the part of governments.

In this context, what is often called the 'environment crisis' refers first of all to the deterioration of physical and biological surroundings as a by-product of the sharp acceleration in the spread of man's ascendancy over the planet and, in particular, of the unbridled exploitation of natural resources. Since that ascendancy and that exploitation are distinctive marks of economic development and population growth, it is impossible to dissociate matters relating to the protection of natural environments from those relating to man's use of the resources they afford. There is accordingly an intrinsic connection between the problems of the environment, those of development and those of population, which cannot be overlooked at any stage in the formulation of programmes of action without entailing serious consequences.

In addition, however, it must be noted that this 'environment crisis' is compelling attention at the very time when the necessity for a new international economic order is becoming apparent and when the classic forms of development, and the ways and means of providing technical assistance for countries in need of it are being challenged. There is talk, for instance, of a 'crisis of civilization', which people are trying to remedy by efforts to improve the 'quality of life'. In this context, where man is brought face to face with himself, the effort to achieve balance and harmony between man and his environment should be looked upon as a further aspect of the endeavour to secure a future for the human race that will be juster, better adapted to man's needs, and in which all people will be more closely united.

When geography dictates international co-operation

Facing all these challenges with which our time has suddenly been confronted, Unesco must make an effective contribution of its own, in all the areas of its competence, to the working out of solutions that are in line with its world-wide humanistic mission.

In the past, Unesco's activities relating to the environment and natural resources have been mainly concerned with scientific research and the training of specialists; for international co-operation, which always helps to advance knowledge, becomes an absolute necessity in the case of disciplines which are geographical in character, since nature recognizes no frontiers between States.

It is thus no accident that the major intergovernmental scientific co-operation programmes for which Unesco provides the Secretariat have developed mainly around such disciplines as geology, ecology, hydrology and oceanography. This scientific effort, designed to lay foundations for a more reliable understanding and more rational use of natural resources, is still of paramount importance. But it is being directed more and more towards interdisciplinary undertakings for improving the quality of the human environment in general, which call for increased and decisive contributions from the social sciences, the humanities, culture, education and communication, as well as for close co-ordination of all these activities. Co-ordination of this kind goes beyond Unesco's own purview and involves all the other governmental or non-governmental organizations concerned, particularly the United Nations Environment Programme.

The definition of Unesco's objectives in this field takes account of the importance of geographical factors, and reflects the research structures and administrative structures set up by most Member States for the study and management of natural resources and the various components of the human environment. The sectors involved are as follows: the sub-soil (with its mineral resources), the soil (with its various eco-systems and biological resources), continental waters (from the point of view of their manifold uses), the oceans (with their resources and special legal status), human settlements (man-made environments in which the population is becoming increasingly concentrated), and lastly, the areas, sites, monuments or works to be afforded special protection as parts of the natural or cultural heritage of mankind. At the same time, the study of the way these various components of the environment are perceived, together with general education and public information, should be approached globally; for this reason they are presented in this chapter under a separate section (see page 315 ff.).

Knowledge of the earth's crust and of its resources

Minerals and fossil fuels are key raw materials of the industrial age. The fuels provide heat and energy; metals and non-metals the materials for machines, buildings, transportation networks, communication systems and other indispensable things. Most chemicals are based on mineral raw materials; the fertilizers that enable agriculture to keep pace with expanding population derive mainly from minerals and fossil fuels. Virtually none of the enormous increase in the standard of living in the industrialized nations would have been possible without the use of vast quantities of minerals, and still greater amounts will be needed for both developing and industrialized countries.

Deposits which are being rapidly exhausted

Whereas ancient civilizations satisfied their limited requirements from deposits found more or less at random on the surface of the earth, the situation has radically changed since the industrial revolution. The ever-increasing demand for raw materials has led to the invention of more and more sophisticated techniques to find the necessary quantities of oil, coal, gas, ores, etc. from hidden deposits increasingly difficult to locate.

The mineral raw materials and fossil fuels are non-renewable. Reserves of some are seriously depleted and provision for agricultural, industrial and domestic needs at a time of rapid population growth will tax the world's ability to supply them.

At the present time, more than 95 per cent of the world's energy supply comes from fossil fuels (oil, coal and gas). Unlike most other economic minerals, these fuels are biochemical compounds which are not part of the bulk composition of the earth but have been formed and accumulated in limited quantities in certain parts of the earth's crust in the course of geological time. These compounds serve not only as fuels, but as an important source of raw materials for many industrial processes, including plastics and pharmaceuticals. The reserves of coal are substantial, but the 'lifetime' of petroleum reserves is said to be thirty-five years and that of natural gas forty years.

Increasingly inaccessible reserves

The following 'lifetimes' for the known reserves of a number of key mineral resources are often quoted: fifteen years for mercury, twenty years for tin and silver, twenty-five years for lead and zinc, thirty-five years for copper. These 'lifetimes' are considerably reduced when account is taken of the present exponential growth in demand. It should be remembered, however, that accurate information on many reserves is not available and these figures are best thought of as indicators of possible short-term shortages. Experience also shows that a slight increase in price makes exploitation of lower-grade ores economical and that a similar result is achieved through improvements in technology. Nevertheless, we may be approaching the lower limit of economically exploitable ores for some metals (for example material containing as little as a quarter of one per cent of copper is now being mined), and many of the more obvious anomalies found by geophysics and geochemistry have been tested. The time is fast approaching, if it is not already here, when ore deposits exposed on the surface or easily found by routine methods will no longer be available, and future discoveries must be based on precise understanding of the geological factors that determine the concentration of elements and minerals into localized ore deposits.

Geological correlation—the key to future discoveries

To achieve this understanding will require consideration of the entire body of geological knowledge about our planet, particularly: (a) correlation of data developed by all the physical sciences, for each can contribute to deciphering the details of ore genesis; (b) stratigraphical correlation, to identify significant geological features in areas where they are well developed or exposed, and to use them to guide mineral exploration elsewhere; and (c) correlation in time, both absolute and relative, to determine the sequence of events that led to formation of mineral deposits. Because deposits of the types discussed above occur on every continent, international co-operation is indispensable.

The geological sciences must derive general principles from the analysis and understanding of geological processes which may have their clearest expression in widely distant parts of the globe. Research in these sciences bears, therefore, a distinct mark of origin and cannot be extrapolated as readily as the results of research in the physical and chemical sciences. For example, one of the most important concepts in geology is the relationship between geological time and sequences of rock strata. This concept has usually been modelled on traditional national thinking and has to be harmonized from country to country for a correct understanding of the history of the planet. Detailed correlation of all parts of the 'stratigraphic column' is of paramount importance for the exploration of numerous resources deposited with and assembled in sediments. Correlation of the sequences of palaeozoic formations of West Africa and South America now being undertaken may, for instance, provide further information on movement of the earth's crust and lead to discoveries of iron ores, hydrocarbons, etc. Correlations being made on both sides of the North Atlantic are concentrated on sulphide ores linked to geological strata.

On the other hand, standards, terminology and classification differ from country to country. The geological sciences thus develop along different lines and, with the ever-increasing amount of locally accumulated knowledge, these paths keep on diverging. Therefore, the solution of many, if not all, basic geological problems will be greatly facilitated and accelerated when data from adjoining areas, or even from distant continents, is made more intelligible to geologists all over the world, and more applicable in economic geology.

Remote sensing techniques, computer science techniques and cartography in the service of the geologist

Environmental data handling

The development of earth sciences research produces a new flow of information, on a global scale, which is accelerated by the use of new research and observation tools such as remote sensing. The handling of huge amounts of data poses difficult technical problems if all countries are to benefit from them.

In recent years there has been an increasing effort by geologists to analyse and interpret many types of geological information in quantitative terms. This leads to the more precise application of correlative and other data-based studies in geology and will provide a more quantitative base for many branches of the geological sciences.

A broad range of statistical and other mathematical methods can now be used in geology, thanks to the availability of modern computers, which makes it possible to reduce large amounts of geological data into manageable forms.

Unfortunately computer keys vary not only from country to country but even from one research centre to another within a country. For proper use to be made of the mass of earth sciences data now available, a great effort in methodological standardization along the lines advocated by COGEODATA is still required.

However, the techniques of remote sensing, data acquisition, handling, storage and presentation are not unique to the earth sciences and follow similar developments in water and marine sciences and in the overall study of land and soil resources.

The synthesis and handy presentation of current knowledge in the earth sciences is best presented in the form of earth science maps on various scales, these being carriers of compiled, concentrated, digested and homogenized information, which lends itself to rapid evaluation of complex regional and thematic problems, thus assisting practical action. Such maps summarize in readily comprehensible form, particularly if they encompass large areas, a vast amount of knowledge accumulated over a long period in numerous publications, reports, etc. Regional and continental earth science maps are invariably based on sources from various countries, and therefore give eloquent evidence of what can be achieved by international scientific co-operation. Moreover, since the preparation of such maps must involve the geologists and geological surveys of the countries covered, their preparation and publication is best achieved under the auspices of an international organization.

Forecasting sudden eruptions of the earth's crust

The processes in the earth's crust which are responsible for the observed distribution of mineral resources also give rise to natural hazards such as earthquakes and volcanic eruptions, which take a heavy toll in human lives and inflict severe economic losses each year. On the average, since the beginning of the present century, over 10,000 persons have been killed each year in such natural disasters and the losses inflicted by earthquakes alone are measured in hundreds of millions of dollars. Greater knowledge of crustal processes will lead to a better understanding of these phenomena and to improved means of protection against them: firstly by allowing more precise delimitation of danger zones and estimation of the risks to life and property within them; secondly, through the development of systems of alert and warning of impending events; thirdly, by providing architects and engineers with the data that they require in order to design and construct earthquake-resistant buildings and public works.

Closely linked to all the problems outlined above is the problem of the training of geologists, geophysicists and geochemists both in geological mapping and mineral resource exploration and in seismological and other geophysical methods of research into natural hazards such as earthquakes, volcanic eruptions and landslides.

Although there is no overall world shortage of geologists, many of the developing countries in which large quantities of mineral resources are to be found and many that are subject to natural hazards still lack the trained earth scientists needed to devise and implement national programmes of resource exploration and management. These countries tend to depend on expertise from outside for the development of mineral resources, since they lack personnel having practical field experience. The establishment of training and research institutes of national or regional vocation, oriented towards the solution of local problems, such as the Institute for Applied Geology established with Unesco/UNDP assistance at Jeddah, Saudi Arabia, appears to meet these needs. This applied approach must not, however, detract from the strengthening of more conventional training in the earth sciences directly linked to national universities (for example, Unesco has helped in the establishment of Geological Departments of Universities in

Sri Lanka and the United Republic of Tanzania) thus permitting the production of well-trained specialists within the country itself and also enabling the teaching staff, through the linking of university research to industry, to participate actively in the development of their countries' economies.

A progressive X-ray of the planet Earth

Co-operation in the fundamental aspects of the earth sciences has a fairly long history. A major step forward in international action was taken with the launching, in 1957, of the International Geophysical Year, a major co-operative research effort that involved 30,000 scientists and technicians from some seventy countries. During the IGY the whole of the planet Earth, from its central core to its magnetosphere far out in space, was subject to intense scrutiny. Later, other international programmes under the sponsorship of the International Council of Scientific Unions (ICSU) concentrated on the study of the solid earth. The Upper Mantle Project (1963-1971) was followed by the Geodynamics Project.

But although these projects received the support of many governments, and some support from Unesco, they were essentially sponsored by the scientific community for purposes of basic research. However, their success pointed to the need for a sustained international effort in the geological sciences.

At the national level, it is clear that the problems outlined above are of vital importance to the economy of countries, and immense resources are already being devoted to their study by governments and industry in most Member States. At the international level, under the guidance of the Committee on Natural Resources of the United Nations Economic and Social Council, numerous studies have already been carried out by the United Nations, by its regional Economic Commissions, by other intergovernmental bodies such as the OECD, and by international non-governmental bodies. Many of these studies have been devoted to the assessment of global, regional or national reserves of minerals or fossil fuels, based on existing knowledge.

Within the United Nations, the Centre for Natural Resources, Energy and Transport is responsible for such economically-based studies, as well as for prospecting for mineral and fuel resources and for general strengthening of geological and mineral resources surveys. Its work is therefore complementary to the activities in scientific research, specialized training and institution-building conducted by Unesco.

Since its inception, Unesco's earth sciences programme has had as its two major objectives the promotion of international co-operation and the provision of assistance to Member States to build up their scientific potential in this field.

Unesco has supported, both morally and financially, two large-scale international research programmes, the Upper Mantle Project (1963-71) and the Geodynamics Project (1973-79) launched by the International Council of Scientific Unions. These have yielded scientific results which have made it possible, for the first time, to draw a comprehensive picture of the continuing evolution of the earth's crust throughout geological time.

The international exchange of earth sciences data has been promoted and improved through support given to such international bodies as the Committee on Storage, Automatic Processing and Retrieval of Geological Data (COGEODATA) and the International Seismological Centre.

In co-operation with the Commission for the Geological Map of the World, the preparation and publication of an important series of small-scale geological and earth science maps has been undertaken. The series includes the Geological Atlas of the World on a scale of 1 : 10,000,000, the Geological Map of Europe on a scale of 1 : 1,500,000 and other continental maps of tectonics, geomorphology, metallogenesis, metamorphism, etc.

The International Geological Correlation Programme

While these activities still continue, a large-scale programme in geology known as the International Geological Correlation Programme (IGCP) was launched in 1973. The main objective of this programme is to achieve a better understanding of the phenomena within the earth's crust which need to be observed and evaluated through international co-operation, and which have a direct bearing on the origin and distribution of mineral and fuel resources.

Two aspects of this Programme need to be stressed: firstly, that it is an interdisciplinary endeavour in which specialists of all branches of the earth sciences participate, through the various commissions, committees and organizations affiliated to the International Union of Geological Sciences (IGCP); secondly that the participation of Unesco gives the Programme an intergovernmental nature.

Although the IGCP started operating only in 1974, the first results are emerging: they concern, for instance, classification of tin/tungsten/beryllium-bearing granites, the correlation of the late Tertiary sediments of the Mediterranean region with those of the Black Sea and Caspian, the definition of the Proterozoic/Phanerozoic boundary, and so on.

Trying to counteract natural hazards

The study of natural hazards, especially earthquakes and volcanic eruptions and of the means of protection against them, has been pursued by Unesco since 1961. After a number of preparatory missions had visited the main seismic regions of the world, a first intergovernmental meeting on seismology and earthquake engineering was held at Unesco in 1964. This meeting laid the foundations of the programme which Unesco has endeavoured to implement during the past twelve years with the limited resources available in its own budget but with substantial support from the United Nations Development Programme. Among the results achieved, may be noted the establishment of the International Seismological Centre in Edinburgh (United Kingdom) in 1970, the creation of the Regional Seismological Centre for South America in 1966 and its incorporation as a regional intergovernmental organization in 1971; the establishment, with the support of UNDP and the Government of Japan, of the International Institute of Seismology and Earthquake Engineering in Tokyo, where over 200 seismologists and earthquake engineers from some forty developing countries have since received advanced training; the completion, again with UNDP support, of a Survey of the Seismicity of the Balkan Region, and of an important research programme in soil dynamics at the National University of Mexico; another large-scale UNDP project, at present under way, is aimed at the modernization of the regional seismological network in four countries of South-East Asia. Quantitative and numerical information on earthquakes, volcanic eruptions and other natural disasters is contained in the Annual Summary of Information on Natural Disasters published each year by Unesco. One of the important aspects of this programme has been the sending of missions of experts to the sites of natural disasters, such as earthquakes, volcanic eruptions, landslides and avalanches, as soon as possible after their occurrence, in order to study in detail the mechanisms and effects. The scientific and technical value of such missions has been widely recognized.

International, multidisciplinary action

The dimensions of the problem are such that it is indispensable, if significant results are to be achieved, to define the limits within which Unesco will confine its action. In brief, it is assumed that Unesco will concentrate its efforts on those scientific aspects which are best dealt with by an intergovernmental organization, bearing in mind the need for close and continuous co-operation with the competent international non-governmental scientific unions and associations.

Four *main themes* may be defined: firstly, the acquisition, handling and analysis of the vast amount of data required for the study of this problem; secondly, international co-operation and co-ordination of geological research into the evolution of the earth's crust; thirdly, the synthesis and application of the knowledge thus acquired to the discovery and rational use of mineral resources; and fourthly, the study of natural hazards and of the means of protection against them.

For the planning and execution of the activities corresponding to these main themes, the three principal *modes of action* will be: the continuation of the International Geological Correlation Programme, for which Unesco will provide the planning and co-ordination machinery, whereas the actual scientific research will be carried out by the participating Member States and will be largely financed by them; a series of international co-ordination, consultation and liaison activities particularly in the field of cartography; lastly, assistance to Member States particularly for the training of specialists in the earth sciences through post-graduate courses and seminars.

The multidisciplinary approach, involving not only natural scientists and engineers but also human, social and economic scientists, will therefore be an important feature of all the programmes devoted to the achievement of the objective. This will help to ensure that public opinion and decision-making on matters relating to mineral and energy resources and to natural hazards will be based on sound scientific information.

The biosphere: man's influence on his environment

The thin layer of soil, water and air surrounding our planet, to which all life is confined and in which man lives and has evolved, consists of a number of complex, self-sufficient units or ecosystems within which a certain equilibrium is maintained through the interactions between communities of animals, plants and other organisms and the chemical and physical elements of their habitat.

How far can man modify his environment?

As a gatherer of food and an occasional hunter, man had, at first, no greater impact on these ecosystems, of which he formed an integral part, than any other mammal species. Yet from the moment he mastered fire and invented tools and agriculture, he began to alter the 'natural' environment and affect its original equilibrium. These technological advances enabled man to modify his immediate environment in ways generally more favourable to himself; it is only through increasingly extensive modification of ecosystems, through making them more and more 'artificial', that man has achieved the high productivity levels of modern agriculture, without which human populations could not have been sustained at present levels. In modifying these ecosystems, man made them simpler through the intentional or accidental elimination of animal and plant species. At the same time man has created his own habitat, his own artificial ecosystems, those vast industrial complexes and urban agglomerations in which nearly half the population of the world now lives.

The key question is, how far can man go in the manipulation of the environment. The progressive simplification of agricultural ecosystems carries with it the risk of disruption and breakdown since a simplified ecosystem is generally less able to react to invasion by pest or disease or to accommodate unexpected events. As the size of human populations and economic activities increases, so does man's potential for disrupting such systems. With the world's population doubling during the next thirty years and economic activity at least tripling, man's total impact on his environment could soon be overwhelming.

Feeding the world population: saving land from erosion and the encroachment of towns

Resources are limited and unevenly distributed. Although we refer to the whole planet as our habitat, the land surface of the earth, which forms man's ecological habitat, constitutes about a quarter (some 13,000 million hectares) of the total surface of the globe. But of this total only one hectare in ten is arable land under cultivation. With very considerable labour and capital investment, only one additional hectare out of ten, at present covered by pastures or forests, could conceivably be brought under cultivation. Another one and a half hectares would be left for rough grazing while the rest (six and a half hectares) is not suitable for any significant food production. In other words, we are already making use of the land that is most productive and easy to exploit. More important, some of the land already in use is showing signs of deterioration; it has been estimated that about five million hectares are currently lost for food production each year, mainly through the expansion of man's built environment and through processes such as erosion and salinization.

Thus man remains very largely dependent on the plant and animal yield from a relatively fixed area of land. The urgently required increases in useful biological production must therefore be sought through making more rational use of those terrestrial resources that are available, that is, by utilizing ecosystems in the best possible way while making sure that they remain resilient (i.e. capable of absorbing stress) and that their renewable resources are not used on a non-renewable basis and thus lost for all time.

Within the land areas now used by man, biological resources are distributed in an unequal way. While opinions differ among countries on how a society can best plan and organize the use of its biological resources (there is often a conflict between the need to satisfy acute, short-term demands and long-term conservation requirements), there is general agreement on the need for more equitable use and distribution of these resources.

No matter what improvements are brought to the production and distribution of biological resources, particularly of food, there are limits to the numbers of men that planet Earth can support, to the number of cattle one hectare of land can feed, to the extent to which soils can be used and plant and animal species can be destroyed without endangering the life support mechanisms on which man depends. We must now make use of all the resources of our environment in a more rational way if we are to ensure our own social and economic development as well as the survival of future generations.

Fragility of the ecosystems

Limits of resources but also limits of our knowledge. A considerable amount of scientific and practical knowledge has been accumulated over the centuries concerning soils, animals and plants, and about the use of biological resources; there have been some remarkable success stories in the fields of land utilization, agricultural production and forest management, particularly in the temperate zones. But contrary to what most people believe, even in these priveleged areas of high and sustained yields, little is known of the long-term effects of some developments of major significance, such as the massive use of pesticides and fertilizers or the introduction of new crop varieties.

This lack of knowledge is, however, much more acute in relation to tropical and sub-tropical ecosystems; for instance, how a tropical rain forest ecosystem actually works and what best use can be made of it is far from being well known. With their many species and rich range of interactions, still imperfectly understood, tropical rain forests are dynamically fragile and although they are well adapted to maintaining themselves in the relatively stable environment in which they have evolved, they are much less resistant to disturbances caused by man than are the simpler, more robust temperate forest ecosystems. Covering as they do some 560 million hectares, tropical rain forests are coming under heavy pressure in a timber-hungry world. But in tropical forests the greater part of the nutrient capital of the ecosystem is contained in the trees themselves. As a consequence, it is generally not easy to achieve permanent cultivation in these areas, where production forestry remains one of the most rational forms of land use. Unfortunately, areas where timber has been felled in quantity are subject to severe soil erosion or to the process of laterization, and the area concerned can be invaded by coarse grasses which turn it into a kind of barren savannah.

Acquisition of basic knowledge on the structure, functioning and productivity of ecosystems is therefore needed at the same time as development of safe methods for their continued utilization. It is widely known that badly chosen land use practices, or wrongly applied management techniques, have led to decreasing agricultural yields in several parts of the world and have sometimes even transformed once productive land into wasteland and desert. Thus the decline of the great Mesopotamian civilization—which was based on irrigated grain production—has been in part attributed to increasing soil salinization resulting from imperfect drainage.

There is, however, an even more urgent need in all regions for information which directly links the resource and environmental problems found in a given area with the social, cultural, economic and biological characteristics and aspirations of the local populations. In particular, information is required on such questions as the social and environmental consequences of alternative land use practices in a particular area and the scientific basis for achieving the optimum sustained yield from ecosystems over the longest possible period.

In the Sahel, for example, the encouragement of sedentary farming reduced the areas of grazing land available to nomadic herdsmen, while the digging of deep wells and the elimination of many of the diseases to which cattle were prone led to overgrazing and destruction of the fragile pasture land with catastrophic results for men and animals during the recent five-year drought.

In short, population/environment/natural resources balance is the key problem area where further information is required in all parts of the world. Although considerable amounts of data exist on individual aspects of this problem, the use made of them has often fallen short of expectations. Research findings have often proved of limited value within the context of development planning and indeed have been unusable by the decision-maker in the mono-disciplinary form in which they are generally gathered and presented. Furthermore, available data are often concerned with particular situations in temperate zones, and the application of knowledge and techniques developed under temperate conditions in the humid tropics and in the arid zones has resulted, and continues to result, in undesirable and sometimes disastrous consequences for the environment and for sustained yield productivity.

International co-operation dictated by nature

Although environmental and resource use problems take on a specific form in different geographic areas of the world, they should nevertheless be viewed in their global or regional perspectives, since the same type of problem is often shared by a number of countries. Information gained in one country on how to halt the spread of desert areas, for example, has a major bearing on the ecological, economic and social future of the country concerned, but is also of obvious interest to other countries facing similar conditions and difficulties. Furthermore, no single country has all the expertise required to tackle all the complex problems involved in population/environment/natural resources interrelationships.

The idea that international scientific co-operation could help develop the knowledge necessary to make better use of areas whose resource potential had previously been insufficiently considered was first developed under the Arid Zone Research programme, sponsored by Unesco in the 1950s and early 1960s. Although the efforts devoted to this activity remained relatively small, they demonstrated the usefulness of integrated land resources surveys which constituted a truly ecological and interdisciplinary approach to the study of potential resource development. They showed at the same time the value of mobilizing scientific manpower from developed countries to assist developing countries affected by a same environmental problem, in this case aridity. They also attempted to link basic research with actual land use problems and to consider the human side of these problems at the same time as their physical and biological aspects.

Through a quite different approach, in the 1960's, the International Biological Programme endeavoured to focus the attention of the scientific community on the then little-known subject of ecosystem studies, in which plants and animals were not considered independently as they had usually been in previous biological research.

Experience acquired showed that emphasis should be placed on the need for an interdisciplinary approach, extended to the social and human sciences, and for collaboration not only with scientists and academics but also with government departments and decision-makers. It also revealed the advantage of a *problem-oriented approach* which will focus research on the resolution of problems of high public priority which have social, economic and environmental dimensions.

In semi-arid zones, for example, problem-oriented research will often be designed to determine and improve the carrying capacity of extensive rangelands and to help stop desert creep.

In mountain areas it will be concerned with economic and environmental effects of increased tourism. How far can the equipment of an Alpine resort with additional ski lifts be continued without degrading the high meadows and thus interfering with the livelihood of local farmers and spoiling the natural attractions of the resort? It will be concerned with the problem of migration from high altitude settlements in the Andes and its repercussions on the lowland coastal and humid tropical ecosystems.

Specialists as equal partners in research

The complexity of these problems calls for a broadening of the range of expertise applied in their solution. Natural scientists on their own can supply only partial and inadequate answers, which increasingly need to be related to a range of social phenomena, needs and conditions. This requires that natural and social scientists take part as equal partners in the planning and implementation of research projects. In a current study on population/environment/resources interrelations in small islands of the Pacific, for example, the research team includes ecologists, pedologists, nutrition experts, human geographers, biogeographers and marine biologists. The study of irrigated lands, requires the co-operation not only of water engineers, hydrologists and agronomists but also chemists, soil physicists, biometeorologists, medical doctors, sociolists, anthropologists, economists and planners. The difficulties involved in creating such interdisciplinary research teams—and in integrating fully the results achieved—should not be underestimated: their effectiveness depends on detailed planning at the outset.

At the same time the achievement of an integrated and interdisciplinary approach to research is facilitated by the development of new tools in land and eco-systems studies. These tools consist first of new methods, including remote sensing, which allow for an overall appraisal of land features and which can show the evolution of an area through continuous monitoring. They also derive from the methods of system analysis and from the utilization of ecological models. Remote sensing, aerial photography and airborne radar are all being used or are about to be used in the classification and continuous monitoring of tropical forests, vast areas inaccessible to normal inventorying and surveying techniques. Advanced systems and mathematical approaches have been applied to the study of total ecosystem functions. At several grazing land sites in North America, for example, systems dynamics techniques have been used to predict the responses of an ecosystem to natural or man-made stress, particularly from the viewpoint of optimizing the yield that can be obtained from these areas.

The specificity of ecological problems demands endogenous scientific development

Of necessity, *governments and decision-makers* will be increasingly involved in assigning priorities, shaping the orientation of research and facilitating the mechanisms of scientific co-operation. A start has been made in promoting an approach which has the twin advantages of projecting the practical face of science to government leaders and of involving decision-makers in the formulation and implementation of research projects. Mechanisms are being developed through which the planner can express his precise information needs during the design phase of a research project and which can, in turn, be used for the timely insertion of the synthesized results of research into the decision-making machinery. Certain aspects are less positive, however, particularly as concern the *build-up of local capabilities and information exchange*. It is essential to promote the endogenous development of science and technology in all fields related to terrestrial biological resources and the natural environment. Unfortunately, there remains a debilitating shortage of indigenous expertise and local infrastructure available to developing countries for environmental survey, research and management. Here is yet another example of the instability which, in so many fields of development, penalizes the developing Third World: the training of specialized personnel who are familiar with the ecological and socio-economic problems of their countries, is undertaken mainly in foreign institutions under different ecological conditions, and the experience gained is not fully relevant to the problems of the region from which the trainee has come.

An intimately linked problem is the major shortage in many regions of centres or institutes for integrated research and training applied to land development.

At the same time, there are obvious advantages to be gained from the exchange of research information, particularly among and between countries having similar ecological and bioclimatic conditions and socio-economic problems. For example, countries of West and Central Africa containing areas of humid tropical forest can contribute greatly to, and gain considerably from, 'transversal' co-operation and transfer of knowledge with Latin American and South-East Asian countries which contain similar areas of humid tropical forest. Unfortunately, until recently, mechanisms and procedures for promoting such exchanges of knowledge and experience have been hampered by differences in culture, language and level of scientific capability. A considerable effort to build up vertical and transversal channels where common problems exist can be envisaged which will complement the long-established mechanisms for communication that exist within the international scientific community.

Interdisciplinary structures and approaches

The national context
In most countries, responsibility for the formulation and implementation of policies for the use of land has traditionally been split between various government agencies, each one being concerned with a particular sector of the economy or with the management of a particular resource for a specific purpose. Thus decisions concerning the various uses of water are often taken independently by different agencies, forests are not always handled by a single organization and land comes under the jurisdiction of local, regional or national administrations having different objectives. Development and management projects have often been justified on the basis of anticipated benefits in one economic sector only and adequate mechanisms for comprehensive appraisal of a particular project—and for genuine comparison of alternatives—have generally been lacking. Over the past ten years or so, however, there have been signs that integrated and co-operative approaches to planning are being increasingly promoted by countries. For example, the importance which governments attach to a comprehensive approach to environmental and natural resource matters is witnessed by the establishment of national machineries for the purpose. By the end of 1975, it was estimated that some sixty countries had established national environmental ministries, departments, councils or secretariats, and the

concept of land use planning, or *aménagement du territoire* has gained considerable momentum.

Greater emphasis is being given to social goals and to qualitative measures of development in planning the use of biological resources and in managing the natural environment. A number of countries are taking positive and concerted action to stop land degradation and resource deterioration and to reclaim territories that once were productive but have now become desert and wasteland. There is also a trend for governments to join together in co-operative activities, as, for instance, the countries of the Sahel have done for both short-term and long-term solutions to the drought problem. Intergovernmental co-operation between countries has been established in a large number of fields, in certain cases at the highest level, as instanced by the 1974 summit agreement between the United States of America and the Union of Soviet Socialist Republics to establish biosphere reserves in consonance with the goals of the MAB Programme of Unesco.

In a number of countries, an effort has been made to establish survey, research and training institutions taking an integrated approach to the study of the potentialities of land. Pioneer work in this direction was undertaken some twenty years ago while centres dealing with aerial survey have expanded their activities. In the developing countries, the idea of interdisciplinary national resources research centres has gained momentum. This effort at the research and training level is, however, still hampered by the reluctance of existing 'traditional' and sectoral institutions to relinquish some of their authority in favour of a co-operative approach.

Convergent action within the United Nations system

Activities within the United Nations family
At the international level, the particular spheres of activity of most organizations of the United Nations reflect the structures which have been developed and which still prevail in most national governments. This specialized approach remains adequate to deal with many of the problems connected with the use of natural resources. At the same time there has been in recent years a trend toward interdisciplinary and inter-agency approaches in such fields as pest management and control, with co-operation between FAO and WHO, the management of grazing lands, with co-operation between FAO and Unesco, and the effects of major schemes of river basin development on man and his surroundings, where many agencies have a contribution to make. Thus, the activities of a number of United Nations agencies include environmental considerations, and the work of FAO in the field of agriculture, forestry and fisheries and of WHO in health and sanitation can be underlined in this respect. In addition, mechanisms for co-operation have been developed within the United Nations system in order that Specialized Agencies can draw on the particular expertise and spheres of competence of each other. To take one example, FAO and Unesco are recognized as focal points for land resources management and ecosystem research respectively, and have made arrangements to help ensure that their programmes in these fields are complementary and mutually supporting.

The convening in Stockholm in June 1972 of the United Nations Conference on the Human Environment represented a new impetus for efforts in this field and served to focus the attention of governments and public alike on the urgent need for action. The establishment, following this Conference, of the United Nations Environment Programme (UNEP) has provided the machinery for the co-ordination and support of relevant international activities. It should be noted that one of the priority subject areas of UNEP is concerned with terrestrial ecosystems, and their management and control. Activities within this subject area are mainly concentrated for the moment on arid lands and grazing lands ecosystems and on tropical forests and woodlands. The role of UNEP, which is not an 'operational' organization, is to stimulate and co-ordinate environmental programmes within the entire United Nations system and thanks to its Environment Fund it can support joint ventures with co-operating agencies such as Unesco in areas of common interest.

Finally, Ecosoc itself has called for co-operation between the United Nations organizations in the search for solutions to a number of environmental and resources problems. This has led to the recent significant development in inter-agency and inter-sectoral approaches. This includes resolution 1878 (LVII) concerning the problem of drought in Africa and resolution 1898 (LVII) concerning science and technology for arid zone problems. As a follow-up to the latter resolution, Unesco has led an inter-agency workshop for the production of a report on the obstacles to the development of arid and semi-arid regions. Finally the United Nations Conference on Desertification, called for by General Assembly resolution 3337 (XXIX), has also led to the reinforcement of this co-operative approach.

International non-governmental initiatives

At the non-governmental level, the International Council of Scientific Unions (ICSU) has played, and continues to play, a major role in harnessing the effort of the international scientific community. Thus, the International Biological Programme (IBP) of ICSU, which terminated in 1974, represented a valuable start and precedent in international co-ordinated research on biological productivity and human welfare. It has been followed by other relevant ICSU undertakings, such as the Scientific Committee on Problems of the Environment (SCOPE) and the International Association of Ecology (INTECOL). Activities on the conservation of natural ecosystems are promoted through the International Union for the Conservation of Nature and Natural Resources (IUCN), which Unesco was instrumental in founding in 1948.

From the synoptic studies by Unesco on the arid zones and the humid tropics . . .

Unesco has a special and perhaps unique responsibility for responding to the changing needs of a changing world in the field of the natural environment and its resources. This responsibility is based on the traditional role of the Organization in respect to the scientific, cultural and educational aspects of the environment, and to the fact that this broad mandate preadapts the Organization for a comprehensive and non-sectoral approach to the basic problems of development.

The Arid Zone Programme, launched by Unesco in 1951, was the starting point of many present-day actions to combat desertification. A wide public was reached by synoptical studies dealing, for example, with the natural resources of arid and semi-arid Africa, the utilization of land and water and the related human problems including nomadism. Concurrently, Unesco devoted attention to the other side of the problem, namely humid tropics research. A series of actions for stimulating scientific research relating to the humid tropics and for promoting international co-operation in this respect, were implemented.

This work has been closely linked with a programme for preparation and publication of thematic maps and surveys relating to the environment and its resources which has been implemented in co-operation with relevant United Nations agencies. These activities have often developed from one of Unesco's traditional roles, that of promoting international scientific understanding through helping the development of comparable methodologies and agreed nomenclatures. In the course of the preparation of the Unesco/FAO Soil Map of the World, for example, the difficulties encountered in producing a legend owing to the widely varying approaches of the different pedological schools of thought led eventually to a fruitful development of ideas.

. . . to the Biosphere Conference (1968) and the Programme on Man and the Biosphere (MAB)

Unesco has also for a number of years helped in the training of specialists from developing countries in modern approaches and techniques for integrated ecological research and survey. A number of international post-graduate training courses are sponsored on a continuing basis, while *ad hoc* training courses and seminars for scientists and resource managers and decision-makers are also organized. Another aspect of Unesco's work in helping increase the indigenous capabilities of countries for integrated ecological research and training relates to assistance in the building-up of infrastructures. Typical of what has been achieved in this respect are the Institute for Applied Research on Natural Resources at Abu Ghraib, Iraq, and the Central Arid Zone Research Institute in Jodhpur, India, which were established with Unesco and UNDP assistance, and which provide a focal point for work in these countries on research and survey of resources linked to economic development. Another example is the creation of a centre, for the analysis of documents on natural resources of the Niger basin, set up in Niamey in the framework of the Niger River Commission.

Within this context of activities Unesco convened, in 1968, a major intergovernmental conference of experts on the scientific basis for rational use and conservation of the resources of the biosphere. The Biosphere Conference helped launch the then radical assertions that the problems of accelerating the rates of economic and social development of countries were intimately connected with problems of the rational use of biological resources, that conservation of these resources should be considered as an element of their rational use and not in opposition to it, and that the improvement in quantitative and qualitative terms of the prosperity and well-being of societies was intermerged with the quality of the relationships between man and his global environment. The Conference recommended the development of a co-operative research programme in this field which was formally launched by the General Conference in November 1970 as the Programme on Man and the Biosphere (MAB). This programme provides a major interdisciplinary focus at the intergovernmental level for improving knowledge of terrestrial biological resources and of interrelationships between human activities and terrestrial ecosystems. The programme, in which both developed and developing countries are playing an active part, has now moved into its operational phase and is conducted in close co-operation with the other United Nations organizations concerned (UNEP, FAO, WHO, WMO) as well as with ICSU and IUCN.

1982 objective: a three-part plan of action

Unesco's programme action in this field will emphasize the study of the structure and functioning of ecological systems and their mode of reaction when exposed to human intervention. It will stress the impact of man on the environment but also the impact of the environment on man, considered as a biological and adaptive creature and as a social, cultural and economic being. Unesco's actions will be primarily concerned with research, training and information exchange. They will not be concerned with the operational aspects of management of terrestrial resources where FAO has a lead responsibility. Rather these actions will seek to provide the objective scientific information—from within both the natural and social sciences—on which sound management can be based. They will be oriented to the solution of concrete practical problems.

Action will be conducted along three main lines: First, activities will be promoted within the framework of an intergovernmental and interdisciplinary programme of scientific co-operation on Man and the Biosphere (MAB). The implementation of this international programme is expected to result in qualitative and quantitative changes in the way in which countries manage and exploit their natural resources, through providing the objective scientific data that are required by decision-makers and planners.

Supervision of the programme will be assured by a representative intergovernmental body, while co-ordination and harmonization of countries' contributions to the international scientific effort will be promoted through flexible mechanisms for project support and information exchange and by making available the technical advice and guidance requested by countries. As the six-year period progresses, there will be an increasing shift in programme actions from the elaboration of guidelines and frameworks for co-operation to the implementation of concrete field activities and integrated pilot research projects, to be undertaken in co-operation with UNEP. These projects will be mainly focused on arid and semi-arid zones and on tropical and subtropical forest areas, though certain projects will be sited in other areas which are particularly fragile and vulnerable to man's impacts, such as high mountain systems and small islands in tropical zones.

The second part of the programme is aimed at an integrated approach to land resources research and management, through development of appropriate methodologies and synthesis of existing information.

The desired impact is first to improve the tools available to Member States for planning purposes through development of methodologies for integrated land studies and for research on ecological processes. Secondly, it is planned to make more efficient use of existing knowledge on land resources and ecological processes through the collation, synthesis and dissemination of information relating to the natural environment. By 1982, regional and sub-regional maps on soil, climate and vegetation will have been prepared for most regions of the world. These maps and related ecological documentation and techniques will serve to strengthen the body of methods and information which can be used for integrated land use planning and development.

The third part of the programme concerns the promotion and development of national and regional capacities for research and management on problems associated with the environment and with the integrated use of biological terrestrial resources.

The desired impact is to increase the indigenous capabilities and capacities available to Member States for an integrated approach to the use of natural resources and to facilitate the adoption of this approach through making planners aware of the value and importance of this approach for balanced development.

This impact will be approached in part, by training of specialists and technicians in the field of integrated ecological research and management. It is intended that, by 1982, and in co-operation with UNEP, the organization of training courses and seminars and provision of study grants for *in situ* training will have resulted in a significant contribution being made to the training of over 800 resources scientists and managers, ecologists and other environment specialists, from over sixty developing countries. The incorporation of environmental concerns as an integral part of the decision-making process on the use and development of natural resources will also be promoted through the convening of seminars and the preparation of guidelines for decision-makers.

Finally, if this programme of stimulation and co-ordination is well conducted, countries will by then have a larger number of competent and indigenous personnel and will be in a better position to develop and strengthen their national infrastructures for ecological and environmental research. By 1982, it is hoped that twenty institutes for integrated development of natural resources will exist in at least ten countries of the humid tropics, and at least ten countries in arid and semi-arid zones. It is further expected that twelve of these institutes will by 1982 be fulfilling a regional role and a regional function.

Sharing water resources

The development of human societies, and of the cities where these societies blossomed out, has always been conditioned by the availability of the water resources essential for their existence; and, despite all its technological transformations, the modern world has not changed this immutable law. On the contrary, the problem of water has, in our days, assumed new dimensions, due partly to the growth of the population but even more to the rapid increase in the needs of agriculture and industry and to the phenomenon of urbanization. The solution of this problem has become a key factor in economic and social development, and it calls for the installation of special structures in national administrations. More and more countries are facing a water crisis, affecting both the quality and the quantity of the water supply.

World water consumption in 1975: 3,000 cubic kilometres

Needs and resources

The most urgent aspect of this problem is the continuous increase of water consumption, which is rising in geometric progression, doubling over a period of twenty years or so, and therefore outstripping by far the population growth. The concentration of people in towns and changes in the way of living are partly responsible for this increase: the needs of a large modern city may be as much as 1,000 litres per person per day (New York), although domestic and municipal consumption continues to represent only a relatively small proportion of the total water consumption (approximately 5 per cent). It is industry which represents the most dynamic factor, particularly the relatively new branches of industry, which demand vast quantities of water: the production of one ton of synthetic fibre, for instance, may require from 3,000 to 5,000 tons of water. But the greatest consumer of water continues to be agriculture (about 70 per cent of the total) especially since, as opposed to the situation in numerous industries, most of the water used for irrigation is evaporated and so cannot be re-used. At the same time, the extension of irrigated areas and the general adoption of new agricultural techniques—such, for instance, as those of the 'green revolution'—which are essential for improving the world food situation, necessitate a continuous increase of water consumption.

The total quantity of water used in the world in 1975 is at a fairly rough estimate some 3,000 km³, representing about 7 per cent of the total mean discharge of the rivers which constitute the bulk of the renewable water resources. Between now and the year 2000, it is reckoned that water consumption will double, rising to about 6,000 km³. This would constitute only about a quarter of the volume of water in Lake Baikal, or a tenth of the deep ground water reserves under the north-west Sahara. Viewed on a world scale and in mean hydrological conditions, these figures do not appear disquieting, but there are two points to be considered. The first is that the doubling of the quantity of water made available to users represents for the world a vast investment, far greater than that already made for current utilization on account of the decreasing yield of the necessary works. The second is that water resources are very unevenly distributed throughout the various regions of the world and in different years and seasons, so that there are many countries where the situation is already critical. Water shortage is chronic in arid or semi-arid regions where use has to be made of non-renewable (and consequently precarious) underground sources or of non-traditional sources (such as desalinized sea water, which necessitates a heavy consumption of energy). Temperate regions, too, are affected by water shortage, due to fluctuations of the hydrological régime.

Floods and drought

Not only do these fluctuations imply restrictions on water usage; their two extremes— floods and drought—give rise to natural disasters which have grave effects on society. Floods occur frequently and affect most parts of the world. They are particularly violent in zones that are subject to tropical cyclones: the cyclone which struck the Gulf of Bengal in November 1970 caused the death of 300,000 people in Bangladesh, in addition to incalculable material damage. Even the most developed countries, possessing excellent prediction services and efficient technical resources, do not escape the effects of floods; for instance, the hurricane Agnes, which ravaged part of the territory of the United States of America in June 1972, caused damage estimated at $3,000 million. Drought has very different hydrological causes and characteristics, and its effects are less spectacular than those of floods; but they are more insidious and lasting, perhaps even more disastrous, since they are closely connected with endemic famine in the world, and may in addition undermine for years and years the prosperity of an entire region (case of the Sahel).

The quality of water

The age-old practice of using rivers and streams for evacuating refuse has not only subsisted to the present day, but has assumed such proportion as to lead to very disquieting results. The same water is subjected, successively, to domestic, industrial and agricultural uses, causing varying degrees of pollution, and is then required to carry down to the sea all the organic and inorganic waste inevitably produced by large population centres and in particular by complex industrial works. This chemical and other waste collects in the rivers and lakes which are no longer able to destroy them by a natural cleansing process, so that they even seep through into the ground water. The resulting deterioration of the water makes it less fit for further use, besides creating a serious threat to public health and adversely affecting the fauna, flora and natural environment. This considerably increases the gravity of the water problem, since it is no longer a question only of whether the required quantity of water is available in a given place and at a given time, but also of whether the *quality* of the water available makes it suitable for the purpose for which it is required. Thus the water crisis becomes a major component of the environment crisis. It should be noted that the deterioration of the quality of water is due not only to the quantitative increase of consumption with the resulting increase of refuse; it is above all a consequence of the development of new products and new production technologies (use of detergents, development of the chemical industry, increasing use of chemical manures and pesticides in agriculture, etc.), releasing into the environment substances that are all the more harmful for not being always biodegradable. It may be said that the problem of combating water pollution, at least in the industrialized countries, has become more difficult than that of ensuring an adequate quantitative supply of water. There is, unfortunately, a risk of the same situation arising in the developing countries, where the factors making for pollution are tending to increase.

The need for a water policy

Rational water management

The water problem, only a few of whose multiple aspects have been listed above, is such as to make it imperative for every country to adopt a *water policy* to ensure the *rational management of water resources*, in regard both to their quantity and their quality. This water policy must be based on the geographical, economic, social and cultural characteristics of each individual country, and it will have to be integrated with the fundamental options governing the development of the country in question. At the same time, there are certain common measures relating to efficient water management that must be included in all countries' water policies. The first is to assess as accurately as possible both the water resources available in the principal basins and in the country as a whole, and also the country's needs, present and future; the second is, by using the technical means which engineers have at their disposal though they may involve large investments, to redistribute these resources, in space and in time, so as to meet the specific requirements in respect of water for domestic, agricultural, industrial and recreational use; the third is to regulate the use of water for these various purposes, bearing in mind the question of pollution; the fourth is to take steps to anticipate or alleviate the disastrous effects—floods or drought—of fluctuations of the hydrological régime; and the last is to preserve sufficient water of sufficient quality for further use, so maintaining a certain quality of the environment.

The evolution of hydrology

Traditional hydrology was directed to the study of the natural water régime and its interactions with the other elements of the geographical milieu. In our day it is rather rare to find rivers, lakes or groundwater in absolulely 'natural' conditions. Hydrology, therefore, has now to be concerned more especially with the effects of man's activities on water resources. The hydrological régime is influenced today by changes in land use, urbanization, soil and water conservation measures, diversion of surface and ground-water discharges, works for regularization of the flow of rivers and protection against flooding, etc.

Moreover, such changes also affect the quality of the water and, in that connection, modern hydrology must study the effects of the discharge of pollutants or waste heat into water, as well as its natural capacity for self-cleansing.

Other disciplines also are concerned with the global approach to these ever-increasing problems and their interactions: hydraulics, the study of water pollution and methods of treating it, hydraulic engineering, etc. At the same time, the development of water resources is increasingly confronted by environmental problems, due to modifications of the hydrological régime and the water quality, as well as by changes in natural sites. For the solution of these problems a pluridisciplinary approach is required, based also on the ecological, biological, pedological and other sciences.

For the decision-makers, the problem consists in using the available water to further the development of a specific region or population group with due regard to their socio-economic and socio-cultural characteristics. Thus the elaboration of strategies in which optimum use is made of water resources involves analysing social, economic and cultural factors as well as purely hydrological or ecological ones, besides foreseeing the overall consequences to which technological decisions may lead; consequently it is extremely important, for optimum results, to work out a scientific basis for water resources management, taking account of all the physical, economic and sociological parameters. This may be described as an integrated approach to the development of water resources, wherein modern methods of systems analysis can usefully be applied.

International co-operation in this connection is not only desirable, but dictated by physical features. Although the practical aspects of water management and use vary greatly from one country to another, according to the abundance and type of water resources, and according to the nature of the economy of the respective countries which determines the actual needs in the matter of water and the ways in which those needs can be met, hydrological phenomena and scientific approaches to water problems are sufficiently similar to make international action in this field particularly useful. In addition, the very nature of the global water cycle demands concerted action on a large scale for assessing its elements and making possible a better knowledge of available resources. Then again, for better or for worse, many countries have to share common resources. This obviously applies in the case of large river basins which comprise the territory of several countries and where co-operation at the level of the whole basin is essential. It also applies in the less evident case of ground water basins. And in general it may be said that the hydrological régime of each country is characterized by fluctuations—either natural or resulting from human activities—which depend on the global water cycle, so that all countries have a common interest in the rational management of this precious resource.

Water management and institutional integration

The measurement of variations in river levels dates back to the earliest civilizations, but it was not until towards the end of the eighteenth century that a beginning was made with the application of hydrology to practical problems; the science of hydraulics was by then sufficiently developed, to be used in the establishment of technical projects, and hydrological observations were sufficiently methodical to supply the necessary information for hydraulic calculations. National hydrological services were set up in the developed countries from the nineteenth century onwards, and such services now exist in a large number of countries. But there are other countries which do not yet possess the technical resources and the personnel that are needed for integrating hydrological activities in their overall economic and social development. Water management and the planning of water use were for a fairly long time subordinated to the needs of each particular sector concerned: municipalities, agriculture, industries, etc. Only recently has it begun to be realized that the management of water resources is a national problem which necessitates an integrated approach taking account of the characteristics both of the water régime and of economic and social development as a whole. Countries sharing major river basins have concluded international agreements and, from the nineteenth century onwards, co-ordinating bodies were established, first for questions of navigation (Rhine, Danube) and then for other aspects of water use. There are now co-ordinating commissions and committees for most of the international basins (Mekong, Niger, Senegal, La Plata, etc.).

A series of international organizations has begun to deal with the scientific, technological, economic and legal aspects of water resources. From 1922 onwards, steps were taken to establish what was to become the International Association of Hydrological Sciences. Other non-governmental scientific organizations have been set up to deal with other aspects (International Association for Hydraulic Research, International Association of Hydrogeologists, International Commission on Large Dams, International Association on Water Pollution Research, International Commission on Irrigation and Drainage, etc.). An endeavour was made to co-ordinate them by setting up within ICSU in 1964 a Scientific Committee for Water Research (COWAR) and by the creation, in 1971, of an independent body, the International Water Resources Association. At the same time, the regional governmental organizations, such as OECD, CMEA OAS, ALESCO, etc., are paying increasing attention, in their programmes, to water problems.

Little by little, the United Nations system came to concern itself with the promotion of international co-operation in regard to the development of water resources. The first of the United Nations agencies to recognize the part played by hydrology and water resources in economic growth was perhaps the United Nations Economic Commission for Asia and the Far East. In 1950 the Bureau of Flood Control, later to become the Water Resources Development Division, was established. From 1954 onwards, in particular, Ecosoc paid special attention to the assembly of hydrological data and the techniques of watershed management. Subsequently, the United Nations and more particularly the regional Economic Commissions stressed the economic, legal and institutional aspects of the development of water resources.

FAO, which is responsible for problems relating to the use of water for the development of agriculture, stock-raising and inshore fishery, carried out studies of various questions of bio-climatology, applied hydraulics and hydrology, providing the basis for applied research necessary for the pursuit of its own particular objectives. WHO concentrates on problems of the water supply for towns and villages and the quality of water, with particular reference to the health aspect. WMO has, since 1955, extended its meteorology programme to certain aspects relating to the assembly of hydrological data methods of hydrological observation and prediction. Since 1971, WMO has included in these activities an 'Operational Hydrology Programme' concerning more especially the operation of observation networks, the assembly and use of hydrological data, and the functioning of hydrological information and prediction services. IAEA is responsible for aspects of international co-operation involving the use of nuclear techniques in hydrological studies and in the development of water resources. The establishment of UNEP, following the United Nations Conference on the Human Environment, stimulated interest in the management and conservation of water resources, as a factor relating to environment.

From the International Hydrological Decade (1965-74) to the International Hydrological Programme

Unesco has from its earliest days taken an interest in the problems of water resources. In 1950, it launched a programme of research on the arid zone, in which hydrology occupied a prominent position. The interest taken by governments in the management of water resources, and the realization of the scientific problems involved therein that this implies, led the General Conference of Unesco, at its thirteenth session, to decide upon the launching of the International Hydrological Decade (1965-74). The programme of this Decade constituted a remarkable example of international co-operation; it contributed to understanding of the processes and phenomena occurring in the hydrosphere, assessment of surface and groundwater resources and their variability, and adoption of a rational attitude towards water use. The theoretical and practical training of hydrologists occupied a very important place in the programme. Over a thousand nationals of developing countries, during the Decade, attended training courses organized or sponsored by Unesco, and National Committees for the IHD were set up in 110 Member States.

The evaluation of the results of the IHD, made in September 1974, revealed the advances which the Decade had made possible in scientific knowledge, in the practical training of hydrologists, in international and regional co-operation in hydrology, and in the promotion of hydrological activities in the developing countries, whose needs the programme was mainly designed to meet. But gaps were noted, more particularly in regard to the application of scientific advances at international level to the solution of the practical problems confronting the developing countries. At the same time it was realized, in view of the gravity of the new problems resulting from the fluctuations of the hydrological régime in tropical zones and the increasingly evident threat of 'water crises' in certain countries, that the international co-operation instituted during the IHD must be continued. The General Conference of Unesco therefore decided, at its seventeenth session, to launch a long-term intergovernmental programme, known as the 'International Hydrological Programme' (IHP). Close co-operation will be maintained between the IHP and other Unesco programmes relating to the environment, such as the programme on Man and the Biosphere (in its aspects concerning the ecological value of water resources) and the oceanographical research programme (in its aspects concerning coastal zones).

Towards competent management of a vital natural element

Unesco's action in the matter of water resources follows three main lines: The promotion of scientific and technical research and of education and practical training in the disciplines concerned, with the object of improving knowledge regarding water resources from the point of view of their interrelation with natural environments and human activities; the promotion of an integrated approach to the problems entailed by the rational management of water resources; the strengthening of the infrastructures for training, study and research in Member States, with a view to increasing their capacity to assess and manage their resources in a scientific manner.

Most of the projects to be implemented under this three-part plan of action, particularly those in the first part, will come within the framework of the International Hydrological Programme. The activities will cover a whole range of highly specialized fields, from methods of estimating water balances to the prediction of changes in the water cycle and to the evaluation of the ecological effects of chemical or thermal pollution—since the cumulative effects of individual behaviour and the disruption caused by industry now affect the planet as a whole. Although there are 'water magistrates' only in Venice at least the above-mentioned activities aim to make men sensible and conscientious managers of what is not only a threatened raw material but a vital natural element.

Man and the sea

The oceans of the world have been variously termed 'inner space' and 'the last unexplored frontier', sobriquets which evoke their immense volume and expanse, their vast resource potential and the rich vein of information about the entire planet which they constitute. The ocean masses cover some 70 per cent of the globe, yet, until the mid-century they were little explored outside the main shipping routes. New and unusual tools had to be invented to plumb their mysterious depths.

Barriers to knowledge

The hostility and magnitude of the marine elements constituted real barriers to their thorough and comprehensive scientific study. Because of these factors progress was slow in developing the conceptual framework needed for the understanding of the physical, chemical, biological and geological processes taking place in this complex realm of interacting natural systems. Many of these systems are in dynamic equilibrium so that any disturbance can have ramifying consequences—for example, the construction of a harbour breakwater can have profound effects on nearby beaches as it can modify the longshore transport of sediment upon which the presence of the beach is dependent. Acquisition of knowledge for the exploitation of these complex natural systems therefore requires methodical, often quite advanced, scientific investigation, both fundamental and applied.

The sea influences man directly through its effect on weather and climate and as a cause of natural disasters such as hurricanes and tsunamis. It has also had a profound effect on human society. Man makes use of the sea in a wide variety of ways—as a source of natural resources (food, chemicals, water, sand, petroleum from beneath its sea bed, etc.), as a source of pleasure and recreation, as a path for commerce, etc.

An environment exposed to disastrous pollution

The contribution of the oceans to human needs is already considerable and can be further developed in many respects. Between 1948 and 1970 the world food catch increased by over 250 per cent and the world live weight catch of marine products now totals about 70 million metric tons. However, the mineral wealth of the oceans, such as manganese nodules, remains virtually untapped and its potential as a source of thermal and hydrodynamic energy has yet to be fully explored.

We should, however, be wary of regarding the sea as an inexhaustible resource store. We extract huge quantities of oil from beneath the sea floor but these are far from being inexhaustible. We have harvested fish to such an extent that in many cases we have interfered with normal cyclical replenishment. In many regions, we have already spoilt the coastal areas where some 60 per cent of the world population lives and where heavy pressures for harbours, industry, tourism and recreation are felt. The oceans, therefore, may alleviate, but cannot provide a complete answer to possible world resource shortages.

A major concern of our time relates to pollution of the sea. The oceans serve as a common, uncontrolled sink for the world's waste products. Sewage, oil cargo residues, domestic, industrial, even radioactive, wastes are indiscriminately dumped in the sea or in rivers which finally transport them to the sea. It has been estimated, for example, that human action introduces 4,000 to 5,000 tons of the toxic pollutant mercury into the oceans each year and that 500,000 tons of crude oil are leaked or deliberately dumped into the oceans annually. The effect is particularly critical in coastal areas with large human settlements. A major problem facing nations therefore is how to balance rationally all of these myriad uses in ways that do not degrade the environment.

Few nations unfortunately are today in a position to cope with the problems raised by the marine environment. Out of 113 countries (excluding some islands) with coastlines, forty-nine have coastlines longer than 1,000 km and six longer than 10,000 km. Nineteen countries have continental shelves equal to or larger than their land area, with an additional forty-five countries with shelves greater than 10 per cent of their land area.

The question appropriate to Unesco is how to enable Member States to acquire the necessary knowledge basis to enable them to exploit the resources of the sea rationally and with a proper balance of the different uses so as to ensure long-term survival and enhanced quality of life. An allied problem is how to help Member States create the necessary infrastructure, to acquire the scientific knowledge base and to apply that knowledge to the management of man's activities in the marine environment.

Outside national jurisdictions: the open sea—an area of bitter conflict but also of international co-operation

Falling as it does outside national jurisdictions, the open sea presents a number of complicated problems of rights and ownership. One particularly thorny problem concerning the law of the sea, and one which has yet to be resolved, relates to the question of international research at sea, especially in the coastal zones where national interests are dominant. On the other hand, this special status of the open sea presents unequalled opportunities in the field of international co-operation, through such bodies as the Intergovernmental Oceanographic Commission (IOC). It has helped to underline the fact that the ocean can only be understood through international scientific efforts and has given a stimulus to international oceanographic research.

Recognition of the sea as a vital element in human affairs has been underscored by the importance that the States of the world have attached to the Third United Nations Conference on the Law of the Sea. Throughout the Conference runs a single binding concept: the relationship of man to the properties and the uses of the sea and its interfaces. This is because all human utilization of the sea depends upon two factors: (a) knowledge of the basic properties of the sea, its life and its bed obtained through fundamental scientific research; and (b) the knowledge of the existence of both living and mineral resources in any particular area which is obtained through survey and exploration.

International co-operation relating to the sea began with such vital, practical matters as nautical charting, marine weather forecasting, fisheries development and protection, and maintenance and protection of submarine telegraph cables. Such was the importance of these practical matters to nations that they were immediately included in the activities of the specialized international agencies as they were formed, such as FAO, ITU, WMO, IAEA, IHO and IMCO.

Before the advent of satellites, remote sensing and sophisticated observation buoys, oceanographic research was mainly conducted aboard specialized research ships. This had the beneficial side-effect of encouraging international co-operation since few countries could afford to build and maintain these expensive vessels; for countries without them, oceanographic research was only possible through joint projects. A second side-effect has been the reinforcement of the inherently interdisciplinary nature of oceanographic research. The environmental systems of the oceans interact closely with one another, and marine biologists, geologists, chemists, physicists and mathematicians are obliged to consult each other. The close confinement of scientists of different disciplines aboard comparatively small ships during long research cruises fosters an atmosphere of unity leading inevitably to closer intellectual collaboration.

International co-operation between marine scientists developed spontaneously, but governments' awareness of the need for international co-operation in marine science grew only as it became apparent that science was essential to solving practical problems and that adequate exploration of the sea and its resources could only be accomplished through co-operative efforts of nations on a global scale. Thus there has been a quickening tempo of international co-operation in marine science since 1945, urged along by the twin pressures of national governments and of scientific organizations.

The demand on human resources to provide the basic data needed to exploit and manage the resources of the marine environment is enormous. Unfortunately, these resources are sparse; in 1970, only eleven countries had more than 100 marine scientists, while only twelve had two or more such scientists per million inhabitants. Efforts are being made to mobilize these resources, but major obstacles still exist.

Marine and human resources

The following figures give some idea of the scale of the manpower problem: in 1950, 750 oceanographers were identified in 48 countries; in 1960, 2,360 oceanographers in 79 countries; in 1970, 5,740 marine scientists in 91 countries; and in 1975, 12,000 marine scientists in 130 countries. This growth in scientific manpower is supplied both by specially trained marine scientists and by scientists and engineers in related fields who acquire their specialized marine knowledge through experience and special training courses.

Much of this growth has occurred in developed countries where a surplus of trained manpower now exists. In contrast, much of the developing world still lacks an adequate marine science base, especially where future coastal development may be substantial. Efforts are being made to bring these two problems together for a mutual solution through regular and extra-budgetary activities by several United Nations agencies and bodies, as well as through bilateral projects.

International co-operation for special short-term marine science training includes courses on special topics and shipboard fellowships aboard research vessels, primarily for trainees from the developing countries. Greater expertise is developed through international fellowships at universities and laboratories abroad. Many developing countries are strengthening their own universities and marine laboratories with international assistance so as to be able to supply their own long-term marine science manpower needs. The latter path can require the building of teaching and research facilities, with libraries and ships, the training of marine scientists with available national and foreign experts, and the provision of jobs afterwards.

After the oceanographic successes of the 1960s, more and more countries, especially in the developing world, came to realize the vital importance of the oceans and of marine science research to their development plans. The marine sciences themselves became more complex as more and more data became available through the introduction of highly sophisticated techniques. Demands on the IOC became correspondingly heavier, its machinery became overburdened and some of the earlier momentum was lost.

These difficulties have been partly overcome through a complete restructuring of the IOC and of marine science within Unesco, but the problems posed by international affairs remain: the unsettled state of national and international jurisdiction of the sea and the sea-bed, the difficult distinction between pure and applied marine science exploration, and the disparate development between nations. These problems, combined with a change in national emphasis from marine scientific exploration to wise management of the sea's resources based on marine science, have caused many initiatives of Unesco and the IOC for international co-operation to be less than effective. Finally, the limited resources of Unesco and IOC have prevented full implementation of various projects with Member States, and thus their high expectations have not always been met.

Plate tectonics, ocean turbulence, dynamics of the oceans

Over the past two decades, vitally important advances have been made in the knowledge of the marine environment. These advances relate first to the actual description of this environment. They further concern such subjects as the revolutionary concepts of global plate tectonics and their consequences for our knowledge of the sea floor, recognition of the phenomenon of ocean turbulence, the study of the interrelated dynamics of the oceans and the atmosphere, of the chemistry of sea water, of the marine food chain and the effects of the glacial lowering of sea level.

Mapping of the sea, its properties, its organisms and its floor has been a major scientific objective of Member States. Through international co-operation under IOC, this objective has been successful on a global scale for many important parameters; much effort is concentrated now on detailed scales. Maps (such as the General Bathymetric Chart of the Oceans) and atlases now faithfully depict such parameters as bottom topography, distribution of sediments by horizontal extent and vertical structure, the magnetic field, the gravity field, sound properties of the ocean and sea floor, oceanic currents and water masses, distribution of marine organisms, distribution of seawater salinity, temperature, density, and numerous other physical-chemical parameters, etc. Such mapping now allows a concentration of effort on identified but unsolved questions, whether they be scientific or applied.

The concepts of 'global plate tectonics' now recognize that the earth's surface is made up of seven huge and several smaller slowly-moving plates. On one side, these plates form at the central rifts of oceanic rises, through volcanic action, while on the far end, at the oceanic trenches, they slowly sink back into the earth's mantle. Land analogues are continental break-up and collision, with attendant earthquakes and volcanoes. The discovery has opened the way to major advances in petroleum exploration and in ore formation theories. Key components of the concept were developed during the first co-operative action of the IOC Member States, the very successful International Indian Ocean Expedition (IIOE) (1959-65), organized through the twin mechanisms of IOC and SCOR (Scientific Committee on Oceanic Research). Evidence of the scientific impact of IIOE is provided by the eight volumes of collected scientific reprints and the thirteen large atlases which appeared in the second half of the following decade. The IIOE also had a lasting beneficial effect in developing the infrastructures of some Member States of the region.

A deep-drilling programme has extensively sampled the sediments and volcanic basement of all the world's oceans except the Arctic Ocean. Unesco and its IOC have been involved in directly related activities such as organizing the necessary general investigations, supporting symposia at the quadri-annual oceanographic congresses, and publishing certain resulting charts. The programme has made major contributions: confirmed the plate tectonic theory by finding compatible ages for the volcanic basement, reconstructed the location of rifts and continents through time, shown major and violent changes in the ocean's circulation, shown world-wide extinction and correlations in various marine organisms as well as their evolution, shown major changes in the salinity of the oceans with the possibility of the ocean even drying up in places, discovered vast deposits of salt, shown the distribution of manganese nodules in space and time, shown indications of petroleum and ores, etc.

Fewer and fewer secrets

Recognition that the ocean is highly turbulent on all scales and at all depths represents another important scientific advance. For instance, surface and near-surface currents have been shown to be highly dynamic, meandering in space and transient in time, besides giving rise to large offshoot eddies. Furthermore, fast deep currents hug the western borders of deep basins; these currents have had profound effects on the sea floor by moving bottom sediments. The Co-operative Investigation of the Kuroshio (CSK) has been impressively successful in determining the dynamics of the mighty Kuroshio Current. The IIOE showed that the equatorial undercurrent varied with the monsoon season. The Atlantic tropical experiment (GATE) examined the current structure of the whole water column. The Mid-Ocean Dynamic Experiment (MODE) examined a single giant deepwater eddy.

A major international scientific effort by Member States, through IOC in co-operation with WMO, is now going into the study of the interrelated dynamics of the oceans and atmosphere, as well as long-term changes in climate. Such studies should allow more reliable prediction of the weather, both short-term and seasonal.

Studies of the chemistry of sea water, marine sediments and marine organisms through co-operative investigations have traced the pathways of various chemical compounds through both simple systems, and complex systems, not only for the major constituents such as sodium, calcium, chloride and carbonate, but also for trace elements such as mercury, fluorine, the rare earths and various radioactive elements. This has laid a firm base for the study and control of marine pollution, a field in which Unesco and its IOC have been active. The nations of the world are co-operating in observation and in rapid data exchange, through the Integrated Global Ocean Station System (IGOSS) which aims to provide immediate access by Member States to ocean temperature and certain oil pollution data. A global plan for the investigation of marine pollution (GIPME) guides the IOC pollution studies. A major effort in collaboration with UNEP and FAO is designed to bring Mediterranean pollution under control.

Studies on marine food chains, nutrient limitations and species identification have provided major advances in ecological knowledge. This knowledge, together with fishery statistics, has allowed nations to co-operate effectively and realistically in regional and global management of marine fisheries, thus providing an effective link between the scientific activities of Unesco and the fisheries activities of FAO.

Nearshore, some equally striking scientific advances have been made; much more is now understood about the effects of the glacial lowering of sea-level (some 200 metres), about complex marine ecological systems such as coral reefs, seaweed and plankton communities, and about geochemical mass balances and chemical gradients, nearshore marine geological processes and currents, the physical dynamics of beaches, etc. These advances form a sound basis for the management of man's coastal activities by individual Member States.

Machinery for international co-operation: the Intergovernmental Oceanographic Commission

From its inception, Unesco has promoted research and infrastructure development in marine science, mostly in co-operation with the International Council of Scientific Unions (ICSU) and FAO during the early years.

Since then, the most striking advance has been the establishment of the Intergovernmental Oceanographic Commission (IOC), for the purpose of promoting scientific investigation through the concerted action of its Member States. At the same time, an Office of Oceanography was created within the Unesco Secretariat to execute a work plan aimed at stimulating and assisting research and training in marine sciences, as well as to act as the Secretariat of the IOC.

In 1972, the Office of Oceanography was administratively separated from the IOC Secretariat, becoming the Division of Marine Sciences. Although the work of the IOC Secretariat and the new Division is inevitably still closely linked and carefully dovetailed, the change was made to enable the Division to give closer attention to the long-standing and rapidly growing programme on the development of national marine science infrastructure and the training of specialists.

The Sub-Committee on Marine Sciences and its Applications of the Administrative Committee on Co-ordination was established in 1960 to co-ordinate oceanographic activities for all the Specialized Agencies of the United Nations. To further improve co-ordination the Inter-Secretariat Committee on Scientific Programmes Relating to Oceanography, consisting of five United Nations agencies, was formed in 1969.

The United Nations Conference on the Human Environment, Stockholm, June 1972, recommended that governments expand their support to components of the United Nations system concerned with research and monitoring in the marine environment and adopt the measures required to improve the constitutional, financial and operational basis under which the Intergovernmental Oceanographic Commission (IOC) is at present operating, so as to make it an effective joint mechanism for the governments and the United Nations organizations concerned (Unesco, FAO, WMO, IMCO, United Nations).

The United Nations Economic and Social Council, through resolutions in 1973 and 1975, requested activities with regard to coastal area development in co-operation with the competent organizations of the United Nations system. For a number of years, the United Nations has been grappling with the legal and jurisdictional problems of the sea, the sea bed and marine resources. In 1958, four Conventions on the law of the sea were adopted. In 1968, the General Assembly established the influential Committee on the Peaceful Uses of the Sea-Bed and the Ocean Floor. In 1970, the General Assembly adopted the Declaration of Principles Governing the Sea-Bed and Ocean Floor. In 1973, the Third United Nations Conference on the Law of the Sea was convened and is still carrying on its deliberations. This Conference has prepared the ground for decisions which, if taken, will have a major impact on Unesco's programme concerning the oceans.

Towards a better knowledge of the marine environment and a more rational use of marine resources

Through mobilization of national efforts and those of United Nations organizations by development and co-ordination of international co-operative projects, the Intergovernmental Oceanographic Commission will work toward: (a) solution of significant identified oceanographic problems utilizing a multidisciplinary approach; (b) establishment of functioning global monitoring and prediction systems, including data and information systems; (c) identification of the training, education and mutual assistance needs in marine science of Member States, including co-ordination of efforts of international organizations to meet those needs.

Unesco will also take steps to identify and fill significant gaps in basic knowledge of natural marine systems through international scientific co-operation, to have transferred effectively such knowledge, and to have established a firm marine scientific basis for coastal area development.

Finally, Unesco will promote, through international co-operation, the establishment of adequate national marine scientific capacity, as a minimum, to advise the national governments on national needs and priorities and to provide the marine science knowledge necessary for intellectual advancement, for economic development and for the rational management of national marine affairs, including the use of the natural environment.

Man and the city

The relationships that man maintains or establishes with his environment are generally described today as conflictual. It cannot be denied that the man-made environment, that of towns and villages, is changing with such ruthless speed that the public authorities in many countries admit to being powerless to control the process. The forecast that the population will have doubled by the end of the century, the advance of industrialization and the almost universal trend towards urbanization all combine to increase this anxiety.

Accelerated urbanization and its consequences: the mushrooming of shanty towns . . .

Although urbanization statistics must only be used with the greatest caution, and can hardly be regarded as comparable from country to country in the absence of agreement concerning the size to be attained by a built-up area before it may be considered a town, the following figures indicate trends and give an idea of the rapidity with which the situation is changing.

In the industrialized countries the majority of the population is already composed of town-dwellers. Certain census returns prior to 1970 give urban population percentages of the order of 70 per cent or even approaching 80 per cent. According to the 1974 report on the world social situation issued in 1975 by the United Nations, the annual average growth rate of the urban population in the so-called 'developed' regions, which stood at 2.1 per cent between 1960 and 1970, was estimated at 2.0 per cent for the period 1970-75, the individual rates being, respectively, 1.6 per cent and 1.4 per cent in Europe, 2.7 per cent and 2.3 per cent in the U.S.S.R., and 1.9 per cent and 1.5 per cent in North America.

In the developing countries, the urbanization process is accelerating. According to the above sources, the annual average growth rate of the urban population between 1960 and 1970 was 4.1 per cent in South Asia, 3.3 per cent in East Asia, 4.8 per cent in Africa and 4.3 per cent in Latin America; the projections for 1970-75 indicated, respectively, 4.3 per cent, 4.0 per cent, 4.9 per cent and 3.9 per cent. These figures mean that in twenty years the urban population of these regions has doubled or even tripled.

In many developing countries, the evidence of this accelerated urban growth is concentrated in a few big cities, where the population is increasing quite inordinately. In one of these countries, for example, the nine largest towns represent today almost one-quarter of the total population. It is hardly suprising that the development of infrastructures cannot keep pace with expansion at such a high rate. Hence the mushrooming of shanty towns where non-integrated population groups crowd into makeshift, insanitary shelters, lacking water, drainage, gas and electricity and with no protection against the hazards of fire and flood, which breed a sense of insecurity. In one town formerly famed for its beauty, one inhabitant in three lives in a shanty town.

. . . and the disappearance of historic centres

In every case, the increasing density of the urban population is accompanied by a radical disruption of the very layout of the town: traditional functions (communication, trade, political affairs, leisure activities) are segregated in different districts; historic quarters disappear either as a result of speculative building projects or because the overcrowded streets are abandoned to the least privileged social categories and quickly deteriorate; fast transport networks tear the urban fabric apart. The inability to cope simultaneously with the use of land, the creation of jobs and improvements in communication systems leads to a steady deterioration of urban living conditions. Thus the town—once pre-eminent as a hub of civilizing influences—is nowadays decried as a place rife with every form of pollution, time-wasting difficulties, segregation, psychological stress, solitude and occasionally even danger.

Far-reaching modifications of the environment are also due to the tourist industry which, in certain countries, dominates the private and public building sectors and destroys the natural equilibrium by setting up massive installations with no regard for the sites and traditions of the so-called 'host' population. Land is often taken over at the expense of such communities in a scandalously arbitrary manner; the distorting and disrupting effects on the economy, and on life-styles and social and moral structures are not perhaps any less disastrous for being less obvious.

Planning—yes, but how?

Since such problems always have inseparable ecological, social, ethical and cultural aspects, physical plans determined by purely economic calculations cannot solve them. And yet this pseudo-planning, extolled like a panacea, still presides over the creation and management of human settlements. It is remarkable that it should have been possible to hold it responsible, just as much as anarchical liberalism, for the destruction of the architectural heritage, sacrificed to the interests of private or State enterprises, the slow death of rural centres and the cultures they nurture, the congestion of subsidized housing estates sited in remote suburbs, the concentration of administrative and industrial establishments and the dreary migrations of workers which they involve and, lastly, the uniformity of a type of town-planning for residential areas tyrannized by the motor-car, whose inhabitants lose both the feeling of belonging to a community and their cultural identity.

True planning, such as shows by its use of land and its layout of urban areas that it cares for the quality of life, will consider human settlements as extremely complex systems which demand patient research in many different fields if they are to be dealt with on scientific lines. Only a synthesis of the findings of this research can take account of the interactions of all the ecological, economic, social, anthropological and psychological factors involved. This implies that such planning will become less and less categorical and authoritarian: too many decisions affecting the rural or urban environment are still taken in ignorance or even contempt of the needs and aspirations of the communities concerned. We know that illogical interrelationships between man and the environment go together with unsatisfactory communication between people. It is no longer admissible that in questions of building and land use decision-making processes should appear incomprehensible to the majority of the population, which accordingly believes its only choice to lie between resignation and revolt.

Studies concerning these problems should be inseparable from all those which deal with the future of the communities affected and should embrace the philosophical, legal, political and technical aspects of development, human rights and a new economic order and, more generally, of the fight against injustice.

From the Athens Charter to the conferences of Stockholm and Vancouver: widening the field of study

Until recent years, considerations of this kind rarely shaped policies regarding the administration and growth of towns or villages. In theory and in practice, the approach to the question of planned human settlements has been dominated since the Second World War, in most countries, by the town-planning principles drawn up prior to 1940 by the CIAM (International Congresses for Modern Architecture) which are known as the Athens Charter. Because they were interpreted in over-simplified terms and reduced to cut-and-dried formulae, these principles led unfortunately to the mechanical development of industrial, residential and business zones, etc. which were subsequently criticized on account of the social segregation they perpetuate or create. Methods which aimed to produce, instead, living forms of urbanization so designed as to integrate harmoniously all the functional aspects of town life were worked out by teams whose attempts at interdisciplinarity have met some success in a very small number of new towns. More conclusive results have been achieved in the treatment of old city centres or quarters which town-planners are rehabilitating for economic as well as cultural reasons.

At the same time, from the very beginning of the First United Nations Development Decade, the phenomena of large-scale development, whose full magnitude had seldom been foreseen, have obliged politicians and professional experts to pose the problems of human settlements in terms that are more complex than those of housing and employment conditions. Although the provision of decent dwellings for the whole population is still a distant aim in many countries, it is apparent that this aim represents only one stage in the effort required. This is shown by the copious documentation accumulated by the Regional Economic Commissions, OECD, COMECON, the European Community and the Organization of American States on urban transport, social and public health facilities, administration, the economy of large towns and regulations governing land use.

The United Nations Conference on the Human Environment (Stockholm, 1972) stressed the complexity of these problems, ranking them with those of energy and linking the future development of human settlements, considered as ecosystems, with the equilibrium of the biological environment. The perils of urban life then became the focal point of the concern expressed in official statements.

From the various forms of pollution to the creeping paralysis of urban traffic, from employment crises to mental health in towns, from rural disorganization to criminality in the large housing estates, the study of all these perils has given rise to a great many research programmes, the establishment of several public and private national institutions and the implementation of decisions taken in this field by international organizations. The Centre for Housing, Building and Planning (CHBP) (United Nations Department of Economic and Social Affairs) is engaged in many operational projects concerning physical planning and building techniques, its responsibilities as regards assistance and financial programmes having been transferred to the new International Habitat and Human Settlements Foundation (United Nations). Mention should also be made of the surveys and projects which will have been carried out under international co-operation arrangements in various countries, largely on a regional basis, as part of the preparatory work for the United Nations Conference on Human Settlements (Vancouver, 1976).

On the agenda: the human settlement considered as an ecosystem

In the light of this proliferation of activities. Unesco did not find it difficult to define its field of competence. Although it had no comprehensive programme relating to 'Man and his Environment', prior to the 1975-1976 biennium various projects dealt, at least partially, with the problems covered by this term. They concerned research in the social sciences, the training of architects, and the protection of the natural and cultural heritage, which was the subject of international instruments adopted by the General Conference in 1972. A specific line of approach was thus being mapped out: inquiries were held into perception of the environment (among children and adults) and public participation in environmental decisions. Work has started on systems of indicators of the quality of the environment. Studies are being conducted on the social and cultural effects of tourism. Programming exercises are being developed for authorities responsible for questions concerning the environment. Other studies are contributing to knowledge about traditional architecture and the problems involved in its adaptation to the needs of present-day life. Lastly, a school of architecture established by Unesco is in operation and is beginning to undertake its regional task in West Africa.

Since 1970, to stimulate and co-ordinate research on the interrelationships between man and the major ecosystems has been the objective of the 'Man and the Biosphere' (MAB) programme, (see pages 283-4 above) an intergovernmental and interdisciplinary programme which consists at present of fourteen main research projects in
which the Programme's National Committees are taking part. One of the themes is more
directly concerned with planning relating to human settlements. The purpose is to consider how urban systems function as actual ecosystems, using more especially measurement of energy, water and waste product circuits as a method of analysing the functioning of these systems. Several large conurbations, such as Hong Kong and Frankfurt,
have already been taken as the subject of studies and models using these methods
under the MAB programme.

Lastly, certain operational projects have provided other bases for theoretical
work. Since 1960 more especially, Unesco has been collaborating with several Member
States in the preservation and presentation of monuments and sites, and historic quarters
and towns. The practical experience gained in this way shows that operations designed
to improve the environment by what are regarded as purely technical methods do not
succeed unless they take due account of the interrelationships which exist between men
(political authorities, managers, inhabitants and users) and between them and the
environment.

In the next few years, action should bear upon the processes of growth, or
rather the continuous creation of human settlements. Towns, old or new, villages and
capitals will develop according to conceptions of man and society that must be clearly
defined. The options that guide physical planning always end by affecting both the natural
environment and human life. By creating towns, men create new ecological systems.
What is more, land use, architecture, and town-planning have reciprocal relationships
with social structures and practices, as they have with the intellectual, emotional and
moral development of individuals.

Guiding the town planner: social indicators

So as to contribute, therefore, to a clearer conception of human settlements, research
work based on pilot projects will be conducted on the whole set of problems linked with
the complex interrelationships between man, the urban environment and the biosphere.
Research will also seek to shed light on the social and cultural processes of decision-
making in specific cases of activities concerned with the administration, preservation
and construction of urban complexes, rural development and the promotion of tourism.
In liaison with this research, studies will be continued with a view to establishing social
indicators; the purpose of these studies should be to procure the means of appraising
the quality of the actual relationships of various groups with their rural or urban environment.

Analyses of forms and functions of urban systems will serve to determine how
this environment, which may be conducive in a greater or lesser degree to social and
cultural activities, can also be a cultural creation, adapted to the psychological needs and

aspirations of the inhabitants. The data obtained should be used as the basic material for a synthesis to be attempted in order to arrive at a type of town-planning which is capable of revitalizing lifeless settlements, combating insignificance and uniformity and creating towns propitious to good human relationships.

In the same spirit, the studies on what is called 'traditional' architecture will contribute not only to meeting the obvious housing needs of rural and peri-urban areas but also to enabling the population in many countries to rediscover and assert their cultural identity.

All these studies and the related experiments will be carried out in collaboration with educational and research institutions and regional or international professional associations of architects, artists and town-planners. It is also in these fields—research ir projects concerning town-planning and training work—that aid will be provided to Member States.

Safeguarding the heritage of mankind and preserving the natural environment

The basic principles constituting the maxim of all action to preserve and enhance the cultural and natural heritage are twofold.

In the first place, the preservation and presentation of works of art, monuments and archaeological or natural sites which belong to the heritage of a particular people or region reflect not only a natural instinct to arrest the processes of destruction and decay, the ancestral desire to protect the most outstanding relics of the past from the depredations of time and wanton human destructiveness: it also contributes to the awareness and affirmation of the cultural identity of the country or region of which these artistic, archaeological or natural treasures form an essential part.

Monuments which are more than mere stones

One cannot, therefore, over-emphasize the fact that the idea of cultural heritage, in its broadest sense, covers not only the visible and material manifestations of this heritage— and monuments in particular—which may be the pride of a country or region, but also the oral traditions, the musical and ethnographic heritage, the folklore, indeed the laws, customs and ways of life which express the essence of ethnic or national temperament. However, the methodological approaches and the practical—including where appropriate, normative—means employed that are suited to the preservation of these less tangible values are different in nature to the much more 'operational' measures required to safeguard a work of art, a monument or a site, and these more diffuse elements of the cultural heritage, *lato sensu*, are not therefore included in the discussion that follows, which covers only objects and monuments in which culture is manifested in a visible and concrete form.[1]

But although the connotations of the concept of 'cultural heritage' extend beyond works of art, monuments and sites, the relationship between the culture of a nation and the monuments in which it is embodied is sufficiently direct and fundamental for their safeguarding and presentation to constitute a major contribution towards affirming the cultural specificity of a country in its own eyes as well as in those of the international community, and one of the first areas in which it seeks to enlist the co-operation of the institutions competent to deal with such matters.

Dual action: safeguarding specific cultural identities and preserving the common heritage of mankind

In the second place, the preservation and presentation of the cultural and natural heritage must not be seen as measures which benefit only the countries directly concerned; the international prestige of certain monuments and historic sites or of certain national parks, their importance as tourist attractions and the concern felt throughout the world when they are imperilled by natural disasters or those of human origin—not to speak of the more general phenomenon of the telescoping of distances and the improvement of communications which makes the world a more compact unit in all respects—these are all so many indications that it is no longer at the purely national but at the world-wide level that the cultural and natural heritage of the different nations must be viewed, as the common heritage of mankind, and steps taken to safeguard its future and ensure its survival.

This way of looking at the problem seems to be further justified by the fact that the centres of civilization with which the various cultural heritages are associated do not always coincide with national frontiers. While the monuments and works of art

---

1. In accordance with the definitions adopted by the 1972 Convention for the Protection of the World Cultural and Natural Heritage, the terms 'cultural heritage' and 'natural heritage' are to be understood as follows:

   Cultural heritage: monuments (architectural works, works of monumental sculpture and painting, elements or structures of an archaeological nature, inscriptions, cave dwellings and combinations of features, which are of outstanding universal value from the point of view of history, art or science); groups of buildings (groups of separate or connected buildings which, because of their architecture, their homogeneity or their place in the landscape, are of outstanding universal value from the point of view of history, art or science); sites (works of man or the combined works of nature and of man, and areas including archaeological sites which are of outstanding universal value from the historical, aesthetic, ethnological or anthropological points of view).

   Natural heritage: natural features consisting of physical and biological formations or groups of such formations, which are of outstanding universal value from the aesthetic or scientific point of view; geological and physiographical formations and precisely delineated areas which constitute the habitat of threatened species of animals and plants of outstanding universal value from the point of view of science or conservation; natural sites or precisely delineated natural areas, of outstanding universal value from the point of view of science, conservation or natural beauty.

in question belong to the people of the country in which they are located, they are often part of a cultural entity whose geographical sphere of influence may extend or have at some time in the past extended far beyond present political boundaries. The same applies to the problem of the natural heritage, as clearly neither geography nor wildlife is a respector of national frontiers.

Conversely, the cultural heritage of a single country is often related to several different civilizations which have each in their turn left substantial evidence of their splendour on its soil. In such circumstances the sensitive problem of priorities may arise.

These various considerations have, over the last few years, resulted in a considerable change in the approach to the problem of safeguarding and enhancing the cultural and natural heritage. Conservation operations are now tending more and more to be placed within the framework of a world-wide preservation policy or at least philosophy grounded on these concepts of transnational civilizations and the common heritage of mankind.

Preservation today: a more comprehensive approach and action on a wider scale

But while the general approach to the problem of safeguarding the cultural and natural heritage has been set on an international basis, the actual situation of the individual countries *vis-à-vis* the problem could hardly be less uniform. Disparities do not only occur in respect of material resources; they are further complicated by the fact that material poverty may coincide with a wealth of cultural or historical monuments and a rich heritage of works of art or the existence of plant or animal species which are in danger of extinction: the countries which are most richly endowed from the artistic, archaeological or ecological point of view are not always the most prosperous. If a division were to be made between the poor and the rich countries in respect of cultural and natural heritage, the resulting categories would be very different from those based essentially on the possession and production of material goods. In fact the countries or regions that are wealthiest as far as cultural or natural heritage are concerned are often among the most handicapped in their action to preserve and enhance it owing to their lack of qualified staff and of investment capital.

Another development—this time of a technical nature—has added a further dimension to the problem, although in itself it represents progress from the methodological point of view: this is the fact that rescue operations are now becoming more ambitious and much wider in their scope. Measures to preserve and enhance the presentation of a particular monument or site are giving way to a broader approach. It is no longer a single monument but the whole of a historic quarter which is afforded protection. One may even wish to preserve the whole of a particular architectural heritage. Nature conservation measures no longer affect a single animal species, but aim to preserve in its integrity the ecosystem of which this species forms part, an approach which is not without a beneficial effect on the 'quality of life'. The wider scale of such operations naturally calls for detailed and stringent planning and more co-operation between the different disciplines; it also makes for more complex technical problems and stronger capital backing in support of a rational and well-judged preservation policy.

An increasingly difficult traffic

The economic disparity between the industrialized countries and those whose lack of financial resources prevents them from taking effective measures to protect their wealth of cultural property has had and continues to have its effect on what is known as 'illicit trading' in cultural property and protected animal species. There is a growing market in industrialized countries for works of art and archaeological objects mainly from developing countries. Veritable networks have been set up to remove cultural property or purchase it at minimal prices, export it—more often than not illicitly—and sell it at great profit to wealthy connoisseurs. The same is true of animal furs and trophies. Legislative and administrative measures taken at national level and more and more extensively at international level have not yet succeeded in suppressing this illicit traffic.

Some cultural property, moreover, was transferred from its country of origin as part of the spoils of war or at a time when these countries were not self-governing, thus depriving them of valuable examples of their cultural life in past or in present times.

Flora and fauna threatened with extinction

The problems posed by protection of the values connected with nature are, *per se,* possibly even more complex. Although the threats to the quality and extent of the natural heritage are generally themselves the result of natural processes which it is often difficult to counteract, they nevertheless call for urgent countermeasures co-ordinated at international level. Loss of wild plants and animals is a serious loss for mankind, not only because of their inherent value as 'natural heritage', but for economic reasons as well. Every domestic plant and animal used by mankind is descended from wild species, and sources of wild genetic material will continue to be needed in the future for improvement of existing domesticates or for new utilizations. The only really effective means of preserving wild plants and animals is through preservation of their habitat—through establishment of ecological reserves or through similar means.

In this sphere, as in that of the preservation of works of art and cultural monuments, changes of attitude and approach have taken place in recent years. In the past the desire to preserve outstanding landscapes and spectacular animal species has led to the creation of national parks, particularly in America and Africa, which are in themselves remarkable achievements and a great tourist attraction. However, it has only been very recently that an ecological rationale for reserve establishment has attained widespread acceptance. Thus it is not surprising that the parks and reserves of the world, though outstanding for their scenic qualities, do not provide for the needs of ecological preservation. They are far from constituting a network which adequately represents the major ecosystem types. Such a network is essential particularly for: (a) providing for preservation of the genetic material of wild animal and plant species, and (b) providing baselines or standards against which change can be measured and the performance of other ecosystems judged.

Conservation and development—overcoming clashes of interest

At the same time the conservation of the cultural and natural heritage—hence of the environment in general—sometimes conflicts with the requirements of economic development in the narrowest definition of the term. The conservation of the cultural heritage may lead to clashes of interest regarding the use to be made of historic areas or sites within or adjoining these areas. In the same way, the conservation of the natural heritage may lead to differences of opinion regarding land use, as it is difficult for the rural population to accept the designation as a conservation area of land which could be used for agriculture or grazing. This problem is common to both industrialized and developing countries, and in the attempt to find solutions which make due allowance for the conservation of the heritage without hindering development difficulties are encountered which are often the most serious which decision-makers at national, regional or local level have to face. It should, however, be borne in mind that improved presentation of the heritage—besides contributing towards the education and leisure opportunities of the local population and towards the affirmation of cultural identity which is an essential ingredient of any well-planned development—may itself be a not insignificant factor in economic development, in that it attracts tourists, including foreign tourists, and can thus constitute a source of invisible exports. But although tourism can help to provide the finance needed for investment it is not without its dangers: where it is not closely supervised it may cause a historic area or town to lose its character and become spoilt, have an adverse effect on the ecology of a reserve or natural park or erode certain socio-cultural values.

The restoration of a historic town or a historic quarter of a modern town may have social repercussions, such as the displacement of its inhabitants, just as the creation of a national park or nature reserve may affect traditional grazing patterns. Various social problems may arise as a result of such action and it is therefore important to take appropriate counter-measures, based on detailed socio-economic surveys, in good time.

Such are the main characteristics of the problem of safeguarding and presenting the cultural and natural heritage. In both cases, if action is to be enlightened and judicious, it must be based on preliminary surveys and inventories; if it is to be comprehensive and binding it must have a legislative and administrative basis; if it is to be technically feasible and effective it must have specialized institutions and equipment at its disposal, while if it is to be scientific in its method and lasting in its effect it must involve specialized research and the training of personnel. In point of fact, it is still very deficient in all these spheres and subject to all sorts of hindrances and restrictions.

The inventory of cultural property: an instrument to be developed; the inventory of the natural heritage: much to be done before it is too late

As regards the identification of cultural property, many States have begun protective inventories—lists with brief descriptions of the cultural heritage to be preserved on a national scale. However, such inventories are still lacking or very incomplete in many countries of the world.

Systematic surveys of species of plants and animals whose survival is in question have been carried out on a world-wide scale although much remains to be done, particularly with ecological systems. In the case of the latter detailed studies of the mutual interdependence of organisms in a given ecological system are still rare and limited to the simpler ones. In complex systems such as a tropical forest with very many species, attention is still concentrated on identification, although broad lines of relationships can and have been determined. Even limiting the scope to plant and animal species whose immediate survival is in jeopardy, the estimated number of threatened species is so large (about 20,000 species for flowering plants alone, for example) that relatively little has yet been done in the way of measures to provide protection. In tropical and subtropical forests, where the flora is rich and poorly known, ecosystem modification is progressing so rapidly that species are probably being eliminated before they become known to science.

Legal protection and administrative problems

Almost every country affording statutory protection of the cultural heritage has laws and regulations, but the nature of the protection thus afforded is often incomplete and nearly everywhere difficulties of implementation are encountered. These are due in the main to the fact that the scope of the provisions is frequently limited, there are no preventive measures or penalties are ineffective. The protective system is sometimes based on out-of-date concepts. Moreover, the practice in regard to laws and regulations varies considerably according to type of government and national traditions. Even within a single country, particularly those with a federal structure, there are sometimes differences in the degree of protection afforded and the administrative machinery available for the preservation of the cultural heritage.

Analysis of the legal situation in Member States reveals that only about one-fifth of them provide satisfactory protection of all the property constituting the cultural heritage. Many governments are aware of these deficiencies, and revision of the laws and regulations so as to give added protection of the cultural heritage is planned or already under way in several countries.

As far as the legal protection of the natural heritage is concerned much remains to be done to ensure the maximum possible conservation of the world's natural areas and genetic resources. Although considerable progress has been made towards establishing a world network of reserves, the majority of protected areas are concentrated in relatively few countries and biotic regions. Thus, even in those continents where conservation interests are strong, national parks or their equivalents are few or lacking in important habitat types. In Africa, a well-developed network of national parks and reserves represents only about one-third of the continent's biotic regions while in all other parts protected areas are few or lacking. Similarly in Europe and North America the number and distribution of natural reserves are such that needs of ecosystem and genetic preservation are not met. In most of Asia, Latin America and the Arab region natural reserves are particularly inadequate.

As regards the national administration required for conservation, many States have established national authorities responsible for the administration of monuments and sites (in several States they are also responsible for the administration of national museums). Of these 29 are found in Europe and North America, 11 in Asia and the Pacific, ten in the Arab States, six in Africa south of the Sahara, and seven in Latin America. In general the authority responsible for the cultural heritage is not the same as that responsible for the natural heritage, although there are some notable exceptions to this rule (in North America, for example). The cultural heritage often comes under the jurisdiction of a ministry responsible for cultural or educational affairs while the natural heritage is the responsibility of the Ministry of Agriculture or the Forestry Department or, more recently, a department with official responsibility for the environment.

Almost ten thousand museums in Europe and North America, less than two thousand in the rest of the world

Public and private museums, as institutions devoted to the collecting, preservation and presentation of the cultural and natural heritage, are widespread, but concentrated primarily in Europe and North America. The statistics of the Unesco/International Council of Museums (ICOM) Documentation Centre show 5,787 museums devoted to fine and applied arts in Europe and North America in 1975 as against 586 in Asia and the Pacific, 276 in Latin America, 78 in Africa south of the Sahara and 37 in the Arab States. The figures for archaeological and history museums show 3,692 in Europe and North America, 442 in Asia and the Pacific, 221 in Latin America, 103 in the Arab States and 94 in Africa south of the Sahara. A very similar imbalance exists in respect of natural history museums, which, until very recently, have suffered from scientists' lack of interest in taxonomy and the inventorying of species, two disciplines which enjoyed great popularity throughout Europe in the eighteenth century. Some collections which were formed in tropical countries have not been properly looked after, as their importance for economic development, which is considerable, had not been realized. The important part that collections of insects, molluscs, plants, etc. play in the prevention of human and plant diseases and the selection of crop varieties is now better understood. This increased interest in the world of nature is likely to attract larger numbers of the public to natural history museums.

Specialized laboratories have also been created in many States to ensure the preservation of cultural property. However, development has been uneven: seven are found in Africa, six in Latin America and 12 in Asia, while Europe and North America dispose of at least 110 laboratories.

With respect to the natural heritage over 1,000 national parks and equivalent reserves were listed in the 1974 United Nations List of National Parks and Equivalent Reserves. However, their total area includes only about one per cent of the earth's surface and many biotic regions receive no representation in parks or reserves so that much remains to be done. The current rate of reduction of species diversity is impoverishing living resources essential for the economic, environmental and cultural existence of man.

In the field of the conservation of cultural property, considerable strides have been made in the past few decades. The use of chemical and physical methods of analysis has become increasingly common. In order to make use of such data, restorers who had previously carried out much of their work using traditional methods and material are given training to use the new data. Specialists are also required and for this reason some of the leading museums and monuments, administrative services, as well as universities, now have programmes to train personnel.

Similarly, there is a need for training specialists capable of handling natural history collections, both in developed and developing countries, and a need for managers of national parks and nature reserves concurrent with the development of the number of such parks and reserves.

A series of standard-setting instruments

To refer only to the most recent past, international action has operated through an ever growing range of international instruments, both legal and standard-setting in character; it has comprised work in the field of documentation and publications and has also been directed to extending the geographical coverage of the international bodies concerned and arranging the planning and financing of operations, without neglecting the creation of an international network of nature reserves.

The growth of technology during the preceding century has also multiplied the effects of warfare. Internationally, The Hague Conventions of 1899 and 1907 sought, *inter alia*, to define cultural property and to ensure that it would not be molested during warfare. The Washington Pact (1935), for the Protection of Artistic and Scientific Institutions and of Historic Monuments (Roerich Pact), also sought similar goals. During the Second World War large-scale aerial bombardment and the use of weapons of mass destruction took place on an unprecedented scale, destroying or damaging many outstanding sites and monuments. In the light of this experience a new Convention was drafted at The Hague in 1954, on the Protection of Cultural Property in the Event of Armed Conflict. Other instruments include the Convention on the means of prohibiting and preventing the illicit import, export and transfer of ownership of cultural property (1970) and the Convention concerning the protection of the world cultural and natural heritage (1972).

At the intergovernmental level, FAO has traditionally played a major role, in co-operation with Unesco, in the field of conservation of nature and wild life because of the relation between this problem and the overall problem of land use, and because of the particular role of forest services in this domain. As regards the cultural heritage, the role of the International Centre for the Study of the Preservation and Restoration of Cultural Property, established in Rome in 1959 in co-operation with the Government of Italy as an intergovernmental organization, in order to stimulate and to co-ordinate international research on conservation and on training, has been steadily growing. The Centre has also contributed to many projects such as the campaign for the preservation of cultural property damaged by the 1968 floods in Florence and Venice. Other intergovernmental organizations which may be mentioned include the Organization of American States, the Council of Europe and the Commission of the European Communities.

An international museographic documentation centre was established in 1952, in collaboration with the International Council of Museums, and another on monuments and sites was started in 1972 in co-operation with the International Council of Museums and Sites (ICOMOS). A documentation centre on natural history and environmental problems is run by the International Union for the Conservation of Nature and Natural Resources (IUCN).

Publications played an important part in the diffusion of information, and the quarterly *Museum*, started in 1948, has helped to spread information on museographic subjects and museum activities on a world-wide scale. The 'Museums and Monuments Series', which includes such titles as *The Organization of Museums, The Conservation of Cultural Property, Underwater Archaeology—A Nascent Discipline* and the *Conservation and Restoration of Monuments and Historic Buildings*, surveyed the problems and techniques involved. Other publications include: the *World Cultural Heritage Bulletin* (Unesco's programmes and activities); *Nature and Resources* (natural area protection); technical reports by the International Centre for the Study of the Preservation and Restoration of Cultural Property (Rome), including the manual entitled *The Conservation of Cultural Property*; information on technical development and national programmes, issued by ICOM, ICOMOS and IUCN.

Regional training centres have been developed which are geared to local needs in terms of the experience and equipment required. Today, the following exist for the preservation of cultural property: Jos, Nigeria; Churubusco, Mexico; Cuzco, Peru; New Delhi, India; Baghdad, Iraq; and Tokyo, Japan.

Advanced international courses for the training of restoration architects and for the restoration of mural paintings were organized by the Rome Centre in co-operation with appropriate Italian institutions. A new course for the preservation of stone, organized with the co-operation of the Italian authorities and the Rome Centre, was begun in Rome and Venice in 1976 to meet primarily European needs, although some fellowships will be provided to enable the training of specialists coming from other regions of the world. Substantial support has also been given to training programmes related to the preservation of the natural heritage.

From Philae to Venice, from Mohenjo-Daro to Borobudur: the planning and financing of international campaigns

International planning and financing

The costs of preservation and presentation are high, the technical skills required for the restoration of monuments are complex. States which have a rich heritage in traditional arts need museums for their preservation and display. The setting aside of national parks and reserves also calls for widespread planning and an administrative infrastructure to ensure conservation and presentation to the public. In the light of these needs, missions of experts or teams of experts to co-operate with Member States in planning and financing projects are among the priority areas of Unesco. These projects are needed so-called developed as well as developing countries. Since the launching in 1960 of the first International Campaign which was directed at saving the monuments of Nubia and which has now reached its final objective—the preservation of the temples of the island of Philae—the operational activities of the Organization, which were previously carried out on a relatively modest scale, have continuously expanded. Other large-scale projects include: saving of Venice, conservation and development of the site of Mohenjo-Daro (Pakistan); restoration and development of monuments in the Cuzco-Puno area (Peru); preparation of master plans for Fès (Morocco) and for the preservation of the cultural and natural heritage of the Katmandu Valley; preservation and presentation of the monuments in Ethiopia, preservation of the monuments on the Acropolis of Athens.

Development of an international system of natural reserves

The need to establish a world-wide network of natural reserves encompassing representative areas of the world's ecosystem has been generally recognized as having high priority. It has long been a central concern of Unesco, which aided the establishment of the International Union for Conservation of Nature and Natural Resources (IUCN) in 1948. Since that time, Unesco has continued to work towards this objective, in concert with IUCN and FAO and, more recently, with the International Biological Programme (IBP) and the United Nations Environment Programme (UNEP). This endeavour was given new impetus with the launching of the Man and the Biosphere (MAB) programme, particularly through MAB Project 8 on 'Conservation of natural areas and of the genetic material they contain', and the establishment of an international network of biosphere reserves. The concept of biosphere reserves has received strong intergovernmental support. The implementation of MAB efforts in this field is being undertaken in close co-operation with UNEP, FAO and IUCN. During 1975 Unesco joined with these organizations in forming an Ecosystem Conservation Group, designed to facilitate co-operation and co-ordination between the four main international organizations concerned in relation to protected areas for nature conservation and ecosystem conservation in general.

The principles of preservation

Action by Unesco will be based on the following principles:

The conservation of the cultural and the natural heritage is one of the most important factors in the assertion of a people's cultural identity. At national level this heritage must therefore be identified, protected, preserved and presented effectively. Access to it must be ensured on as wide and democratic a basis as possible and organized cultural activities centred on it.

Loss of or damage to a part of the cultural or natural heritage impoverishes the whole of mankind and for this reason its protection and presentation should be the responsibility of the whole international community, whatever the civilization with which the cultural heritage in question may be associated.

The preservation and presentation of the cultural and natural heritage should be based on legal, administrative, scientific and technical standards which are internationally accepted.

Action taken in this field does not conflict with social and economic development as one is part of the other and each must complement the other.

The preservation and presentation of the cultural and natural heritage is a dynamic process which involves the participation of all levels of society under continuous and imaginative leadership.

The preservation and presentation of the cultural and natural heritage is a contribution to the work of education, which should take advantage of the educational opportunities offered by monuments, historic sites, museums, national parks, etc.

The preservation and presentation of the cultural and natural heritage helps to improve the quality of life. Cultural tourism can improve international understanding, but must be accompanied by measures to counterbalance its possible adverse effects on the physical environment and socio-cultural values.

The protection of mankind's cultural heritage requires action to be taken by all to suppress illicit traffic in works of art and archaeological objects.

Principles must be laid down for the restitution, to those countries which so desire, of cultural property transferred from their territory during the colonial period.

The protection of mankind's natural heritage, including the genetic reserves of plant and animal species, must be considered an essential part of any rational use of the earth's resources.

Unesco's multidisciplinary programme: international regulations and encouragement of scientific aspects, technological dissemination and promotional activities

Efforts will be made to promote the establishment and application of international standards for the conservation of the cultural and natural heritage of mankind, through the wider application of existing international conventions and recommendations;

through the preparation of possible new international instruments, e.g. for the prevention and coverage of risks to movable cultural property, the conservation of moving images and the principles applicable to underwater archaeology; and through measures to secure the restitution of cultural property.

The preservation and presentation of the world cultural heritage will be encouraged through improved methods and new conservation techniques, the establishment of national inventory systems, the increase in the number of museums and conservation laboratories and the expansion of training facilities for conservation specialists. Studies will be carried out on subjects such as standardized inventory systems, conservation of historic quarters, museum planning in developing regions, the preservation of cinematographic material, etc. Information will be exchanged between the various international documentation centres, a standardized cataloguing system developed and regional documentation networks established. Existing publications such as *Museum*, the *World Cultural Heritage Bulletin*, *Monumentum* and the technical handbooks series will be continued, as will promotional activities such as the international campaigns for the preservation of Philae, Venice, Borobudur, Mohenjo-Daro, Katmandu and the Parthenon.

Measures for the preservation of the world's natural heritage will be aimed at establishing, through the Man and the Biosphere (MAB) National Committees in participating countries, a world-wide network of 'biosphere reserves', protected areas dedicated to international co-operation in ecosystems and genetic material preservation.

Action will be taken to help establish international research programmes and to stimulate national efforts at setting up new reserves in major ecosystem types. A newsletter will be published for the exchange of information between biosphere reserves and short-term missions organized to deal with specific problems. The MAB National Committees will be assisted in the development of courses for training conservation personnel.

Knowing how to live : education on the environment

Many analyses have shown a variety of economic, political, social and technological causes for current environmental problems. In all regions throughout the world there are programmes aimed at focusing attention on these problems and such concerns as the lack of ecologically oriented development, the seriousness of pollution problems and the importance of developing more environmentally harmonious life-styles and social behaviours.

There is, furthermore, an older environmental problem which is increasingly entering the awareness of humanity, namely, the disparity in the quality of life and the conditions of the environment not only between the less developed and the more developed nations, but also among areas within individual countries.

A key factor: perception of the environment and environmental changes

The world to date is largely in the formative stages of resolving its many environmental dilemmas. Innovative and ecologically sound technology and rigorous regulatory measures have been found for helping to solve immediate problems, such as vehicular emissions in crowded cities and high-stack transfrontier pollution. There is, however, the abiding problem of man's attitudes, values and behaviour.

Man's behaviour in the biosphere is a function of his understanding and perception of the environment and of his own position within it. Choices for action are made in the context of uncertainty concerning the 'objective' characteristics of the biosphere and the degree of uncertainty is a function both of the variability and changing characteristics of the environment itself and of man's knowledge of these characteristics. Environmental change, therefore, depends, at least in part, upon the ways in which people perceive their environments and upon their objectives in using, modifying and creating environments within which they can satisfy their material and spiritual needs.

Man can, of course, tolerate a wide range of environmental conditions, many of which are of his own making and the boundaries of which are set by his ability to live in conditions of both climatic and biosocial extremes, to earn a livelihood, and to satisfy his psycho-cultural needs. Within this broad range, however, human beings consider some environmental conditions more satisfactory than others, and their patterns of preference for environments are a function of culture and of individual personality. It is important, therefore, not only to understand the nature and direction of environmental change and its effect on man and society, but also the extent to which the new environments resulting from such change are compatible with the objectives and preference patterns of men. The nature of the individual's perception of his environment is therefore a key factor in the establishment and eventual achievement of environmental goals.

Man's power to disrupt his environment

With the tremendous advances that have been achieved in science and technology and the rapid growth of modern industry they have made possible, coupled with the population explosion and the spread of huge urban agglomerations in which nearly half the population of the world now lives, man's impact on his environment has become so great that unconsidered action could disrupt the environmental life support system upon which he depends.

The scientist's response to this problem has been to step up ecological research, through such undertakings as Unesco's Man and the Biosphere (MAB) Programme, in an attempt to provide a scientific basis for the rational use and conservation of the resources of the biosphere and for the improvement of the relationship between man and the environment. The aim here is to provide decision-makers with solid scientific advice on which to base their choice of action.

For the ordinary individual, however, the complexity of modern life is so great that he tends to feel powerless to exert any real influence upon his environment, which he sees as being manipulated by the impersonal forces of science and technology, industry and government.

At the same time, the individual has become more aware of a decline in the quality of life, a concept which he tends to confuse with freedom from environmental pollution, since pollution is more strikingly evident and more easily measured than overall quality. Unfortunately, this rather vague awareness of a lowering of the quality of life is usually accompanied by a failure to perceive the existence of actual environmental problems. Many people are born and raised in already deteriorated environments which to them seem perfectly normal. Even if they are aware of a local problem they are often unable to relate this to wider environmental considerations and may be unaware that in relieving one of their own environmental problems, for example in getting rid of waste products by dumping them in a river, they may be creating a severe environmental problem for others.

In the final analysis, however, it is upon the will of individuals who together make up the general public that both scientists and decision-makers depend. It is evident therefore that there can be no hope of finding viable solutions to environmental problems unless and until general education, at all levels, is suitably modified to enable people from all walks of life to comprehend, from childhood, the fundamental interactions and interrelationships between man and his environment.

How to devise and conduct environmental education

Within the beliefs and attitudes of modern man, his very non-perception of the environmental condition and its deteriorating state, lie the behavioural roots of such problems as pollution, energy wastage, and the destruction of the natural environment. There is a general lack of a universal ethic encompassing the globe and its life-supporting mechanisms, an ethic which espouses attitudes and behaviours on the part of individuals and societies which are consonant with humanity's place and critical role in the biosphere.

The principal problem for educators and all those concerned about humanity's environment is how best to help people at all levels—individual, corporate or governmental—to make sound social choices and decisions. There is a general lack of educational programmes which plan the environmental education process from the beginning, inside and outside the formal school system. 'The environment' cannot be treated as a subject in the same sense as, for example, mathematics, biology, or languages. The need is to provide education in problem-solving so that, faced with an environmental problem, the pupil will quickly come to understand that sound environmental decisions depend upon a host of interacting factors—scientific principles, available technology, personal and social values, financial resources, local constraints, etc. Thus emphasis should be placed on the interdisciplinary nature of environmental education, which means that it should become a part of every subject taught. In studying pollution, for example, a biology class might consider its effect on health, a chemistry class might examine certain techniques for combating it, while an economics class might look at the costs of pollution and of anti-pollution measures.

Failure to plan the environmental education process in this manner involves the failure to conceive all formal and non-formal education as mutually complementary in developing an environmentally aware and competent generation. The result is general failure in assisting both youth and adults to become more knowledgeable concerning the total environment and its associated problems, more perceptive, aware and skilled in efforts to solve these problems, and more highly motivated to work towards their solutions. To inculcate awareness and understanding of the problems of the environment is not enough; it is not enough to affect the individual in his beliefs, attitudes and values unless there is a carry-over into his behaviour, into the everyday decisions that he makes.

Thus the continuing environmental crisis is confronting educators and communicators with a new and urgent challenge. In the past they have tended to indoctrinate generations with values emphasizing human power over nature and expansion and growth which have led to our present condition. Many of these values were necessary and even desirable; their productive results have been beneficial in many respects. However, those values which eventually proved unfavourable to the quality of life or will not in the future favour humanity's harmonious and continued existence on the planet earth will need to be replaced by new values and concepts, a new global ethic and universal concern for a shared planet. Generally speaking, environmental education will aim at inserting more harmoniously each person or group in the environmental system of which they form a part and on which they depend for their lives.

Against pollution and wastage: the action of courageous pioneers and the progressive use of legal measures

Progress in environmental education has been very uneven—both between and within Member countries. As early as 1949, there was evidence that at least twenty-four countries were beginning to show concern for the development of well-designed environmental education programmes; twenty years later some eighty countries had started to develop action programmes. However, in the majority of these countries, the growth of environmental education programmes was hindered by insufficient programme coordination and resources. Predictably, the countries with the greatest socio-economic resources tended to have the most serious problems and the most comprehensive programmes.

Many Member States have passed environmental laws intended to control pollution and a number have signed agreements laying down the principles and guidelines of a regional environmental policy. Some countries have agreed on a voluntary basis and without legal restraint to notify their neighbours of measures they are about to take, or have recently taken, for the control of substances likely to have undesirable effects on man or his environment. Actions of this nature require aware, informed, and concerned public officials and citizens. For this reason, many Member States have developed instructional programmes to create an environmentally literate public.

In a number of industrialized countries, environmental problems have been brought to public attention and elevated to community or national issues through the mass media, often acting in close collaboration with community groups. In others, pioneering actions have been undertaken by courageous individuals who have gradually won the support of media. Among the more familiar issues dealt with by these means are the population phenomena, deforestation, paper consumption, chemical poisoning, exhaust emission, noise, fish and wild-life protection.

From the Stockholm recommendations (1972) . . .

Within the *United Nations system*, many of the Specialized Agencies are concerned with environmental matters, and publication of their research results and of the proceedings of symposia, expert panels and working groups they have sponsored over the past thirty years has played an important role in generating public awareness of environmental problems. Several United Nations agencies—particularly Unesco, United Nations Environmental Programme (UNEP), WHO, WMO, ILO and FAO—have been conducting research, public information campaigns, the implementation of formal and non-formal programmes of education and training in areas directly related to environmental education. Interagency collaboration has made significant progress in the development of an overall framework and direction for a co-operative international programme in environmental education.

At the 1972 United Nations Conference on the Human Environment, in Stockholm, this concern for generalized environmental education was clearly formulated. The conference recommended the establishment of 'an international programme in environmental education, interdisciplinary in approach, in school and out of school, encompassing all levels of education and directed toward the general public, in particular the ordinary citizen living in rural and urban areas, youth and adult alike, with a view to educating him as to the simple steps he might take within his means, to manage and control his environment'.

Environmental education efforts have been made from the Organization's very beginnings. In the immediate past, efforts related to environmental education have been recorded in every sector with an increasing emphasis on inter-sectoral programming and activity. Many of the programmes in the field of education have been directly involved in general environmental education, e.g., the programmes for integrated science, biology, education for international understanding and peace, and population education.

. . . to the MAB surveys on the perception of the environment

Unesco's Man and the Biosphere Programme (MAB), has made 'Perception of Environmental Quality' one of its key project areas. In the framework of this project and with a very significant contribution from the social science programme, research teams in three

Member States have looked at the way small groups of young adolescents use and value their spatial environment. The report of this study recommends that the studies utilized, with slight modifications, be extended to a number of countries, in a long-range programme of international research. The intention of this research was to help document the human costs and benefits of economic development, by showing how the child's use of the resulting micro-environment affects his life. The results of this research were published in 1976. Environmental perception also pervades all the other international themes of MAB, and—in co-operation with SCOPE—field guidelines for environmental perception studies were being tested during 1976 in a variety of rural and urban settings.

The most recent Unesco initiative in this field is the general environmental education programme, launched in response to the above-mentioned recommendation of the United Nations Conference on the Human Environment and developed in co-operation with UNEP. The focus of this new programme has been to enlist all the relevant resources in the Secretariat, and to collaborate with other United Nations agencies and appropriate international bodies, so as to develop an overall framework and direction for a co-operative international programme to further environmental education globally.

Education and information: the joint action of the United Nations Environmental Programme . . .

One of the first actions taken within the framework of this new programme was the sending, early in 1975, of a questionnaire on environmental needs and priorities to the education ministers of all Unesco Member States. In the replies received 110 Unesco Member States expressed interest in environmental education, with 63 per cent expressing relatively high levels of environmental education needs. Of this group, 84 per cent were in Africa, Asia, Arab States and Latin America. Important and significant environmental education needs were also clearly expressed in other more developed regions.

This was followed by the convening by Unesco/UNEP, in October 1975, of a major international workshop in Belgrade, attended by some 100 educational specialists from 64 countries, at which the overall framework and direction for a co-operative international programme to further environmental education was worked out.

In another joint venture with UNEP an important programme of environmental education for engineers of all disciplines has been initiated and similar programmes are being developed for architects, town-planners, managers and economists.

. . . and of Unesco's efforts to change attitudes

Unesco will continue its efforts to improve public knowledge and understanding of environmental problems. The approach will be interdisciplinary and comprehensive, in the sense that it will view the problem of man in his environment in its totality, including all aspects of the environment: ecological, economical, technological, social, cultural and aesthetic. The approach will be based on most recent and concrete results of scientific research and experience. Particular emphasis should be laid on local, national and international co-operation in the solution of environmental problems. Environmental education should be a continuous lifelong process both in school and out of school, with a view to securing the active participation of all individuals in preventing and solving environmental problems. Research on perception of environmental quality and on attitudes towards the environment will therefore be developed. After the intergovernmental Conference on Environmental Education held in 1977, the programme is entering its operational phase, during which it will probably receive financial assistance from UNDP.

8 Population: individual and collective problems

Among a series of recent world conferences convened to shed more light on some important issues relevant to the development process, the World Population Conference (Bucharest, 1974) was opportune in bringing about a much needed consensus regarding the fact that population questions, complex and important though they are—and precisely because of their complexity and importance—must not be considered in isolation. On the contrary, they have to be seen within the framework of overall socio-economic development, and approached with the closest concern for human rights, cultural integrity and national sovereignty.

Population, development, human rights

Too little is known regarding the interrelations between population and development factors. This lack of knowledge, and in particular ignorance as to the effects of the former on the latter, precludes simplistic attempts to explain or solve development problems in terms of demographic reasons or programmes. There is, however, some evidence that rapid population growth and mass poverty do coincide in time and space, and that they are mutually reinforcing. Where the second obtains, birth rates tend to be high and, together with declining mortality, lead to rapid population increase. Per contra, under the conditions and policies obtaining in many developing countries, rapid rates of natural increase may make the reduction of poverty more difficult. Thus for many of these countries, whether for reasons of natural endowment or of patterns of agrarian tenure and structure, fertile new land available to absorb and support fast-growing populations is limited, as are the investment resources required for its exploitation and development. Nor has the alternative possibility of absorption through industrialization been largely effective, especially given the highly uneven incidence of the kind of industrialization which has taken place, and unemployment has in consequence mounted. The resultant picture is often summarized in terms of a high dependency ratio, i.e.: an age structure in which the numbers of the very young and the very old are large in relation to the economically active population which supports them. This economic burden impairs the level of living for all, most particularly for the children and the aged. Other problems seen as arising from rapid growth have to do with social and political stability, with the supply of food and natural resources, or again, especially under certain conditions, with environmental degradation. The range of needs thus affected is closely linked with human rights at every level from individual to global, involving mental and physical health, nutrition, housing, education, employment, income, recreation and more generally speaking the relationship of man to his immediate socio-cultural and natural environment and ultimately to the resources of the planet.

The foregoing should not be taken to imply that the rate of population growth, together with the age composition and demographic structure with which it is associated and to some extent produces, is the only demographic variable related to the development process. Thus absolute size of the population clearly has a close bearing on, *inter alia*, the extent of a country's internal division of labour. And a question of major importance, only now beginning to receive adequate attention, is that of the physical distribution of the population, its density, localized concentrations and spatial movements, particularly urban-rural migrations.

Seven billion people in the year 2000

The above elements of analysis, including the fact that in many countries the main population issues have to do more with distribution, migration, sub-fecundity and the like than with population growth, still have to be seen against the reality of an unprecedented population growth at global level. World population is now around 4 billion, having grown with considerable rapidity over the last century or so. Its age structure is particularly favourable to further growth: fewer than 6 per cent of the total population are more than 65 years old, a large proportion of women are in the child-bearing ages, and relatively large numbers of women will enter the reproductive ages in the next decades, since some 36 per cent of the people in the world are less than 15 years old. The present overall rate of growth is about 2 per cent per year, and there is every indication that there will be a global population of around 7 billion by the end of the century.

These are global dimensions, and while limitations of space preclude their detailed breakdown the following further indications of change over the period 1970-75 are of interest. Among major demographic areas, Europe has the lowest rate of population growth, estimated at 0.64 per cent per year. The highest rate, over 2.7 per cent, is estimated for Latin America, with both Africa and South Asia accelerating almost to this level. The rate for East Asia is estimated to be some 1.6 per cent.

The World Plan of Action adopted by the Bucharest Conference stresses the importance of improving knowledge of demographic and socio-economic interrelations, and with this as a base, of promoting, by education and information, awareness of the issues and options related to population questions, both among the general public (including persons of school age) and among those responsible for formulating policies and programmes in population and related areas. These emphases were clearly endorsed by the eighteenth session of the General Conference, which saw such a focus of activities as a prerequisite of responsible choice, freedom of response, and respect both for the human rights of the individual and the development needs and objectives of the wider community.

Another reason which prompts Unesco to continue acting in fields connected with population is the high level of relevance of such fields to its mandate concerning education, information and the social sciences. In the case of education, for instance, the introduction of population related components into educational contents offers an excellent instrument for the renewal of those contents inasmuch as these components, concerning vital topics, are of the highest relevance for the individual, as well as for the local and national communities concerned.

Regional aspects

All regions have faced similar difficulties in varying degrees, in policy/programme formulation: there are serious gaps in the basic demographic data; there are continuing uncertainties about the causes and consequences of fertility behaviour, particularly at the family level; more is known about the effects of socio-economic change and development on demographic variables than about the impact of population trends on development. There has been a certain disappointment with family planning programmes, which, whether adopted for reasons of family limitation, spacing or health, are apparently tapering off in effectiveness. This is variously attributed to faults of management, technology or techniques, including inadequate education and information; to too narrow a concentration on population control at the cost of ignoring the total process of developmental change which should accompany or precede it and may even—some would assert—make it unnecessary; to insufficient attention to the rights, values and cultural dignity of the individuals and societies for whom the programmes are intended. In addition, as noted earlier, demographic situations differ widely from country to country—and even within a given country—and so in consequence do both the perception of problems and the steps taken to overcome them. Thus in the African region a major concern has been the collection of basic demographic data and the training of technical personnel required for their analysis. In the Latin American region, attention has been concentrated on the interrelations of social and economic variables within the highly differentiated development styles and patterns of socio-economic change which characterize the region. In the Western Asian region, action has been defined by such factors as high birth rates, rapidly declining mortality, large-scale rural exodus to capital cities, intra-regional migration, and social imbalances arising from the movement of skilled workers and technicians. In Asia and the Pacific, where there is the largest growth in absolute numbers and some of the highest densities in the world, over 95 per cent of the population live in countries which have adopted family planning programmes as a major arm of official population policies.

The contribution of the international organizations

Large-scale attention to population questions by the United Nations system dates from the mid-1960s when the attention of the international community was aroused by high population growth projections, with Member States beginning to be increasingly concerned with the interrelations of demographic factors and socio-economic development. (See preceding paragraph for an outline of some of the major foci of recent action in different regions). The relevant activities of the United Nations agencies and organizations form a joint interagency, interdisciplinary programme articulated through the co-ordinating machinery of the Inter-Agency Consultative Committee of the United Nations Fund for Population Activities (UNFPA). The resources available to the system were considerably increased by the establishment in 1969 of the United Nations Fund for Population Activities (first established in 1967 as a Trust Fund of the United Nations). The purposes of UNFPA are, briefly, to promote awareness of the implications of national and international population problems and to enhance the knowledge and capacity of the United Nations system to respond to Member States' requests for assistance in the population field.

It is of importance to stress here the work of international non-governmental organizations interested in the population field. A number of them have a long history of involvement with both research and educational activities and have been particularly efficacious because of their operational flexibility and their multiplicity of contacts at local levels. Not all are as directly concerned as, for example, the International Union for the Scientific Study of Population, or the International Planned Parenthood Federation, but an indication of their numbers may be gathered from the fact that some thirty NGOs were actively associated with Unesco's programme in support of World Population Year.

Following important decisions taken by the General Conference and Executive Board in 1966 and 1967 respectively, Unesco was given a detailed mandate in the population field by the General Conference in November 1968. The overall purpose of Unesco's population programme, as defined in this and subsequent resolutions of the General Conference, is to improve knowledge and to increase awareness of the causes and consequences of population change, of their interrelations with other aspects of social, cultural and environmental change, and of their implications for human rights and the quality of life. The programme thus involves activities in education, as well as communications and the social and natural sciences.

Unesco's expanded operations in the population field effectively began in 1970, at which point an urgent task was the development of the necessary programme concepts, infrastructure and capacity for action in what was largely a new field for the Organization. Among the most important operational trends to date has been the introduction, through Unesco's existing field structure, of staff and programmes in education and information at regional level, with the aim of directly stimulating and supporting national programmes. Activities have included advisory and documentation services in education and communication related to population programmes, training workshops in education and communication, and the publication of education and communication materials. A source book on population education has been published for immediate use by curriculum specialists and as a basis for the development of materials packages and kits for specific national programmes in population education. At the teacher-training level, instruction on population and population education has been integrated into teacher educator courses and a substantial volume of related materials has been developed. These activities represent significant progress in a hitherto largely untouched field, but it is perhaps even more important to note that they have directly stimulated the development of and requests for aid to substantial national programmes in the education and communication fields in relation to population.

Research activities have proceeded more slowly, on the whole, with attention focused on the following: interrelations between demographic trends and education development and opportunity; the family and socio-economic change in relation to demographic trends; population/environment relations in island situations; human rights and cultural values in relation to population programmes; development of social indicators of the quality of life, including the analysis of related demographic and environmental factors; content and methodology of education and information activities in the population field.

Beyond purely demographic goals: the recommendations of the Bucharest Conference (1974)

As with the recommendations of the World Population Conference, the most recent decisions of the General Conference enjoin a much wider conceptual basis as a general principle of action in this field. The true goals of population policies go beyond the purely demographic, and population problems are in consequence closely linked with many, if not all, of the major world problems. It is thus not population in isolation, population *per se*, but—in the broadest terms—population in relation to human rights concerning education, information and the socio-cultural and natural environment, which should be the distinctive focus and basic principle of Unesco action. Put more succinctly, population programme activities should be fully integrated within the wider context of development and the concern for a new economic order. (This concern with placing population matters in context extends to every level of programme conceptualization and action, e.g. population education is seen within the wider setting of educational innovation and renovation).

Recognition of national sovereignty in determining population policies, and of the marked specificity of demographic situations and contexts might be taken as separate principles of action; considered together, they converge with great force and require, *inter alia*, that the programme reflect the large importance of activities at national and local level. Within this framework the regional infrastructure also plays an important role.

Intercultural studies, strategies adapted to the different societies

From 1977 to 1982 efforts will be made to improve scientific knowledge of the inter-relations of demographic phenomena and natural environment and resources, thus providing a better knowledge-base for policy-makers, planners, educators, communicators and others concerned with these areas; Unesco will also seek to improve co-operation and exchange of data and information among researchers from both developed and developing countries. Unesco's action will mainly take the form of studies, including a series of comparative, cross-cultural studies on family structures, and the causes, dynamics and consequences of migration; studies on pedagogical and learning theory in relation to population education; regional and national studies on such subjects as relations between population and human rights issues, etc.

Moreover, the Organization will produce educational and information materials for school and out-of-school use, including a number of regional and national source books and audio-visual material. Advisory services in programme preparation will be available to Member States; seminars and training courses will be organized, etc. Primary attention will be given to the development of effective programme strategies adapted to regional and national settings and particularly their socio-economic and cultural characteristics.

These are clearly two complementary aspects of a whole, the former helping to provide the knowledge-base necessary to ensure the intellectual adequacy of the latter.

9 Communication

From the outset, the United Nations, seeking ways of establishing a lasting peace in a world which had just been shaken by a bloody war, acknowledged the role of communication as a potentially decisive factor in international understanding and as a means of promoting better mutual understanding between peoples. The idea that the mass media should be enlisted in the task of promoting 'the mutual knowledge and understanding of peoples' is embodied in the Organization's Constitution and it was for this reason that, as soon as it was founded, Unesco tackled the problem of finding out the conditions under which the development of communication throughout the world might be likely to strengthen 'the defences of peace' in the minds of men. Since then, the Organization has become increasingly aware of the possibilities which communication techniques have to offer within its fields of competence, in particular in education; even before the First United Nations Development Decade, the idea took shape of applying these techniques of development, making use of their power to bring about integration and to motivate people and bring them together.

Information media throughout the world: for long the exclusive preserve of a minority

Since 1946, developments have been swift and no one any longer doubts that we are entitled to expect a great deal more of the mass media than 'the free flow of ideas'. But it must be emphasized that, historically, the mass media were ill prepared for the task which now devolves upon them. Being products of industrialization, they scarcely affected the peoples of Asia and Africa who, by reason of their low purchasing power and an inadequate electricity supply system (the transistor had not then been invented), were deprived of access to them. These information media therefore remained the exclusive preserve of a minority—the citizens of the colonial powers and a very restricted local élite. Even in Latin America, although it had been politically independent for more than a century, the press, which had been in existence since the seventeenth century, was also reserved for a minority, whether governmental or revolutionary, and was not accessible to the broad masses of the illiterate population.

A correct approach to the problem of communication also needs to take into account the far-reaching transformations which the information media have undergone, since the coming into being of means other than verbal communication and correspondence, that is to say since the appearance of the first newspapers. The press was initially conceived as a means of *disseminating ideas* in the political gazettes and pamphlets of the seventeenth and eighteenth centuries. But, from the mid-nineteenth century onwards, a radical change occurred: the invention of the high-speed printing press, and later of the rotary press, and the introduction of advertising, which radically changed the financial circumstances of production, making possible the mass low-cost circulation of newspapers. Considerations of a commercial nature then came to the fore and affected even the *content* of the organs of the press, which endeavoured to increase their advertising revenue by appealing to the widest possible public. From then on the press sought to entertain just as much as to inform and persuade, and these three considerations governed its development in the twentieth century up to the time when the press came into competition with the audio-visual both as regards its information and entertainment role and also as regards advertising markets.

Since their inception, indeed, the cinema, radio and television were obliged in the majority of cases to adjust their activities in the light of commercial considerations. Even in a number of European countries in which radio and television are non-profit State monopolies, the need to attract a large audience has resulted in programmes which are designed mainly as entertainment. Whether this was a necessary development or a case of taking the easy way out, it must, in any case, be recognized that for several decades such stations have been increasingly vying with competing commercial channels. While these radical changes were taking place, the press was to some extent recovering its initial function as a medium for dissemination and debate, for news comment and in-depth analysis.

Misuse: oppression, propaganda and profit, one-way communication

In parallel to their traditional functions, the information media began to be used deliberately as instruments of *mass persuasion*, whether for political or commercial ends, as early as the First World War. Although modern research findings have qualified the old mechanistic stimulus-response theories according to which a given message must necessarily produce a particular effect, such theories prevailed for a long time and even now are all too often used, even if unwittingly, to sanction the use of the information media for mercenary or even oppressive ends, for propaganda or profit. These attempts at manipulation have given rise to a certain mistrust of the mass media, to which an almost mythical omnipotence is attributed, quite irrespective of the environment in which the target audience lives and moves.

Although the notion of 'the free flow of information' goes back some fifty years, it has been invoked as a concept in international documents only since the end of the Second World War. At that time it was generally and sincerely believed that the universal dissemination of information would be enough to ensure understanding and respect among peoples and to allay conflicts. But euphoric optimism of this kind overlooks certain essential facts, not the least of which is the uneven international availability of facilities for press communication, which makes it illusory to aim at universal dissemination and which opens the way for a one-way flow of information. Even when ulterior political motives did not sway the relevant decisions or taint the basic ideas, no account was taken of the needs and aspirations of numerous peoples still under colonial domination, unable to make their voice heard at a time when the principles which might form the basis of a philosophy of communication were taking shape. Although the word 'communication' was already current at that time in English language texts, what was meant in fact was a rather one-sided *dissemination of information*. It was only much later that there emerged the concept of communication in its true sense (from the Latin 'communicare': to make common, to share), no longer implying an active transmitter and a passive receiver, but allowing for feedback from the latter of a kind likely to modify the behaviour of the former or, better still, requiring the active participation of all concerned in the communication process, which thus becomes a pluridimensional flow of information with multiple feedback.

Communication, whatever the medium which carries it, is essential and has always been essential to any society. A human community sharing the same ideas, beliefs and concerns can only come into being through a system of communication which puts its members in touch with each other and can only continue in existence within such a system. The human group and communication are coextensive, a fact which has been confirmed on an increasingly broad scale in the last few decades, during which communication has expanded to cover the entire globe as the problems of mankind have increasingly come to be seen on a world-wide scale, in spite of the ideological and institutional differences which continue to split human society.

A source of misapprehension or a decisive factor in mutual understanding between peoples

In a world in which, whether one likes it or not, everything has repercussions on everything else—often in an inappropriate or harmful way—the communication media have thus become instruments of considerable significance and effectiveness, and the different aspects of their development and use need to be studied at international level: this presupposes a willingness on the part of States, in spite of their national interests and allegiances, to transcend their immediate interests when necessary and to agree to collaborate in order to harness the media for the common good and to build bridges of information and knowledge between communities and peoples wherever such bridges are lacking.

This brings us a long way from communication as a means of entertainment or as an instrument of persuasion, roles to which it was long wished to confine it. Communication, as a potent means of integration, is capable, if judiciously used by States and peoples and provided that there is a sincere desire for concertation, of forming, in the world of tomorrow, the basis for better international understanding, for more humane and more balanced development, and for greater knowledge and appreciation of different cultures, thus conducing to the maintenance of peace. But it would be pointless to overlook the fact that the abuse or totally uncontrolled use of the mass media might easily provoke or prolong states of tension and mutual misunderstanding and reinforce inequalities and compromise the new economic and social order which is being established.

The difficulties with which Unesco will have to contend in order fully to carry out its task in the field of communication are obviously numerous. One such difficulty, and by no means the least, lies in the fact that, historically speaking, the mass media have served other objectives than that of making possible real communication between people. There is a widespread tendency to mistrust the media and to see them only in terms of the misuses to which they can be put. A change of approach is undoubtedly called for in the way in which they are used, and it is Unesco's duty to enlist every effort to achieve this end, an end which should be attained through bold action, both in the ethical sphere and on the level of practical demonstration, particularly with regard to the use of simple, low-cost equipment which can be used at community level and which enables individuals to take a more active part in the daily life of the group.

Information at the heart of modern problems

Energy and information are regarded in modern theory as the two basic principles of any system. In order for Unesco to carry out its task in fuller awareness, the Organization should therefore study the problems of communication at the level of the *individual* who, being himself an energy and information system, feels a biological need to communicate with those around him; at the level of the various *communities*, in which it is essential to offset the effects of monolithic mass information by enabling small groups to voice their aspirations; lastly, at the level of *countries*, which face the internal problem of how to use the communication media for educational purposes and for promoting development, and the external problem of finding ways of expressing themselves directly so as to project for the benefit of others an appropriate image of themselves, to preserve their cultural integrity and to contribute to the inception of a new and more equitable international order which shows greater consideration for particular interests.

The four sections of this Chapter therefore reflect first of all a concern to continue the activities flowing from those provisions of the Constitution of Unesco in which the Member States proclaimed their desire to promote the free exchange of ideas and knowledge, to develop and extend the means of communication among their peoples in order to promote mutual knowledge and understanding and to draw up international agreements for these purposes which will allow the free flow of ideas in words and images. But, at the same time, they reflect the new demands which have made themselves felt in recent years: with the beginning of the Second Development Decade it has become clear to Member States that modern communication technology— and, in particular, space communications—might impinge, with disturbing consequences, on the various world markets and interfere unduly with national information media, thereby jeopardizing the national culture and independence of countries which have only just freed themselves from other forms of subjection. At the same time, the concept of the free flow of information has worked to the disadvantage of such countries, for which, in the last analysis, it has meant primarily opening the gates to a flood of information from outside whilst they themselves have been unable to make their voice heard. This is why several resolutions adopted by the General Conference have prescribed a course of action to be undertaken by the Organization in an endeavour to establish a *more balanced flow* of information and ideas at international level, respecting the various cultures and individual priorities of each country.

Towards a free, balanced flow of information

Economic and political developments, coupled with striking progress in transport and telecommunications, have led to a vast increase in the volume of international communication and exchange of information as well as in the international movement of persons and the circulation of educational, scientific and cultural materials. Global communications networks, expanded by the development of satellite technology, provide the possibility for instantaneous exchange of news both by word and image among all countries linked to the systems. Services providing global coverage of news and events are available to media throughout the world from several large news agencies based in industrialized countries. Television news exchanges are arranged on a systematic basis within and between regional broadcasting unions in Europe while a beginning has been made in organizing similar exchanges in some other regions, notably the Arab States, Asia and Latin America. Likewise, regional groupings of national news agencies in Asia and Africa have been endeavouring to arrange systematic pooling and exchange of news and feature material.

Imbalances in information sources and the cultural implications of imported programmes

Despite the technical possibilities and the efforts for co-operation, however, the flow of information presents a serious imbalance and a large part of the world continues to be deprived of adequate means and structures for the transmission and reception of information and ideas. The global survey of the mass media recently published by Unesco in *World Communications* drew attention to 'the imbalances in the flow of information between countries and in the content of what flows'. The flow is predominantly from a small number of technologically developed and highly industrialized countries to the rest of the world. For example, a recent analysis by Unesco of the international flow of television programme material indicated that in a majority of developing countries with television systems at least half their programmes were imported. Of the total world imports of television programmes, some 75 per cent originated in North America.

To a large extent the flow of news and entertainment and the supply of technical equipment and materials are the result of international commercial activities, which, while providing essential services and the transfer of technical knowledge and experiences, raise questions of cultural identity and technological dependence.

While the importance of the free flow of information is widely accepted as the basis of mutual understanding, many developing countries are concerned that their lack of access to world communication channels denies them the opportunity of informing the world of their problems, aspirations, and contribution to the culture of mankind. At the same time, the fact that they are the recipients of a disproportionate volume of information and entertainment from foreign sources leaves them concerned about the preservation of their cultural integrity and system of values. The future possibility of direct broadcasts via satellites has intensified this concern.

The immense size of the audiences reached by the mass media, and particularly by radio and television, and the ease and speed with which information and ideas can spread throughout the whole world, transcending national frontiers, have brought an increasing preoccupation with the content and quality of what is published and broadcast, and with the effects of the mass media on relations between peoples. Hence the need to promote respect for differences in cultural and social values; and the development of acceptable criteria on the rights, duties and responsibilities of communication institutions and individual professionals in their international relationships.

Communication, moreover, is an essential component in a new social and economic order, and equal access to information sources and flows between and within societies is necessary for its establishment.

Obstacles to the circulation of educational material and to the movement of persons

With regard to educational, scientific and cultural materials, their international circulation is hampered by a variety of tariff, trade and transport obstacles at a time when the economic and social development plans of many countries call for a significant increase in the quantity of such materials. While a number of international instruments have been formulated to facilitate their importation and some action has been taken to reduce transport costs, the measures proposed have not been universally adopted and many difficulties remain in the way of the distribution of books, films, media equipment, printing paper, scientific instruments and other materials for educational, cultural and scientific purposes.

As to the movement of persons, while modern means of transport, though unevenly distributed throughout the world, have made international travel easier, there are often, in practice, obstacles impeding the circulation of persons from one country to another. Granted the educational and cultural value of travel and its importance for international understanding there is a manifest need for further measures to promote exchanges, remove obstacles and facilitate travel and study abroad.

Detaxation of means of communication and development of multilateral exchange of information

In the wake of the Second World War, with the widespread destruction of mass media facilities and the vivid recollection of wartime censorship and controls, there was a powerful impulse to rebuild links between people through all means of communication. Also of immediate concern in these years were the high tariffs, postal and transport costs and other trade barriers to the free movement of educational, scientific and cultural materials. Increasingly, governments recognized that the revenues which they might derive from tariffs and taxes levied on the transfer of knowledge were of small importance in comparison with the gains to be reaped from its freer circulation.

Since the late 1960s, partly as a result of technical advances and partly because of growing recognition of the role of communication in the shaping of a new world order, attention has been directed to the need for a more equitable 'two-way' flow of information and to the importance of the content and quality of the information transmitted. Technological developments such as broadcasting satellites have brought into sharp focus the need for all cultures to have a proper representation in this world-wide information exchange. Concurrently the explosive increase in travel facilities has been accompanied by a recognition that they should be used to increase and enrich personal contacts in an international context.

These trends towards freer movement of persons and increased cultural and information exchanges have been stimulated in recent times by the spirit of détente and positive steps to foster international co-operation despite ideological differences.

Important initiatives to promote co-operation have been taken by professional organizations which have provided an institutional base for international and regional co-operation.

Beneficial effects of the easing of customs regulations and postal rates

A number of international bodies have been concerned in the work of formulating, negotiating and implementing practical measures to improve the circulation of educational, scientific and cultural materials. The organizational framework for tariff reductions has been provided by the General Agreement on Tariffs and Trade (GATT), and by the Customs Co-operation Council. Postal and air transport rates for the dispatch of such materials have been eased by measures adopted by the Universal Postal Union (UPU) and the International Air Transport Association (IATA), while the United Nations Conference on Trade and Development (UNCTAD) has continuously co-operated with Unesco in the promotion of such measures as special loans and compensatory financing schemes to help developing countries acquire materials needed for their educational and social development.

Impetus to the international facilitation of travel by persons engaged in educational, scientific and cultural activities, was given by the United Nations Conference on International Travel and Tourism convened in Rome in 1963 which suggested the simplification of procedures concerning visas, foreign residence permits, the transfer of foreign exchange, etc.

In the field of freedom of information, responsibility for the political aspects of the question rests with the United Nations, where since its first General Assembly which declared freedom of information 'the touchstone of all freedoms' and a 'fundamental human right' a series of debates and resolutions has touched upon the rights, obligations and practices of the mass media. Among these, the Universal Declaration of Human Rights, proclaimed in 1948, included in Article 19 the right to freedom of opinion and expression. A Draft Convention and a Draft Declaration on Freedom of Information were transmitted to the General Assembly in 1952 and 1960 respectively but have remained on the agenda with little progress being made.

From standard-setting action to study grants and programmes by satellite . . .

Unesco has co-operated with both Member States and the United Nations in this field in terms of its constitutional obligation to 'collaborate in the work of advancing the mutual knowledge and understanding of peoples, through all means of mass communication and to that end recommend such international agreements as may be necessary to promote the free flow of ideas by word and image'.

The first international instrument to be adopted by the Organization, in 1948, was the Agreement for Facilitating the International Circulation of Visual and Auditory Materials of an Educational, Scientific and Cultural Character, which now has twenty-eight contracting States. It was followed, in 1950, by the Agreement on the Importation of Educational, Scientific and Cultural Material, which now has sixty-eight contracting States, while its scope may soon be extended through a protocol to cover new materials resulting from modern technology.

The General Conference, at its seventeenth session (1972), proclaimed a Declaration of Guiding Principles on the Use of Satellite Broadcasting for the Free Flow of Information, the Spread of Education and Greater Cultural Exchange, a problem which is concurrently receiving intensive consideration by the United Nations Committee on the Peaceful Uses of Outer Space. In addition a text of a Draft Declaration on Fundamental Principles Governing the Use of the Mass Media in Strengthening Peace and International Understanding and in Combating War Propaganda, Racism and Apartheid is under consideration.

International exchange arrangements have been promoted with the co-operation of professional bodies. Projects concerning the development and linking of national news agencies to give a greater voice to the developing countries, the pooling and exchange of news, features, news films and broadcasts to their mutual advantage, have been undertaken. Groups of countries have been assisted in surveying the possibilities of regional co-operation to establish satellite broadcasting systems for education and development.

... so many paths towards the exchange of ideas and closer international relations

Programmes of research have been undertaken on the international flow of information, including television programme traffic, world news agencies, external radio broadcasting, and on the marketing patterns of transnational film and television distribution.

Lastly, with a view to facilitating the movement of persons, the Organization has carried out studies and published a number of works: *Study Abroad, Travel Abroad, The Handbook of International Exchanges*, etc. and is continuing its fellowship and exchange programme. Unesco's self-appointed task for the next few years will consist of strengthening its action in favour of a more equitable two-way flow of information, particularly between developing and developed countries. Through research and study, the Organization proposes to further understanding of the world situation as regards the international flow of information, one important aspect of which is the understanding of the role and impact of transnational corporations. In association with the appropriate professional organizations, criteria will be established for a wider international use of mass communications. Efforts will be made to promote regional co-operation for the development of news agencies and the exchange of news, articles and programmes.

Action will also be taken to remove obstacles to the international circulation of educational, scientific and cultural materials and to promote measures designed to facilitate the exchange of persons whose activities relate to these fields.

Copyright and dissemination of works

Copyright is a necessary stimulus to the creation of works of the mind. The system on which it is based—the payment to the author of a small percentage of the purchase price of a book or the admission charge paid to see a play or hear a concert—gives him an income which is obtained from his public. When such income is sufficiently large to ensure the author's livelihood, it enables him to devote all his energies to his creative work, in the field of letters, arts, sciences or techniques.

Protection and dissemination

The need to protect copyright however is not the sole aspect of the problem. For an author does not create only for himself or to provide himself with a living; he creates in order to communicate his thought and works to the public.

The direct protection of creative artists is but one of the problems arising from the dissemination of works of the mind in the contemporary world. Various related activities contribute to this dissemination, particularly those of performers in the case of works that are not solely meant for reading, those of producers of phonograms, which give a certain duration to interpretations, and those of broadcasting agencies, which eliminate distance.

Unesco, whose Constitution assigns it the task of giving 'the people of all countries access to the printed and published materials produced by any of them', has an obligation to encourage the activities of creative artists by safeguarding their material and moral interests and by taking into account the role played by works of the mind in general development, as well as in the promotion of education, science and culture. If we examine the present situation in the world as regards creative activity, it becomes clear that there are two *de facto* points to be taken into account which call for action on the part of the international community.

To reduce disparities in intellectual production and increase access to all intellectual works

It is apparent, in the first place, that there is a great disparity between the various countries with respect to intellectual production, and that the developing countries are increasingly dependent upon the industrialized countries for access to the works most needed for progress in education, science and culture. Thus, for example, estimates of world book production in 1973 show that the number of titles published per million inhabitants varies from 553 in Europe to 27 in Africa, the figures being 50 in Asia and 87 in South America.

This being so, the developing countries have to import or translate, at considerable cost, works published in the advanced countries—and such works, moreover, are not always suited to their needs. As for translations, it is likewise symptomatic that, according to the latest statistics, approximately three-quarters of the works translated annually throughout the world were originally written in English, French, Russian or German (in that order), and, with the exception of the Spanish-speaking countries of Latin America, only 3 per cent were written in the languages of developing countries.

... a less static conception of copyright

The second point that must be taken into account relates to the diversification of problems connected with copyright protection due to the development of techniques for the dissemination of creative works (reprography, computers, satellites, television by cable, video-cassettes, etc.). These techniques and audio-visual media are now so widely used that it is urgently necessary to find solutions which reconcile the rights of authors or their assignees with users' interests. For while it is important to protect the legitimate interests of copyright proprietors, since such protection is essential to their intellectual productivity, the control that they exercise over the use of protected works must not be allowed to become an obstacle to the development and improvement of documentation and education systems, or even of systems for the circulation of their works. It is important that opportunities for obtaining documentation should be increased to the maximum, particularly in the scientific and technical field, through the application of new methods specially adapted to meet the growing demand for information.

It is therefore essential, on the one hand, to establish legal norms designed to encourage the development of national cultures and also to ensure that works of the mind are circulated as widely as possible and, on the other hand, to formulate strategies which make it possible to promote their circulation. To do so, we must not be content with a purely static conception of copyright in which legislation is regarded simply as a means of defending the creators of intellectual works against unjust attack; we must encourage the adoption of a dynamic and purposeful approach, so that the legitimate and necessary protection of authors becomes a means of fostering intellectual creation—an important factor in the development of human knowledge, the benefits of which should be made available to all peoples, and primarily to economically and technically underprivileged States.

From the Berne Union (1886) to the Geneva Convention (1952) and the Paris Revisions (1971)

Efforts to establish an international statute for works of the mind go back to the end of the 19th century, when—in 1886—the Berne Convention for the Protection of Literary and Artistic Works was adopted. It was administered by the United International Bureaux for the Protection of Intellectual Property (BIRPI) and the governments of the World Intellectual Property Organization (WIPO). A number of Pan-American conventions, administration of which was subsequently entrusted to the Organization of American States, were also concluded between 1889 and 1946. Thus it was possible to distinguish between three groups of States, according to the measures they had taken to regulate their international relations in this regard: (a) Member States of the International Union constituted by the Berne Convention; (b) States parties to one or more of the Pan-American conventions; (c) States which had not acceded to any system of international copyright protection, some of which regulated their relations in this respect through bilateral agreements.

In view of the need for a universal diplomatic instrument that would be approved by all countries, the General Conference, at its second session (Mexico, 1947), decided that the Organization should study the problem of improving copyright at the universal level, existing conventions being taken into account. The work done in this connection by the Secretariat led, in 1952, to the adoption of the Universal Copyright Convention, which did not replace the Berne Convention or the Pan-American Conventions, but established a system of protection that enabled the countries of the Berne Union and the American continent to maintain stable and clearly defined conventional relations, and which could also be acceded to by countries with widely differing economic and cultural situations.

... sustained action for the universal improvement of copyright

By 1963 it had become clear that special provisions for developing countries should be included in multilateral copyright conventions. To this end, on the occasion of the revision of certain basic provisions of the Berne Convention, a protocol thereto was adopted in 1967, in Stockholm, providing a special status for the developing countries. The General Conference, for its part, at its fourteenth session (1966), invited the Director-General to ask the competent bodies to study the possibility of revising the Universal Convention. The revised text of that Convention was adopted on 24 July 1971 and entered into force on 10 July 1974. In view of the difficulties encountered in applying the Stockholm Protocol, the Berne Convention was also revised, in July 1971, so that the developing countries might enjoy advantages of the same nature as those provided for in the Universal Convention as revised. The revisions thus made did not alter the complementary nature of the two instruments, since on many points the Berne Convention established protection norms that were superior to those of the Universal Convention as revised (length of protection, moral right, formalities, broadcasting rights, etc.).

Moreover, at its sixteenth session (1970), the General Conference decided to establish an international Copyright Information Centre. The function of this centre is to implement a programme of action to facilitate, on the practical level and within established legal norms, the access of developing States to protected works, in particular by aiding those States to overcome the difficulties they meet with in the collection of data (bibliographical information, selection of works, identification of copyright proprietors), in negotiations to obtain the necessary authorization for translation, reproduction, adaptation or any other use of an intellectual work, and in the search for qualified translators, as well as the difficulties they encounter as a consequence of the economic situation.

... extended today to the audio-visual field

The protection of certain auxiliaries of intellectual creation has also been recognized at the international level. Thus in 1961 Unesco, in conjunction with the International Labour Organisation (ILO) and the United International Bureaux for the Protection of Intellectual Property (BIRPI), convened a diplomatic conference which adopted the International Convention for the Protection of Performers, Producers of Phonograms and Broadcasting Organizations, and in 1971 and 1974, in conjunction with the World Intellectual Property Organization (WIPO), it convened two international conferences of States, which adopted respectively the Convention for the Protection of Producers of Phonograms against Unauthorized Duplication of their Phonograms and the Convention relating to the distribution of programme-carrying signals transmitted by satellite.

Since WIPO administers the Berne Convention and a certain number of other international instruments relating to the legal protection of intellectual property, it was deemed necessary to co-ordinate the activities carried on in the field of copyright by Unesco and WIPO. This was the subject of an agreement approved by the Executive Board of Unesco at its 93rd session (93 EX/Decision 6.8) and by the Co-ordination Committee of WIPO on 27 November 1973, which was signed by the two Directors-General on 12 March 1974. The application of this agreement enables the two Organizations to co-ordinate their activities in such a way that duplication of effort is avoided and to carry out a number of joint activities.

Complementary and therefore reconcilable—the protection of authors' rights and users' interests

The Organization's approach is characterized by a desire to ensure the recognition of the complementary nature of two kinds of rights—those of authors and those of the public, research and knowledge—by paying particular attention to the social significance of intellectual property. Unesco's role consists in organizing the protection of copyright so as to enable works to reach an increasingly wide public, with a view to promoting the development of education, science and culture. The Organization, therefore, should not consider copyright, at either the international or the national level, solely from the point of view of commutative justice towards authors in their relations with users of their works; it should also take into account the educational and cultural needs of the international community, particularly the least favoured members of that community, and strive to find solutions which reconcile authors' rights and users' interests. In this connection, it should be recalled that the Universal Copyright Convention, in guaranteeing 'adequate and effective' protection to the creators of works of the mind, though at a lower level than that of the Berne Convention, enables such works to be widely circulated.

With a view to meeting these two demands, Unesco seeks first to develop standards designed to encourage the creation of intellectual works, to protect such works and to facilitate their dissemination, and secondly to promote access to protected works.

On the one hand, efforts will be made to study the field of application of the international instruments on copyright, to establish standards relating to the ways and means of applying copyright regulations in view of the development of communication techniques and to study new problems such as those concerning respect for works in the public domain or the promotion of folklore.

On the other hand, steps will be taken to improve information on copyright proprietors, in particular through the establishment of copyright information centres, and to encourage closer co-operation between copyright proprietors and copyright users, with special emphasis on the relations between developed and developing countries and on the financial aspects of the problems.

Impact and significance of the media

An understanding of the communication process and of the structures, motivations and effects of the media of mass communication is fundamental to the improvement of communication between persons and between peoples. In addition to the social role of the media—as channels for the dissemination of information, culture and education, in the socialization process, in the conferral of status and in their agenda-setting function —it has been recognized since the beginning of the First Development Decade that they play an important part in economic development and can contribute to the establishment of a new economic and social order. Research is therefore a prerequisite to the formulation of policies for the development of communication media which will govern the allocation of often scarce resources towards socially desirable ends.

From the printed news-sheet to the transistor revolution: mass communication, the offspring of technology

The media of mass communication are a product of technology. They have been developed, at different periods of history in different societies, in an almost haphazard way. Although concern over the effects of the communication media on society has been voiced in the past, it is only in the last fifteen years that the acceleration of technological development and fundamental social and economic changes have provoked a real apprehension of the problem to be faced. The transistorized (and hence portable) radio receiver, faster telecommunication transmissions, and ultimately satellite communication have heightened the urgency of the problem.

Research programmes have to be redefined to include a multidisciplinary approach and to study communication media not as something separate but as an essential part of the social fabric. This entails research into the complete continuum of the communication process rather than into isolated parts of it. However, in many countries, the whole scientific base structure for such communication research is, at present, too weak to support the needed research. There are not enough institutions in a position to carry out empirical work nor enough trained researchers. Established relations between research institutions and government departments or between institutions and funding agencies are lacking. For example in Asia, Africa and Latin America a small number of competent research centres have grown up only in the last few years. While in North America and certain parts of Europe there is a great amount of research being undertaken, much of it is uncoordinated and has largely led to the accumulation of discrete findings. Frequently, throughout the world there is duplication of research programmes since until recently there was no systematic approach to the exchange of information.

Media and society: political aspects and deontological implications

Moreover research findings are not always taken into account by decision-makers and media producers. Decisions are being made daily about media policies and programme output, but the needs of people and the requirements of national development are not always the criteria upon which these decisions are made. There seems to be an increasing realization among policy-makers and development strategists of the importance of scientific research about those aspects of development which are not strictly economic, technological and ecological in nature, but policy-oriented programmes of research into all aspects of communication as a social and economic process are urgently required.

A better understanding of the role of communication in society should also help communicators themselves to redefine their responsibilities and assist in the formulation and adoption of standards of professional conduct.

Finally, the public as a whole, as receiver of media messages, needs to understand the processes that lead to their formulation, to evaluate them and to participate actively in the communication flow.

Stemming from different orientations, communication research has developed along separate paths in the various regions of the world. This has prevented the formulation of a satisfactory theoretical base for what is now recognized as essentially an interdisciplinary field of study rather than a discipline in its own right. Secondly the financing made available to research has influenced its direction: the media industries themselves have tended to promote 'service' research amounting to little more than counting audience coverage while both commercial and political interests have called for quick returns on investments and have thus led to the proliferation of 'effects' studies designed to assess the impact of messages on their audiences, with little attention to the goals and motivations of the communicators themselves, to the effects of the structures of the communication channels, or to the broader social environment in which communication takes place.

From 'functional' research and studies on impact to a new approach aimed at national objectives

A growing dissatisfaction with the results achieved led in the late 1950s to doubts about the future for communication research; it was only in the late 1960s that a new approach was formulated which is now gaining general acceptance. Certain broadcasting organizations, for example, reoriented their research departments as tools for programme formulation; a number of countries have established commissions or financed research programmes to re-examine the communication needs of their countries; universities have established new institutions or redesigned their programmes towards policy-oriented research; schools of journalism have broadened their curricula and are seeking to become schools of social communication.

Research, education, deontology

Regional organizations, both governmental and non-governmental, are contributing to this new dimension. The Council of Europe has undertaken a programme of studies on the implications of new communication technology; the Arab States Broadcasting Union has taken initiatives for the establishment of a regional research organization; the Asian Mass Communication Research and Information Centre (AMIC) has played an important role in promoting research and the exchange of research findings; most recently, a start has been made toward the establishment of an African communication research organization. At the international level, the International Association for Mass Communication Research, the International Institute of Communications, the World Council of Christian Communication and other such bodies have contributed by providing forums for discussion and channels for dissemination of ideas in this field. For the future, it is possible that the United Nations University may have an important role to play in this respect.

Moves to inculcate an understanding and appreciation of the media in the general public began mainly with film education, and much practical work was undertaken by a number of national film institutes which ran special courses for students and produced curricular materials for use in schools and adult education centres. In the 1970s this approach has been widened to extend to all communications media— for example there has been interest in certain countries in teaching understanding of the press in schools—but this has as yet penetrated only to a limited extent in the developed and hardly at all into the developing world.

Standards of professional conduct for the media have been codified since the early 1920s and now exist in a considerable number of countries in all continents. Their form and scope vary considerably: separate codes for the press, the broadcast and the film media, often drawn up and voluntarily adopted by the professions themselves but in other cases imposed by law or governmental decree. Press or media councils—the earliest dating from 1916—now exist in over twenty-five countries.

In the United Nations, between 1950 and 1952 the Sub-Commission on Freedom of Information and of the Press drafted an international code of ethics for information personnel. At its ninth session in 1954 the General Assembly decided to take no further action in this regard, and requested the Secretary-General to transmit the draft to information enterprises and professional organizations for such action as they might deem appropriate.

At Unesco: clarification of processes, emphasis on practical objectives

Unesco itself has been active in these various fields. The General Conference of Unesco, at its fifteenth session in November 1968, had authorized the Director-General to 'undertake a long-term programme of research and to promote the study of the role and effects of the media of mass communication in modern society'. In June 1969 a meeting of experts convened by Unesco in Montreal recommended that Unesco 'consider a major international study of the present and future effects of communication on the relations between changing societies and social groups, and on the individuals comprising them, to identify the ways in which the mass media can best serve the needs of present and future society'. This recommendation was approved by the General Conference of Unesco at its sixteenth session in November 1970. Since that date, Unesco, with the help of an international panel of consultants, has formulated proposals for an international research programme, has contracted studies on communication in the community, and has helped to establish mechanisms for the international exchange of research findings.

A Unesco report in 1964 was concerned with teaching a critical approach to cinema; more recently studies of media education in Europe and North America were initiated in 1974 with an emphasis on curriculum and methodology, leading to the development of a model curriculum for testing (initially at the school level) in 1976.

In recent years the Organization has carried out studies of the functioning of national media councils and, in consultation with appropriate professional organizations, has formulated guidelines for national codes of ethics for the media, stressing the right to information and the responsibilities of those collecting and disseminating it.

In the field of communication research, Unesco's first task is the promotion of the new current of thinking that has recently become manifest, and to which the Organization has indeed largely contributed. Experience has shown that Unesco is perhaps the only body able to play a catalytic role in obtaining international recognition of the need for new research, leading to a better understanding of the process and role of communication in society, and to a more precise definition of the questions that need to be asked. Emphasis must also be placed on policy-oriented research which will assist decision-makers in the allocation of resources for communication development.

Given the lack of institutional bases and of trained researchers which still persists in certain regions, despite the encouraging trends which have been noted above, an important area of Unesco's action during the coming period will consist of assistance to Member States in overcoming these obstacles.

On the regional and international levels, Unesco should continue to promote co-operation between research institutes and a fuller interchange of research findings through a network of documentation centres.

It is important, if communication is to be better understood, for all citizens to have an opportunity to investigate communication forms and, where possible, to have personal and practical experience of communications technologies. This experience should begin as part of formal education, but opportunities for the study of communication processes should be included in all aspects of lifelong education. Unesco can assist in this respect by encouraging a better exchange of information, methods and techniques.

Unesco should continue to contribute to the improvement of professional standards for the mass media, particularly through co-operation with the professional organizations concerned.

Communication and development

Policy-makers in many countries, developed and developing, are faced with problems related to the integration of communication media into national development programmes.

Associating the public in national affairs, informing the decision-makers

In the newer developing countries, the principal task is to ensure greater participation of the people in economic and national affairs, enhance their skills and knowledge, weld them to nationhood, and enable them to find their cultural and personal identity. Without full use of the modern mass media in conjunction with more traditional ways of social communication, there is little hope that urgent goals can be reached in a short time, especially when the effort involves many millions of people. Development programmes have too often been confronted with failure because they were designed without giving proper consideration to social, political, cultural and communication factors.

In the more highly industrialized countries, a revolution in communication technology is upsetting many existing institutions. Potentially, it makes it possible for every citizen to benefit from cheap and plentiful opportunities to choose what he would like to see, hear, or read, and to express his views to others; but it also threatens older social values and ways of life. However, the main problem is that policy-makers interested in the development of the communication media do not have the fundamental information upon which to base their decisions. This information can only be provided by objective and scientific research.

Communication policies provide the principles and guidelines on which communication systems are built. They have to be translated into action plans which touch many aspects of the organization of society—indeed all activities related to the acquisition, distribution and productive use of information and experience. The efficient use of communication for social, cultural and economic development as well as for administrative purposes, therefore, requires comprehensive long-term integrated planning. There is growing recognition of the need for development of planning methodologies in this field, for mechanisms for co-ordination and integration of communication plans in overall national development planning, and new training programmes to provide the necessary skills.

Electronic facsimiles, the satellite, television by cable: possible aids to development

If the communication media are to play their full role, both as channels for a free and balanced flow of information and as agents of economic development and social progress, there is an urgent need for the developing countries to overcome the existing deficiencies in their communication infrastructures and availability of trained personnel. Moreover, new media provide opportunities of social use for which new programme formats need to be devised and tested.

Over the past ten years there has been a significant spread of communications media, especially of mass communication forms. Marked progress has been made in the use of electronic transmission of facsimiles, offset printing, communication satellites, simpler lightweight production equipment, video and audio recording and the distribution of television programmes by multi-channel cables. These have a potential for diversifying production and distribution to serve the interests of differing groups, providing individuals with greater freedom of choice in what they receive and improving exchanges between countries; they could be of value to many countries in expanding and accelerating the use of mass communication for social and economic development. However, this progress is mainly seen in the industrialized world, and over the decade the differential between developed and developing countries has actually enlarged.

Thus, even though television services now exist in many more countries than 10 years ago, in most the number of receivers is still small. In some 30 countries of Asia and Africa there are no television services at all. In Africa 9 countries and territories have no daily newspapers; only 15 of the remainder have a daily circulation of more than 10 per 1,000 of the population and in none does it exceed 100. In 40 African countries the number of radio receivers is less than 100 per 1,000. In Asia, daily newspaper circulation is less than 100 per 1,000 in 12 countries, and in only 6 is it more than 100. The ratio of radio receivers in 17 countries is far less than 100 per 1,000, and in only 8 is it more than 200. In only 7 of the Spanish-speaking countries of North and South America is daily newspaper circulation more than 100 per 1,000 and while the number of radio receivers in 8 of them is more than 100 per 1,000, and in another 5 more than 300, the number of television receivers is less than 100 per 1,000 in 10 countries and in only 2 is it more than 200. There are no national news agencies in 15 countries of Africa, 11 Spanish-speaking countries of North and South America and 6 Asian countries.

In the Third World: inadequate infrastructures and shortage of specialists . . .

The first problem for communication development is therefore to prevent, as far as possible, any further widening of this gap. Appropriate infrastructures and institutions have to be created to allow for media expansion in the developing countries of Africa, Asia and Latin America, and facilities established for staff training.

This is not to say that there has been no communication training: in fact, training provisions have increased considerably over the decade. In Asia, for example, an advanced regional training programme for broadcasting professionals has met, over the past three years, 38 per cent of estimated regional training requirements. But at a more basic national level, quantitative needs have been met only to the extent of 4 per cent and many of the programmes arranged have been *ad hoc* and in-service. Relatively little attention has been paid to training techniques and methodologies. There is still a lack of basic curricula and materials and considerable waste and duplication in the transfer of training aids from one environment to another.

A further problem stems from the rigidity in patterns of control over communication media. There is still relatively littele opportunity for audiences, both individuals and groups, to become involved in the business of production and management, to have access to media tools and materials, or to have an explicit choice in the selection of media programmes. Communication media still tend to be monolithic, with limited developments at the local or community level and considerable imbalances between urban and rural environments.

. . . and sometimes neglect of low-cost media

Equally, the weight of both interest and investment is still attached primarily to mass communication forms, with some neglect of low-cost, small-format media which might be of special value to the developing world. There is comparatively little evaluation of new communication technologies and few attempts to adapt these to non-industrial settings. Moreover, in those cases where new technologies are introduced experimentally into a developing country, their introduction is often too rapid, with insufficient attention paid to the problems of evaluation and of technology transfer. Yet it is already clear that new communication forms, particularly those based on group or community media which allow greater public participation, call for a re-examination of the role of the communicator himself, and this in turn has implications for future training programmes.

The interaction between the development of communication tools and their application to a variety of problem areas and audiences still produces the most recalcitrant problems. While the processes of diffusion have been extensively researched, the results of these researches have not been fed back practically to the media producer, or incorporated as a matter of course into project design. To maximize the contribution of the communication media to social and economic development, improved methods of analysis, a greater emphasis on the evaluation of materials and more working criteria in controlled environments are still required.

The sophistication of the electronic media in contrast to the lack of newpapers in many rural areas

Mass communication media have developed in the different countries and regions of the world under highly varying legal and organizational provisions and to serve very different purposes; only in very rare cases has there been a concerted approach to the problem of communication itself. It would be impossible to summarize the different modalities that have been adopted throughout the world, but typically it may be said that measures concerning different aspects of communication have been drawn up in a host of different agencies and ministries: telecommunication, information, education as well as those concerned with the development of commerce and industry. All too often these activities have gone on independently; it is only in recent years that, largely due to the sudden advance in communication and information technology, the need for explicit policies and co-ordinated planning has begun to be recognized.

In overall figures, there has been a steady increase in the physical means available for communication all over the world, and it can be said that far more people are receiving information through the mass media than ten years ago. This general picture needs, however, to be analysed more closely; the main development has been in the electronic media, while the press and cinema have remained stationary. Again, within countries, development has occurred mainly in urban centres, so that to the gap between the developed and the developing countries must be added the gap between the urban and rural populations. Only in recent years has there been a move, notably in Africa, to establish rural newspapers and provide a specifically rural broadcasting service. Another important initiative is the Satellite Instructional Television Experiment begun in an Asian country in 1975, designed to bring educational programmes to rural areas through the use of the most modern technology.

New technology, however, is not only a matter of physical equipment; its introduction raises far-reaching questions of institutional structure and of planning and managerial skills. The management problems involved in satellite transmission have, for example, been the subject of special study in North America, in connection with certain satellite projects. Computer technology has been adopted, both in broadcasting management and in the press, in North America, Europe and Japan.

At the other end of the scale, low-cost and community media are being progressively introduced: local broadcasting and community cable networks 'videograph', to cite but a few examples. An experiment in the use of portable video-recorders has been carried out in certain African villages.

As already noted, there has been a considerable increase in the provision of training facilities the world over, and particularly in Africa, Asia and Latin America. Especially important has been the recognition that the communicator in today's society requires a broad general education going far beyond narrow technical training, with the result that teaching programmes in communication have increasingly appeared in the offerings of universities.

The attraction of the cinema and the rise in radio and television broadcasting in the developing countries

International and regional organizations, both governmental and non-governmental, have played a growing role in the development of communication. Thus the Joint African and Mauritanian Organization (OCAM) has decided on the establishment of a cinema consortium for French-speaking African countries, the Agence de Coopération Technique et Culturelle has recently started work in the field of rural communication, the Organization of American States has supported journalism training projects, and the African, Arab States and Asian regional broadcasting unions have actively promoted broadcasting training. The Latin-American Centre for Higher Studies in Communication (CIESPAL) has played an important part in reorienting communication education in the region. On another level, organizations such as the International Institute of Communications and the International Film and Television Council have undertaken studies on the possibilities offered by new technologies and the consequences of their introduction.

Several of the United Nations agencies themselves are concerned with various aspects of this problem. The International Telecommunications Union is not only responsible for world-wide planning of the use of the broadcasting spectrum but also through its technical assistance programme has over the past two decades assisted in planning regional telecommunications networks and is active in training engineering staff in individual countries. FAO has long been concerned with the use of media for agricultural education and has organized many training courses and seminars on this subject. WHO and ILO, each within its sphere of competence, have also carried out activities in this field. The United Nations Development Programme recognized the importance of communication support to development projects and, in the late 1960s, set up a special service to provide assistance to Member States for this purpose.

Within Unesco, the importance of a planned approach to communication was stressed in 1970, when the sixteenth session of the General Conference authorized the

Director-General to 'help Member States in the formulation of their mass communication policies'. Since then, Unesco has undertaken studies of the methodological basis for communication planning and of the requirements for the training of communication planners. It has published the first monographs of a series of studies, undertaken in co-operation with National Commissions, on national communication policies in selected countries and convened in 1976 in Latin America the first of a series of regional intergovernmental conferences on communication policies and undertaken preliminary work for a similar conference in Asia.

Limits and scope of Unesco's planning action

Since the early 1950s assistance to Member States in planning and training for mass communication has been a continuing feature of the Organization's programme, and systematic efforts have been made since the early 1960s to help establish national and regional institutions for this purpose. These have led, for example, to the creation of several university-based communication institutes. Since 1973 emphasis has been given to the area of communication management, both in studies and practical workshops, and in 1974 the production and evaluation of a series of manuals and training aids was undertaken.

Innovation (both in communication technology and in its application to specific problem areas) has been a major interest spanning two decades, especially in the area of non-formal and informal education. Characteristic examples are assistance given to farm forum experiments in Asia and Africa, to a multi-media experiment for rural audiences in an African country and to an integrated approach to rural development in a Latin American country. Projects financed from extra-budgetary sources have been concerned with research into prototype programme production, with the creative use of film in a development context, and more recently with the interactive uses of film and video programming. In the applied area of population education, the potent ial of folk media and low-cost aids has been investigated, and in Africa there has been a series of experiments with the rural press.

A major emphasis since 1974 has been upon community media and the problem of access to media materials and participation by audiences. In this context, special emphasis has been placed upon local forms of radio and television and on small-format technologies. A study of new models in Europe and North America was accompanied by an experimental project in the Caribbean involving the community press, local radios and video work, thus approaching at first hand the problem of technology transfer.

... trying out the machinery for formulating national policies

The policies adopted to govern the development of communication in any country are essentially a matter for decision of the Member State concerned; Unesco cannot therefore formulate such policies nor draw up rules for their formulation. Unesco has, however, a key role to play in promoting the concept of communication policies and in assisting in the establishment of mechanisms for their formulation and implementation. Options need to be studied, sophisticated methodologies developed, a corps of planners trained and assistance provided in the elaboration of integrated communication plans. National policies need to be harmonized with regional objectives and international agreements.

Communication policies and planning should not be identified with centralized direction, but should be considered as a framework for the rational development of communication activities in society, allowing for alternative approaches, permitting flexibility and innovation, and giving full rein to creativity. Unesco therefore works closely with media and professional bodies with a view to promoting the adoption of policies at the professional level which will contribute to overall policy formulation in the whole area of communication.

The development of communication forms, technologies and infrastructures should be planned taking into account their application to specific problem areas or to particular social groups. This requires interaction between the technologist, the communicator, the development worker, the researcher and the planner; the introduction of formative evaluation so that findings can be translated into practical recommendations for the media practitioners, and proper consideration of the problems of technology transfer.

A special emphasis should be placed on experimental work with new communication technologies, including their continuous evaluation in experimental situations so that they may be relevantly adapted to social, educational and economic purposes in the developing world.

In considering the role and potential of communications media, the problems of users must be emphasized; priority should be given to new approaches to communication organization and management which improve individual access to communication channels and materials, and involve audiences more fully in production and decision-making processes.

10 Managing mankind's knowledge

Information has become an essential basis for the progress of civilization and society. Lack of information and of effective means of exchanging it are now widely recognized as being limiting factors in the economic and social development of peoples. Thus, the problem of information is none other than the problem of managing mankind's knowledge—the collective memory which society must learn to control effectively and utilize fully in order to progress.

An international duty: the control and equitable use of the collective memory

In the present world context there can be no doubt, as is underscored by resolutions of the General Assembly of the United Nations in its recent special (VIIth) and ordinary (XXXth) sessions, of the crucial immediate importance of scientific and technological information transfer for the developing countries. These resolutions call upon all countries to ensure the freest and fullest possible access of developing countries to needed technologies and call upon the United Nations system to take steps to ensure that relevant technology and experience are widely disseminated. Similarly the Conference on Security and Co-operation in Europe, Helsinki (1975), stressed the importance of the wider dissemination of information of all kinds among countries.

Statistical information is also recognized as an indispensable element in the rational planning of economic and social development as well as in the assessment of progress toward established goals in education, science, culture and communication at the national, regional and world levels.

Thus, in the context of national information needs at all levels, the United Nations system is now expected to take the leading role in promoting new institutional arrangements for the effective assignment, control and exchange of information.

The development of information transfer mechanisms by Member States can be grouped into three distinct problems: how to gain access to information, how to manage information and how to make effective use of information resources.

Access, management, exploitation: the three major problems of the transfer of knowledge

The problem of access involves identifying a country's information needs, matching these to relevant internal and external sources of information and evolving a national information policy and plan to ensure maximum availability of the relevant information at all levels. In the development of information exchange across national borders, international information systems are increasingly seen as a vital element in dealing with this problem.

Effective management of information implies the existence of a national information system with appropriate networks and modern services—information and documentation services, libraries of all kinds, archives—suiting the requirements of different countries and the development of good communication between them. Equally important is the availability of adequately trained personel able to fulfil the role of communicators.

In discussing information, it should be pointed out that it is often not the scarcity of information but rather its very complexity and volume that prevents effective control. The proliferation of information and also the increasing complexity of its physical form—films, tapes, video, etc.—necessitate the development and application of sophisticated information-handling technologies.

The question of effective use of information is the third and most important aspect of the information transfer process, since it is only through appropriate use that benefit can accrue. Feedback from the user communities thus becomes an essential element in the design and evaluation of information transfer systems.

National and international co-ordination

A further world trend which should be noted is the need felt by Member States to develop closer co-ordination in building information systems responsive to national needs, and especially to co-ordinate their information services through an effective national information policy. In implementing a policy it is most often the sharing of responsibility through networks of institutions which is proving to be the most viable method for reducing costs of access to information and of information-handling.

International information systems, dealing with specific areas, are in a sense the ultimate refinement of the co-ordination process in information transfer, assuring access according to the needs of participating countries, who also provide inputs to the system and share the costs. They imply the co-operation of relevant national institutional components.

Co-ordination of these national counterparts is an important factor enabling each country, whatever its stage of development, to reap the full benefit from international information systems and to participate in a two-way flow of the information resources available to the world community.

Unesco's role should be, within the context of the United Nations system and its own charter, to foster a general framework for the wider use and control of information through the development of specialized information services, documentation, library and archives infrastructures and of the interconnection of information systems at the national and international levels.

Indeed, Article I of its Constitution stipulates that the Organization shall 'maintain, increase and diffuse knowledge ... by encouraging co-operation among the nations in all branches of intellectual activity ... the exchange of publications, ... and other materials of information; and by initiating methods of international co-operation calculated to give the people of all countries access to the printed and published materials produced by any of them'.

The programme will deal with all types of information within the context of national priorities for research or technological application for education and cultural development and for management and planning.

Emphasis will be placed on improving national capabilities for management and use of available information and on facilitating the exchange of information among Member States, not only in priority fields, such as science and technology, but also to foster better communication between peoples to improve knowledge of each other's culture and thus contribute to peace and understanding.

Unesco efforts will also be directed towards the assembly of statistics necessary to the rational planning and evaluation of programmes concerning the expansion of education, the application of science and technology the development and the co-ordination of cultural development with overall economic and social progress. In particular, a statistical infrastructure will be created or expanded at the national, regional and world levels to quantify activities in education, science, culture and communication and also to measure progress toward goals established for the Second Development Decade and the New International Economic Order.

Information, its systems and services

Information has become an essential element in knowledge of all the problems which determine or affect the lives of peoples and the evolution of societies as well as relations among nations. It constitutes a key element in decision-making at the most varied levels on account of the growing complexity of modern societies and the rapid changes to which they are subject. As knowledge advances and its applications become more diverse and call for further research, precise information concerning the state of a question, and even of how it is likely to evolve, is necessary before any action can be undertaken in no matter what field. This being so, the rational utilization of natural and human resources, scientific and technological development as well as agricultural and industrial progress, the advance of culture and social welfare are inseparable from access to the most diversified and comprehensive information. The problem thus arises not only of the collection, processing and dissemination of information in each country, but also of information exchange among the different countries of the world.

Thus the problem of information is none other than the problem of managing mankind's knowledge, and any reflection or action concerning economic, social and cultural development—in the widest sense of the term—must necessarily take that into account.

Exponential growth of the mass of information; rapid advance of technology

Without attempting to open a discussion here on the various complex aspects of the problem of information at national, regional and international levels, it is possible to mention briefly a few of its essential characteristics. The steady increase of information available is a fact borne out by the study of recent developments; we are caught up in a process which has been called the 'exponential growth' of the mass of information available, and it is to be expected that this growth will continue in the coming years. This will be the case, in particular, in the fields of science and technology, because of the increase in the number of research workers, scientists and engineers and the diversification of the fields of science and technology. Generally speaking, the output of new knowledge is growing, side by side with economic and social development.

A second feature is the rapid development of the technologies used to store, retrieve or communicate information. The increasingly extensive application of computer science goes hand in hand with the use of telecommunications and modern techniques of filing, indexing and reproduction. It is also generally recognized that this process is bound to accelerate and that the decade 1980-1990 will be marked by the general use of computerized information, on a virtually industrial scale, which will take the place of the amateurish methods still in use at the present time. There is also reason to believe that progress in all the branches of scientific and technological knowledge which may be subsumed under the heading 'informatics' will lead to the emergence of new relations, new concepts and new syntheses. This will undoubtedly have important effects not only on the quest for knowledge and on its communication, but also on the organization of society.

Lack of information in developing countries

Despite these advances, which are, moreover, interconnected—since only the use of modern data processing methods makes it possible to 'manage' the growing volume of knowledge available, and since the production of new knowledge is, in turn, accelerated by the availability of a mass of data which is made possible by the application of technology—inequalities in this area are serious. The shortage of information in the developing countries is one of the important aspects of the gap dividing them from the industrialized countries; there is no possible comparison today between the immense capacities of the industrialized countries and the embryonic services possessed by the developing countries. This situation exacerbates both their relative poverty and their dependence, and should be considered as one of the major obstacles to their economic, technological, social and cultural development. It would be unrealistic, indeed impossible, to think of simply 'transferring' the huge volume of information available to those regions which lack it. Yet steps must be taken to ensure that those regions have access to all the available sources and are able to choose freely the information which they wish to obtain. In return, and for the sake of all concerned, the developing countries should also be encouraged to make their own contribution to the continuous expansion of information.

Interdependence and complementarity

The interdependence of information activities at the national and international levels is a fact of central importance. Knowledge is essentially universal; it is obvious that the industrialized countries in isolation cannot be self-sufficient, especially with regard to scientific and technical information, and it is no less obvious that the transfer of such information to the developing countries is of capital importance, as is emphasized in the resolutions adopted by the United Nations General Assembly at its seventh special session and at its thirtieth regular session. But, conversely, international exchange and transfer are not really possible unless there are appropriate national structures and unless such structures are compatible with what may be called the 'rules of the game', i.e., the technical norms governing the international movement of information.

It would appear that there is at present a twofold trend towards integration in information. Where disciplines are concerned, isolated approaches are no longer justifiable; the principles, methods and norms of information processing are the same, whatever the subject being dealt with; hence, the methodological tools developed to process scientific and technological information can be applied to all fields of knowledge. Similarly, where institutions are concerned, apart from the specific problems connected with the particular responsibilities of various bodies such as libraries, documentation centres and archives, there are common procedures, methods and technologies, so that all information services may be regarded as forming a system whose functioning and development call for similarity of approach.

Improving the transfer of information between nations

As a result of the attention given to the problems of information, the work to be accomplished in this area at both the national and the international levels has been defined;

it can be divided into four fields corresponding to the four sub-objectives of the main objective.

First, policies must be defined and plans worked out in the light of the needs of the national communities—and of the international community in all its diversity. Secondly, methodological tools must be produced, improved, or simply chosen by common agreement, which will enable information to be transferred and systems to be interlinked, by ensuring their compatibility. Thirdly, there is the question of the development of information infrastructures, services and systems, i.e., the structures, institutions and bodies of all kinds which form the links in the chain of the processing and transfer of information. This includes the development of libraries, documentation centres, archives, abstracting, indexing and translation services, world-wide and regional specialized information centres and international specialized systems. Lastly, consideration must be given to training, not only for information personnel but also for information users.

These four fields, or sub-objectives, correspond to the various courses of action open to Unesco. For Member States, the Organization can be a place for holding discussions leading to the development of common policies or the harmonization of existing policies; through advisory services, it can also help Member States to define their policies and their plans in the light of international experience, to which it can give them access.

Unesco can also be a centre for international reflection on technical matters, the studies undertaken and the exchange of ideas and discussion in various forms enabling methods, norms or guidelines to be worked out which are generally accepted by the international community of specialists and experts.

Thirdly, at the request of Member States Unesco can contribute, through advisory services, pilot projects or, in some cases, operational activities, to the establishment of structures or institutions in the national context. It may contribute both to the organization of institutions and to technologies, together with their applications. At the international level, the Organization can also take the initiative in setting up specialized information networks or systems in its fields of competence (for example: education, social sciences, science policy and culture) or participate in similar activities for which another institution—particularly one or more agencies of the United Nations system—is primarily responsible.

Lastly, Unesco can contribute in various ways to the training of specialized personnel or of information users, which is in keeping with its general educational vocation.

Thus the four main axes defining the tasks to be accomplished correspond, on the one hand, to goals which are being pursued by the different countries and by the international community, and on the other, to action which Unesco can take. For some years, Member States have been making major efforts in respect of information, but starting from very unequal bases. Moreover, the situation within the developed countries themselves, from the point of view of circulation, standardizatio and interconnection, is far from satisfactory.

The organizations of the United Nations system all accord particular importance to the collection and international exchange of information in their respective fields of competence. Almost all have developed specialized international information systems or are in the process of doing so. In this connection, however. Unesco has a particular role which stems from its Constitution and which is largely recognized within the United Nations system, with regard in particular to: the establishment of international accounting standards, the organization of research and the pooling of research findings, the organization of training and of advisory services for Member States with respect to general policy and planning, and the granting of operational assistance with a view to the creation or the improvement of national information infrastructures and services.

The conceptual framework of UNISIST

The major specialized information systems, such as those of the nuclear sciences or agriculture, have accepted the conceptual framework of the UNISIST programme. This programme is aimed, generally speaking, at promoting 'co-ordinated and sustained international action to facilitate transfer of scientific and technical information for the economic and social development of nations'.

The national infrastructures: pillars of the international networks

Unesco's action in the field of documentation, libraries and archives has been slanted towards promotional activities and international co-operation and also towards measures to foster the systematic development of infrastructures and the training of personnel in Member States. An intergovernmental conference, meeting in 1974, accepted 'the general concept of national infrastructures of documentation services, libraries and archives (NATIS)'.

Furthermore, Unesco's activities include the development and improvement of various specialized information systems such as the data bank (DARE) for the social sciences, the information exchange network of the International Bureau of Education, for which a central data bank is to be established, or again the Science and Technology Policies Information Exchange System (SPINES), for which preparatory studies have been carried out.

Facing the future with an overall programme

The interest shown in information transfer and scientific and technological information interconnections and exchanges under the UNISIST programme on the one hand, and the magnitude of the needs in respect of documentation, libraries and archives to be met by national information systems (NATIS) on the other, make it necessary for an overall programme to be defined which will also include Unesco's specialized information systems, be they already in operation or in the process of being developed.

Unesco's programme between now and 1982 is intended to promote the formulation of information policies at national, regional and world levels; to encourage the establishment of norms and their dissemination and to assist in the development of information infrastructures and specialized international information systems. Parallel to this the Organization will take steps to promote through all forms of encouragement and teaching, the practical and theoretical training and education of professionals and users of information.

Although the pursuit of these objectives demands much patience and sustained concentration, it is worth making the effort to achieve the goal: namely, that information should no longer be a privilege and that it should be universally understood.

Tuning statistics to requirements

Modern methods and techniques of analysis for development planning as well as for monitoring of programmes and assessment of progress require an ever-increasing access to and use of statistical data. Statistical work and the necessary infrastructures have grown in response to these needs, but this growth has been rather uneven.

Lack of balance between 'social statistics' and 'economic statistics', and areas little suited to quantification

The situation in this respect varies considerably between countries. In many developing countries, there is still a lack of reliable, up-to-date and sufficiently detailed data. This is due to a large extent to the shortage of adequately trained personnel for the statistical services, both as regards statisticians and related personnel, such as computer analysts and programmers.

There are also considerable differences in development according to the areas covered. For a long time statistics in education, science, culture and communication have been neglected in comparison with demographic and economic statistics. In general, there is still a lack of balance between 'social statistics' and 'economic statistics'. Yet, the former prove more and more necessary as development policy and planning attempt to achieve a better balance between economic, social and cultural factors, so as to avoid a concentration on economic growth alone, measured by the Gross National Product and related statistical indicators.

Policies and planning in education, science, culture and communication have to take into account factors which are difficult to quantify. Thus, in addition to the efforts made for improving the coverage, accuracy and reliability of the basic data, work has to be undertaken to build up new tools and indicators covering the widest possible fields, in accordance with a multidisciplinary and integrated approach to development. Methodological studies are required to this effect.

'Sine qua non' condition for co-operation: international comparability

Achieving international comparability of statistical data is a basic requirement for international and regional co-operation—whether in the form of intellectual co-operation, consisting of exchanges of information and experiences, with a view to promote policies and innovations, or multilateral or bilateral assistance programmes which require an adequate knowledge of the degree of development in aid-seeking countries. This need for comparability is particularly felt in connection with all the analyses, projections and studies carried out in pursuance of the objectives of the Second Development Decade and to contribute to the establishment of a new international economic order, especially in the areas of Unesco competence. A major obstacle lies in the wide differences in the nature and presentation of statistical data available in the different countries. Specific efforts must therefore be made to achieve a reasonable degree of standardization.

Since 1960, there has been a marked improvement in the ability of most Member States to provide statistics on education, science, culture and communication. This improvement is reflected in national publications as well as in the amount and quality of data reported in questionnaires and published in the *Unesco Statistical Yearbook*, and in the statistical content of background papers prepared for international meetings and conferences. Unesco has contributed to this development through technical assistance, international standardization, methodological studies, seminars, publications and pilot projects.

Education opened the way

Unesco's involvement in statistics on education dates back to the 1950s, and the first major international action was the adoption by the General Conference in 1958 of the Recommendation concerning the International Standardization of Educational Statistics. Since 1968, work has been undertaken to develop the International Standard Classification of Education (ISCED), which culminated in the resolutions of the 35th Session of the International Conference of Education (Geneva, 1975), calling upon Member States and Unesco to adopt ISCED for the international reporting of statistics in the field of education. A major change has occurred in the evolution from the purely descriptive 'age of stocks' to the more policy-oriented flow analysis and efficiency assessments. An important part has been played also by education projections based upon trend extrapolations as inputs for planners and policy-makers.

The need for statistics on science and technology was first recognized at the time of the United Nations Conference on the Application of Science and Technology to Development (1962). Unesco responded to the expressed need for data on present and future scientific and engineering manpower by initiating a manifold programme to assist Member States in the collection and analysis of statistical data on the numbers of scientists, engineers and technicians and their deployment in the economy as well as the sources and distribution of funds for research, experimental development and other scientific and technical activities. This work was based on methodology elaborated by developed countries but adapted to the needs and resources of countries with different socio-economic systems and at varying levels of development and was co-ordinated with related statistical activities in other international organizations.

As more developing countries establish national research councils or other centralized bodies for decision-making in the field of science and technology, they are calling on Unesco with increasing frequency for assistance in collecting and analysing the data they need for effective utilization of their resources. In the Ministerial Conferences on the Application of Science and Technology to Development (CASTALA, CASTASIA, CASTAFRICA), detailed statistical analyses within the limits of available data have been prepared for background use and for incorporation in the working documents.

In the fields of culture and communication, recommendations were adopted by the General Conference of Unesco for the international standardization of statistics relating to book production and periodicals (1964) and of library statistics (1970). Nevertheless, statistics on culture and communication are often fragmentary, and do not constitute a coherent and comprehensive system. Only recently—because of the increasing recognition of the role of culture and communication in overall policies for development—has the need for adequate quantitative information for policy, planning and research purposes been felt. The existing statistics, however, are still far from meeting the requirements of this rapidly growing demand. It is thus necessary to reinforce them and to integrate them in the overall system of demographic and social statistics being developed by the United Nations and the associated agencies.

Assistance from the United Nations and Unesco within the framework of a five-year plan

Special reference may be made here to the inter-agency work currently being carried out within the United Nations system towards developing an integrated System of Social and Demographic Statistics (SSDS). The procedure will be similar to that followed for the System of National Accounts (SNA) or the Material Products System (MPS). Since education and culture will form important subareas of the new System (SSDS), Unesco has a major role to play in the long-term statistical development work.

In the context of the Second Development Decade, particular attention is being focused in the United Nations system on the need to reinforce considerably technical assistance activities. At the initiative of the Statistical Commission, and in conformity with Resolution 1533 (L) of the Economic and Social Council, concerted action has been initiated by the United Nations organizations to develop an expanded and integrated five-year scheme for technical assistance in statistics. As far as Unesco is concerned, this work is, however, still in its very first beginning, as its technical assistance activities so far have been limited mostly to providing statistics on education. In view of Member States' interest in a broader analysis of socio-economic development for planning purposes, it is expected that they will be requesting assistance in developing the remaining fields, i.e. those relating to science, culture and communication.

The statistical work of Unesco depends largely on the degree of development and capacity of the national statistical systems. The role of Unesco is to help in strenthening national statistical services through such measures as the training of specialists and the development of the network of regional advisors. Methodological work will be improved through the elaboration of new methods for collecting, processing and presenting data and the publication of studies and reports to disseminate information about the new methods.

Data collection will be expanded to include new areas, such as capital investments in education, scientific activities related to research and experimental development, public expenditure for cultural activities, etc. The standardization and international comparability of data will be improved, due to the application in an increasing number of Member States of the International Standard Classification of Education.